T0326294

AN ELEMENTARY TREATISE
ON
ACTUARIAL MATHEMATICS

AN ELEMENTARY TREATISE
ON
ACTUARIAL MATHEMATICS

by

HARRY FREEMAN, M.A., F.I.A.

CAMBRIDGE

Published for the Institute of Actuaries

AT THE UNIVERSITY PRESS

1931

CAMBRIDGE
UNIVERSITY PRESS

University Printing House, Cambridge CB2 8BS, United Kingdom

Cambridge University Press is part of the University of Cambridge.

It furthers the University's mission by disseminating knowledge in the pursuit of
education, learning and research at the highest international levels of excellence.

www.cambridge.org
Information on this title: www.cambridge.org/9781316611784

First published 1931
First paperback edition 2016

A catalogue record for this publication is available from the British Library

ISBN 978-1-316-61178-4 Paperback

CONTENTS

PROBABILITY

INTRODUCTION

WHILE to a mathematician the actual knowledge of pure mathematics required for a student to pass the Examinations of the Institute of Actuaries may not be large, to the average candidate who is breaking fresh ground the amount appears to be heavy, and when that knowledge has to be gained by reading parts only of standard works on mathematics his difficulties are multiplied.

It was for this reason that the Council invited Alfred Henry to produce his book on *Calculus and Probability*. That book is now out of print and Henry is no longer with us. Had he been alive he would have been the first to acknowledge that his book did not cover all the ground that is now required.

The Council have thought it to be very desirable that a new Text Book of a more comprehensive design should be published for the benefit of our students, and in looking round for a man of sufficient experience to undertake such difficult and laborious work, they were happy in giving a unanimous invitation to Mr Freeman.

This book is the result and it will, I am confident, be found to be a comprehensive work, at any rate so far as the student is concerned, on Finite Differences, Summation, Differential and Integral Calculus and Probability.

Mr Freeman has, I am glad to see, commenced with a chapter on Elementary Trigonometry, a knowledge of which, as he states himself, is essential to a proper understanding of the Differential and Integral Calculus.

The whole work should prove to be a Text Book of great value to actuarial students.

H. M. T.

AUTHOR'S PREFACE

IT has been my experience in dealing with the subjects of the syllabus for Part I of the Examinations of the Institute of Actuaries that it is essential to interest the student in the subject and then, when his interest has been aroused, to supply him with numerous examples illustrative of the principles that have been expounded. This is of particular importance when treating of Finite Differences and Probability, which are almost invariably new to the student.

In pursuance of the first of these aims, I have had no compunction when occasion has arisen in wandering from the strict confines of the examination syllabus. For example, a little information on modern symbolic notation, or a paragraph on osculatory interpolation, while not essential to the immediate needs of the Part I student, may however prove of interest to him and, it is hoped, may stimulate him to further researches. Again, in accordance with my belief for the necessity for examples, I have included in the text many varied types of question and have set numerous examples for solution. The student should find considerable scope for his industry and ingenuity in working the examples set after each chapter and at the end of the book.

I have been fortunate in the assistance rendered me by my friends. In the first place, my sincerest thanks are due to Mr D. C. Fraser and Mr G. Green, who read through the book in manuscript and who were always willing to confer with me at any time and on any subject connected with the book. Then again, my colleagues on the panel of Tutors, Mr C. D. Rich and Mr C. W. Sanger, have rendered me much help at various stages of the work, for which I am very grateful. Finally I am deeply indebted to Mr S. H. Alison and Mr G. J. Lidstone for their expert advice. Mr Alison's suggestions on the chapters dealing with Limits and the elements of the Calculus were particularly valuable. Mr Lidstone not only read the whole of the proofs, but put at my disposal his unique knowledge of actuarial mathematics. It would not be too much to say that certain of the chapters on Finite Differences would have presented a comparatively meagre appearance had it not been for the inspiration afforded by the published writings and the helpful suggestions of Mr Fraser and Mr Lidstone.

H. F.

December, 1930

NOTE ON SYMBOLS

The following symbols and abbreviations have been used in the text:

$n!$ "factorial n." $n! = n(n-1)(n-2)\ldots 3.2.1$, where n is a positive integer.

n_r $\dfrac{n(n-1)(n-2)\ldots(n-r+1)}{r(r-1)(r-2)\ldots 3.2.1}$, where n may be positive or negative, integral or fractional, and r is a positive integer.

$\equiv$ "is equivalent to." Thus $E \equiv 1 + \Delta$ means that the operation E is equivalent to the operations $1 + \Delta$.

$\rightarrow$ "tends to the value." For example, $\underset{n\to\infty}{\mathrm{Lt}} \left(1 + \dfrac{1}{n}\right)^n$ is an abbreviated form of "the limit of $\left(1 + \dfrac{1}{n}\right)^n$ as n tends to infinity."

J.I.A.   *Journal of the Institute of Actuaries.*

T.F.A.   *Transactions of the Faculty of Actuaries.*

J.S.S.   *Journal of the Institute of Actuaries Students' Society.*

CHAPTER I

ELEMENTARY TRIGONOMETRY

1. A knowledge of trigonometrical functions is essential for the proper understanding of various formulae of the differential and integral calculus. The present chapter is therefore devoted to the development of the elementary functions and their properties. The account is short, and for the purpose of studying the functions generally recourse should be had to a recognized textbook. The chapter has been included only with the object of enabling those who have not studied trigonometry to obtain sufficient knowledge to follow the remainder of the book.

2. Definitions.

Consider a straight line X_1OX of indefinite length fixed in a plane. At a point O in the straight line is hinged another straight line OA, also of indefinite length, capable of being revolved about the hinge at O, but only in an anti-clockwise direction. Then, as OA revolves, it sweeps out an angle XOA.

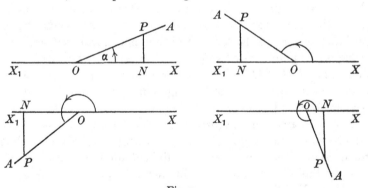

Fig. 1.

Take any point P on the moving line OA and drop a perpendicular PN on to the fixed line X_1OX. Then, by the properties of similar triangles, the ratios between the sides of the right-angled triangle PON will be the same for all positions of P, for any one

position of the line OA. These constant ratios are the trigonometrical ratios of the angle XOA, and are defined thus, where α
stands for the angle XOA:

$\dfrac{NP}{OP}$ is the sine of the angle XOA and is written sin α,

$\dfrac{ON}{OP}$ „   cosine   „   „ XOA „   „   cos α,

$\dfrac{NP}{ON}$ „   tangent   „   „ XOA „   „   tan α.

These are the principal ratios, and most trigonometrical problems
can be solved by the use of these three ratios only. It is often
convenient, however, to use the reciprocals of the ratios: the
respective reciprocals are

$\dfrac{OP}{NP}$, the cosecant of the angle XOA, written as cosec α,

$\dfrac{OP}{ON}$, the secant   „   „ XOA,   „   „   sec α,

$\dfrac{ON}{NP}$, the cotangent   „   „ XOA,   „   „   cot α.

3. It is important to note that, even if the two triangles PON in
the first two diagrams of Fig. 1 are geometrically equal, it does not
follow that the trigonometrical ratios of the two angles given by the
positions of OP are the same. In elementary plane geometry, the
straight line joining any two points L and M may be indifferently
denoted by LM or ML. On the other hand, the straight lines which
enter into the definitions of the trigonometrical ratios have *sign* as
well as magnitude, and the direction of the straight line determines
the sign. To ascertain the correct sign to be given to a straight line,
we proceed in the following manner. Imagine the plane in which
the fixed line has been drawn to be divided into four sections by the
straight line X_1OX and a straight line YOY_1 through O perpendicular to X_1OX.

If OP be any position of the revolving line, we can arrive at the
point P from O either by proceeding along OP or by the double
journey ON, NP. In order to develop a logical system we must
adopt a convention based on the direction to be taken to arrive at

P from O, and on the particular quadrant in which the point P lies. The convention is that lines drawn from O in the directions OX or OY are positive and that those drawn from O in the directions

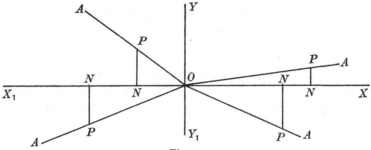

Fig. 2.

OX_1 and OY_1 are negative. The line OA is called the radius and is always to be considered as positive. The perpendicular line NP is to be regarded as drawn in the direction $N \to P$, i.e. from the line OX to the radius OA, and not from P to N.

In Fig. 2, therefore, we have

1. Quadrant XOY: ON positive and NP positive;
2.   ,, X_1OY: ON negative and NP positive;
3.   ,, X_1OY_1: ON negative and NP negative;
4.   ,, XOY_1: ON positive and NP negative.

These quadrants are called the first, second, third and fourth quadrants respectively.

4. It is evident that the trigonometrical ratios, being derived from the ratios between ON, NP, OP, will have sign as well as magni-

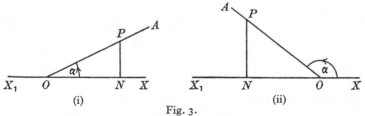

Fig. 3.

tude. For example, for the angle α in Fig. 3 (i) all the sides of the triangle ONP are positive in direction and as a result all the trigonometrical ratios of the angle will be positive.

On the other hand, in Fig. 3 (ii) we shall have

$$\sin \alpha = NP/OP \quad \text{(positive)/(positive)} \quad \text{i.e. } positive,$$
$$\cos \alpha = ON/OP \quad \text{(negative)/(positive)} \quad \text{i.e. } negative,$$
$$\tan \alpha = NP/ON \quad \text{(positive)/(negative)} \quad \text{i.e. } negative,$$

and similarly for the reciprocal ratios.

5. Negative angles.

If the revolving line be constrained to move in a *clockwise* direction, it is said to trace out a negative angle. For example, let the straight line OA_1 take up the position indicated, not by a

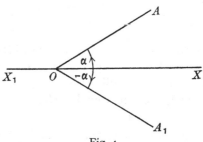

Fig. 4.

revolution passing first through the position OA, but by passing in the opposite direction direct to OA_1; then the angle XOA_1 is a negative angle.

In the figure the angle XOA is α, and the angle XOA_1 is $-\alpha$.

6. Relations between the ratios.

From the definitions of the ratios we have at once

$$\tan \alpha = NP/ON = \frac{\dfrac{NP}{OP}}{\dfrac{ON}{OP}} = \frac{\sin \alpha}{\cos \alpha} \qquad \ldots\ldots\text{(i)}.$$

Similarly, $$\cot \alpha = \frac{\cos \alpha}{\sin \alpha} \qquad \ldots\ldots\text{(ii)}.$$

Again, from any of the diagrams in Fig. 1,

$$NP^2 + ON^2 = OP^2.$$
$$\therefore \ (NP/OP)^2 + (ON/OP)^2 = 1,$$

i.e. $$(\sin \alpha)^2 \ + (\cos \alpha)^2 \ = 1.$$

A more convenient method of writing $(\sin \alpha)^2$, $(\cos \alpha)^2$, etc. is by omitting the brackets and denoting the squares of the ratios by $\sin^2 \alpha$, $\cos^2 \alpha$, etc. The above relation is therefore

$$\sin^2 \alpha + \cos^2 \alpha = 1 \qquad \ldots\ldots\text{(iii)}.$$

Similarly, by dividing both sides of the identity

$$ON^2 + NP^2 = OP^2$$

by ON^2 we shall have

$$1 + (NP/ON)^2 = (OP/ON)^2$$

or $\qquad\qquad 1 + \tan^2 \alpha \quad = \sec^2 \alpha \qquad \ldots\ldots\text{(iv)}.$

Again, dividing by NP^2, we shall obtain

$$1 + \cot^2 \alpha \quad = \operatorname{cosec}^2 \alpha \qquad \ldots\ldots\text{(v)}.$$

7. Identities.

Just as algebraic identities can be proved by the application of various fundamental rules, so the relations between the trigonometrical ratios can be applied to the proof of trigonometrical identities.

Example 1.

Prove that $\quad \tan \alpha + \cot \alpha = \sec \alpha \operatorname{cosec} \alpha$.

$$\begin{aligned}
\tan \alpha + \cot \alpha &= \sin \alpha/\cos \alpha + \cos \alpha/\sin \alpha \\
&= (\sin^2 \alpha + \cos^2 \alpha)/\cos \alpha \sin \alpha \\
&= 1/\cos \alpha \sin \alpha \\
&= (1/\cos \alpha)\,(1/\sin \alpha) \\
&= \sec \alpha \operatorname{cosec} \alpha.
\end{aligned}$$

Example 2.

Prove that $\quad \sec^2 \alpha - \operatorname{cosec}^2 \alpha = \tan^2 \alpha - \cot^2 \alpha$.

$$\begin{aligned}
\sec^2 \alpha - \operatorname{cosec}^2 \alpha &= (\tan^2 \alpha + 1) - (\cot^2 \alpha + 1) \\
&= \tan^2 \alpha - \cot^2 \alpha.
\end{aligned}$$

Example 3.

Prove that $\qquad \dfrac{\tan \alpha - \tan \beta}{\cot \alpha - \cot \beta} + \tan \alpha \tan \beta = 0$.

Multiply through by $\cot \alpha - \cot \beta$ and the expression becomes

$$\tan \alpha - \tan \beta + \cot \alpha \tan \alpha \tan \beta - \tan \alpha \tan \beta \cot \beta$$

or $\qquad \tan \alpha - \tan \beta + \tan \beta - \tan \alpha$, which is zero.

Alternatively:

$$\cot \alpha - \cot \beta = \frac{1}{\tan \alpha} - \frac{1}{\tan \beta} = - \frac{\tan \alpha - \tan \beta}{\tan \alpha \tan \beta}.$$

$$\therefore \frac{\tan \alpha - \tan \beta}{\cot \alpha - \cot \beta} = - \tan \alpha \tan \beta.$$

8. Magnitude of angles. Degrees.

The unit angle in elementary geometry is the *degree*. An angle of x degrees is denoted by $x°$. The degree is defined as the angle subtended at the centre of a circle by an arc equal in length to $1/360$ of the circumference. For arithmetical calculation the degree is a convenient unit, and we can obtain the values of the trigonometrical ratios of many angles by reference to simple geometrical figures.

Example 4.

Find the sine, cosine and tangent of (i) $45°$, (ii) $30°$, (iii) $60°$.

(i) Let ONP be an isosceles triangle, right-angled at N, so that $ON = NP$. Then, if ON be of unit length,

$$OP^2 = ON^2 + NP^2 = 1 + 1 = 2,$$

so that $OP = \sqrt{2}$.

Therefore, easily,

$$\sin 45° = 1/\sqrt{2}, \quad \cos 45° = 1/\sqrt{2}, \quad \tan 45° = 1.$$

(ii) Take the angle XOA to be $30°$. Then the angle NPO is $60°$ and the figure ONP is one-half of an equilateral triangle of side equal in length to OP.

If, therefore, NP be of unit length, $OP = 2$ and $ON = \sqrt{3}$, so that

$$\sin 30° = \tfrac{1}{2}, \quad \cos 30° = \sqrt{3}/2,$$
$$\tan 30° = 1/\sqrt{3}.$$

(iii) From a consideration of the above figure it is evident that

$$\sin 60° = \sqrt{3}/2, \quad \cos 60° = \tfrac{1}{2}, \quad \tan 60° = \sqrt{3}.$$

9. Magnitude of angles. Radians.

A more convenient unit for analytical purposes is the angle subtended at the centre of a circle by an arc equal in length to the radius: this angle is called a *radian*. Since the ratio between the angle at the centre and the arc on which it stands is constant for all circles, it follows that the radian is the same whatever the radius of the circle: the radian may therefore be taken as a unit of measurement.

To obtain the number of radians corresponding to the number of degrees in an angle, all that is necessary is to multiply the number of degrees by $\frac{\pi}{180}$. This is easily seen to be so, for if x be the number of degrees corresponding to a radian, we have

$$\frac{\text{angle subtended by the arc equal in length to the radius}}{\text{angle subtended by half the circumference}} = \frac{\text{radian}}{180°}$$

i.e. $r/\pi r = x/180,$

so that $x = 180/\pi$, or π radians $= 180°.$

In applying the calculus to trigonometrical functions it is essential that angles should be expressed in terms of an absolute unit of measurement. Consequently, in all the work that follows, unless otherwise stated, angles must be taken to be measured in radians.

10. Periodicity of the trigonometrical ratios.

If we consider the definitions of the ratios, taking into account the signs as well as the magnitudes, it can easily be shown that there will be more than one angle having the same particular ratio. To take a simple example: in the following figure, let the radius

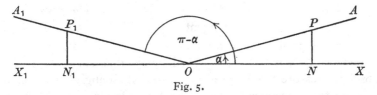

Fig. 5.

take up the positions OA and OA_1, where the angle XOA is the angle α and the angle XOA_1 is the supplement of XOA, i.e. $\pi - \alpha$.

Then, attending to the directions of the lines involved, we shall have

$$\sin \alpha = NP/OP = N_1P_1/OP_1 = + \sin (\pi - \alpha),$$

$$\cos \alpha = ON/OP = - ON_1/OP_1 = - \cos (\pi - \alpha),$$

and $\tan \alpha = NP/ON = N_1P_1/- ON_1 = - \tan (\pi - \alpha).$

Again, from the figure it can be shown similarly that

$$\sin \alpha = - \sin (\pi + \alpha) = - \sin (2\pi - \alpha),$$
$$\cos \alpha = - \cos (\pi + \alpha) = + \cos (2\pi - \alpha),$$
$$\tan \alpha = + \tan (\pi + \alpha) = - \tan (2\pi - \alpha).$$

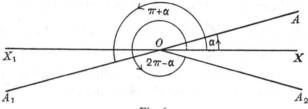

Fig. 6.

If now the radius make a complete revolution, so that, starting from the position OX it takes up the position OA after first tracing out the angle 2π, then it is evident that $\sin \alpha = \sin (2\pi + \alpha)$; $\cos \alpha = \cos (2\pi + \alpha)$; $\tan \alpha = \tan (2\pi + \alpha)$.

We have, therefore, that

$$\sin \alpha = \sin (\pi - \alpha) = \sin (2\pi + \alpha) = \sin (3\pi - \alpha) = \ldots\ldots,$$
$$\cos \alpha = \cos (2\pi - \alpha) = \cos (2\pi + \alpha) = \cos (4\pi - \alpha) = \ldots\ldots,$$
$$\tan \alpha = \tan (\pi + \alpha) = \tan (2\pi + \alpha) = \tan (3\pi + \alpha) = \ldots\ldots$$

These relations may be generalised in the forms:

all angles having the same sine as α are the values of $n\pi + (-1)^n \alpha$,

,,   ,,   cosine   ,,   ,, $2n\pi \pm \alpha$,

,,   ,,   tangent   ,,   ,, $n\pi + \alpha$,

where n is a positive integer.

For example, it has been proved above that $\sin 30° = \frac{1}{2}$. In absolute measure this is $\sin \pi/6 = \frac{1}{2}$, so that all angles whose sine is $\frac{1}{2}$ are the successive values of $\{n\pi + (-1)^n \pi/6\}$, i.e. $\pi/6$, $5\pi/6$, $13\pi/6$, $17\pi/6$, and so on.

It will be seen that if we replace n by $2m$, so that only even values of the positive integers are taken into account, the general angle for $\sin \alpha$ is $2m\pi + \alpha$; this brings the property of the sine into line with those of the other ratios. For all the trigonometrical functions, therefore, we may say that

$$f(x + 2m\pi) = f(x).$$

If a function have this property it is said to be a *periodic function* with period 2π.

A graphical representation (Fig. 7) shows quite clearly the periodic property of the sine, cosine and tangent.

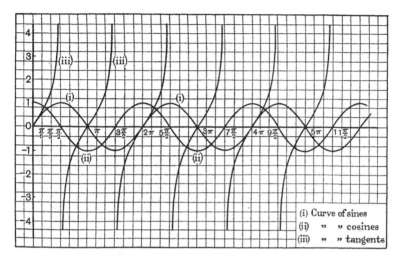

Fig. 7.

Notes: (i) The tangent and cotangent are periodic with period π.

(ii) It can be shown quite easily by the consideration of a diagram similar to Fig. 6 that the generalised forms hold equally for negative integral values of n.

11. Ratios of $(\tfrac{1}{2}\pi \pm a)$.

(i) If in Fig. 8 the angles XOP and XOP_1 are a and $\tfrac{1}{2}\pi - a$ respectively, and we make $OP_1 = OP$, then by considering the geometry of the two triangles ONP and ON_1P_1 it is easily seen that

$$ON/OP = N_1P_1/OP_1,$$
$$NP/OP = ON_1/OP_1,$$
$$NP/ON = ON_1/N_1P_1;$$

so that
$$\cos a = \sin (\tfrac{1}{2}\pi - a),$$
$$\sin a = \cos (\tfrac{1}{2}\pi - a),$$
$$\tan a = \cot (\tfrac{1}{2}\pi - a).$$

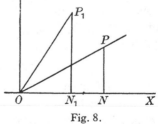

Fig. 8.

Similarly, $\cot \alpha = \tan (\tfrac{1}{2}\pi - \alpha)$ and $\operatorname{cosec} \alpha = \sec (\tfrac{1}{2}\pi - \alpha)$.

The angles α and $\tfrac{1}{2}\pi - \alpha$ are called *complementary* angles, the "co" in cosine, cotangent and cosecant corresponding to the *complementary* angle.

(ii) If the angle $XOP_1 = \tfrac{1}{2}\pi + \alpha$ as in Fig. 9

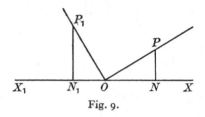

Fig. 9.

we shall have $ON/OP = N_1P_1/OP_1$, $\therefore \cos \alpha = \sin (\tfrac{1}{2}\pi + \alpha)$;

also $\qquad\qquad NP/OP = - ON_1/OP_1$, $\therefore \sin \alpha = - \cos (\tfrac{1}{2}\pi + \alpha)$;

and $\qquad\qquad\qquad\qquad\qquad \tan \alpha = - \cot (\tfrac{1}{2}\pi + \alpha)$.

(iii) When the angle XOP is so small that ON and OP coincide,

$$\sin 0 = 0, \ \cos 0 = 1, \ \tan 0 = 0;$$

and from the above

$$\sin \tfrac{1}{2}\pi = \cos 0 = 1, \ \cos \tfrac{1}{2}\pi = \sin 0 = 0, \ \tan \tfrac{1}{2}\pi = \infty.$$

12. Inverse functions.

From the identity $\sin \pi/6 = \tfrac{1}{2}$ we can obtain the inverse relation, namely, that $\pi/6$ is the angle whose sine is $\tfrac{1}{2}$. The notation adopted for this is

$$\sin^{-1} \tfrac{1}{2} = \pi/6.$$

This inverse notation is not to be confused with the algebraic notation for negative indices. Although a^{-1} is equivalent to $1/a$, $\sin^{-1} x$ is not $1/\sin x$, but the angle whose sine is x. We have generally from the above, that if $\sin \alpha = x$, then

$$\sin^{-1} x = n\pi + (- 1)^n \alpha.$$

As a general rule it is convenient to take the inverse function as the numerically smallest angle (with the proper sign) giving the required value of the direct function.

Example 5.

Write down (i) the smallest positive angle, (ii) the general formula for the angle x, given that $x = \cos^{-1} 0 + \cos^{-1} \sqrt{3}/2 + \cos^{-1} 1/\sqrt{2}$.

$$\cos \tfrac{1}{2}\pi = 0, \qquad \therefore \; \cos^{-1} 0 = \tfrac{1}{2}\pi;$$

$$\cos \pi/6 = \sqrt{3}/2, \qquad \therefore \; \cos^{-1} \sqrt{3}/2 = \pi/6;$$

$$\cos \pi/4 = 1/\sqrt{2}, \qquad \therefore \; \cos^{-1} 1/\sqrt{2} = \pi/4.$$

Therefore $x = \tfrac{1}{2}\pi + \pi/6 + \pi/4 = 11\,\pi/12$, which is the smallest positive angle. The general angle is $2n\pi \pm 11\pi/12$.

13. Projection.

If from the extremities of a straight line AB perpendiculars be dropped on to another straight line LM, produced if necessary,

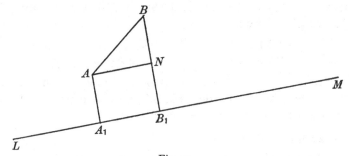

Fig. 10.

the part intercepted on LM by the feet of the perpendiculars is called the *projection* of AB on LM.

In Fig. 10 A_1B_1 is the projection of AB and B_1A_1 is the projection of BA. If AN be drawn through A parallel to LM, then $A_1B_1 = AN$. Call the angle NAB β; then $AN/AB = \cos \beta$, so that

$$A_1B_1 = AN = AB \cos \beta.$$

In other words, the projection of the line AB on the line LM is $AB \cos \beta$, where β is the angle between the lines AB and LM, both produced if necessary. As in para. 3, the lines are supposed to have signs according to the direction in which they are drawn: thus $BA = - AB$ and so on.

The following proposition is important.

The sum of the projections of the sides of a triangle XYZ, taken in order, on any straight line in the same plane, is zero.

The projection of XY is LM,

„ YZ is MN,

„ ZX is NL,

so that the sum of the projections of XY, YZ, ZX is

$$LM + MN + NL = 0.$$

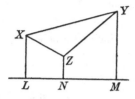 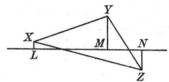

Fig. 11.

As a corollary to this, we have at once that the sum of the projections of XY and YZ = the projection of XZ. For, denoting the
projection of XY by (XY), etc.,

$$(XY) + (YZ) + (ZX) = 0,$$

i.e. $\qquad (XY) + (YZ) \qquad = -(ZX) = (XZ).$

It is easily seen that if $ABCD...K$ be any closed figure, the sum
of the projections of the sides AB, BC, CD, ... taken in order on
any straight line in the same plane is zero.

14. The addition theorems.

Let the revolving line sweep out the angle α by taking up the
position OA, and subsequently the angle β by the new position OB.

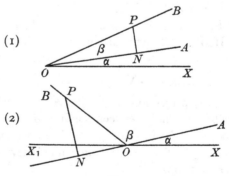

Fig. 12.

Drop a perpendicular PN from any point P in OB on to OA.
Project the sides of the triangle ONP on to OX.

(1) $(OP) = (ON) + (NP)$
$$= ON \cos \alpha + NP \cos (\tfrac{1}{2}\pi + \alpha)$$
$$= ON \cos \alpha - NP \sin \alpha.$$

$\therefore OP \cos (\alpha + \beta) = OP \cos \beta \cos \alpha - OP \sin \beta \sin \alpha.$

(2) $(OP) = (ON) + (NP)$
$$= ON \cos (\pi + \alpha) + NP \cos (\tfrac{1}{2}\pi + \alpha)$$
$$= ON (- \cos \alpha) - NP \sin \alpha.$$

$\therefore OP \cos (\alpha + \beta) = OP \cos (\pi - \beta)(- \cos \alpha) - OP \sin (\pi - \beta) \sin \alpha$
$$= OP \cos \beta \cos \alpha - OP \sin \beta \sin \alpha.$$

Therefore in both cases we have that
$$\cos (\alpha + \beta) = \cos \alpha \cos \beta - \sin \alpha \sin \beta \qquad \ldots\ldots\text{(vi)}.$$

By changing the sign of β,
$$\cos (\alpha - \beta) = \cos \alpha \cos \beta + \sin \alpha \sin \beta \qquad \ldots\ldots\text{(vii)},$$

since it can be shown easily from the relations in para. 10 that $\cos (- \beta) = \cos \beta$, and that $\sin (- \beta) = - \sin \beta$.

Again, by changing α to $\tfrac{1}{2}\pi + \alpha$ in (vi),
$$\cos (\tfrac{1}{2}\pi + \alpha + \beta) = \cos (\tfrac{1}{2}\pi + \alpha) \cos \beta - \sin (\tfrac{1}{2}\pi + \alpha) \sin \beta,$$

i.e. $\qquad \sin (\alpha + \beta) = \sin \alpha \cos \beta + \cos \alpha \sin \beta \qquad \ldots\ldots\text{(viii)},$

and, by writing $- \beta$ for β in (viii),
$$\sin (\alpha - \beta) = \sin \alpha \cos \beta - \cos \alpha \sin \beta \qquad \ldots\ldots\text{(ix)}.$$

The corresponding formulae for the tangents of the compound angles may be obtained thus:

$$\tan (\alpha + \beta) = \frac{\sin (\alpha + \beta)}{\cos (\alpha + \beta)} = \frac{\sin \alpha \cos \beta + \cos \alpha \sin \beta}{\cos \alpha \cos \beta - \sin \alpha \sin \beta}$$

$$= \frac{\dfrac{\sin \alpha \cos \beta}{\cos \alpha \cos \beta} + \dfrac{\cos \alpha \sin \beta}{\cos \alpha \cos \beta}}{\dfrac{\cos \alpha \cos \beta}{\cos \alpha \cos \beta} - \dfrac{\sin \alpha \sin \beta}{\cos \alpha \cos \beta}} = \frac{\tan \alpha + \tan \beta}{1 - \tan \alpha \tan \beta} \qquad \ldots\ldots\text{(x)},$$

and similarly $\tan (\alpha - \beta) \qquad = \dfrac{\tan \alpha - \tan \beta}{1 + \tan \alpha \tan \beta} \ldots\ldots\text{(xi)}.$

Note. We have proved the addition theorems for the following ranges of angles: (1) $\alpha < \tfrac{1}{2}\pi$ and $\beta < \tfrac{1}{2}\pi$; (2) $\alpha < \tfrac{1}{2}\pi$ and $\beta > \tfrac{1}{2}\pi < \pi$. The method of projection can be applied in a similar manner to prove the theorems for angles of any magnitude.

15. Sum and Difference formulae.

We have

$$\sin(\alpha + \beta) = \sin\alpha\cos\beta + \cos\alpha\sin\beta,$$
$$\sin(\alpha - \beta) = \sin\alpha\cos\beta - \cos\alpha\sin\beta;$$

therefore, by addition,

$$\sin(\alpha + \beta) + \sin(\alpha - \beta) = 2\sin\alpha\cos\beta.$$

Let $\alpha + \beta = \gamma$ and $\alpha - \beta = \delta$.

Then $\quad \sin\gamma + \sin\delta = 2\sin\frac{1}{2}(\gamma + \delta)\cos\frac{1}{2}(\gamma - \delta)$ ......(xii).

By subtraction, we have, similarly,

$$\sin\gamma - \sin\delta = 2\cos\frac{1}{2}(\gamma + \delta)\sin\frac{1}{2}(\gamma - \delta) \quad ......(\text{xiii}).$$

From formulae (vi) and (vii) it can be shown in the same manner that

$$\cos\gamma + \cos\delta = 2\cos\frac{1}{2}(\gamma + \delta)\cos\frac{1}{2}(\gamma - \delta) \quad ......(\text{xiv}),$$
$$\cos\gamma - \cos\delta = 2\sin\frac{1}{2}(\gamma + \delta)\sin\frac{1}{2}(\delta - \gamma)$$
$$= -2\sin\frac{1}{2}(\gamma + \delta)\sin\frac{1}{2}(\gamma - \delta)......(\text{xv}).$$

These formulae can be proved by projection on the same lines as those adopted for the proofs of the addition formulae.

16. Double angles and half angles.

From formula (vi) we have, by putting $\beta = \alpha$,

$$\cos 2\alpha = \cos^2\alpha - \sin^2\alpha,$$

or, since $\cos^2\alpha + \sin^2\alpha = 1$,

$$\cos 2\alpha = 2\cos^2\alpha - 1 = 1 - 2\sin^2\alpha \quad ......(\text{xvi}).$$

Again, from the formula for $\sin(\alpha + \beta)$, putting $\alpha = \beta$,

$$\sin 2\alpha = 2\sin\alpha\cos\alpha \quad ......(\text{xvii}).$$

The tangent formula (x) gives

$$\tan 2\alpha = 2\tan\alpha/(1 - \tan^2\alpha) \quad ......(\text{xviii}).$$

By replacing 2α by α convenient formulae in terms of half angles can at once be obtained, thus:

$$\sin\alpha = 2\sin\tfrac{1}{2}\alpha\cos\tfrac{1}{2}\alpha,$$
$$1 = \cos^2\tfrac{1}{2}\alpha + \sin^2\tfrac{1}{2}\alpha;$$

$$\therefore \sin \alpha = \frac{2 \sin \tfrac{1}{2}\alpha \cos \tfrac{1}{2}\alpha}{\cos^2 \tfrac{1}{2}\alpha + \sin^2 \tfrac{1}{2}\alpha}$$

$$= \frac{\dfrac{2 \sin \tfrac{1}{2}\alpha \cos \tfrac{1}{2}\alpha}{\cos^2 \tfrac{1}{2}\alpha}}{\dfrac{\cos^2 \tfrac{1}{2}\alpha}{\cos^2 \tfrac{1}{2}\alpha} + \dfrac{\sin^2 \tfrac{1}{2}\alpha}{\cos^2 \tfrac{1}{2}\alpha}}$$

$$= \frac{2 \tan \tfrac{1}{2}\alpha}{1 + \tan^2 \tfrac{1}{2}\alpha} \qquad \ldots\ldots(xix).$$

Similarly $\qquad \cos \alpha = \dfrac{1 - \tan^2 \tfrac{1}{2}\alpha}{1 + \tan^2 \tfrac{1}{2}\alpha} \qquad \ldots\ldots(xx),$

and, by division, $\quad \tan \alpha = \dfrac{2 \tan \tfrac{1}{2}\alpha}{1 - \tan^2 \tfrac{1}{2}\alpha} \qquad \ldots\ldots(xxi).$

17. Examples.

Some examples illustrative of the use of the above formulae for the proving of identities and for the solution of trigonometrical equations are given below.

Example 6.

Prove that $\qquad \dfrac{\sin 5a + \sin a}{\sin 3a - \sin a} = 1 + 2 \cos 2a.$

$$\frac{\sin 5a + \sin a}{\sin 3a - \sin a} = \frac{2 \sin \tfrac{1}{2}(5a + a) \cos \tfrac{1}{2}(5a - a)}{2 \cos \tfrac{1}{2}(3a + a) \sin \tfrac{1}{2}(3a - a)}$$

$$= \frac{2 \sin 3a \cos 2a}{2 \cos 2a \sin a} = \frac{\sin 3a}{\sin a}.$$

But $\sin 3a = \sin(2a + a) = \sin 2a \cos a + \cos 2a \sin a$

$$= 2 \sin a \cos^2 a + (1 - 2 \sin^2 a) \sin a$$

$$= 2 \sin a (1 - \sin^2 a) + (1 - 2 \sin^2 a) \sin a$$

$$= 3 \sin a - 4 \sin^3 a.$$

$\therefore \sin 3a/\sin a = 3 - 4 \sin^2 a = 3 + 2(1 - 2 \sin^2 a) - 2$

$$= 1 + 2 \cos 2a.$$

Example 7.

If $\qquad \cos \alpha + \cos \beta + \cos \gamma + \cos \alpha \cos \beta \cos \gamma = 0,$

prove that $\qquad \tan \tfrac{1}{2}\alpha \tan \tfrac{1}{2}\beta \tan \tfrac{1}{2}\gamma = \pm 1.$

Now $\qquad \cos \alpha = \dfrac{1 - \tan^2 \tfrac{1}{2}\alpha}{1 + \tan^2 \tfrac{1}{2}\alpha}.$

Let $\qquad \tan \tfrac{1}{2}\alpha = a, \ \tan \tfrac{1}{2}\beta = b, \ \tan \tfrac{1}{2}\gamma = c.$

Then the condition that
$$\cos \alpha + \cos \beta + \cos \gamma + \cos \alpha \cos \beta \cos \gamma = 0$$
is the same condition as
$$\frac{1 - a^2}{1 + a^2} + \frac{1 - b^2}{1 + b^2} + \frac{1 - c^2}{1 + c^2} + \frac{(1 - a^2)(1 - b^2)(1 - c^2)}{(1 + a^2)(1 + b^2)(1 + c^2)} = 0.$$

By a simple algebraic transformation this becomes
$$\frac{4(1 - a^2 b^2 c^2)}{(1 + a^2)(1 + b^2)(1 + c^2)} = 0,$$

i.e.
$$1 - a^2 b^2 c^2 = 0,$$
$$\therefore a^2 b^2 c^2 = 1,$$
$$abc = \pm 1,$$

i.e.
$$\tan \tfrac{1}{2}\alpha \tan \tfrac{1}{2}\beta \tan \tfrac{1}{2}\gamma = \pm 1,$$
which proves the proposition.

Example 8.

Prove that, if $\alpha + \beta + \gamma = \pi$, then
$$\frac{1 - \cos \alpha + \cos \beta + \cos \gamma}{1 - \cos \beta + \cos \gamma + \cos \alpha} = \frac{\tan \tfrac{1}{2}\alpha}{\tan \tfrac{1}{2}\beta}.$$

If $\alpha + \beta + \gamma = \pi$, then $\tfrac{1}{2}\alpha = \tfrac{1}{2}\pi - \tfrac{1}{2}(\beta + \gamma)$, so that
$$\sin \tfrac{1}{2}\alpha = \cos \tfrac{1}{2}(\beta + \gamma) \quad \text{and} \quad \cos \tfrac{1}{2}\alpha = \sin \tfrac{1}{2}(\beta + \gamma).$$
$$\frac{(1 - \cos \alpha) + (\cos \beta + \cos \gamma)}{(1 + \cos \alpha) + (\cos \gamma - \cos \beta)} = \frac{2 \sin^2 \tfrac{1}{2}\alpha + 2 \cos \tfrac{1}{2}(\beta + \gamma)\cos \tfrac{1}{2}(\beta - \gamma)}{2 \cos^2 \tfrac{1}{2}\alpha - 2 \sin \tfrac{1}{2}(\beta + \gamma)\sin \tfrac{1}{2}(\gamma - \beta)}.$$

Substituting for $\sin \tfrac{1}{2}\alpha$ and $\cos \tfrac{1}{2}\alpha$ as above, and dividing through by
$\dfrac{\cos \tfrac{1}{2}(\beta + \gamma)}{\sin \tfrac{1}{2}(\beta + \gamma)}$, i.e. by $\cot \tfrac{1}{2}(\beta + \gamma)$ or $\tan \tfrac{1}{2}\alpha$, we obtain

$$\cot \tfrac{1}{2}(\beta + \gamma)\frac{\cos \tfrac{1}{2}(\beta + \gamma) + \cos \tfrac{1}{2}(\beta - \gamma)}{\sin \tfrac{1}{2}(\beta + \gamma) + \sin \tfrac{1}{2}(\beta - \gamma)}$$
$$= \tan \tfrac{1}{2}\alpha \frac{2 \cos \tfrac{1}{2}\gamma \cos \tfrac{1}{2}\beta}{2 \cos \tfrac{1}{2}\gamma \sin \tfrac{1}{2}\beta} = \frac{\tan \tfrac{1}{2}\alpha}{\tan \tfrac{1}{2}\beta}.$$

Example 9.

Solve the equation $\sin 9x + \sin 5x + 2 \sin^2 x = 1.$

$$\sin 9x + \sin 5x = 1 - 2 \sin^2 x$$
$$= \cos 2x,$$

i.e.
$$2 \sin 7x \cos 2x = \cos 2x;$$

therefore, either
$$\cos 2x = 0 \qquad \qquad \ldots \ldots (a),$$

or
$$\sin 7x = \tfrac{1}{2} \qquad \qquad \ldots \ldots (b).$$

From (a) $\qquad 2x = \tfrac{1}{2}\pi,$

or $\qquad\qquad x = \pi/4$ and generally $x = \tfrac{1}{2}\left(2n \pm \tfrac{1}{2}\right)\pi,$

and from (b) $\qquad 7x = \pi/6,$

or $\qquad\qquad x = \pi/42 \qquad$,, $\qquad x = \tfrac{1}{7}\left[n + (-1)^n \tfrac{1}{6}\right]\pi.$

Example 10.

Express the function $A \cos \gamma + B \sin \gamma$ in terms of a single function of a single angle.

Let $A = r \cos \delta$, and $B = r \sin \delta$.

Then, since $\cos^2\delta + \sin^2\delta = 1$, we have $A^2 + B^2 = r^2$,

and, by division, $\qquad \tan \delta = B/A,$

i.e. $\qquad\qquad\qquad \delta = \tan^{-1}(B/A).$

We may write, therefore,

$$A \cos \gamma + B \sin \gamma = r \cos \gamma \cos \delta + r \sin \gamma \sin \delta = r \cos(\gamma - \delta),$$

where $\qquad\qquad\qquad r = \pm\sqrt{A^2 + B^2}.$

Similarly $\qquad A \cos \gamma - B \sin \gamma = r \cos(\gamma + \delta).$

Example 11.

To expand $\cos nx$ in an ascending series of powers of $\cos x$ and $\sin x$, where n is a positive integer.

Now, $\cos 2x = \cos^2 x - \sin^2 x,$

$$\cos 3x = 4\cos^3 x - 3\cos x$$
$$= \cos^3 x + 3\cos^3 x - 3\cos x$$
$$= \cos^3 x - 3\cos x\,(1 - \cos^2 x)$$
$$= \cos^3 x - 3\cos x \sin^2 x = \cos^3 x - \frac{3\cdot 2}{2!}\cos x \sin^2 x,$$

$$\cos 4x = \cos^2 2x - \sin^2 2x$$
$$= \cos^4 x - 2\cos^2 x \sin^2 x + \sin^4 x - 4\sin^2 x \cos^2 x$$
$$= \cos^4 x - 6\cos^2 x \sin^2 x + \sin^4 x$$
$$= \cos^4 x - \frac{4\cdot 3}{2!}\cos^2 x \sin^2 x + \frac{4\cdot 3\cdot 2}{4!}\sin^4 x.$$

This suggests the general form

$$\cos nx = \cos^n x - n_2 \cos^{n-2} x \sin^2 x + n_4 \cos^{n-4} x \sin^4 x - \ldots$$
$$+ (-1)^m n_{2m} \cos^{n-2m} x \sin^{2m} x + \ldots,$$

where n_r stands for $\dfrac{1}{r!}n(n-1)\ldots(n-r+1).$

Similarly, by expressing $\sin 2x$, $\sin 3x$ and $\sin 4x$ in terms of powers of $\cos x$ and $\sin x$, the general form for $\sin nx$ would appear to be

$$\sin nx = n_1 \cos^{n-1} x \sin x - n_3 \cos^{n-3} x \sin^3 x + \ldots$$
$$+ (-1)^{m-1} n_{2m-1} \cos^{n-(2m-1)} x \sin^{2m-1} x + \ldots.$$

F

Assume these two formulae true for the positive integral value n. Then

$$\cos (n + 1) x = \cos nx \cos x - \sin nx \sin x$$
$$= \cos x (\cos^n x - n_2 \cos^{n-2} x \sin^2 x + \ldots)$$
$$- \sin x (n_1 \cos^{n-1} x \sin x - n_3 \cos^{n-3} x \sin^3 x + \ldots),$$

where the coefficient of $\cos^{n-2m+1} x \sin^{2m} x$ is $(-1)^m (n_{2m} + n_{2m-1})$, which is $(-1)^m (n + 1)_{2m}$.

Similarly for $\sin (n + 1) x$.

If, therefore, the series are true for n they are true for $n + 1$. But they are true for 2, 3, 4, …; therefore they are true for 5, 6, … and for any positive integer.

EXAMPLES 1

1. Write down the sine, cosine and tangent of the following angles:
$$150^\circ, \qquad 135^\circ, \qquad 750^\circ, \qquad 210^\circ.$$

2. Express the angles in the above question in radian measure.

3. Explain carefully why the following relations are impossible:
(a) $\sin A = 1.2$;   (b) $\sin^2 A = 2 - \cos^2 A$;
(c) $\sin A = .8$ and $\cos A = .7$;   (d) $\tan A = .8$ and $\sec A = .9$;
(e) $\sin A = .5$, $\cos A = .4$ and $\tan A = .6$.

4. Give in radians the smallest positive angle satisfying the equations:
(a) $\sin x = \frac{1}{2}$;   (b) $\sin \frac{1}{2}x = \sqrt{3}/2$;
(c) $\tan 4x = 1$;   (d) $\operatorname{cosec} x = \sqrt{2}$;
(e) $\cos 8x = 1$.

5. Determine $\operatorname{cosec} \beta$:
(a) $\sec \beta = 8$;   (b) $\cos \beta = .108$;   (c) $\tan \beta = .501$.

6. Prove the identities:
(i) $\sin^4 \alpha - \sin^2 \alpha = \cos^4 \alpha - \cos^2 \alpha$;
(ii) $\cos^2 \alpha - \sin^2 \alpha = 2 \cos^2 \alpha - 1 = 1 - 2 \sin^2 \alpha$;
(iii) $\sin^3 \alpha - \cos^3 \alpha = (1 + \sin \alpha \cos \alpha) (\sin \alpha - \cos \alpha)$;
(iv) $\sin \gamma \cos \gamma = \tan \gamma/(1 + \tan^2 \gamma)$;
(v) $\sin^2 \beta \tan^2 \beta + \sin^2 \beta = \tan^2 \beta$;
(vi) $(\tan A - \tan B) \cos A \cos B = \sin A \cos B - \cos A \sin B$;
(vii) $\cos^2 \beta (3 - \tan^2 \beta) = 3 - 4 \sin^2 \beta$;
(viii) $\dfrac{\cos^2 \beta - \sin^2 \gamma}{\sin^2 \beta \sin^2 \gamma} = \dfrac{1 - \tan^2 \beta \tan^2 \gamma}{\tan^2 \beta \tan^2 \gamma}$;
(ix) $2 \cos A - \sec A = (\cos A - \sin A) (1 + \tan A)$;
(x) $(\sec \beta + \tan \beta) (\operatorname{cosec} \beta - \cot \beta) = (\sec \beta - 1) (\operatorname{cosec} \beta + 1)$.

7. Write down the complete solutions of the following equations:

(i) $\sin x = 1/\sqrt{2}$; (ii) $\sec x = 2$;

(iii) $\tan x = -1/\sqrt{3}$; (iv) $\cos\left(\tfrac{1}{4}\pi + \theta\right) = 0$;

(v) $\sin\theta = \cos\theta$.

8. Complete the identities:

(i) $\sin^{-1}\tfrac{1}{2} + \sin^{-1}\sqrt{3}/2 =$ (ii) $\cos^{-1} 0 + \cos^{-1} 1 =$

(iii) $\tan^{-1}\sqrt{3} + \tan^{-1} 1/\sqrt{3} =$

(iv) $\sin^{-1}(-1) + \cos^{-1} 0 =$ (v) $\cos^{-1}\tfrac{1}{2} + 2\sin^{-1}\tfrac{1}{2} =$

(vi) $\cot^{-1}\infty + \tan^{-1} 1 =$

(vii) $\cos^{-1}\left(-\tfrac{1}{2}\right) + 4\sec^{-1}\left(-2/\sqrt{3}\right) =$

(viii) $\sin^{-1}(-1) + \sin^{-1}\left(-\tfrac{1}{2}\right) =$

(ix) $\sec^{-1} 2 + \sec^{-1}(-2) + \sec^{-1}(-1) =$

(x) $3\operatorname{cosec}^{-1} 2 + \operatorname{cosec}^{-1}(-2) + \operatorname{cosec}^{-1}(-1) =$

9. Solve the equations:

(i) $\cos 4x = \sin 5x$; (ii) $\sin x = \cos 10x$;

(iii) $\tan x = \cot\left(\tfrac{1}{4}\pi + x\right)$; (iv) $\operatorname{cosec} x = \sec(3\pi - 2x)$;

(v) $\sin(n\pi - 3x) = \cos(2n\pi - 4x)$.

10. Write down, in terms of ratios of the angle θ alone,

$\sin(3\pi/2 + \theta)$; $\cos(3\pi/2 - \theta)$; $\tan(5\pi - \theta)$; $\cot(5\pi/2 - \theta)$;

$\operatorname{cosec}(2\pi + \theta)$; $\sec(7\pi/2 + \theta)$; $\cot(-\theta)$; $\sin(-3\pi - \theta)$;

$$\cos\left(-\tfrac{1}{2}\pi + \theta\right).$$

11. Show that

(i) given $A = \sin^{-1} 3/5$, $\cos A = 4/5$;

(ii) ,, $B = \cos^{-1} 12/13$, $\sin B = 5/13$;

(iii) ,, $C = \sin^{-1} 8/17$, $\tan C = 15/17$;

(iv) ,, $D = \tan^{-1}\tfrac{1}{2}$, $\sin D = 1/\sqrt{5}$.

12. Find the values of

$\sin(A + B)$ where $A = \sin^{-1} 3/5$ and $B = \cos^{-1} 12/13$;

$\cos(A + B)$,, $A = \cos^{-1} 3/5$ $B = \sin^{-1} 8/17$;

$\sin(A - B)$,, $A = \sin^{-1} 12/13$ $B = \sin^{-1} 1/\sqrt{5}$;

$\cos(A - B)$,, $A = \sin^{-1} 5/13$ $B = \tan^{-1}\tfrac{1}{2}$;

$\sin 2A$,, $A = \sin^{-1} 15/17$;

$\cos 2A$,, $A = \cot^{-1} 2$;

$\tan(A + B)$,, $A = \sec^{-1} 5/4$ $B = \cot^{-1} 12/5$;

$\tan(A - B)$,, $A = \sin^{-1} 3/5$ $B = \operatorname{cosec}^{-1}\sqrt{5}$;

$\tan 2A$,, $A = \sin^{-1}\cdot 83$;

$\cot(A - B)$,, $A = \cos^{-1}\cdot 7$ $B = \sec^{-1}\cdot 3$.

Prove the following identities:

13. $\sin (A - B) \cos B + \cos (A - B) \sin B = \sin A$;

14. $\dfrac{\tan (A + B) - \tan A}{1 + \tan (A + B) \tan A} = \tan B$;

15. $\sin 3a = 3 \sin a - 4 \sin^3 a$;

16. $\tan 3a (1 - 3 \tan^2 a) = 3 \tan a - \tan^3 a$;

17. $\sin \pi/6 + \sin \pi/3 = 2 \sin \frac{1}{4}\pi \sin \pi/12$;

18. $\sin 3\beta + \sin 5\beta = 2 \sin 4\beta \cos \beta$;

19. $\tan \frac{1}{2}\theta = (1 - \cos \theta)/\sin \theta$;

20. $\sin (\theta + \frac{1}{4}\pi) - \cos (\theta - \frac{1}{4}\pi) = 0$;

21. $\cos (\frac{1}{4}\pi + \theta) + \cos (\frac{1}{4}\pi - \theta) = \sqrt{2} \cos \theta$;

22. $\cos (a + \beta) + \sin (a - \beta) = 2 \sin (\frac{1}{4}\pi + a) \cos (\frac{1}{4}\pi + \beta)$;

23. $\cos A + \cos 3A + \cos 5A + \cos 7A = 4 \cos A \cos 2A \cos 4A$;

24. $(\cos A + \cos 3A) \cos 4A = (\cos 3A + \cos 5A) \cos 2A$;

25. $\tan A + \tan B = \sin (A + B)/\cos A \cos B$;

26. $\cos 2\beta \cos \beta - \sin 4\beta \sin \beta = \cos 2\beta \cos 3\beta$;

27. $\cos 4\delta = \cos^4 \delta - 6 \cos^2 \delta \sin^2 \delta + \sin^4 \delta$;

28. $(a + b) + (a - b) \tan^2 \theta = (a + b \cos 2\theta) \sec^2 \theta$;

29. $\cos 4A = 3 + 4 \sin 2A - 2 (\cos A + \sin A)^4$;

30. $\tan \frac{1}{2} (A + B) - \tan \frac{1}{2} (A - B) = 2 \sin B/(\cos A + \cos B)$;

31. $(\tan A + \tan B) \sin (A - B) = (\tan A - \tan B) \sin (A + B)$;

32. $(\cot^2 A - \cot^2 B) \sin^2 A \sin^2 B = \cos (A + B) \cos (A - B)$.

Solve the equations:

33. $2 \sin x + 5 \cos x = 2$;

34. $\cos (a + x) - \sin (a + x) = \sqrt{2}$;

35. $\cos^{-1} x = \frac{1}{4}\pi - \cot^{-1} 2$;

36. $4 \cos x = 2 \tan x + 3 \sec x$;

37. $\sin x \sin 3x = \sin 5x \sin 7x$;

38. $\tan^{-1} \dfrac{x + 1}{x - 1} + \tan^{-1} \dfrac{x - 1}{x} = \tan^{-1} (- 7)$;

39. $\cos x + \cos 2x + \cos 3x + \cos 4x = 0$.

40. $x = \tan^{-1} \frac{1}{2} + \tan^{-1} \frac{1}{4} + \tan^{-1} \frac{1}{13}$. Express x in the form $\tan^{-1} k$.

41. Prove by projection that
$$\cos A + \cos (2\pi/3 + A) + \cos (2\pi/3 - A) = 0.$$

42. Plot the curve $\sin x/\cos 2x$ from 0 to π and hence solve approximately the equation $\quad\quad\quad 2x \cos 2x = \sin x.$

43. Show that
$$2 \cos \tfrac{1}{2}A = (\pm \sqrt{1 + \sin A} \pm \sqrt{1 - \sin A}).$$

How would you find the cosine of the half-angle, given the sine of the whole angle, from this formula? Explain your answer by obtaining $\sin \pi/12$.

44. If $A + B + C = \pi$, prove that $\Sigma \tan A = \tan A \tan B \tan C$. Prove also that $\Sigma \sin 2A = 4 \sin A \sin B \sin C$.

45. Prove that $2 \tan^{-1} \left\{ \dfrac{(a-b)}{(a+b)} \tan \tfrac{1}{2}x \right\} = \cos^{-1} \left\{ \dfrac{b + a \cos x}{a + b \cos x} \right\}$.

46. Solve the equation $8 \sin x + \sqrt{3} \sec x = \operatorname{cosec} x$.

47. If $\sin (B + C - A)$, $\sin (C + A - B)$, $\sin (A + B - C)$ are in arithmetic progression, prove that $\tan A$, $\tan B$, $\tan C$ are also in arithmetic progression.

48. Solve the equation $\sin^{-1} (1 - x)^{\frac{1}{2}} + \tan^{-1} 2x = \tfrac{1}{2}\pi$.

49. Obtain α and β from the equations
$$\sin (\alpha + \beta) \cos (\alpha - \beta) = \tfrac{3}{4},$$
$$\cos (\alpha + \beta) \sin (\alpha - \beta) = \tfrac{1}{4}.$$

50. By multiplying all the way through by $2 \sin \tfrac{1}{2}\beta$, sum the series $\sin \alpha + \sin (\alpha + \beta) + \sin (\alpha + 2\beta) + \dots$ to n terms.
Show that
$$\cos \alpha + \cos (\alpha + 2\pi/n) + \cos (\alpha + 4\pi/n) + \dots + \cos (\alpha + \overline{2n - 1}\pi/n) = 0.$$

CHAPTER II

FINITE DIFFERENCES

DEFINITIONS AND FUNDAMENTAL FORMULAE

1. In most mathematical operations there are two classes of quantities. One class consists of those quantities which have the same value throughout the operation, and the other of quantities which may take different values. The first class are *constants* and the second are *variables*. If for example throughout a particular investigation $y = 5$, then wherever y occurs we may substitute the value 5 and y is said to be constant. If however $y = x + 2$, then to any particular value of x there corresponds a different value of y. In this example, if x may take up any value that we care to give it, then x is called an *independent variable*. On the other hand, y will vary according to the value that we assign to x and is said to be a *function* of x, or simply a *dependent variable*. A function of x is generally expressed in either of the following notations: $f(x)$, $F(x)$, $\phi(x)$, ... or u_x, v_x, U_x, ... There may be more than one independent variable on which the value of the function depends. Suppose that $y = x \sin \alpha + z \cos \beta$, where x, z, α, β all vary: then x, z, α, β are the independent variables and y may be written as $f(x, z, \alpha, \beta)$ or $u_{xz\alpha\beta}$.

A rational integral function is a simple form of function depending upon one variable.

$y = a + bx + cx^2 + dx^3 + ... + kx^n$ is a *rational integral function* of the nth degree in x, where a, b, c, d, ... k are constants and the indices are positive integers, n being the greatest.

It should be noted that for any one value of x in such a function there is one and only one value of y.

An alternative name for a rational integral function is a *parabolic* function. When represented graphically the curve

$$y = a + bx + cx^2 + ...$$

is said to be of the parabolic form.

2. Consider the function $y = u_x = 1 + x + x^2$. It is quite easy to obtain the value of y corresponding to any value of x by substituting that value of x on the right-hand side of the equation. For example

x	0	1	2	3	4	5	6	7	8
y	1	3	7	13	21	31	43	57	73

It will be noticed that for successive integral values of x in the above table the values of y follow a certain definite law. If from each value of y the previous value of y be subtracted, we obtain a new set of figures:

$$(\alpha) \quad 2 \quad 4 \quad 6 \quad 8 \quad 10 \quad 12 \quad 14 \quad 16$$

and if the subtraction be performed on these figures in the same way the new differences are

$$(\beta) \quad 2 \quad 2 \quad 2 \quad 2 \quad 2 \quad 2 \quad 2$$

The sequence of 2's in (β) is not a mere coincidence: it will be shown later that when y has the value supposed all the terms in (β) have the same value, 2, however far the series extends.

This leads us to another method of obtaining values of y. Suppose that we write down the original table in a different form, and include in the table the two sets of figures (α) and (β) thus:

x	y	(α)	(β)
0	1		
		2	
1	3		2
		4	
2	7		2
		6	
3	13		2
		8	
4	21		2
		10	
5	31		2
		12	
6	43		2
		14	
7	57		2
		16	
8	73		

We can now find any further value of y by extending the columns (α) and (β). We must however work from (β) to (α) and then to

y instead of from y to (α) and then to (β) as has already been done. For example, to obtain the value of y when x has the value 9, i.e. to obtain u_9, a new 2 must be inserted in the (β) column: the new value in the (α) column will be $16 + 2 = 18$, and the required value of y will be $73 + 18 = 91$. To find u_{10} the process is continued. Any value of y corresponding to an integral value of x can be obtained in a similar manner.

3. The above is a particular instance of a far more general set of operations. We have used the simplest possible numerical values of x, namely the natural numbers, and we have evolved our example from a known quadratic function $y = u_x = 1 + x + x^2$. As a general rule the form of the function is not known and the given values of x are not necessarily consecutive integers.

4. Now suppose that instead of numerical values of x differing by unity we have the following consecutive values of x:

$$a,\ a + h,\ a + 2h,\ a + 3h,\ \ldots,$$

where the values of x differ by a quantity h instead of by unity.

Then if the function be still $y = u_x$ the values of y corresponding to the above values of x will be

$$u_a,\ u_{a+h},\ u_{a+2h},\ u_{a+3h},\ \ldots.$$

In order to form a column similar to column (α) above we shall have to write down

$$u_{a+h} - u_a,\ u_{a+2h} - u_{a+h},\ u_{a+3h} - u_{a+2h},\ \ldots.$$

These are the *first differences* of the function $y = u_x$ and are denoted by

$$\Delta u_a,\ \Delta u_{a+h},\ \Delta u_{a+2h},\ \ldots,$$

where Δ is not a quantity but a symbol representing an "operation."

Column (β), being the differences of column (α), will be

$$(u_{a+2h} - u_{a+h}) - (u_{a+h} - u_a),$$
$$(u_{a+3h} - u_{a+2h}) - (u_{a+2h} - u_{a+h}),$$
$$\ldots\ldots\ldots\ldots\ldots\ldots\ldots\ldots$$

or, more shortly,

$$\Delta u_{a+h} - \Delta u_a,$$
$$\Delta u_{a+2h} - \Delta u_{a+h},$$
$$\ldots\ldots\ldots\ldots\ldots\ldots\ldots\ldots$$

These are the *second differences* of u_x and are denoted by

$$\Delta^2 u_a, \ \Delta^2 u_{a+h}, \ \Delta^2 u_{a+2h}, \ \ldots,$$

where, it must be emphasized, the symbol Δ^2 does not represent the square of a quantity but denotes the repetition of an operation. Similarly, third, fourth, ... nth differences are denoted by

$$\Delta^3 u_a, \ \Delta^4 u_a, \ \ldots \Delta^n u_a.$$

5. Before forming a *difference table* similar to that in para. 2, it is convenient to introduce alternative names for x and y in our equation $y = u_x$. Where our ultimate object is to obtain numerical values of x or y, the independent variable is often termed the *argument*, and the corresponding value of y the *entry*.

In a table of logarithms the number itself is the argument and the logarithm the entry. The converse holds in a table of antilogarithms, where the logarithm is the argument. Similarly in a table of sin a, a is the argument and the sine the entry, whereas a is the entry in a table of $\sin^{-1} a$.

6. Our new difference table is therefore

Argument	Entry	First differences	Second differences	Third differences
a	u_a			
		Δu_a		
$a + h$	u_{a+h}		$\Delta^2 u_a$	
		Δu_{a+h}		$\Delta^3 u_a$
$a + 2h$	u_{a+2h}		$\Delta^2 u_{a+h}$	
		Δu_{a+2h}		$\Delta^3 u_{a+h}$
$a + 3h$	u_{a+3h}		$\Delta^2 u_{a+2h}$	
		Δu_{a+3h}		$\Delta^3 u_{a+2h}$
$a + 4h$	u_{a+4h}		$\Delta^2 u_{a+3h}$	
		Δu_{a+4h}		
$a + 5h$	u_{a+5h}			

The first term in the table (u_a) is called the *leading term*, and the differences which stand at the head of the respective columns, namely Δu_a, $\Delta^2 u_a$, $\Delta^3 u_a$, ..., are called the *leading differences*.

7. Although we have expressed the terms in the difference table by the use of Δ symbols, it is quite easy to obtain any difference in terms of the function alone.

For example, $\Delta^3 u_a$ is the difference between $\Delta^2 u_{a+h}$ and $\Delta^2 u_a$, or $\Delta^3 u_a = \Delta^2 u_{a+h} - \Delta^2 u_a$.

Again, $\Delta^2 u_a$ is the difference between Δu_{a+h} and Δu_a, or

$$\Delta^2 u_a = \Delta u_{a+h} - \Delta u_a,$$

and as　$\Delta u_a = u_{a+h} - u_a,$

we have $\Delta^3 u_a = \Delta^2 u_{a+h} - \Delta^2 u_a$

$$= (\Delta u_{a+2h} - \Delta u_{a+h}) - (\Delta u_{a+h} - \Delta u_a)$$

$$= \Delta u_{a+2h} - 2\Delta u_{a+h} + \Delta u_a$$

$$= (u_{a+3h} - u_{a+2h}) - 2(u_{a+2h} - u_{a+h}) + (u_{a+h} - u_a)$$

$$= u_{a+3h} - 3u_{a+2h} + 3u_{a+h} - u_a.$$

8. It is a simple matter to construct a difference table from a given set of data.

Consider the following examples:

Example 1.

Construct a difference table from the following values, where y is a function of x:

x	y	Δy	$\Delta^2 y$	$\Delta^3 y$
1	1			
		7		
2	8		12	
		19		6
3	27		18	
		37		6
4	64		24	
		61		6
5	125		30	
		91		6
6	216		36	
		127		
7	343			

Example 2.

Show that, in the following table of annuity-values, third differences are practically constant:

Argument x	Entry a_x	Δa_x	$\Delta^2 a_x$	$\Delta^3 a_x$
35	14·298			
		$-$ ·154		
36	14·144		$-$ ·004	
		$-$ ·158		$+$ ·001
37	13·986		$-$ ·003	
		$-$ ·161		·000
38	13·825		$-$ ·003	
		$-$ ·164		$+$ ·001
39	13·661		$-$ ·002	
		$-$ ·166		$+$ ·001
40	13·495		$-$ ·001	
		$-$ ·167		
41	13·328			

It will be observed that in Ex. 1 third differences are invariably the same. In the second example, however, third differences are not quite constant, although the error in assuming them to be so is very small. The difference in the two examples lies in the fact that, while the first function is $y = x^3$, the table of annuity-values from which the data in the second example have been taken does not conform to a mathematical law.

Example 3.

Assuming third differences constant, find the values of u_2 and u_3 from the data:

x	4	5	6	7	8
u_x	·35	·88	1·71	2·90	4·51

Construct the difference table from the given values, and fill in the vacant spaces in the $\Delta^3 u_x$ column with the constant third difference, thus:

x	u_x	Δu_x	$\Delta^2 u_x$	$\Delta^3 u_x$
2	− ·05			
		·11		
3	+ ·06		·18	
		·29		·06
4	+ ·35		·24	
		·53		·06
5	+ ·88		·30	
		·83		·06
6	+ 1·71		·36	
		1·19		·06
7	+ 2·90		·42	
		1·61		
8	+ 4·51			

9. Now it has been stated above that a convenient method for expressing the difference between two successive values of a function u_{a+h} and u_a is by the symbol Δ prefixed to u_a, so that $\Delta u_a = u_{a+h} - u_a$. It will be seen therefore that to find Δu_a we perform two operations: we change u_a to u_{a+h} and subtract u_a from it. The new function u_{a+h} resulting from the first of these operations is denoted symbolically by Eu_a, and the double operation may be written

$$\Delta u_a = Eu_a - u_a.$$

This gives $\qquad Eu_a = u_a + \Delta u_a.$

Eu_a may therefore otherwise be expressed as the sum of u_a and its first difference.

Suppose that in either of the above relations the u_a which occurs in each of the terms be omitted. Then we can state that the two operations denoted by "E" and "Δ" are connected by the symbolic equation

$$E \equiv 1 + \Delta.$$

It must be distinctly understood that we have not "factorized out" u_a in the relation $Eu_a = u_a + \Delta u_a$, and that we must relate the symbols to the functions on which they operate. If, therefore, we were using the equivalence $\Delta \equiv E - 1$, and we operated on the function sin x, it would be wrong to say that Δ sin $x = E$ sin $x - 1$. The correct statement is Δ sin $x = E$ sin $x -$ sin x. Since we are dealing with symbols we cannot increase or decrease either of them by unity, and on forming the algebraic or trigonometrical identity the function must be included in all three terms. In other words, in the identity $E \equiv 1 + \Delta$ the 1 is a symbol of operation just as are E and Δ, and its meaning is that the function on which it operates is to be taken once without alteration.

10. In the same way as Δ^2 denotes, when operating on a function, the difference of the difference of the function, i.e. the second difference, so E^2 denotes the operation of repeating E. That is to say

$$E^2 u_x = E.Eu_x = Eu_{x+h} = u_{x+2h},$$

$$E^3 u_x = u_{x+3h},$$

$$\dots\dots\dots\dots\dots$$

and, generally, $E^n u_x = u_{x+nh}.$

Care must be taken not to confuse the expression $E^2 u_x$ with $(Eu_x)^2$. For example,

$$E^2 (x^2) = (x + 2h)^2 = x^2 + 4hx + 4h^2,$$

but $(Ex)^2 = (x + h)^2 = x^2 + 2hx + h^2.$

11. It is evident that the first difference of a function of the form cx, where c is a constant, is constant: for $\Delta cx = c(x + h) - cx = ch$, which is constant.

Let us consider the effect of differencing a function of x of higher degree than the first.

Example 4.

Difference successively the functions (i) $y = bx^2$ and (ii) $y = ax^3$.

(i) $\Delta bx^2 = b(x + h)^2 - bx^2 = 2bhx + bh^2$,

$\qquad \Delta^2 bx^2 = \Delta(2bhx + bh^2) = 2bh(x + h) + bh^2 - 2bhx - bh^2 = 2bh^2$,

and since $2bh^2$ is constant all further differences will be zero.

(ii) $\Delta ax^3 = a(x + h)^3 - ax^3 = 3ahx^2 + 3ah^2x + ah^3$,

$\qquad \Delta^2 ax^3 = 6ah^2x + 6ah^3$,

and $\Delta^3 ax^3 = 6ah^3$, further differences vanishing.

Collating the above results, we have that

the first differences of functions of the form cx are constant,

the second $\qquad$,, $\qquad$,, $\qquad$,, $\qquad bx^2 \qquad$,,

the third $\qquad$,, $\qquad$,, $\qquad$,, $\qquad ax^3 \qquad$,,

It follows therefore that third differences of $ax^3 + bx^2 + cx + d$ are constant, for before we reach the third differences the terms bx^2, cx and d will have been eliminated.

12. The above considerations lead us to the following important proposition:

If u_x be a rational integral function of the nth degree in x, then the nth difference of the function is constant.

Let the function be

$$u_x = ax^n + bx^{n-1} + cx^{n-2} + \dots + s;$$

then $\quad \Delta u_x = a(x + h)^n + b(x + h)^{n-1} + c(x + h)^{n-2} + \dots + s$

$$- ax^n - bx^{n-1} - cx^{n-2} - \dots - s$$

$$= anx^{n-1}h + b'x^{n-2} + c'x^{n-3} + \dots + r',$$

where $b', c', \dots r'$ are coefficients not involving x.

Similarly,

$$\Delta^2 u_x = an(n-1)x^{n-2}h^2 + b''x^{n-3} + c''x^{n-4} + \dots + q'',$$

and so on.

Each time that we difference we lower the degree of the function by unity. After differencing n times no terms after the first will appear, and we shall be left with

$$\Delta^n u_x = an(n-1)(n-2)(n-3) \dots 2 \cdot 1 \cdot h^n \text{ or } an! \, h^n,$$

which is independent of x and is therefore constant.

As a corollary we may note that $\Delta^{n+1} u_x = 0$, a property of a rational integral function of the nth degree which is of value in the practical application of the work.

The converse proposition is of importance: if the nth difference of a function is zero, the function is a rational integral function of the nth degree.

13. It should be remembered that we are dealing here with a particular form of function. Should the function be other than a rational integral function the nth difference will not vanish however great n may be. Thus, we have

Example 5.

Find the nth difference of e^x.

$$\Delta e^x = e^{x+h} - e^x = e^x (e^h - 1),$$
$$\Delta^2 e^x = (e^h - 1)(e^{x+h} - e^x) = e^x (e^h - 1)^2.$$

Similarly, $\Delta^3 e^x = e^x (e^h - 1)^3,$

$$\dots\dots\dots\dots\dots$$

Ultimately $\Delta^n e^x = e^x (e^h - 1)^n$, which is still a function of x, and is therefore not constant.

14. Although it has been said that the symbols Δ and E are in no sense algebraic quantities, our definitions, namely that Δ^n denotes the operation of differencing the function n times, and that E^n denotes the operation of obtaining a new function when the argument is increased by n unit differences, enable us to apply to these symbols the ordinary algebraic laws. For example,

$$\Delta (u_x + u_y) = u_{x+h} + u_{y+h} - u_x - u_y \quad \text{or} \quad u_{x+h} - u_x + u_{y+h} - u_y,$$

which is $\Delta u_x + \Delta u_y$. This relation is exactly similar to the ordinary algebraic identity $3(x + y) = 3x + 3y$.

The three simple algebraic laws are the laws of (i) distribution, (ii) commutation, (iii) indices.

(i) $\Delta (u_x + v_x + w_x + \dots)$

$$= (u_{x+h} + v_{x+h} + w_{x+h} + \dots) - (u_x + v_x + w_x + \dots)$$
$$= (u_{x+h} - u_x) + (v_{x+h} - v_x) + (w_{x+h} - w_x)$$
$$= \Delta u_x + \Delta v_x + \Delta w_x + \dots.$$

Similarly,

$$E (u_x + v_x + w_x + \dots) = E u_x + E v_x + E w_x + \dots.$$

(ii) The symbols Δ and E are commutative in their operation as regards constants. For if c be a constant,

$$\Delta c u_x = c u_{x+h} - c u_x = c\,(u_{x+h} - u_x) = c\Delta u_x,$$

and $\qquad E c u_x = c u_{x+h} \qquad = c E u_x.$

(iii) The application of indices to the symbols Δ and E may be shown thus:

If m be a positive integer, then Δ^m represents the operation of differencing u_x m times.

$$\Delta^m u_x = (\Delta\Delta\Delta\Delta \ldots m \text{ times})\, u_x,$$

$$\Delta^n (\Delta^m u_x) = (\Delta\Delta\Delta\Delta \ldots n \text{ times})\,(\Delta\Delta\Delta\Delta \ldots m \text{ times})\, u_x$$

$$= (\Delta\Delta\Delta\Delta \ldots \overline{m + n} \text{ times})\, u_x$$

$$= \Delta^{m+n} u_x.$$

Similarly, $\qquad E^m u_x = u_{x+mh},$

$$E^n (E^m u_x) = E^n u_{x+mh} = u_{x+mh+nh} = E^{m+n} u_x.$$

15. In connection with the law of indices we must be careful to define Δ^m, Δ^n, E^m, ... when m and n are not positive integers. So far, the symbols Δ^m and E^m are intelligible only when we can actually perform the operations defined above and obtain the values of the new functions. We have not yet defined these symbols when the indices are negative. Consider for example the symbol Δ^{-1}. Since we have assumed that the symbol Δ obeys the ordinary algebraic laws, Δ^{-1} must be such that $\Delta\,(\Delta^{-1}u_x)$ gives $\Delta^0 u_x$, i.e. u_x.

Let m be a positive integer. Then we define $\Delta^{-m} u_x$ as a function such that if it be operated on by Δ^m the result will be $\Delta^{m-m} u_x$, i.e. u_x. In the same way we have a meaning for $E^{-m} u_x$, namely, that E^m operating on $E^{-m} u_x$ produces u_x. But if m be a positive integer, E^m operating on u_{x-mh} produces $u_{x-mh+mh}$, i.e. u_x. Therefore the same result is obtained by operating with E^m on $E^{-m} u_x$ as on u_{x-mh}. In other words just as $E^m u_x$ gives u_{x+mh} so $E^{-m} u_x$ gives u_{x-mh}.

The symbols E and Δ may be manipulated in a manner similar to algebraic quantities provided that it is always remembered that they are operators and that they have no actual values. There are, however, two important points in which algebraic precedent cannot be safely followed. These are:

(1) Operators are not commutative with regard to variables. E.g., $\Delta(u_x v_x)$ does not as a rule equal $u_x \Delta v_x$.

(2) It is fundamental in algebra that if a function vanishes, then one of its factors must vanish. It is not true that if the result of a series of operations on u_x is equivalent to $\mathrm{o}.u_x$ (i.e. zero), then some one of the operations on u_x must produce $\mathrm{o}.u_x$. For example, if $x^2 = \mathrm{o}$, then $x = \mathrm{o}$; it does not necessarily follow, however, that if $\Delta^2 \equiv \mathrm{o}$, then $\Delta \equiv \mathrm{o}$.

In many problems it is convenient to use operators alone and to omit the functions on which they operate. Where this practice is followed the sign $\equiv$ (is equivalent to) should be adopted in place of $=$ (equals). Thus, $Eu_x = (\mathrm{I} + \Delta)\,u_x$, but $E \equiv (\mathrm{I} + \Delta)$.

For further information on the difficulties connected with the use of operators the student may refer to *J.S.S.* vol. II, pp. 237 *et seq.* (S. H. Alison).

16. Proceeding from the definition of differencing, it has been shown that

$$u_{x+h} = u_x + \Delta u_x,$$

$$u_{x+2h} = u_{x+h} + \Delta u_{x+h}$$

$$= u_x + \Delta u_x + \Delta(u_x + \Delta u_x)$$

$$= u_x + 2\Delta u_x + \Delta^2 u_x,$$

$$u_{x+3h} = u_{x+h} + \Delta u_{x+2h}$$

$$= u_x + 2\Delta u_x + \Delta^2 u_x + \Delta(u_x + 2\Delta u_x + \Delta^2 u_x)$$

$$= u_x + 3\Delta u_x + 3\Delta^2 u_x + \Delta^3 u_x.$$

The coefficients of the various terms in these expansions are the coefficients of x in the expansions of $(\mathrm{I} + x)$, $(\mathrm{I} + x)^2$, $(\mathrm{I} + x)^3$ by the binomial theorem. If we assume, for positive integral values of x, that the general relation between u_{x+nh} and u_x and its differences follows the same law, we can prove the truth of the assumption by the method of mathematical induction.

Assume therefore that

$$u_{x+nh} = u_x + n_1 \Delta u_x + n_2 \Delta^2 u_x + \ldots + n_r \Delta^r u_x + \ldots + \Delta^n u_x$$

is true for the value n.

Then, since $\quad u_{x+(n+1)h} = u_{x+nh} + \Delta u_{x+nh},$

we have

$$u_{x+(n+1)h} = u_x + n_1\Delta u_x + n_2\Delta^2 u_x + \ldots + n_r\Delta^r u_x + \ldots + \Delta^n u_x$$
$$+ \Delta\left(u_x + n_1\Delta u_x + n_2\Delta^2 u_x + \ldots + n_r\Delta^r u_x + \ldots + \Delta^n u_x\right)$$
$$= u_x + \Delta u_x\left(n_1 + 1\right) + \Delta^2 u_x\left(n_2 + n_1\right) + \ldots$$
$$+ \Delta^r u_x\left(n_{r+1} + n_r\right) + \ldots + \Delta^{n+1}u_x.$$

But $\qquad\qquad n_{r+1} + n_r = (n+1)_r,$

$\therefore\ u_{x+(n+1)h} = u_x + (n+1)_1\Delta u_x + (n+1)_2\Delta^2 u_x + \ldots$
$$+ (n+1)_r\Delta^r u_x + \ldots + \Delta^{n+1}u_x,$$

which is of the same form in $(n+1)$ as was the original expression in n.

Therefore if the assumption is true for n it is true for $n+1$.

But the theorem holds when $n = 1, 2, 3$.

Therefore it is true when $n = 4, 5, \ldots$ and for all positive integral values.

Therefore, for positive integral values of x,

$$u_{x+nh} = u_x + n_1\Delta u_x + n_2\Delta^2 u_x + n_3\Delta^3 u_x + \ldots + n_r\Delta^r u_x + \ldots + \Delta^n u_x.$$

17. When the relation between the operator Δ and E was discussed it was stated that our definition of these operations enables us to apply the ordinary algebraic laws to these symbols. We may therefore use the equivalent relation

$$E \equiv (1 + \Delta),$$

and if we operate on the function u_x we shall have

$$u_{x+nh} = E^n u_x = (1 + \Delta)^n u_x$$
$$= (1 + n_1\Delta + n_2\Delta^2 + \ldots + n_r\Delta^r + \ldots + \Delta^n)\, u_x.$$

If we introduce the fact that the symbols follow the algebraic distributive law, we may write

$$u_{x+nh} = u_x + n_1\Delta u_x + n_2\Delta^2 u_x + \ldots + n_r\Delta^r u_x + \ldots + \Delta^n u_x,$$

which is the relation proved above for positive integral values of n.

This result is true whatever the form of the function so long as n is a positive integer. If n be other than a positive integer we cannot adopt the binomial expansion without further investigation. For the purposes of this chapter it will be sufficient to assume that the relation $E^n \equiv (1 + \Delta)^n \equiv 1 + n_1\Delta + n_2\Delta^2 + n_3\Delta^3 + \ldots$ holds without restriction. The question of the validity of the expansion will be discussed at a later stage (see Chap. III).

F

18. We are now in a position to state that if $n+1$ consecutive values of a rational integral function of the nth degree are given, then, by the method of finite differences, we can obtain the actual function in the form

$$u_x = u_0 + x_1\Delta u_0 + x_2\Delta^2 u_0 + \dots + x_n\Delta^n u_0,$$

where
$$x_r \equiv \frac{x\,(x-r)\dots(x-r+1)}{r!},$$

or
$$u_x = A + Bx_1 + Cx_2 + \dots + Kx_n,$$

where the coefficients $A, B, C, \dots K$ are obtained by inspection of a table of differences.

Now if we are given $n+1$ corresponding values of x and u_x it does not immediately follow that u_x is a rational integral function of the nth degree.

For example, suppose that we have the following data:

x	0	1	2	3	4	5
u_x	1	4	9	16	25	36

Since six values are given there are the following possibilities:

(i) they may be actually given as values of the function $(1+x)^2$;

(ii) they may be given as values of a rational integral function of the *second degree* in x, and it may be required to find the function;

(iii) they may be given as values of a rational integral function of the nth *degree, where n is less than* 6, and it may be required to find the function;

(iv) they may be given as values of a rational integral function without any information as to degree;

(v) no information regarding the nature of the function may be available.

The answer to (ii) and (iii) is obviously $u_x = (1+x)^2$.

The answer to (iv) is $u_x = (1+x)^2 + \dfrac{1}{6!}\,x\,(x-1)\dots(x-5)\,A_x$

or $(1+x)^2 + A_x x_6$, where A_x is a rational integral function of x which does not become infinite at any of the points 0, 1, 2, 3, 4, 5. $\dfrac{1}{6!}\,x\,(x-1)\dots(x-5)\,A_x$ will then obviously vanish for these values.

The answer to (v) is the same as to (iv) except that A_x need not be a rational integral function.

It is of importance to realise that we can always find a value for

A_x which will make the function $u_x = (1 + x)^2 + A_x x_6$ agree with any additional value whatever. For example, if $u_{4.5} = 100$ the function $u_x = (1 + x)^2 + 2^9 x_6$ will agree with the given values and also with the additional value which has been inserted at the point $x = 4\cdot5$.

Conversely we can say that whatever be the complete form of the function of which the six given values are samples, the value at any other point is the value of the function $(1 + x)^2$ at that point with an error $A_x x_6$. Whether the value is a good approximation or not depends on the magnitude of A_x, and we may or may not have reason to suppose that A_x is so small that it can be neglected. It should be understood that we are not at liberty to say that $(1 + x)^2$ gives an approximate value at the point in question unless we can give such a reason.

19. If instead of writing $E^n \equiv (1 + \Delta)^n$ and expanding this by the binomial theorem, we write $\Delta^n \equiv (E - 1)^n$ and expand, a new series is obtained:

$$\Delta^n u_x = (E - 1)^n u_x$$
$$= [E^n - n_1 E^{n-1} + n_2 E^{n-2} - n_3 E^{n-3} + \ldots + (-1)^r n_r E^{n-r}$$
$$+ \ldots + (-1)^n] u_x$$
$$= u_{x+nh} - n_1 u_{x+(n-1)h} + n_2 u_{x+(n-2)h} - \ldots$$
$$+ (-1)^r n_r u_{x+(n-r)h} + \ldots + (-1)^n u_x.$$

Just as the relation established in para. 16 enables us to obtain the value of u_{x+nh} in terms of u_x and its leading differences, so the above relation gives any required difference of the function u_x in terms of successive values of the function.

20. A few simple illustrations of the use of these two formulae are given below.

Example 6.

Find u_6, given $u_0 = -3$, $u_1 = 6$, $u_2 = 8$, $u_3 = 12$; third differences being constant.

The leading differences are easily found to be $\Delta u_0 = 9$; $\Delta^2 u_0 = -7$; $\Delta^3 u_0 = 9$.

$$u_6 = (1 + \Delta)^6 u_0 = (1 + 6\Delta + 15\Delta^2 + 20\Delta^3) u_0$$
$$= u_0 + 6\Delta u_0 + 15\Delta^2 u_0 + 20\Delta^3 u_0$$
$$= -3 + 54 - 105 + 180 = 126.$$

Note. There is no need to continue the expansion beyond third differences, as further differences are zero.

Example 7.

Find u_2, given $u_4 = 0$, $u_5 = 3$, $u_6 = 9$; second differences being constant.

Here the initial term of the known series is u_4, so that in order to find u_2 we must use the relation

$$u_2 = u_{4-2} = E^{-2}u_4 = (1 + \Delta)^{-2} u_4 = (1 - 2\Delta + 3\Delta^2) u_4,$$

as far as second differences.

$$u_2 = u_4 - 2\Delta u_4 + 3\Delta^2 u_4$$
$$= 0 - 6 + 9 = 3,$$

since $\Delta u_4 = 3$ and $\Delta^2 u_4 = 3$.

Example 8.

From the following values of u_x, calculate $\Delta^5 u_0$:

$$u_0 = 3, \ u_1 = 12, \ u_2 = 81, \ u_3 = 200, \ u_4 = 100, \ u_5 = 8.$$

Since we require one value only of $\Delta^5 u_x$, we do not need to form a difference table, but may write at once

$$\Delta^5 u_0 = (E - 1)^5 u_0$$
$$= (E^5 - 5E^4 + 10E^3 - 10E^2 + 5E - 1) u_0$$
$$= E^5 u_0 - 5E^4 u_0 + 10E^3 u_0 - 10E^2 u_0 + 5E u_0 - u_0$$
$$= u_5 - 5u_4 + 10u_3 - 10u_2 + 5u_1 - u_0$$
$$= 755.$$

Note that before we can find the fifth difference six terms of the series must be given.

21. Separation of symbols.

In obtaining the value of $E^n u_x$ in terms of u_x and its differences we have used the symbolic relation $E \equiv (1 + \Delta)$ and have expanded $(1 + \Delta)^n$ by the binomial theorem without introducing the function u_x until the last stage. This method, in which in fact u_x is omitted from both sides of the identity, is known as the method of *separation of symbols*, and enables many relations involving u_x and differences of u_x to be readily established.

Example 9.

Show that

$$u_0 + u_1 + u_2 + \ldots + u_n$$
$$= (n + 1)_1 u_0 + (n + 1)_2 \Delta u_0 + (n + 1)_3 \Delta^2 u_0 + \ldots + \Delta^n u_0.$$

$$u_0 + u_1 + u_2 + \ldots + u_n$$
$$= u_0 + Eu_0 + E^2u_0 + \ldots + E^nu_0$$
$$= (1 + E + E^2 + \ldots + E^n)\, u_0$$
$$= \frac{E^{n+1} - 1}{E - 1}\, u_0$$
$$= \frac{E^{n+1} - 1}{\Delta}\, u_0$$
$$= \frac{(1 + \Delta)^{n+1} - 1}{\Delta}\, u_0$$
$$= \frac{1}{\Delta}\,[1 + (n+1)_1\Delta + (n+1)_2\Delta^2 + (n+1)_3\Delta^3 \ldots + \Delta^{n+1} - 1]\,u_0$$
$$= [(n+1)_1 + (n+1)_2\Delta + (n+1)_3\Delta^2 + \ldots + \Delta^n]\,u_0$$
$$= (n+1)_1\,u_0 + (n+1)_2\,\Delta u_0 + (n+1)_3\,\Delta^2u_0 + \ldots + \Delta^n u_0.$$

Example 10.

Prove by the method of separation of symbols that

$$u_x = u_{x-1} + \Delta u_{x-2} + \Delta^2 u_{x-3} + \Delta^3 u_{x-4} + \ldots + \Delta^{n-1}u_{x-n} + \Delta^n u_{x-n}.$$

$$u_x - \Delta^n u_{x-n} = u_x - \Delta^n E^{-n}u_x = \left\{1 - \left(\frac{\Delta}{E}\right)^n\right\} u_x = \frac{E^n - \Delta^n}{E^n}\, u_x$$
$$= \frac{1}{E^n}\left\{\frac{E^n - \Delta^n}{E - \Delta}\right\} u_x, \quad \text{since } E - \Delta \equiv 1,$$
$$= E^{-n}\left(E^{n-1} + \Delta E^{n-2} + \Delta^2 E^{n-3} + \ldots + \Delta^{n-1}\right) u_x$$
$$= \left(E^{-1} + \Delta E^{-2} + \Delta^2 E^{-3} + \ldots + \Delta^{n-1}E^{-n}\right) u_x$$
$$= u_{x-1} + \Delta u_{x-2} + \Delta^2 u_{x-3} + \ldots + \Delta^{n-1}u_{x-n}.$$
$$\therefore \quad u_x = u_{x-1} + \Delta u_{x-2} + \Delta^2 u_{x-3} + \ldots + \Delta^{n-1}u_{x-n} + \Delta^n u_{x-n}.$$

Since this is true for all values of n we have the convenient formulae

$$u_x = u_{x-1} + \Delta u_{x-1} \text{ (which is otherwise evident)},$$
$$u_x = u_{x-1} + \Delta u_{x-2} + \Delta^2 u_{x-2},$$
$$u_x = u_{x-1} + \Delta u_{x-2} + \Delta^2 u_{x-3} + \Delta^3 u_{x-3},$$

and so on.

Example 11.

Obtain a formula based on u_n similar to that given by the relation

$$E^x u_0 = (1 + \Delta)^x\, u_0.$$

$$E^x u_0 = u_x = E^{x-n}u_n = \left(\frac{1}{E}\right)^{n-x} u_n = \left(\frac{E - \Delta}{E}\right)^{n-x} u_n, \quad \text{since } E - \Delta \equiv 1,$$
$$= \left(1 - \frac{\Delta}{E}\right)^{n-x} u_n$$
$$= [1 - (n-x)_1\Delta E^{-1} + (n-x)_2\Delta^2 E^{-2} - \ldots]\,u_n$$
$$= u_n - (n-x)_1\Delta u_{n-1} + (n-x)_2\Delta^2 u_{n-2} - \ldots.$$

It will be found that this is an ordinary formula which could be obtained by using the values in the reverse order $u_n, u_{n-1}, u_{n-2}, \ldots u_0$. There is as much justification for using one order as the other. It should be noticed that the same numerical values appear in the table of differences, but that they are in the reverse order with a change of sign for the odd differences.

Example 12.

Find the value of

$$\Delta x^m - \tfrac{1}{2}\Delta^2 x^m + \frac{1 \cdot 3}{2 \cdot 4}\Delta^3 x^m - \frac{1 \cdot 3 \cdot 5}{2 \cdot 4 \cdot 6}\Delta^4 x^m + \ldots \text{ to } m \text{ terms.}$$

Since $\Delta^{m+1} x^m$ and higher differences of x^m are zero, the sum of the series to m terms is the same as the sum to infinity.

Omitting the function x^m, and working on symbols alone, we have

$$\Delta - \tfrac{1}{2}\Delta^2 + \frac{1 \cdot 3}{2 \cdot 4}\Delta^3 - \frac{1 \cdot 3 \cdot 5}{2 \cdot 4 \cdot 6}\Delta^4 + \ldots \equiv \Delta\left(1 - \tfrac{1}{2}\Delta + \frac{1 \cdot 3}{2 \cdot 4}\Delta^2 - \frac{1 \cdot 3 \cdot 5}{2 \cdot 4 \cdot 6}\Delta^3 + \ldots\right)$$

$$\equiv \Delta\left(1 - \tfrac{1}{2}\Delta + \frac{\tfrac{1}{2} \cdot \tfrac{3}{2}}{2!}\Delta^2 - \frac{\tfrac{1}{2} \cdot \tfrac{3}{2} \cdot \tfrac{5}{2}}{3!}\Delta^3 + \ldots\right)$$

$$\equiv \Delta(1 + \Delta)^{-\frac{1}{2}} \equiv \Delta E^{-\frac{1}{2}}.$$

The value of the given series is therefore

$$\Delta E^{-\frac{1}{2}} x^m = \Delta(x - \tfrac{1}{2})^m = (x + \tfrac{1}{2})^m - (x - \tfrac{1}{2})^m,$$

if the interval of differencing be taken as unity.

Further examples of the application of the method of separation of symbols to the operators Δ and E and to other operators will be found in Chapters VII and VIII.

22. Factorial notation.

For convenience in working it is often useful to use a notation for the product of m factors of which the first is x and the successive factors decrease by unity by means of which the differences of the function can be readily written down.

$$u_x = x(x - 1)(x - 2)(x - 3) \ldots (x - \overline{m - 1})$$

is denoted by $x^{(m)}$.

$$\Delta x^{(m)} = (x + 1)x(x - 1) \ldots (x - \overline{m - 2}) - x(x - 1)(x - 2) \ldots$$

$$(x - \overline{m - 1})$$

$$= mx(x - 1) \ldots (x - \overline{m - 2})$$

$$= mx^{(m-1)}.$$

Similarly $\qquad \Delta^2 x^{(m)} = m\,(m-1)\,x^{(m-2)},$

and, eventually, $\qquad \Delta^m x^{(m)} = m!.$

The reciprocal function

$$\frac{1}{x\,(x+1)\,(x+2)\,...\,(x+m-1)},$$

where the successive factors increase by unity, is denoted by $x^{(-m)}$, and by proceeding as above it can be shown that

$$\Delta x^{(-m)} = -\,mx^{(-\overline{m+1})};\quad \Delta^2 x^{(-m)} = m\,(m+1)\,x^{(-\overline{m+2})},$$

and so on.

It should be noted that the result of differencing $x^{(-m)}$ is to increase the degree of the denominator, and that, as a result, $\Delta^m x^{(-m)}$ is not constant.

A special case of $x^{(m)}$ is where x is a positive integer. We have then that

$$x^{(m)} = x\,(x-1)\,(x-2)\,...\,(x-m+1) = x!/(x-m)!\ \text{ or }\ {}^x P_m.$$

It is also of interest to note that the result of differencing $x^{(m)}$ is analogous to that of differentiating x^m. We have

$$\Delta x^{(m)} = mx^{(m-1)}\quad \text{and}\quad \frac{d}{dx}x^m = mx^{m-1},$$

$$\Delta^m x^{(m)} = m!\qquad \text{and}\quad \frac{d^m}{dx^m}x^m = m!.$$

Example 13.

Express $2x^3 - 3x^2 + 3x - 10$ and its differences in factorial notation.

Let

$$u_x = 2x^3 - 3x^2 + 3x - 10 = Ax\,(x-1)\,(x-2) + Bx\,(x-1) + Cx + D.$$

Putting $x = 0, 1, 2$ in succession, we obtain easily that

$$D = -10;\quad C = 2;\quad B = 3.$$

By equating coefficients of x^3 on both sides of the identity we find that $A = 2$.

$$\therefore\quad 2x^3 - 3x^2 + 3x - 10 = 2x^{(3)} + 3x^{(2)} + 2x^{(1)} - 10.$$

$$\Delta u_x = 6x^{(2)} + 6x^{(1)} + 2,$$

$$\Delta^2 u_x = 12x^{(1)} + 6,$$

and $\qquad\qquad \Delta^3 u_x = 12.$

23. An alternative method for expressing a rational integral function of x in the factorial notation is by use of *detached coefficients*. By this method any such function can be written down in the form $Ax^{(n)} + Bx^{(n-1)} + Cx^{(n-2)} + \ldots + K$ with very little trouble.

The principle can best be illustrated by an actual example.

Example 14.

Write down $11x^4 + 5x^3 + 2x^2 + x - 15$ in factorial notation.

Let

$$u_x = 11x^4 + 5x^3 + 2x^2 + x - 15 = Ax^{(4)} + Bx^{(3)} + Cx^{(2)} + Dx^{(1)} + E$$
$$= Ax(x-1)(x-2)(x-3) + Bx(x-1)(x-2)$$
$$+ Cx(x-1) + Dx + E.$$

If we divide u_x by x, the quotient will be

$$11x^3 + 5x^2 + 2x + 1$$

and the remainder $\qquad -15 \qquad\qquad\qquad = E.$

Divide $11x^3 + 5x^2 + 2x + 1$ by $x - 1$:

$$
\begin{array}{r|ll}
x - 1 & 11x^3 + 5x^2 + 2x + 1 & \quad 11x^2 + 16x + 18 \\
& \underline{11x^3 - 11x^2} & \\
& \quad\ 16x^2 + 2x & \\
& \quad\ \underline{16x^2 - 16x} & \\
& \qquad\quad 18x + 1 & \\
& \qquad\quad \underline{18x - 18} & \\
& \qquad\qquad\ 19 & \qquad\qquad = D.
\end{array}
$$

Divide $11x^2 + 16x + 18$ by $x - 2$:

$$
\begin{array}{r|ll}
x - 2 & 11x^2 + 16x + 18 & \quad 11x + 38 \\
& \underline{11x^2 - 22x} & \\
& \quad\ 38x + 18 & \\
& \quad\ \underline{38x - 76} & \\
& \qquad\quad 94 & \qquad = C,
\end{array}
$$

and so on.

The above processes may be appreciably shortened by adopting the following procedure:

(i) Omit the x^4, x^3, x^2, ... and work on coefficients alone;

(ii) Change the sign of the constant term in $x - 1$, $x - 2$, $x - 3$, ..., so that addition takes the place of subtraction.

The required remainders can then be easily obtained. Thus:

1	11	5	2	1	−15
	0	11	16	18	
2	11	16	18	19	
	0	22	76		
3	11	38	94		
	0	33			
4	11	71			
	0				
	11				

$\therefore u_x = 11x^4 + 5x^3 + 2x^2 + x - 15 = 11x^{(4)} + 71x^{(3)} + 94x^{(2)} + 19x^{(1)} - 15.$

This short method is the method of detached coefficients and is of particular advantage in solving certain problems in summation of series (see Chap. VII).

EXAMPLES 2

By constructing difference tables, find:

1. The sixth term of the series 8, 12, 19, 29, 42, ...

2. The seventh and eighth terms of the series 0, 0, 2, 6, 12, 20, ...

3. The first term of the series whose second and subsequent terms are 8, 3, 0, − 1, 0, ...

4. The entry corresponding to the argument 3 from the table:

x (argument)	5	6	7	8	9	10
y (entry)	10·1	18·1	29·5	44·9	64·9	90·1

5. The tenth term of the series 3, 14, 39, 84, 155, 258, ...

6. Given that $y = x^3 - x^2 + x + 10$, verify by constructing a difference table that the value of y when $x = 10$ is 920. Use the following values of x: 1, 2, 3, 4, 5, 6, and the corresponding values of y.

7. Prove that $u_4 = u_3 + \Delta u_2 + \Delta^2 u_1 + \Delta^3 u_1$.

8. Find $\Delta^3 u_x$, where $u_x = ax^3 + bx^2 + cx + d$ and the interval of differencing is h.

9. u_x is a rational integral function of x, the following values of which are known: $u_2 = u_3 = 27$; $u_4 = 78$; $u_5 = 169$. Find the function.

10. Obtain $\Delta^{10} [(1 - ax)(1 - bx^2)(1 - cx^3)(1 - dx^4)]$.

11. Find Δab^{cx} and $\Delta^2 ab^{cx}$. Hence sum the first ten differences of ab^{cx}.

12. What are the functions whose first differences are (1) x; (2) c^x; (3) $9x^2 + 3$?

13. $u_x = (5x + 12)/(x^2 + 5x + 6)$. Find Δu_x and $\Delta^2 u_x$.

14. $u_x = -(x-1)^{-1}(x-2)^{-1}$. Find Δu_x.

15. $u_1 = (12 - x)(4 + x)$; $u_2 = (5 - x)(4 - x)$; $u_3 = (x + 18)(x + 6)$; $u_4 = 94$. Obtain a value of x, assuming second differences constant.

16. Find $\Delta^n u_x$, where u_x is (1) $ax^n + bx^{n-1}$, (2) e^{ax+b}.

17. Show that $u_4 = u_0 + 4\Delta u_0 + 6\Delta^2 u_{-1} + 10\Delta^3 u_{-1}$ as far as third differences.

18. The first four terms of a series are 0, 15, 16, 30. Find the sixth term, using the relation in Qu. 17.

19. Find the value of $\Delta^2 \left[\dfrac{a^{2x} + a^{4x}}{(a^2 - 1)^2} \right]$.

20. Obtain the function whose first difference is
$$x^3 + 3x^2 + 5x + 12.$$
By means of the relation $u_x = (1 + \Delta)^x u_0$, find

21. u_{12} given $u_0 = 3$; $u_1 = 14$; $u_2 = 40$; $u_3 = 86$; $u_4 = 157$; $u_5 = 258$.

22. u_6 given $u_0 = 25$; $u_1 = 25$; $u_2 = 22$; $u_3 = 18$; $u_4 = 15$; $u_5 = 15$.

23. u_9 given $u_0 = 1$; $u_1 = 11$; $u_2 = 21$; $u_3 = 28$; $u_4 = 29$.

24. The tenth term of the series 1, 37, 61, 77, ...

25. The eleventh term of the series 1, 4, 13, 36, 81, 156, 269, ...

26. Prove that the rth difference of a rational integral function of the nth degree is a rational integral function of the $(n - r)$th degree if $r < n$. What happens when (1) $r = n$, (2) $r > n$?

27. Define the functions $x^{(m)}$ and $x^{(-m)}$. Obtain their nth differences, distinguishing between the cases when $n \gtreqless m$.

28. Represent the function $x^4 - 12x^3 + 42x^2 - 30x + 9$ and its successive differences in factorial notation.

29. Find $\Delta^n u_x$ where u_x is

(i) $(ax + b)(a.\overline{x+1} + b)(a.\overline{x+2} + b) \dots (a.\overline{x+m} + b)$ given $m > n$.

(ii) $[(ax + b)(a.\overline{x+1} + b)(a.\overline{x+2} + b) \dots (a.\overline{x+m} + b)]^{-1}$.

30. Obtain $\Delta \sin x$, $\Delta \tan x$ and $\Delta (x + \cos x)$ where the interval of differencing is a.

31. Explain the difference between $\left(\dfrac{\Delta^2}{E}\right) u_x$ and $\dfrac{\Delta^2 u_x}{E u_x}$ and find the values of these functions when $u_x = x^3$.

32. $u_x = \sin x$. Show that $\Delta^2 u_x = k E u_x$ where k is constant.

33. Prove that $\Delta (\tan^{-1} x) = \tan^{-1} \left\{ \dfrac{h}{(1 + xh + x^2)} \right\}$ where h is the interval of differencing.

Use the method of separation of symbols to prove the following identities:

34. $u_1 x + u_2 x^2 + u_3 x^3 + \dots$

$$= \dfrac{x}{1 - x} u_1 + \dfrac{x^2}{(1 - x)^2} \Delta u_2 + \dfrac{x^3}{(1 - x)^3} \Delta^2 u_3 + \dots.$$

35. $\Delta^n u_{x-n} = u_x - n_1 u_{x-1} + n_2 u_{x-2} - \dots.$

36. $u_{x+n} = u_n + x\Delta u_{n-1} + (x + 1)_2 \Delta^2 u_{n-2} + (x + 2)_3 \Delta^3 u_{n-3} + \dots.$

37. $u_0 + x\Delta u_1 + x_2 \Delta^2 u_2 + x_3 \Delta^3 u_3 + \dots = u_x + x\Delta^2 u_{x-1} + x_2 \Delta^4 u_{x-2} + \dots$

38. $u_0 + \dfrac{u_1 x}{1!} + \dfrac{u_2 x^2}{2!} + \dfrac{u_3 x^3}{3!} + \dots$

$$= e^x \left[u_0 + x\Delta u_0 + \dfrac{x^2}{2!} \Delta^2 u_0 + \dfrac{x^3}{3!} \Delta^3 u_0 + \dots \right].$$

39. $u_x - u_{x+1} + u_{x+2} - u_{x+3} + \dots = \dfrac{1}{2} \left[u_{x-\frac{1}{2}} - \dfrac{1}{8} \Delta^2 u_{x-\frac{3}{2}} \right.$

$$\left. + \dfrac{1 \cdot 3}{2!} \left(\dfrac{1}{8} \right)^2 \Delta^4 u_{x-\frac{5}{2}} - \dfrac{1 \cdot 3 \cdot 5}{3!} \left(\dfrac{1}{8} \right)^3 \Delta^6 u_{x-\frac{7}{2}} + \dots \right].$$

40. $u_{2n} - n_1 . 2u_{2n-1} + n_2 . 2^2 u_{2n-2} - \dots + (- 2)^n u_n = (- 1)^n (c - 2an)$, where $u_x = ax^2 + bx + c$.

41. $u_x - \dfrac{1}{8} \Delta^2 u_{x-1} + \dfrac{1}{8} . \dfrac{3}{16} \Delta^4 u_{x-2} - \dfrac{1 \cdot 3 \cdot 5}{8 . 16 . 24} \Delta^6 u_{x-3} + \dots$

$$= u_{x+\frac{1}{2}} - \dfrac{1}{2} \Delta u_{x+\frac{1}{2}} + \dfrac{1}{4} \Delta^2 u_{x+\frac{1}{2}} - \dfrac{1}{8} \Delta^3 u_{x+\frac{1}{2}} + \dots.$$

42. Find the relation between α, β, γ in order that $\alpha + \beta x + \gamma x^2$ may be expressible in one term in factorial notation.

43. Sum to n terms

$$1 . 2 \Delta x^n - 2 . 3 \Delta^2 x^n + 3 . 4 \Delta^3 x^n - 4 . 5 \Delta^4 x^n + \dots.$$

44. If u_x be a rational integral function of x of the third degree and $\Delta x = 1$, prove that

$$u_x = u_0 + x\Delta u_0 + \dfrac{x^{(2)}}{2!} \Delta^2 u_0 + \dfrac{x^{(3)}}{3!} \Delta^3 u_0.$$

45. Prove that

$u_0 + n_1 u_1 x + n_2 u_2 x^2 + n_3 u_3 x^3 + \dots$

$$= (1 + x)^n u_0 + n_1 (1 + x)^{n-1} x\Delta u_0 + n_2 (1 + x)^{n-2} x^2 \Delta^2 u_0 + \dots.$$

46. If n be a positive integer, prove that u_n is the difference between the two series:

$$n_1 u_1 + (n + 1)_3 \Delta^2 u_0 + (n + 2)_5 \Delta^4 u_{-1} + \dots,$$

and $\quad (n - 1)_1 u_0 + n_3 \Delta^2 u_{-1} + (n + 1)_5 \Delta^4 u_{-2} + \dots.$

CHAPTER III

INTERPOLATION FOR EQUAL INTERVALS

1. Interpolation may be defined as the operation of obtaining the value of a function for any intermediate value of the argument, being given the values of the functions for certain values of the argument. The process has been picturesquely described by Thiele as "the art of reading between the lines of a table." Where the form of the function $y - u_x$ is known or can be deduced from the given values, the ordinary algebraic process of substitution can be used, and the required value obtained with little difficulty. In actuarial work the relation connecting the function and the independent variable is seldom evident, and it is then that recourse must be had to finite difference methods.

2. Before proceeding to examine the practical aspect of interpolation the question of negative and fractional values of n in the expression $(1 + \Delta)^n u_x$ must be considered. The proof of the identity $u_{x+nh} = (1 + \Delta)^n u_x$ by means of operators or by induction, as in the previous chapter, ceases to have a meaning if n is negative or fractional, since the reasoning assumes that the argument x advances by steps of h at a time. The assumption that, so long as the ordinary algebraic rules are followed, the expansion is true for all values of the quantities involved and not only for certain specified values, is not necessarily true, and an analogy can be drawn between the application of the binomial theorem to algebraic quantities and to operators. For example, the expansion $(1 + x)^n$ is only convergent, i.e. is arithmetically intelligible, for negative values of n, provided that x is numerically less than unity.

Thus $(1 - x)^{-2} = 1 + 2x + 3x^2 + 4x^3 + \ldots + rx^{r-1} + \ldots$ leads to an absurd result if we put $x = 2$, for then we should have

$$(-1)^{-2} = 1 + 4 + 12 + 32 + \ldots$$

which is impossible, since

$$(-1)^{-2} = 1/(-1)^2 = 1.$$

Similarly we must have regard to the possibility of expanding $(1 + \Delta)^n u_x$ by the use of the binomial theorem.

Consider the two following series of corresponding values of x and u_x:

(i)

x	0	1	2	3'	4	5
u_x	1	4	9	16	25	36

Then to find the value of, say, $u_{\frac{1}{2}}$ we shall have

$$u_{\frac{1}{2}} = E^{\frac{1}{2}} u_0 = (1 + \Delta)^{\frac{1}{2}} u_0$$

$$= u_0 + \tfrac{1}{2}\Delta u_0 + \frac{\tfrac{1}{2}(\tfrac{1}{2} - 1)}{2!} \Delta^2 u_0 + \ldots.$$

The leading differences are $\Delta u_0 = 3$ and $\Delta^2 u_0 = 2$, higher differences being zero.

$$\therefore \quad u_{\frac{1}{2}} = 1 + \tfrac{1}{2} \cdot 3 + \frac{\tfrac{1}{2}(\tfrac{1}{2} - 1)}{2!} \cdot 2$$

$$= 1 + 3/2 - \tfrac{1}{4} = 9/4,$$

which is otherwise evident, since u_x is $(1 + x)^2$, and, for the value $x = \tfrac{1}{2}$, $u_x = (3/2) = 9/4$.

(ii)

x	0	1	2	3	4	5
u_x	1	5	25	125	625	3125

This is evidently a geometrical progression and the function from which the values are derived is $y = u_x = 5^x$. If we attempted to express u_x as a rational integral function of x so that

$$u_x = a + bx + cx^2 + dx^3 + \ldots,$$

and then applied the relation $E^n u_0 = (1 + \Delta)^n u_0$ for the value $n = \tfrac{1}{2}$, we should obtain as above

$$u_{\frac{1}{2}} = E^{\frac{1}{2}} u_0 = (1 + \Delta)^{\frac{1}{2}} u_0$$

$$= u_0 + \tfrac{1}{2}\Delta u_0 + \frac{\tfrac{1}{2}(\tfrac{1}{2} - 1)}{2!} \Delta^2 u_0 + \ldots.$$

Here the leading differences are $1, 4, 16, 64, 256, \ldots$ and tend to become successively larger. But $u_{\frac{1}{2}} = 5^{\frac{1}{2}} = 2 \cdot 24$ approximately, and this cannot be the same as the divergent series found by expanding $(1 + \Delta)^{\frac{1}{2}} u_0$.

Hence unless the function is capable of being expressed as a rational integral function of x we cannot use the relation $E^n \equiv (1+\Delta)^n$ for the value $n = \tfrac{1}{2}$.

3. Let us now consider the problem more generally. If u_x be a rational integral function of degree k in x, we may write

$$u_x = a + bx + cx^2 + \dots + px^k.$$

If we adopt the binomial expansion for expressing u_x in terms of u_0 and the leading differences of u_0, namely,

$$u_x = u_0 + x_1\Delta u_0 + x_2\Delta^2 u_0 + \dots + x_r\Delta^r u_0 + \dots$$

we have two series for u_x which are equivalent for more than k values of the variable, since they are true for all positive integral values of x.

Hence by a well-known algebraic theorem, they are true for all values of x, positive or negative, integral or fractional.

Therefore so long as u_x is a rational integral function of x the binomial expansion is valid for all values of x. It is not necessarily valid for other forms of function, and we are led to the conclusion that we can expand u_{x+nh} in terms of Δu_x, $\Delta^2 u_x$, $\dots \Delta^r u_x$, $\dots$ by the binomial theorem for all forms of the function if n be a positive integer, but only for other values of n if u_{x+nh} is a rational integral function of x.

4. All finite difference formulae which are employed for the purpose of interpolation are based on the hypothesis that the functions in question can be represented by polynomials, i.e. by rational integral functions, with sufficient accuracy for the purpose in hand. This assumption is the justification for using integral formulae for fractional intervals: the processes to be explained in this and subsequent chapters are simply various methods of carrying out the calculations based on this assumption. One special advantage of these methods is that it is unnecessary to fix in advance the degree (n) of the polynomial; the interpolation formulae will be in such a form that to increase n will merely involve the introduction of a fresh term without affecting the other terms. The introduction of additional terms however will not necessarily improve the approximation or justify the assumption. Fortunately, in actuarial work the functions with which we deal are usually such that the assumption is sufficiently accurate for our purpose.

5. In applying the formula in para. 3 to a given set of data the following points should be noted:

(a) If the basic curve is $y = a + bx + cx^2 + \ldots + kx^{n-1}$ there will be n constants, and in order to determine these constants n equations are necessary. For there to be n equations, values of y corresponding to n values of x must be given. Therefore either n points on the curve, or n other corresponding relations between x and y must be known. In that event the curve will be of degree $n - 1$, and nth and higher differences may be assumed zero.

(b) Our investigation has been confined to equidistant values of the argument. If the given values are not equidistant a formula slightly different in form from the expansion $(1 + \Delta)^x u_0$ can be developed with a modified method of differencing (see Chapter IV).

With regard to the statement (a) above that for a curve of degree $n - 1$ there must be n facts given, it is not essential that n points on the assumed curve must be known. We may have given, for example, three points and two values of the differential coefficient $\dfrac{du_x}{dx}$. Here we have five facts; we assume therefore a fourth degree curve, so that fifth and higher differences are zero.

6. Newton's formula.

The formula $u_{x+nh} = u_x + n_1 \Delta u_x + n_2 \Delta^2 u_x + \ldots$ is known as Newton's formula, and is the fundamental formula for interpolation when the given values are at equidistant intervals. The expansion can be applied to solve many forms of the problem of interpolation.

The following variations of the problem may arise:

(i) Where there are n equidistant terms and it is required to find an intermediate term.

(ii) Where there are n equidistant terms of which $n - 1$ are known and it is required to find the missing term.

(iii) Where there are n equidistant terms of which $n - r$ are known and it is required to find the r missing terms.

Note. Some modern writers have adopted the name "Newton-Gregory formula" for the above expansion, as the first publication appears to have occurred in a letter from James Gregory to John Collins on 23 Nov. 1670. The letter is given and the question of Newton's priority is fully discussed by D. C. Fraser in *J.I.A.* vol. LII, pp. 117–35.

7. Examples of the different variations referred to above are given below:

Example 1.

The values of annuities by a certain table are given for the following ages:

Age	x	25	26	27	28	29
Annuity-value	a_x	15·006	15·326	15·630	15·919	16·195

Determine the value of the annuity at age $27\frac{1}{2}$.

Five values are given: we must therefore assume that fourth differences are constant. The difference table is

x	a_x	Δa_x	$\Delta^2 a_x$	$\Delta^3 a_x$	$\Delta^4 a_x$
25	15·006				
		·320			
26	15·326		− ·016		
		·304		+ ·001	
27	15·630		− ·015		+ ·001
		·289		+ ·002	
28	15·919		− ·013		
		·276			
29	16·195				

The leading differences correspond to the argument $x = 25$ and we require the entry for age $27\frac{1}{2}$. Our formula is therefore

$$a_{27\frac{1}{2}} = E^{2\frac{1}{2}} a_{25} = (1 + \Delta)^{2\frac{1}{2}} a_{25}$$

$$= \left[1 + 2·5\Delta + \frac{2·5 \times 1·5}{2} \Delta^2 + \frac{2·5 \times 1·5 \times ·5}{6} \Delta^3 \right.$$

$$\left. + \frac{2·5 \times 1·5 \times ·5 \times (- ·5)}{24} \Delta^4 \right] a_{25}$$

$$= a_{25} + 2·5\Delta a_{25} + 1·875\Delta^2 a_{25} + ·3125\Delta^3 a_{25} - ·03906\Delta^4 a_{25}$$

$$= 15·006 + ·8000 - ·0300 + ·0003 - ·00004$$

$$= 15·776.$$

Note. Since the data are given to three places of decimals, sufficient figures have been used to give three places only in the result. Since our interpolation is based on an assumption, namely, that fourth differences are constant, a result to more than this number of decimal places would be unjustifiable.

Example 2.

From the following data find the value of u_{47}:

$$u_{46} = 19·2884; \quad u_{48} = 19·5356; \quad u_{49} = 19·6513; \quad u_{50} = 19·7620.$$

We cannot form a difference table, since the given terms are not equidistant. As however four terms are available we may assume that third differences are constant, and that as a consequence fourth differences are zero.

If the function is $y = u_x$ we assume therefore that $\Delta^4 u_x = 0$ whatever the value of x. We may write

$$\Delta^4 u_{46} = 0,$$

i.e. $$(E - 1)^4 u_{46} = 0,$$

or $$(E^4 - 4E^3 + 6E^2 - 4E + 1) u_{46} = 0,$$

i.e. $$u_{50} - 4u_{49} + 6u_{48} - 4u_{47} + u_{46} = 0,$$

so that $19\cdot7620 - 78\cdot6052 + 117\cdot2136 - 4u_{47} + 19\cdot2884 = 0,$

from which $$u_{47} = 19\cdot4147.$$

Example 3.

Complete the following table:

x	2·0	2·1	2·2	2·3	2·4	2·5	2·6
u_x	·135		·111	·100		·082	·074

This is similar to Ex. 2. Instead of using the assumption once that $\Delta^5 u_x = 0$, we write down two equations of the same form, thus

$$\Delta^5 u_{2\cdot0} = 0, \quad \text{so that} \quad (E - 1)^5 u_{2\cdot0} = 0,$$

and $$\Delta^5 u_{2\cdot1} = 0, \quad ,, \quad (E - 1)^5 u_{2\cdot1} = 0.$$

Our two equations then become

$$u_{2\cdot5} - 5u_{2\cdot4} + 10u_{2\cdot3} - 10u_{2\cdot2} + 5u_{2\cdot1} - u_{2\cdot0} = 0,$$

and $$u_{2\cdot6} - 5u_{2\cdot5} + 10u_{2\cdot4} - 10u_{2\cdot3} + 5u_{2\cdot2} - u_{2\cdot1} = 0,$$

since the interval of differencing is 0·1.

Inserting the known values of u_x and solving, the required values are easily found to be $u_{2\cdot1} = \cdot123$ and $u_{2\cdot4} = \cdot090$.

Note. The function in this question is $y = e^{-x}$ and the tabular value of $u_{2\cdot4}$ is ·091 correct to two decimal places. This difference is due to the fact that our assumption that the curve $y = u_x$ is a rational integral function of the fourth degree in x is only approximately true.

8. Change of origin.

If we had plotted the curve $y = u_x$ on which the values of u_x in, say, Example 2 were assumed to lie, we should have had values of y corresponding to values of x at 46, 48, 49, 50. Precisely the same curve would result, however, if we changed the origin of our co-ordinates so that 46 was represented by the value $x = 0$, 48 by

$x = 2$, 49 by $x = 3$ and so on, the unit of x being unaltered. This process of changing the origin simplifies our notation considerably. In the three examples above we could have changed the origin and could have altered the questions to read:

Ex. 1. Origin at age 25   Given u_0, u_1, u_2, u_3, u_4
Unit of differencing 1 year of age Required $u_{2\frac{1}{2}}$.

Ex. 2. Origin at $x = 46$ Given u_0, u_2, u_3, u_4
Unit of differencing $x = 1$ Required u_1.

Ex. 3. Origin at $x = 2\cdot0$ Given u_0, u_2, u_3, u_5, u_6
Unit of differencing $x = 0\cdot1$ Required u_1 and u_4.

It is of interest at this stage to note the difference that exists between the ordinary accepted notation in algebra and that in finite differences for successive terms of a series. For example, in an algebraic series such as 1, 2, 4, 8, 16, ..., where each term is twice the preceding one, the terms are generally denoted by u_1, u_2, u_3, u_4, ..., the nth term being u_n. This is because the terms follow strictly the order of the natural numbers: we cannot imagine, say, the $2\frac{1}{2}$th term of such a series. Graphically, the series is represented by a succession of isolated points. On the other hand, if the same series of values of the function $y = u_x$, 1, 2, 4, 8, 16, ..., corresponding to equidistant values of x, were given and we were required to interpolate for a value of the independent variable between two of the given terms, we should assume that a smooth curve could be drawn to pass through the points. Having chosen one of the values of x for our origin, we should then proceed to apply a suitable finite difference formula. For the above data the value of x most convenient for our origin would be the value for which $y = 1$, and our (imaginary) curve would pass through the point whose coordinates are (0, 1). In that event the terms would be denoted by u_0, u_1, u_2, u_3, ..., the nth term being u_{n-1}. This difference between the two sets of notation is of importance when dealing with summation of series.

9. If in Newton's formula

$$u_{x+nh} = u_x + n_1 \Delta u_x + n_2 \Delta^2 u_x + n_3 \Delta^3 u_x + \dots$$

we put $h = 1$, $x = 0$, and replace n by x, we obtain the series

$$u_x = u_0 + x_1 \Delta u_0 + x_2 \Delta^2 u_0 + x_3 \Delta^3 u_0 + \dots.$$

This is generally called the *advancing difference* formula, and gives u_x in terms of u_0 and its leading differences.

If, however, we wish to obtain u_x in terms of u_{-m} and its leading differences, we may write the formula

$$u_x = u_{-m+(m+x)} = E^{m+x}u_{-m} = (1 + \Delta)^{m+x}\, u_{-m}$$

$$= u_{-m} + (m + x)_1\Delta u_{-m} + (m + x)_2\, \Delta^2 u_{-m} + \dots$$

$$+ (m + x)_r\, \Delta^r u_{-m} + \dots.$$

It is often more convenient to use this formula than to obtain u_x in terms of u_0 and differences of u_0, the advantage being that thereby we can make use of values of the argument on either side of the origin.

10. Subdivision of intervals.

A frequent problem in actuarial work is the interpolation for values of u_x at individual points, given every fifth or tenth value of the function. For example, the problem may be to complete the series $u_0, u_1, u_2, u_3, \dots$ from the known values $u_0, u_5, u_{10}, u_{15}, \dots$ or from $u_0, u_{10}, u_{20}, u_{30}, \dots.$

A simple method for obtaining the individual values where quinquennial values are known is given below.

Let δu_x denote the difference for *unit* intervals of x and Δu_x denote the difference for *quinquennial* intervals.

Then u_{x+5} may be expressed as either $(1 + \delta)^5 u_x$ or as $(1 + \Delta)u_x$.

Symbolically $\qquad (1 + \delta)^5 \equiv 1 + \Delta,$

i.e. $\qquad\qquad (1 + \delta) \equiv (1 + \Delta)^{\frac{1}{5}},$

or $\qquad\qquad\quad \delta \equiv (1 + \Delta)^{\frac{1}{5}} - 1.$

From this relation we can find easily that

$$\delta u_x = (\cdot 2\Delta - \cdot 08\Delta^2 + \cdot 048\Delta^3 - \dots)\, u_x.$$

Hence $\qquad \delta^2 u_x = (\cdot 2\Delta - \cdot 08\Delta^2 + \cdot 048\Delta^3 - \dots)^2\, u_x$

$$= (\cdot 04\Delta^2 - \cdot 032\Delta^3 + \dots)\, u_x.$$

Similarly $\qquad \delta^3 u_x = (\cdot 008\Delta^3 - \dots)\, u_x.$

The same principle can be adopted if decennial values are known. In that event $\Delta u_x, \Delta^2 u_x, \dots$ will represent differences for decennial intervals, and the individual differences will be found from the identity $\delta \equiv (1 + \Delta)^{\frac{1}{10}} - 1.$

An example will show the application of the method.

Example 4.

From the following table of yearly premiums for policies maturing at quinquennial ages, estimate the premium for policies maturing at all ages from 45 to 65 inclusive:

Age x	45	50	55	60	65
Premium	2·871	2·404	2·083	1·862	1·712

The leading differences for quinquennial intervals are

Δu_x	$\Delta^2 u_x$	$\Delta^3 u_x$	$\Delta^4 u_x$
− ·467	+ ·146	− ·046	+ ·017

The formulae required are

$$\delta u_x = (\cdot 2\Delta - \cdot 08\Delta^2 + \cdot 048\Delta^3 - \cdot 0336\Delta^4)\, u_x = - \cdot 1078592,$$

$$\delta^2 u_x = (\cdot 04\Delta^2 - \cdot 032\Delta^3 + \cdot 0256\Delta^4)\, u_x = + \cdot 0077472,$$

$$\delta^3 u_x = (\cdot 008\Delta^3 - \cdot 0096\Delta^4)\, u_x = - \cdot 0005312,$$

$$\delta^4 u_x = \cdot 0016\Delta^4 u_x = + \cdot 0000272,$$

assuming fourth differences constant.

We have therefore by completing the table of differences,

Age	u_x	δu_x	$\delta^2 u_x$	$\delta^3 u_x$	$\delta^4 u_x$
45	2·871				
		− ·10786			
46	2·763		+ ·007747		
		− ·10011		− ·0005312	
47	2·663		+ ·007216		+ ·0000272
		− ·09290		− ·0005040	
48	2·570		+ ·006712		+ ·0000272
		− ·08618		− ·0004768	
49	2·484		+ ·006235		+ ·0000272
		− ·07995		− ·0004496	
50	2·404		+ ·005786		
		− ·07417			
51	2·330				

and so on.

Note that since we require the value of the premium to the nearest penny, three decimal places will be required in the u_x column. To obtain results correct to three figures, four decimal places will be needed: δu_x must therefore be given to five decimal places, $\delta^2 u_x$ to six and $\delta^3 u_x$ to seven.

EXAMPLES 3

Given the following data (a), find the missing term or terms (b):

1. (a) $u_0 = 580$, $u_1 = 556$, $u_2 = 520$, $u_4 = 385$; (b) u_3.

2. (a) $u_1 = 386$, $u_3 = 530$, $u_5 = 810$; (b) u_2; u_4.

3. (a) $u_0 = 150$, $u_1 = 192$, $u_2 = 241$, $u_4 = 374$; (b) u_3.

4. (a) $u_1 = 94$, $u_3 = 265$, $u_5 = 415$; (b) u_2; u_4.

5. (a) $u_0 = 6021$, $u_1 = 5229$, $u_2 = 4559$, $u_3 = 3979$; (b) $u_{\frac{3}{4}}$.

6. (a) $u_{50} = 92345$, $u_{51} = 91556$, $u_{52} = 90748$, $u_{55} = 88204$; (b) u_{53}; u_{54}.

7. (a) $u_{-1} = 202$, $u_0 = 175$, $u_1 = 82$, $u_2 = 55$; (b) $u_{\frac{1}{2}}$.

8. (a) $u_0 = 0$, $u_1 = 3$, $u_2 = 10$, $u_3 = 34$, $u_5 = 209$, $u_8 = 1002$; (b) u_4; u_6; u_7.

9. (a) $u_0 = 192 \cdot 1$, $u_1 = 187 \cdot 5$, $u_2 = 184 \cdot 7$, $u_3 = 184 \cdot 6$, $u_4 = 194 \cdot 6$, $u_5 = 199 \cdot 4$, $u_7 = 212 \cdot 7$, $u_9 = 224 \cdot 3$; (b) u_6; u_8.

10. (a) $u_0 = 98203$, $u_1 = 97843$, $u_2 = 97459$, $u_3 = 97034$; (b) $u_{2 \cdot 25}$.

11. The numbers of members of a certain Society are as given in the following table:

Year	Number
1910	845
1911	867
1912	
1913	846
1914	821
1915	772
1916	
1917	757
1918	761
1919	796

Make the best estimate you can of the numbers in 1912 and 1916.

12. Find p_{53} if $p_{50} = \cdot 98428$, $p_{51} = \cdot 98335$, $p_{54} = \cdot 98008$, $p_{55} = \cdot 97877$.

13. If $u_0, u_1, u_2, \ldots u_6$ be consecutive terms of a series, prove that

$$u_3 = \cdot 05 u_0 - \cdot 3 u_1 + \cdot 75 u_2 + \cdot 75 u_4 - \cdot 3 u_5 + \cdot 05 u_6.$$

Supply the missing term:

$u_0 = 72795$ $u_4 = 67919$

$u_1 = 71651$ $u_5 = 66566$

$u_2 = 70458$ $u_6 = 65152$.

14. $u_{235} = 2\cdot37107$ $u_{237} = 2\cdot37474$
        $u_{236} = 2\cdot37291$ $u_{238} = 2\cdot37658.$

Find $u_{235\cdot63}$.

15. Given $u_0 = -\cdot5, u_1 = -\cdot484, u_5 = 0, u_6 = \cdot256$ find the missing terms.

16. Given the following data: $u_0 = 0, u_{10} = 15, u_{20} = 50$; estimate u_{15}.

If you were given in addition $u_0 = 35$ how would your estimate be revised? Illustrate your answer by a diagram.

17. Find the value of an annuity at $5\frac{3}{8}$ per cent. given the following table:

Rate per cent.	Annuity value
4	17·29203
$4\frac{1}{2}$	16·28889
5	15·37245
$5\frac{1}{2}$	14·53375
6	13·76483

18. Obtain approximations to the missing values:

x	50	51	52	53	54	55	56
$f(x)$	3·684			3·756	3·780	3·803	3·826

19. The area A of a circle diameter d is given for the following values:

d	80	85	90	95	100
A	5026	5674	6362	7088	7854

Find approximate values for the areas of circles of diameters 82 and 91 respectively.

20. Calculate a value for sin 33° 13′ 30″ from the following table of sines:

angle $x°$	30	31	32	33	34
sin $x°$	·5000	·5150	·5299	·5446	·5592

21. $u_{75} = 2459$; $u_{80} = 2018$; $u_{85} = 1180$; $u_{90} = 402$. Calculate the values of u_{82} and u_{79}.

22. From the data in Qu. 21 complete the table for values of u_x corresponding to individual values of x from 75 to 85.

23. Four values of a function at decennial points are given. Express $\delta u_x, \delta^2 u_x, \delta^3 u_x$ (the differences for unit intervals) in terms of the differences of the function for decennial intervals.

Find the values u_1 to u_9 inclusive, given $u_0 = 0, u_{10} = \cdot174, u_{20} = \cdot347, u_{30} = \cdot518.$

24. $u_0 = 23\cdot1234$; $u_6 = 23\cdot7234$; $u_{12} = 24\cdot6834$; $u_{18} = 26\cdot1330$. Complete the series u_0 to u_6.

25. If you were asked at very short notice to obtain approximate values for the complete series $f(0), f(1), f(2), \ldots f(20)$, being given that $f(0) = \cdot013$, $f(10) = \cdot248$, $f(15) = \cdot578$, and $f(20) = \cdot983$, what methods would you adopt, and what value would you obtain for $f(9)$?

26. $\quad u_0 + u_8 = 1\cdot9243 \qquad\qquad u_2 + u_6 = 1\cdot9823$

$\qquad\quad u_1 + u_7 = 1\cdot9590 \qquad\qquad u_3 + u_5 = 1\cdot9956$.

Find u_4.

27. Tables are available giving premiums at age 40 at the following rates per cent:

Rate per cent.	3	$3\frac{1}{2}$	4	$4\frac{1}{2}$	5	6
P_{40}	$\cdot025891$	$\cdot024654$	$\cdot023517$	$\cdot022470$	$\cdot021509$	$\cdot019811$

It is desired to obtain P_{40} at $5\frac{1}{2}$ per cent. Obtain this, using (a) two of the above values; (β) four of the above values; (γ) six of the above values.

28. Given

$$\sum_1^{10} f(x) = 500426, \quad \sum_4^{10} f(x) = 329240, \quad \sum_7^{10} f(x) = 175212 \text{ and } f(10) = 40356,$$

find $f(1)$.

29. $u_1 = 1$; $u_2 + u_3 = 5\cdot41$; $u_4 + u_5 + u_6 = 18\cdot47$;

$\qquad u_7 + u_8 + u_9 + u_{10} + u_{11} + u_{12} = 90\cdot36$.

Find the value of u_x for all values of x from 1 to 12 inclusive.

30. If you were given u_0, u_1, u_2 and $\sum\limits_{x=1}^{x=10} u_x$ how would you complete the table of u_x up to u_{10}?

31. Given $u_0 = 117\cdot7$; $u_2 = 110\cdot5$; $u_4 = 102\cdot7$; $u_{10} = 75\cdot4$, obtain the values of u_x for all integral values of x from 0 to 10.

32. Obtain the following relation between nine terms of the series represented by $u_1, u_2, \ldots u_9$:

$$u_5 = \tfrac{4}{5}(u_4 + u_6) - \tfrac{2}{5}(u_3 + u_7) + \tfrac{4}{35}(u_2 + u_8) - \tfrac{1}{70}(u_1 + u_9),$$

and find u_5, given

$u_1 = \cdot74556$; $u_2 = \cdot55938$; $u_3 = \cdot42796$; $u_4 = \cdot32788$; $u_6 = \cdot18432$;

$\qquad u_7 = \cdot13165$; $u_8 = \cdot08828$; $u_9 = 0$.

33. It is asserted that a quantity, which varies from day to day, is a rational and integral function of the day of the month, of less than the fifth degree, and that its values on the first seven days of the month are

$$30, \qquad 30, \qquad 28, \qquad 25, \qquad 22, \qquad 20, \qquad 20.$$

Examine whether these assertions are consistent. If so, assume them to be true, and find (1) the degree of the function, (2) its value on the sixteenth of the month.

34. Extrapolation may be defined as the process of obtaining further terms of a series as opposed to interpolation, which is the process of finding intermediate terms.

The values of a certain function, corresponding to the values 4, 6, 8, 10 of the argument, are 914, 742, 605, 500 respectively; extrapolate to calculate the value of the function corresponding to the value 11 of the argument.

35. Given $u_0 = 1876$, $u_1 = 777$, $u_3 = 19$, $u_6 = -218$, interpolate the values of u_2, u_4 and u_5, and find the form of the function, assuming it to be a rational integral function.

CHAPTER IV

INTERPOLATION WITH UNEQUAL INTERVALS

1. In the previous chapter formulae have been developed on the assumption that the argument proceeded by equal intervals. Although in actuarial problems the data are generally given at equidistant intervals of the independent variable, it sometimes happens that we are required to interpolate when values of the function are known for unequal intervals. In other words, instead of values of u_x for arguments $x + h$, $x + 2h$, $x + 3h$, ... being given, the known values are $x + a$, $x + b$, $x + c$, ..., where $a - b$, $b - c$, ... are not necessarily equal.

2. Divided differences.

Since we cannot take out the differences as hitherto defined, we adopt a process of differencing involving the argument as well as the entry. The differences obtained by this process are called "divided" differences, and are found in the following manner.

Let u_x be given for the values $x = a$, $x = b$, $x = c$, $x = d$, ..., where the intervals need not be equal. Then we have

(i) First divided differences:

$$\frac{u_b - u_a}{b - a}; \quad \frac{u_c - u_b}{c - b}; \quad \frac{u_d - u_c}{d - c}; \quad ...,$$

which may be denoted by

$$\Delta' u_a; \quad \Delta' u_b; \quad \Delta' u_c; \quad ....$$

(ii) Second divided differences:

$$\frac{\Delta' u_b - \Delta' u_a}{c - a}; \quad \frac{\Delta' u_c - \Delta' u_b}{d - b}; \quad \frac{\Delta' u_d - \Delta' u_c}{e - c}; \quad ...,$$

or

$$\Delta'^2 u_a; \quad \Delta'^2 u_b; \quad \Delta'^2 u_c; \quad ....$$

(iii) Third divided differences:

$$\frac{\Delta'^2 u_b - \Delta'^2 u_a}{d - a}; \quad ... \quad \text{or} \quad \Delta'^3 u_a; \quad ...$$

and so on.

A numerical example will make this clear.

Example 1.

Take out the divided differences of u_x given the following table:

x	1	2	4	7	12
u_x	22	30	82	106	206

The table is

x	u_x	$\Delta' u_x$	$\Delta'^2 u_x$	$\Delta'^3 u_x$	$\Delta'^4 u_x$
1	22				
		$\dfrac{30-22}{2-1}=8$			
2	30		$\dfrac{26-8}{4-1}=6$		
		$\dfrac{82-30}{4-2}=26$		$\dfrac{-3\cdot6-6}{7-1}=-1\cdot6$	
4	82		$\dfrac{8-26}{7-2}=-3\cdot6$		$\dfrac{\cdot51-(-1\cdot6)}{12-1}=\cdot192.$
		$\dfrac{106-82}{7-4}=8$		$\dfrac{1\cdot5-(-3\cdot6)}{12-2}=\cdot51$	
7	106		$\dfrac{20-8}{12-4}=1\cdot5$		
		$\dfrac{206-106}{12-7}=20$			
12	206				

It is essential to arrange the work systematically if error is to be avoided. The numerators and denominators must be set out, either in parallel columns or in the form of fractions. Where there is ample space the columnar arrangement is better, especially where the divisors are cumbrous. It should be noted that while the numerators are the first differences of the preceding divided differences, the denominators are all formed directly from the arguments, differencing first in the ordinary way, then in pairs, then in triplets, ... and so on. It will also be seen that the divisor is always the difference between the values of x for the last and first u_x involved in the difference.

3. Newton's divided difference formula.

An alternative notation for divided differences is as follows. Let the function be $f(x)$ and the arguments $x_0, x_1, x_2, \dots x_r$. Then the successive divided differences are

$$f(x_0, x_1) = \frac{f(x_0) - f(x_1)}{x_0 - x_1},$$

$$f(x_0, x_1, x_2) = \frac{f(x_0, x_1) - f(x_1, x_2)}{x_0 - x_2},$$

$$\cdots\cdots\cdots\cdots$$

$$f(x_0, x_1, x_2, \ldots x_r) = \frac{f(x_0, x_1, x_2, \ldots x_{r-1}) - f(x_1, x_2, x_3, \ldots x_r)}{x_0 - x_r},$$

where the arguments are all different.

If we replace $x_0, x_1, \ldots x_r$ by $x, a_0, a_1, \ldots a_n$, we obtain a system that may be written

$$(x - a_0) f(x, a_0) = f(x) - f(a_0),$$

$$(x - a_1) f(x, a_0, a_1) = f(x, a_0) - f(a_0, a_1),$$

$$\vdots \qquad\qquad \vdots$$

$$(x - a_n) f(x, a_0, \ldots a_n) = f(x, a_0, \ldots a_{n-1}) - f(a_0, a_1, \ldots a_n).$$

From this we obtain in succession

$$f(x) = f(a_0) + (x - a_0) f(x, a_0)$$

$$= f(a_0) + (x - a_0) f(a_0, a_1) + (x - a_0)(x - a_1) f(x, a_0, a_1)$$

$$= \ldots,$$

and generally

$$f(x) = f(a_0) + (x - a_0) f(a_0, a_1) + (x - a_0)(x - a_1) f(a_0, a_1, a_2) + \ldots$$

$$+ (x - a_0)(x - a_1) \ldots (x - a_{n-1}) f(a_0, a_1, \ldots a_n) + R,$$

where

$$R = (x - a_0)(x - a_1) \ldots (x - a_n) f(x, a_0, a_1, \ldots a_n).$$

This is Newton's formula with divided differences.

It should be noted that the term preceding R in the expansion is $(x - a_0)(x - a_1) \ldots (x - a_{n-1}) f(a_0, a_1, \ldots a_n)$, there being n factors in the coefficient. In R, however, the coefficient has $n + 1$ factors, the new factor $(x - a_n)$ being introduced.

Reverting to the notation

$$\Delta'^n u_{a_r} = \frac{\Delta'^{n-1} u_{a_{r+1}} - \Delta'^{n-1} u_{a_r}}{a_{n+r} - a_r}$$

the above formula becomes

$$u_x = u_{a_0} + (x - a_0) \Delta' u_{a_0} + (x - a_0)(x - a_1) \Delta'^2 u_{a_0} + \ldots$$

$$+ (x - a_0)(x - a_1) \ldots (x - a_{n-1}) \Delta'^n u_{a_0} + R.$$

For a further investigation of the remainder term R see the article "On certain Formulae of Approximate Summation, etc." in *J.I.A.* vol. LIII, by Prof. Steffensen, to whom the above proof is due.

4. Theorems similar to those proved for the ordinary advancing difference formula can be shown to be true for divided differences. The following important proposition holds equally for divided differences as for differences at equal intervals.

If u_x be a rational integral function of the nth degree in x, then the nth divided difference is constant.

It will be sufficient to consider the function $y = x^n$.

Then, if the values of the argument x be $a, b, c, \ldots$, the first divided difference is

$$(b^n - a^n)/(b - a) = b^{n-1} + b^{n-2}a + b^{n-3}a^2 + \ldots + a^{n-1},$$

a homogeneous function of a and b of degree $(n - 1)$.

Again, the second divided difference is

$$\frac{(c^{n-1}+c^{n-2}b+c^{n-3}b^2+\ldots+b^{n-1})-(b^{n-1}+b^{n-2}a+b^{n-3}a^2+\ldots+a^{n-1})}{c - a},$$

or

$$\frac{(c^{n-1}+c^{n-2}b+c^{n-3}b^2+\ldots+b^{n-1})-(a^{n-1}+a^{n-2}b+a^{n-3}b^2+\ldots+b^{n-1})}{c - a}$$

$$= \frac{c^{n-1} - a^{n-1}}{c - a} + b\,\frac{c^{n-2} - a^{n-2}}{c - a} + \ldots + b^{n-2}\frac{c - a}{c - a},$$

and since $c - a$ is a factor of all the numerators, this is a homogeneous function of a, b, c of the $(n - 2)$th degree.

Generally, the pth divided difference is a homogeneous function of $(p + 1)$ values of the argument of the $(n - p)$th degree.

Therefore the nth divided difference will be of the $(n - n)$th degree, i.e. will be constant.

If nth divided differences are constant, higher divided differences will be zero. In that event the expansion for u_x in para. 3 will stop at the term just preceding R, and we shall have identically

$$u_x = u_{a_0} + (x - a_0)\,\Delta' u_{a_0} + (x - a_0)\,(x - a_1)\,\Delta'^2 u_{a_0} + \ldots$$

$$+ (x - a_0)\,(x - a_1)\,\ldots\,(x - a_{n-1})\,\Delta'^n u_{a_0}.$$

5. Newton's divided difference formula can be applied quite easily in practice, as the following example will show.

Example 2.

From the data in Ex. 1, find u_8.

Assuming fourth divided differences constant, the formula gives

$$u_8 = u_1 + (8-1)\Delta'u_1 + (8-1)(8-2)\Delta'^2u_1$$
$$+ (8-1)(8-2)(8-4)\Delta'^3u_1 + (8-1)(8-2)(8-4)(8-7)\Delta'^4u_1$$
$$= u_1 + 7\Delta'u_1 + 42\Delta'^2u_1 + 168\Delta'^3u_1 + 168\Delta'^4u_1$$
$$= 22 + 56 + 252 - 268{\cdot}8 + 32{\cdot}3$$
$$= 93 \text{ to the nearest integer.}$$

6. Development of Newton's advancing difference formula.

If the interval $b - a = h$, we have

$$\Delta'u_a = (u_b - u_a)/(b-a) = (u_{a+h} - u_a)/h = \Delta u_a/h;$$

also if the interval $c - b =$ the interval $b - a = h$,

$$\Delta'^2u_a = (\Delta'u_b - \Delta'u_a)/(c-a)$$
$$= \frac{(u_{a+2h} - u_{a+h})/h - (u_{a+h} - u_a)/h}{2h}$$
$$= (u_{a+2h} - 2u_{a+h} + u_a)/2h^2 = \Delta^2u_a/2h.$$

Similarly, if the interval $d - c$ is also h,

$$\Delta'^3u_a = (\Delta'^2u_b - \Delta'^2u_a)/(d-a)$$
$$= \frac{(u_{a+3h} - 2u_{a+2h} + u_{a+h})/2h^2 - (u_{a+2h} - 2u_{a+h} + u_a)/2h^2}{3h}$$
$$= (u_{a+3h} - 3u_{a+2h} + 3u_{a+h} - u_a)/3 . 2h^3 = \Delta^3u_a/3! \, h^3,$$

and so on.

The formula for u_x in terms of u_a and its leading divided differences is

$$u_x = u_a + (x-a)\,\Delta'u_a + (x-a)(x-b)\,\Delta'^2u_a$$
$$+ (x-a)(x-b)(x-c)\,\Delta'^3u_a + \ldots$$
$$+ (x-a)(x-b)(x-c)\ldots(x-k)\,\Delta'^nu_a.$$

This becomes, on putting $x - a = nh$,

$$u_{a+nh} = u_a + nh\Delta'u_a + nh\,[nh - (b-a)]\,\Delta'^2u_a$$
$$+ nh\,[nh - (b-a)]\,[nh - (c-a)]\,\Delta'^3u_a + \ldots.$$

If now we have equal intervals, so that

$$b - a = h, \; c - a = 2h, \ldots,$$

and so on,

$$u_{a+nh} = u_a + \frac{nh\Delta u_a}{h} + \frac{nh\,(nh-h)\,\Delta^2 u_a}{2!\,h^2}$$

$$+ \frac{nh\,(nh-h)\,(nh-2h)\,\Delta^3 u_a}{3!\,h^3} + \dots$$

from the relations proved above,

i.e. $$u_{a+nh} = u_a + n_1\Delta u_a + n_2\Delta^2 u_a + n_3\Delta^3 u_a + \dots,$$

which is Newton's formula for advancing differences.

7. Lagrange's interpolation formula.

On the same assumption as has been made hitherto, namely that the function concerned is a rational integral function of x, an interpolation formula can be evolved which is equivalent to the process of splitting up an algebraic fraction into its partial fractions.

Let n values of the function $y = u_x$ be given, so that u_x is supposed to be a rational integral function of the $(n-1)$th degree in x, and let the given values of x be $a, b, c, \dots k$.

Then we may write

$$u_x = A\,(x-b)\,(x-c)\dots(x-k) + B\,(x-a)\,(x-c)\dots(x-k) + \dots$$

$$+ K\,(x-a)\,(x-b)\dots(x-m),$$

where there are n terms each of degree $n-1$ in x.

This is true for all values of x involved. Put therefore $x = a$.

Then $$u_a = A\,(a-b)\,(a-c)\dots(a-k),$$

$$\therefore A = \frac{u_a}{(a-b)\,(a-c)\dots(a-k)}.$$

Similarly, by putting $x = b$,

$$B = \frac{u_b}{(b-a)\,(b-c)\dots(b-k)}.$$

In like manner all the coefficients can be found.

$$\therefore u_x = u_a\frac{(x-b)\,(x-c)\dots(x-k)}{(a-b)\,(a-c)\dots(a-k)} + u_b\frac{(x-a)\,(x-c)\dots(x-k)}{(b-a)\,(b-c)\dots(b-k)} + \dots$$

$$+ u_k\frac{(x-a)\,(x-b)\,(x-c)\dots}{(k-a)\,(k-b)\,(k-c)\dots},$$

or otherwise

$$\frac{u_x}{(x-a)(x-b)\ldots(x-k)} = \frac{u_a}{(a-b)(a-c)\ldots(a-k)}\frac{1}{x-a}$$
$$+ \frac{u_b}{(b-a)(b-c)\ldots(b-k)}\frac{1}{x-b} + \ldots.$$

It is evident that this is exactly the same as splitting the fraction

$$\frac{u_x}{(x-a)(x-b)\ldots(x-k)}$$

into partial fractions.

This alternative expression is due to Euler and was given earlier than Lagrange's formula.

It is interesting to note that Euler's form, when written as

$$\frac{f(x)}{(x-a)(x-b)\ldots} + \frac{f(a)}{(a-x)(a-b)\ldots} + \frac{f(b)}{(b-x)(b-a)\ldots} + \ldots$$

is an expression for the divided difference $f(x, a, b, c, \ldots k)$. It follows therefore that Euler's formula (and consequently Lagrange's) can be evolved from the divided difference formula by equating the nth divided difference to zero.

8. Lagrange's formula is usually laborious to apply in practice and requires close attention to sign; it is generally simpler to employ other finite difference methods. Where the intervals are equal an advancing difference formula may be used, and for unequal intervals it is preferable to use divided differences.

The principles on which this formula has been developed are the same as those assumed for the difference formulae, namely that n values of the function being given, nth differences are assumed zero. The following examples show the application of the formula.

Example 3.

Given the data in Ex. 1, obtain u_8 by the use of Lagrange's formula.

$$\frac{u_8}{(8-1)(8-2)(8-4)(8-7)(8-12)} = \frac{u_1}{(1-2)(1-4)(1-7)(1-12)}\cdot\frac{1}{(8-1)}$$
$$+ \frac{u_2}{(2-1)(2-4)(2-7)(2-12)}\cdot\frac{1}{(8-2)}$$
$$+ \frac{u_4}{(4-1)(4-2)(4-7)(4-12)}\cdot\frac{1}{(8-4)} + \ldots,$$

i.e. $\dfrac{u_8}{7.6.4.1.(-4)} = \dfrac{22}{(-1)(-3)(-6)(-11).7} + \dfrac{30}{1.(-2)(-5)(-10).6}$

$\qquad\qquad + \dfrac{82}{3.2.(-3)(-8).4} + \dfrac{106}{6.5.3.(-5).1}$

$\qquad\qquad + \dfrac{206}{11.10.8.5.(-4)}.$

$\therefore\ u_8 = -10{\cdot}666\ldots + 33{\cdot}6 - 95{\cdot}666\ldots + 158{\cdot}293\ldots + 7{\cdot}865$

$\qquad = 93$ (to the nearest integer) as in Ex. 2.

Example 4.

Find the form of the function $y = u_x$ given that

$$u_0 = 8, \quad u_1 = 11, \quad u_4 = 68, \quad u_5 = 123.$$

By Lagrange's formula:

$\dfrac{u_x}{x(x-1)(x-4)(x-5)} = \dfrac{8}{(-1)(-4)(-5)}\cdot\dfrac{1}{x} + \dfrac{11}{1(-3)(-4)}\cdot\dfrac{1}{x-1}$

$\qquad\qquad + \dfrac{68}{4.3(-1)}\cdot\dfrac{1}{x-4} + \dfrac{123}{5.4.1}\cdot\dfrac{1}{x-5}$

$\qquad = -\dfrac{2}{5}\cdot\dfrac{1}{x} + \dfrac{11}{12}\cdot\dfrac{1}{x-1} - \dfrac{68}{12}\cdot\dfrac{1}{x-4} + \dfrac{123}{20}\cdot\dfrac{1}{x-5}$

$\qquad = \dfrac{1}{20}\dfrac{115x+40}{x(x-5)} - \dfrac{1}{12}\dfrac{57x-24}{(x-1)(x-4)}$

$\qquad = \dfrac{23x+8}{4x(x-5)} - \dfrac{19x-8}{4(x-1)(x-4)}.$

$\therefore\ u_x = \tfrac14\left[(23x+8)(x^2-5x+4) - (19x-8)(x^2-5x)\right]$

$\qquad = x^3 - x^2 + 3x + 8.$

It is instructive to work out this example by divided differences, using two different orders for the values of x, thus illustrating the important principle that the order is indifferent.

(a)

x	u_x	$\Delta' u_x$	$\Delta'^2 u_x$	$\Delta'^3 u_x$
0	8			
		$3 \div 1 = 3$		
1	11		$16 \div 4 = 4$	
		$57 \div 3 = 19$		$5 \div 5 = 1$
4	68		$36 \div 4 = 9$	
		$55 \div 1 = 55$		
5	123			

$\therefore\ u_x = 8 + 3x + 4x(x-1) + 1x(x-1)(x-4) = x^3 - x^2 + 3x + 8.$

(b)

x	u_x	$\Delta'u_x$	$\Delta'^2 u_x$	$\Delta'^3 u_x$
5	123			
		$-115 \div -5 = 23$		
0	8		$-8 \div -1 = 8$	
		$+60 \div +4 = 15$		$-4 \div -4 = 1$
4	68		$+4 \div +1 = 4$	
		$-57 \div -3 = 19$		
1	11			

$$\therefore u_x = 123 + 23\,(x-5) + 8\,(x-5)\,x + 1\,(x-5)\,x\,(x-4)$$
$$= 123 + 23x - 115 + 8x^2 \stackrel{.}{-} 40x + x^3 - 9x^2 + 20x$$
$$= x^3 - x^2 + 3x + 8.$$

9. Newton's formula for divided differences may be considered as the basic formula in finite differences. It has been shown that, by making the intervals equal, the ordinary advancing difference formula follows, and that Lagrange's formula can be evolved from the divided difference formula by equating the nth divided difference to zero. Moreover, by taking the limiting values when the intervals tend to zero, an important theorem known as Taylor's theorem follows. (See Chapter XI.)

EXAMPLES 4

1. Given terms at unequal intervals, explain how to apply the method of divided differences to find an interpolated value: illustrate your answer by finding u_5 given

$$u_{4\cdot50} = 1345, \quad u_{4\cdot55} = 1470, \quad u_{4\cdot70} = 2010, \quad u_{4\cdot90} = 3815, \quad u_{5\cdot15} = 10965.$$

2. $u_{40} = 43833$, $u_{42} = 46568$, $u_{44} = 49431$, $u_{45} = 50912$. Use divided differences to find u_{43}.

3. Given the following table, find log 656.

No.	654	658	659	661
Log	2·8156	2·8182	2·8189	2·8202

4. $u_{50} = 1\cdot6990$, $u_{52} = 1\cdot7160$, $u_{54} = 1\cdot7324$, $u_{55} = 1\cdot7404$. Find u_{53} by divided differences.

5. $u_{35\cdot0} = 1175$, $u_{35\cdot5} = 1280$, $u_{39\cdot5} = 2180$, $u_{40\cdot5} = 2420$. Obtain a value for u_{40} (i) by advancing differences, (ii) by divided differences.

6. $u_{7\cdot0} = 235$, $u_{7\cdot1} = 256$, $u_{7\cdot9} = 436$, $u_{8\cdot1} = 484$. Find $u_{8\cdot0}$.

7. Find the first three divided differences of the function $y = x^{-2}$ for the arguments $x = l, m, n, p$.

Find by Lagrange's formula the value of

8. u_{48} given $u_{40} = 15 \cdot 22$, $u_{45} = 13 \cdot 99$, $u_{50} = 12 \cdot 62$, $u_{55} = 11 \cdot 13$.

9. u_8 given $u_0 = 17 \cdot 378$, $u_5 = 15 \cdot 894$, $u_{10} = 14 \cdot 270$, $u_{15} = 12 \cdot 412$.

10. u_{22} given $u_{10} = 22 \cdot 40$, $u_{15} = 21 \cdot 66$, $u_{20} = 20 \cdot 82$, $u_{25} = 19 \cdot 85$.

11. u_1 given $u_0 = \cdot 400$, $u_2 = \cdot 128$, $u_3 = \cdot 224$, $u_4 = \cdot 376$.

12. Use Lagrange's formula to find the form of the function $y = f(x)$ given

x	0	2	3	6
$f(x)$	659	705	729	804

13. Values of u_x are given for all integral values of x from 0 to $n - 1$. Show that u_x is capable of expression in the form

$$\frac{x!}{(x-n)!\,(n-1)!}\left[\frac{u_{n-1}}{x-n+1} - (n-1)_1\frac{u_{n-2}}{x-n+2}\right.$$
$$\left. + (n-1)_2\frac{u_{n-3}}{x-n+3} - \ldots \pm (n-1)_{n-1}\frac{u_0}{x}\right].$$

Find u_x given $u_0 = 4$, $u_1 = 7$, $u_2 = 12$, $u_3 = 20$, by using the above formula.

14. By means of Lagrange's formula, prove that, approximately,

(1) $u_1 = u_3 - \cdot 3\,(u_5 - u_{-3}) + \cdot 2\,(u_{-3} - u_{-5})$,

(2) $u_0 = \frac{1}{2}\,[u_1 + u_{-1}] - \frac{1}{8}\,[\frac{1}{2}\,(u_3 - u_1) - \frac{1}{2}\,(u_{-1} - u_{-3})]$.

15. Four equidistant values u_{-1}, u_0, u_1, and u_2 being given, a value is interpolated by Lagrange's formula. Show that it may be written in the form

$$u_x = yu_0 + xu_1 + \frac{y\,(y^2 - 1)}{3!}\Delta^2 u_{-1} + \frac{x\,(x^2 - 1)}{3!}\Delta^2 u_0,$$

where $x + y = 1$.

16. If $f(a_1, a_0) = \dfrac{f(a_1) - f(a_0)}{a_1 - a_0}$, $f(a_2, a_1) = \dfrac{f(a_2) - f(a_1)}{a_2 - a_1}$, etc. be divided differences of the first order; $f(a_2, a_1, a_0) = \dfrac{f(a_2, a_1) - f(a_1, a_0)}{a_2 - a_0}$, etc. divided differences of the second order and so on, find $f(2, 4, 9, 10)$, where $f(x) = $ (i) $x^3 - 2x$, (ii) $x^4 + x^2 + 1$.

17. Prove that if u_x be a rational integral function of x of the nth degree, and if values u_a, u_b, u_c, ... of u_x be given, then the expression for u_x in terms of its divided differences is the same whatever the order of arrangement of the u's.

18. Apply Lagrange's formula to find $f(5)$ and $f(6)$, given that
$$f(1) = 2, f(2) = 4, f(3) = 8, f(4) = 16 \text{ and } f(7) = 128;$$
and explain why the results differ from those obtained by completing the series of powers of 2.

19. $u_{-30} = 30$; $u_{-13} = 34$; $u_3 = 38$; $u_{18} = 42$. Find u_0.

20. $u_{70} = 7{\cdot}69$; $u_{72} = 7{\cdot}07$; $u_{73} = 6{\cdot}78$; $u_{75} = 6{\cdot}18$. Interpolate to find u_{71} by divided differences, using the following orders of the argument:

(i) 70, 73, 75, 72; (ii) 72, 75, 70, 73.

21. By means of divided differences, find the value of u_{19} from the following table:

x	11	17	21	23	31
u_x	14,646	83,526	194,486	279,846	923,526

CHAPTER V

CENTRAL DIFFERENCES

1. If a series of values of u_x be given, we can interpolate to find any intermediate value by one of the methods in the preceding chapters. Where the values of the argument x proceed by unit intervals it has been shown that, on certain assumptions, Newton's advancing difference formula can be applied to give satisfactory results. If the value of u_x were required for some value of x between $x = 0$ and $x = 1$, it might be considered that we should obtain a better result if our knowledge of the shape of the curve extended on both sides of the values of x between which we wish to interpolate. That is to say, where we may choose any values of u_x at unit intervals for our data, it might be of advantage if we could use a formula involving values such as u_{-3}, u_{-2}, u_{-1}, u_0, u_1, u_2, u_3, ... rather than $u_0, u_1, u_2, u_3, u_4, \ldots$ By the advancing difference formula we expand u_x in terms of a given value of u_x and its leading differences. In *central difference* formulae we are not confined to leading differences; the formulae are based on differences obtained from values of u_x on either side of the origin.

2. There are various central difference formulae that are of use in actual practice, and the development of the better-known formulae is an exercise in the application of the fundamental principles of finite differences which will be advantageous to the student. It will be assumed that the values of the function correspond to equidistant values of the argument. For unequal intervals the method of divided differences should be adopted.

3. Gauss's formula.

The ordinary advancing difference expansion is

$$u_x = u_0 + x\Delta u_0 + \frac{x\,(x-1)}{2!}\,\Delta^2 u_0 + \frac{x\,(x-1)\,(x-2)}{3!}\,\Delta^3 u_0$$
$$+ \frac{x\,(x-1)\,(x-2)\,(x-3)}{4!}\,\Delta^4 u_0 + \ldots.$$

Now $\Delta^2 u_0 = \Delta^2 u_{-1} + \Delta^3 u_{-1};$

$\Delta^3 u_0 = \Delta^3 u_{-1} + \Delta^4 u_{-1}; \quad \Delta^4 u_{-1} = \Delta^4 u_{-2} + \Delta^5 u_{-2};$

. . . .

Therefore we may write

$$u_x = u_0 + x\Delta u_0 + \frac{x\,(x-1)}{2!}\,(\Delta^2 u_{-1} + \Delta^3 u_{-1})$$

$$+ \frac{x\,(x-1)\,(x-2)}{3!}\,(\Delta^3 u_{-1} + \Delta^4 u_{-1}) + \dots$$

$$= u_0 + x\Delta u_0 + \frac{x\,(x-1)}{2!}\,\Delta^2 u_{-1}$$

$$+ \left[\frac{x\,(x-1)}{2!} + \frac{x\,(x-1)\,(x-2)}{3!}\right]\Delta^3 u_{-1}$$

$$+ \left[\frac{x\,(x-1)\,(x-2)}{3!} + \frac{x\,(x-1)\,(x-2)\,(x-3)}{4!}\right]\Delta^4 u_{-1} + \dots$$

$$= u_0 + x\Delta u_0 + \frac{x\,(x-1)}{2!}\,\Delta^2 u_{-1} + \frac{(x+1)\,x\,(x-1)}{3!}\,\Delta^3 u_{-1}$$

$$+ \frac{(x+1)\,x\,(x-1)\,(x-2)}{4!}\,(\Delta^4 u_{-2} + \Delta^5 u_{-2}) + \dots,$$

since $x_r + x_{r+1} = (x+1)_{r+1},$

$$= u_0 + x\Delta u_0 + x_2\Delta^2 u_{-1} + (x+1)_3\,\Delta^3 u_{-1} + (x+1)_4\,\Delta^4 u_{-2} + \dots.$$

This is known as the Gauss "forward" formula.

A variant of this method is to write the advancing difference formula in the form

$$u_x = u_0 + x\Delta u_0 + \frac{x^{(2)}}{2!}\,\Delta^2 u_0 + \frac{x^{(3)}}{3!}\,\Delta^3 u_0 + \frac{x^{(4)}}{4!}\,\Delta^4 u_0 + \dots.$$

Then, since

$$x_r + x_{r+1} = (x+1)_{r+1}, \quad \text{or} \quad \frac{x^{(r)}}{r!} + \frac{x^{(r+1)}}{(r+1)!} = \frac{(x+1)^{(r+1)}}{(r+1)!},$$

we have

$$u_x = u_0 + x\Delta u_0 + \frac{x^{(2)}}{2!}\,(\Delta^2 u_{-1} + \Delta^3 u_{-1}) + \frac{x^{(3)}}{3!}\,(\Delta^3 u_{-1} + \Delta^4 u_{-1})$$

$$+ \frac{x^{(4)}}{4!}\,(\Delta^4 u_{-1} + \Delta^5 u_{-1}) + \dots$$

$$= u_0 + x\Delta u_0 + \frac{x^{(2)}}{2!}\,\Delta^2 u_{-1} + \left(\frac{x^{(2)}}{2!} + \frac{x^{(3)}}{3!}\right)\Delta^3 u_{-1}$$

$$+ \left(\frac{x^{(3)}}{3!} + \frac{x^{(4)}}{4!}\right)\Delta^4 u_{-1} + \dots$$

$$= u_0 + x\Delta u_0 + \frac{x^{(2)}}{2!}\,\Delta^2 u_{-1} + \frac{(x+1)^{(3)}}{3!}\,\Delta^3 u_{-1} + \frac{(x+1)^{(4)}}{4!}\,\Delta^4 u_{-1} + \dots,$$

whence, by writing $\Delta^4 u_{-1} = \Delta^4 u_{-2} + \Delta^5 u_{-2}$ and so on, Gauss's formula follows.

A proof similar to the above, in which the general term is evolved, and which depends upon the method of separation of symbols, will be found in *J.I.A.* vol. L, pp. 31, 32.

An alternative method of proof, depending on the basic formula for divided differences, follows the lines of the corresponding proof of Newton's formula for equal intervals. If on p. 61 we take arguments $a, a + h, a - h, a + 2h, a - 2h, \ldots$ instead of $a, a + h, a + 2h, a + 3h, \ldots$ and proceed to express the divided differences in terms of ordinary differences, Gauss's formula is at once obtained. This is seen more easily by writing down terms in the order $u_0, u_1, u_{-1}, u_2, u_{-2}, \ldots$ and taking out the leading divided differences.

If we write the terms of the series and their differences thus:

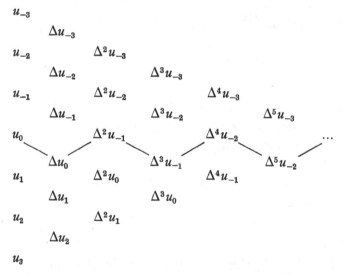

it will be seen that successive differences in the Gauss formula above lie along the zig-zag line indicated. For this reason the formula is often referred to as the "zig-zag" formula.

4. Stirling's formula.

If in Newton's formula we group the terms in a slightly different manner from that above, and use the relations

$$\Delta u_0 = \Delta u_{-1} + \Delta^2 u_{-1};$$
$$\Delta^2 u_0 = \Delta^2 u_{-1} + \Delta^3 u_{-1}; \qquad \Delta^3 u_{-1} = \Delta^3 u_{-2} + \Delta^4 u_{-2};$$
$$\dots \dots \dots \dots \dots \dots \dots \dots \qquad \dots \dots \dots \dots \dots \dots \dots \dots$$

we have

$$u_x = u_0 + x\,(\Delta u_{-1} + \Delta^2 u_{-1}) + x_2\,(\Delta^2 u_{-1} + \Delta^3 u_{-1})$$
$$+ x_3\,(\Delta^3 u_{-1} + \Delta^4 u_{-1}) + \dots,$$

which, on substituting the single function $(x + 1)_{r+1}$ for $x_r + x_{r+1}$ and so on, becomes easily

$$u_x = u_0 + x\Delta u_{-1} + (x + 1)_2\,\Delta^2 u_{-1} + (x + 1)_3\,\Delta^3 u_{-2}$$
$$+ (x + 2)_4\,\Delta^4 u_{-2} + \dots.$$

This is another form of Gauss's formula—the "backward" form.

It should be noted that this is also a zig-zag formula. Here we take an upward step in the diagram from u_0 and then proceed alternately, whereas in the forward formula the first step is downward.

Taking the mean of the two Gauss formulae we arrive at the following expansion:

$$u_x = u_0 + x\tfrac{1}{2}\,(\Delta u_0 + \Delta u_{-1}) + \frac{x^2}{2!}\Delta^2 u_{-1} + \frac{x\,(x^2 - 1^2)}{3!}\tfrac{1}{2}\,(\Delta^3 u_{-1} + \Delta^3 u_{-2})$$

$$+ \frac{x^2\,(x^2 - 1^2)}{4!}\,\Delta^4 u_{-2} + \frac{x\,(x^2 - 1^2)\,(x^2 - 2^2)}{5!}\tfrac{1}{2}\,(\Delta^5 u_{-2} + \Delta^5 u_{-3})$$

$$+ \frac{x^2\,(x^2 - 1^2)\,(x^2 - 2^2)}{6!}\,\Delta^6 u_{-3} + \dots.$$

This is known as Stirling's formula.

5. Bessel's formula.

Transforming the origin in the Gauss backward formula from o to 1, we have

$$u_x = u_1 + (x - 1)\,\Delta u_0 + \frac{x\,(x - 1)}{2!}\,\Delta^2 u_0 + \frac{x\,(x - 1)\,(x - 2)}{3!}\,\Delta^3 u_{-1}$$

$$+ \frac{(x + 1)\,x\,(x - 1)\,(x - 2)}{4!}\,\Delta^4 u_{-1} + \dots.$$

The mean of this and the forward formula is

$$u_x = \tfrac{1}{2}\,(u_0 + u_1) + (x - \tfrac{1}{2})\,\Delta u_0 + \frac{x\,(x - 1)}{2!}\tfrac{1}{2}\,(\Delta^2 u_{-1} + \Delta^2 u_0) + \dots,$$

which is Bessel's formula.

6. Everett's formula.

The Gauss forward formula with interval x and initial term v_1 may be written

$$v_{x+1} = v_1 + x\Delta v_1 + x_2\Delta^2 v_0 + (x+1)_3\,\Delta^3 v_0 + (x+1)_4\,\Delta^4 v_{-1}$$
$$+ (x+2)_5\,\Delta^5 v_{-1} + \dots.$$

The backward formula with interval $(x-1)$ and initial term v_1 gives

$$v_x = v_1 + (x-1)\,\Delta v_0 + x_2\Delta^2 v_0 + x_3\Delta^3 v_{-1} + (x+1)_4\,\Delta^4 v_{-1}$$
$$+ (x+1)_5\,\Delta^5 v_0 + \dots.$$

Subtract the second series from the first: then, since

$$v_{x+1} - v_x = \Delta v_x,$$

we have

$$\Delta v_x = x\Delta v_1 + (x+1)_3\,\Delta^3 v_0 + (x+2)_5\,\Delta^5 v_{-1} + \dots$$
$$- (x-1)\,\Delta v_0 - x_3\Delta^3 v_{-1} - (x+1)_5\,\Delta^5 v_{-2} - \dots.$$

Put $u_x,\ \Delta u_x,\ \Delta^2 u_x,\ \dots$ for $\Delta v_x,\ \Delta^2 v_x,\ \Delta^3 v_x,\ \dots$.
Then

$$u_x = xu_1 + (x+1)_3\,\Delta^2 u_0 + (x+2)_5\,\Delta^4 u_{-1} + \dots$$
$$- (x-1)\,u_0 - x_3\Delta^2\,u_{-1} - (x+1)_5\,\Delta^4 u_{-2} - \dots.$$

When x is less than unity a convenient form of this formula for interpolation between u_0 and u_1 is obtained by putting $\xi = 1 - x$; thus

$$u_x = xu_1 + \frac{x\,(x^2-1)}{3!}\,\Delta^2 u_0 + \frac{x\,(x^2-1)\,(x^2-4)}{5!}\,\Delta^4 u_{-1} + \dots$$
$$+ \xi u_0 + \frac{\xi\,(\xi^2-1)}{3!}\,\Delta^2 u_{-1} + \frac{\xi\,(\xi^2-1)\,(\xi^2-4)}{5!}\,\Delta^4 u_{-2} + \dots,$$

the most common form of Everett's formula.

The above elegant proof is due to G. J. Lidstone (*J.I.A.* vol. LX, pp. 349–52). In his note on this formula Mr Lidstone shows how to obtain another formula similar to the above for interpolation between $u_{-\frac{1}{2}}$ and $u_{\frac{1}{2}}$. The mean of the two Gauss formulae is taken in the same way, but $x\,;\,v_0$ and $x\,;\,v_1$ are used in place of $x\,;\,v_1$ and $x-1\,;\,v_1$ respectively: the formula then becomes

$$u_{p-\frac{1}{2}} = u_0 + \frac{p^2 - \frac{1}{4}}{2!} \Delta u_0 + \frac{(p^2 - \frac{1}{4})(p^2 - \frac{9}{4})}{4!} \Delta^3 u_{-1} + \ldots$$
$$- \frac{q^2 - \frac{1}{4}}{2!} \Delta u_{-1} - \frac{(q^2 - \frac{1}{4})(q^2 - \frac{9}{4})}{4!} \Delta^3 u_{-2} + \ldots,$$

where $p = \frac{1}{2} + x$ and $q = \frac{1}{2} - x$.

This form is generally known as Everett's "second" formula; it is specially adapted for use in statistical work.

7. Sheppard's rules.

Dr W. F. Sheppard has laid down certain general principles for obtaining central difference formulae which are very simple in their application. By adopting a slightly different notation from the usual a difference table is constructed from which the formulae can be written down with little trouble. Thus:

Δu_{-1} is denoted by $(-1, 0)$, $\qquad \Delta^2 u_{-1}$ is denoted by $(-1, 0, 1)$,

$\Delta u_0 \qquad$,, $\qquad (0, 1)$, $\qquad \Delta^2 u_0 \qquad$,, $\qquad (0, 1, 2)$,

$\Delta u_1 \qquad$,, $\qquad (1, 2)$; $\qquad \Delta^2 u_1 \qquad$,, $\qquad (1, 2, 3)$;

$\qquad\qquad \Delta^3 u_{-1}$ is denoted by $(-1, 0, 1, 2)$,

$\qquad\qquad \Delta^3 u_0 \qquad$,, $\qquad (0, 1, 2, 3)$,

$\qquad\qquad \Delta^3 u_1 \qquad$,, $\qquad (1, 2, 3, 4)$;

and so on.

The difference table then becomes

x	u_x	Δu_x	$\Delta^2 u_x$	$\Delta^3 u_x$
x_{-2}	u_{-2}			
		$(-2, -1)$		
x_{-1}	u_{-1}		$(-2, -1, 0)$	
		$(-1, 0)$		$(-2, -1, 0, 1)$
x_0	u_0		$(-1, 0, 1)$	$\ldots$
		$(0, 1)$		$(-1, 0, 1, 2)$
x_1	u_1		$(0, 1, 2)$	
		$(1, 2)$		
x_2	u_2			

The Newton advancing difference formula may be written

$$u_x = u_0 + (x - x_0)(0, 1) + \frac{(x - x_0)(x - x_1)}{1 \qquad 2}(0, 1, 2)$$
$$+ \frac{(x - x_0)(x - x_1)(x - x_2)}{1 \qquad 2 \qquad 3}(0, 1, 2, 3) + \ldots,$$

which is $\quad u_x = u_0 + x\Delta u_0 + x_2\Delta^2 u_0 + x_3\Delta^3 u_0 + x_4\Delta^4 u_0 + \ldots$.

Gauss's forward formula:

$$u_x = u_0 + (x - x_0)\,(0, 1) + \frac{(x - x_0)\,(x - x_1)}{1} \frac{}{2} (- 1, 0, 1)$$

$$+ \frac{(x - x_0)\,(x - x_1)\,(x - x_{-1})}{1 \quad\ 2 \qquad 3} (- 1, 0, 1, 2) + \ldots,$$

or $u_x = u_0 + x\,(0, 1) + x_2\,(- 1, 0, 1) + (x + 1)_3\,(- 1, 0, 1, 2) + \ldots$

$$= u_0 + x\Delta u_0 + x_2\Delta^2 u_{-1} + (x + 1)_3\Delta^3 u_{-1} + \ldots.$$

The rules are

(i) Start with any tabulated value of u_x.

(ii) Pass to successive differences by steps either downwards or upwards.

(iii) The new suffix introduced at each step determines the new factor, involving x, for use in the next term.

By means of these rules the formulae of Newton, Stirling and Bessel can be written down at once, whether for equal or unequal intervals.

8. It will be of interest to compare the results brought out by applying first, a central difference formula, and, secondly, the ordinary advancing difference formula, to the same set of data.

Example 1.

Interpolate by means of Gauss's forward formula to find the present value of an annuity of 1 p.a. for 27 years at 5 per cent. compound interest, given the following table:

No. of years x: 15   20   25   30   35   40

Annuity-value a_x: 10·3797 12·4622 14·0939 15·3725 16·3742 17·1591

If we take 25 years as the origin and 5 years as the unit, the value required will be $u_{.4}$.

x	u_x	Δu_x	$\Delta^2 u_x$	$\Delta^3 u_x$	$\Delta^4 u_x$	$\Delta^5 u_x$
− 2	10·3797					
		2·0825				
− 1	12·4622		− ·4508			
		1·6317		·0977		
0	14·0939		− ·3531		− ·0215	
		1·2786		·0762		·0054
1	15·3725		− ·2769		− ·0161	
		1·0017		·0601		
2	16·3742		− ·2168			
		·7849				
3	17·1591					

The Gauss formula is

$$u_x = u_0 + x\Delta u_0 + x_2\Delta^2 u_{-1} + (x + 1)_3 \Delta^3 u_{-1} + (x + 1)_4 \Delta^4 u_{-2}$$
$$+ (x + 2)_5 \Delta^5 u_{-2}.$$

When $x = \cdot 4$ the successive coefficients are

$$\cdot 4; \quad -\cdot 12; \quad -\cdot 056; \quad \cdot 0224; \quad \cdot 010752$$

and to four decimal places the value of $u_{\cdot 4}$ is $14\cdot 6430$, which agrees with the tabulated value.

To apply the advancing difference formula we take 15 years as the origin and are required to find u_x when $x = 2\cdot 4$.

In the formula

$$u_x = u_0 + x\Delta u_0 + x_2\Delta^2 u_0 + x_3\Delta^3 u_0 + x_4\Delta^4 u_0 + x_5\Delta^5 u_0$$

the coefficients are

$$2\cdot 4; \quad 1\cdot 68; \quad \cdot 224; \quad -\cdot 0336; \quad -\cdot 010752.$$

On evaluating the expansion we obtain for $u_{2\cdot 4}$ the value $14\cdot 6430$ as above.

It will be seen that the two results are in agreement (as indeed they must be, since the same values of u are used), and it may be asked therefore wherein lies the advantage of using the central difference formula. This question will be discussed in the next paragraph.

9. Consider an approximation to a particular value of u_x based on, say, r values out of n available. The error in the approximation, as measured by the first neglected term, is least when the coefficient of that term is least. It can be shown that this happens when the values of u_x upon which the interpolation is based range round the space in which x falls, so that x is as nearly as possible central. The central difference formulae give a systematic method for building up the table subject to these conditions.

Again, the central difference coefficients are as a general rule smaller than those required for the calculations in the advancing difference formula (as will be seen in the Example) and, by a suitable choice of origin, the arithmetical work may be reduced to a minimum.

It should be noted that, in the phrase "as measured by the first neglected term," this measure is not theoretically complete; it is however generally sufficient in practice if the first neglected order of differences is constant or is changing but slowly. When this is not so it will not necessarily be true that a central difference formula beginning with u_0 is more accurate than the advancing difference formula beginning with the same term. [See p. 337 of Sheppard's Paper, cited below.]

10. Relative accuracy of the formulae.

The relative accuracy of the various central difference formulae can be investigated in an elementary manner on the following lines.

The Gauss forward formula is

$$u_x = u_0 + x\Delta u_0 + x_2\Delta^2 u_{-1} + (x+1)_3\,\Delta^3 u_{-1} + (x+1)_4\,\Delta^4 u_{-2} + \ldots$$

It is easy to show that if we expand u_x by Stirling's formula as far as a certain order of even differences we can obtain by a simple transformation the above formula to even differences. Similarly it can be proved that Bessel's formula and Gauss's formula are identical to odd differences. Now the Gauss formula involves only ordinary differences while the other two series involve differences of the form $\frac{1}{2}(\Delta^n u_r + \Delta^n u_{r+1})$: these may be called "mean" differences. If instead of proceeding to constant differences the series stop short at, say, rth differences—which are not constant—the use of any of the formulae will involve an error. It remains to examine which of these formulae gives the best result in different circumstances.

The following demonstration is based on that given in greater detail by Mr D. C. Fraser in *J.I.A.* vol. L, p. 25.

Suppose that x is not greater than ·5. Then, by calculating the coefficients in Gauss's formula, it will be found that for positive values of x none of the coefficients (except that multiplying Δu_0) differs greatly from $\pm$ ·5 times the preceding coefficient. (See Table, *J.I.A.* vol. L, p. 25.) Thus the terms after that involving the third difference are approximately equal to

$$(x+1)_4\,(\Delta^4 + \tfrac{1}{2}\Delta^5 + \ldots)u_{-2},$$

i.e. to

$$(x+1)_4 \cdot \tfrac{1}{2}\,(\Delta^4 u_{-2} + \Delta^4 u_{-1}).$$

If therefore we substitute $\frac{1}{2}(\Delta^4 u_{-2} + \Delta^4 u_{-1})$, the mean difference in line with $u_{\frac{1}{2}}$, for $\Delta^4 u_{-2}$ in Gauss's formula, we make the formula approximately correct to fifth differences, without having to calculate the actual coefficient of the fifth difference. The substitution therefore improves the accuracy of the formula.

When, however, the substitution is made, it will be found to reproduce Bessel's formula to the fourth mean difference. Therefore Bessel's formula to fourth mean differences is usually more accurate than Stirling's to the fourth difference.

It may be shown similarly that Stirling's formula to odd mean differences is more accurate than Bessel's to the same order of differences.

The above demonstration is only approximate: a strict investigation into the relative accuracy of central and advancing difference formulae requires rather more elaborate mathematical discussion. (See Whittaker and Robinson, *Calculus of Observations*, p. 49; Lidstone, *T.F.A.* vol. IX, pp. 246–257; Fraser, *J.I.A.* vol. L, pp. 25–27; Sheppard, *Proceedings of the London Mathematical Society*, vol. IV, Parts 4, 5.)

Mr D. C. Fraser has given the following criteria summarising the properties of interpolation formulae:

(i) Formulae which proceed to constant differences are exact and are true for all values of n whether integral or fractional.

(ii) Formulae which stop short of constant differences are approximations.

(iii) Approximate formulae which terminate with the same difference are identically equal.

It should be noted that these rules, and those given in para. 7, are quite general; they apply to all formulae based on finite differences, not ending with mean differences.

11. Apart from the general superiority of central difference formulae certain of the formulae possess distinct advantages in special circumstances. For example, for the bisection of an interval Bessel's form is convenient, since the alternate terms are zero. We have, at once,

$$u_{\frac{1}{2}} = \tfrac{1}{2}(u_0 + u_1) - \tfrac{1}{8}[\tfrac{1}{2}(\Delta^2 u_{-1} + \Delta^2 u_0)] + \tfrac{3}{128}[\tfrac{1}{2}(\Delta^4 u_{-2} + \Delta^4 u_{-1})] + \dots.$$

Again, in using Everett's formula for the subdivision of intervals the terms are such that they may be used twice: they occur both in the "x" expansion and in the "ξ" expansion. An example will make this clear.

Example 2.

Given

x	30	35	40	45	50	55	60
u_x	771	862	1001	1224	1572	2123	2983

obtain values for u_x for all integral values of x between $x = 40$ and $x = 50$.

The difference table is

x	u_x	Δu_x	$\Delta^2 u_x$	$\Delta^3 u_x$	$\Delta^4 u_x$
30	771				
		91			
35	862		48		
		139		36	
40	1001		84		5
		223		41	
45	1224		125		37
		348		78	
50	1572		203		28
		551		106	
55	2123		309		
		860			
60	2983				

Everett's formula gives

$$u_x = xu_1 + (x + 1)_3\, \Delta^2 u_0 + (x + 2)_5\, \Delta^4 u_{-1} + \dots$$
$$+ \xi u_0 + (\xi + 1)_3\, \Delta^2 u_{-1} + (\xi + 2)_5\, \Delta^4 u_{-2} + \dots,$$

also $u_{1+\xi} = \xi u_2 + (\xi + 1)_3\, \Delta^2 u_1 + (\xi + 2)_5\, \Delta^4 u_0 + \dots$
$$+ xu_1 + (x + 1)_3\, \Delta^2 u_0 + (x + 2)_5\, \Delta^4 u_{-1} + \dots,$$

and the second line in $u_{1+\xi}$ is the same as the first line in u_x.

Since the data are given at quinquennial points and we require values at individual points, we may write $x = \cdot2, \cdot4, \cdot6, \dots$ and $\xi = \cdot8, \cdot6, \cdot4, \dots$. The first line of $u_{\cdot2}$ will be the same as the second line for $u_{1\cdot8}$ and so on.

The coefficients of the terms in the first line of the formula for u_x are, to fourth differences,

$\cdot2$	$- \cdot032$	$\cdot006336$
$\cdot4$	$- \cdot056$	$\cdot010752$
$\cdot6$	$- \cdot064$	$\cdot011648$
$\cdot8$	$- \cdot048$	$\cdot008064$

The work is best arranged in tabular form, thus:

x	xu_1	$\dfrac{x(x^2-1)}{3!}\Delta^2 u_0$	$\dfrac{x(x^2-1)(x^2-4)}{5!}\Delta^4 u_{-1}$	Sum of first three terms (ii) + (iii) + (iv)	Sum of second three terms	Interpolated result (v) + (vi)
(i)	(ii)	(iii)	(iv)	(v)	(vi)	(vii)
·2	200·2	−2·7	0·0	197·5		
·4	400·4	−4·7	0·1	395·8		
·6	600·6	−5·4	0·1	595·3		
·8	800·8	−4·0	0·0	796·8		
·2	244·8	−4·0	0·2	241·0	796·8	1037·8
·4	489·6	−7·0	0·4	483·0	595·3	1078·3
·6	734·4	−8·0	0·4	726·8	395·8	1122·6
·8	979·2	−6·0	0·3	973·5	197·5	1171·0
·2	314·4	− 6·5	0·2	308·1	973·5	1281·6
·4	628·8	−11·4	0·3	617·7	726·8	1344·5
·6	943·2	−13·0	0·3	930·5	483·0	1413·5
·8	1257·6	− 9·7	0·2	1248·1	241·0	1489·1

The only column which needs explanation is column (vi). This column represents the second set of three terms of the formula, correct to fourth central differences, and is obtained by writing down *in the reverse order* the values of the previous column applicable to the sum of the first three terms.

It should be mentioned that the values in column (vii) of the table do not quite agree with the tabular values: the tabular values are 1038, 1081, 1122, 1172, 1281, 1345, 1415, 1490. The reason for this is that the function upon which the original values depend is not a rational integral function of the independent variable and that therefore a formula based on finite differences is only an approximate representation of the function. The example is based on the rates of mortality according to the H^M table, the data being 10^5 times the probability of dying in the year of age x.

12. Just as $\Delta \equiv E - 1$, or $\Delta u_x = u_{x+1} - u_x$, similar symbolic identities may be deduced from the relations existing between u_x, $u_{x+\frac{1}{2}}$ and $u_{x-\frac{1}{2}}$. Dr Sheppard has introduced the following notation, which is widely used by mathematicians:

$$\delta u_x = u_{x+\frac{1}{2}} - u_{x-\frac{1}{2}},$$

and
$$\mu u_x = \tfrac{1}{2}\left(u_{x+\frac{1}{2}} + u_{x-\frac{1}{2}}\right).$$

The relationships between E, δ and μ are quite easy to establish.

$$\delta \equiv E^{\frac{1}{2}} - E^{-\frac{1}{2}} \equiv E^{-\frac{1}{2}} [E - 1] \equiv E^{-\frac{1}{2}} \Delta.$$

$$\therefore \quad \delta^{2n} \equiv E^{-n} \Delta^{2n}.$$

Also $\qquad \mu \equiv \tfrac{1}{2} (E^{\frac{1}{2}} + E^{-\frac{1}{2}}),$

and $\qquad \mu\delta \equiv \tfrac{1}{2} (E - E^{-1}) \equiv \tfrac{1}{2} (\Delta E^{-1} + \Delta),$

$$\mu\delta^{2n+1} \equiv \tfrac{1}{2} [E^{-(n-1)} - E^{-(n+1)}] \Delta^{2n}$$

$$\equiv \tfrac{1}{2} (\Delta E^{-1} + \Delta) \Delta^{2n}.$$

Again $\qquad 2\mu \equiv 2E^{\frac{1}{2}} - \delta,$

or $\qquad E^{\frac{1}{2}} \equiv \mu + \tfrac{1}{2}\delta.$

By means of these symbols the central difference formulae can be written down in very convenient form.

For example, Gauss's forward formula is

$$u_x = u_0 + x\delta u_{\frac{1}{2}} + x_2 \delta^2 u_0 + (x + 1)_3 \, \delta^3 u_{\frac{1}{2}} + (x + 1)_4 \, \delta^4 u_0 + \dots,$$

and Stirling's becomes

$$u_x = u_0 + x\mu \delta^2 u_0 + \tfrac{1}{2}x^2 \delta u_0 + (x + 1)_3 \, \mu\delta^3 u_0 + \dots.$$

EXAMPLES 5

1. Apply a central difference formula to obtain u_{25}, given $u_{20} = 14$, $u_{24} = 32$, $u_{28} = 35$, $u_{32} = 40$.

2. Given $u_2 = 10$, $u_1 = 8$, $u_0 = 5$, $u_{-1} = 10$, find $u_{\frac{1}{2}}$ by Gauss's forward formula.

3. Use Stirling's formula to find u_{28}, given $u_{20} = 49225$, $u_{25} = 48316$, $u_{30} = 47236$, $u_{35} = 45926$, $u_{40} = 44306$.

4. Given $u_{20} = 2854$, $u_{24} = 3162$, $u_{28} = 3544$, $u_{32} = 3992$; find u_{25} by Bessel's formula.

5. $a_{21} = 18\cdot4708$; $\quad a_{25} = 17\cdot8144$; $\quad a_{29} = 17\cdot1070$; $\quad a_{33} = 16\cdot3432$; $a_{37} = 15\cdot5154$. Find a_{30} by Gauss's forward formula.

6. What are the practical advantages arising from the use of central differences in interpolation?

Employ Stirling's formula to obtain successive approximations to $(1\cdot02125)^{50}$, given

$$(1\cdot01)^{50} = 1\cdot64463; \quad (1\cdot02)^{50} = 2\cdot69159; \quad (1\cdot03)^{50} = 4\cdot38391;$$
$$(1\cdot015)^{50} = 2\cdot10524; \quad (1\cdot025)^{50} = 3\cdot43711.$$

7. Find formulae true to third differences for the bisection of an interval

    (i) in terms of the two nearest values of the function and of differences of the functions;

    (ii) in terms of values of the function only.

Apply either formula to find P_{35}, given the values of P_x at 20, 30, 40, 50 to be 1313, 1727, 2392, 3493 respectively.

8. Given the table

x	310	320	330	340	350	360
log x	2·4914	2·5052	2·5185	2·5315	2·5441	2·5563

find the value of log 3375 by a central difference formula.

9. Prove that if third differences are assumed to be constant

$$u_x = xu_1 + \frac{x(x^2 - 1)}{6}\Delta^2 u_0 + yu_0 + \frac{y(y^2 - 1)}{6}\Delta^2 u_{-1},$$

where $y = 1 - x$.

Apply this formula to find the values of u_{11} to u_{14} and u_{16} to u_{19}, given that $u_0 = 3010, u_5 = 2710, u_{10} = 2285, u_{15} = 1860, u_{20} = 1560, u_{25} = 1510$ and $u_{30} = 1835$.

10. From the table of annual net premiums given below find the annual net premium at age 25 by means of Bessel's formula:

Age	Annual net premiums
20	·01427
24	·01581
28	·01772
32	·01996

11. Apply a central difference formula to find $f(32)$, given

$f(25) = ·2707, \quad f(30) = ·3027, \quad f(35) = ·3386, \quad f(40) = ·3794.$

12. Use Gauss's interpolation formula to obtain the value of $f(41)$, given $f(30) = 3678·2, f(35) = 2995·1, f(40) = 2400·1, f(45) = 1876·2, f(50) = 1416·3$.

Verify your result by using Lagrange's formula over the same figures.

13. Buchanan's formula for interpolating between u_0 and u_1 is

$u_{·2} = ·8u_0 - ·048\Delta^2 u_{-1} + ·0128\Delta^4 u_{-2} + ·2u_1 - ·032\Delta^2 u_0 + ·0016\Delta^4 u_{-1}$

$u_{·4} = ·6u_0 - ·064\Delta^2 u_{-1} + ·0144\Delta^4 u_{-2} + ·4u_1 - ·056\Delta^2 u_0 + ·0080\Delta^4 u_{-1}$

$u_{·6} = ·4u_0 - ·056\Delta^2 u_{-1} + ·0080\Delta^4 u_{-2} + ·6u_1 - ·064\Delta^2 u_0 + ·0144\Delta^4 u_{-1}$

$u_{·8} = ·2u_0 - ·032\Delta^2 u_{-1} + ·0016\Delta^4 u_{-2} + ·8u_1 - ·048\Delta^2 u_0 + ·0128\Delta^4 u_{-1}.$

Prove the formula for $u_{·2}$.

F

14. Show that any central difference formula can be developed from Lagrange. Apply a central difference formula obtained thus to find $f(3\frac{1}{2})$, given that $f(2) = 2{\cdot}626$; $f(3) = 3{\cdot}454$; $f(4) = 4{\cdot}784$ and $f(5) = 6{\cdot}986$.

15. Given $u_0, u_1, u_2, u_3, u_4, u_5$ (fifth differences constant), prove that

$$u_{2\frac{1}{2}} = \tfrac{1}{2}c + \frac{25\,(c - b) + 3\,(a - c)}{256},$$

where $\qquad a = u_0 + u_5; \quad b = u_1 + u_4; \quad c = u_2 + u_3.$

16. A series is formed by the division of the terms of the two series

$$
\begin{array}{ccccc}
u_x & 1 & 2 & 6 & 24 \ldots n! \\
v_x & 4 & 20 & 240 & 1680 \ldots \tfrac{1}{6}(n+3)!
\end{array}
$$

Obtain an interpolated value for $u_{2\frac{1}{2}}/v_{2\frac{1}{2}}$ of the new series by a central difference formula and compare the result with the quotient of $u_{2\frac{1}{2}}$ by $v_{2\frac{1}{2}}$ in the component series.

17. The following is a difference table written down in Woolhouse's notation:

$$
\begin{array}{ccccc}
u_{-2} \\
 & a_{-2} \\
u_{-1} & & b_{-1} \\
 & a_{-1} & & c_{-1} \\
u_0 & & b_0 & & d_0 \\
 & a_1 & & c_1 \\
u_1 & & b_1 \\
 & a_2 \\
u_2
\end{array}
$$

If $a_0 = \tfrac{1}{2}(a_{-1} + a_1)$ and $c_0 = \tfrac{1}{2}(c_{-1} + c_1)$, show that Stirling's formula (to fourth differences) can be expressed as

$$u_x = u_0 + Ax + Bx^2 + Cx^3 + Dx^4,$$

where A, B, C, D are functions of a_0, b_0, c_0, d_0 only.

18. Prove that in Woolhouse's notation

$$u_x = u_0 + xa_1 + x_2 b_0 + (x + 1)_3 c_1 + (x + 1)_4 d_0$$

correct to fourth differences.

19. Show that the sum of the terms of the series $u_{-2}, u_{-1}, u_0, u_1, u_2$ can be expressed in the following form

$$Au_0 + B\delta^2 u_0 + C\delta^4 u_0,$$

where $\delta^2 u_0$ and $\delta^4 u_0$ denote the second and fourth central differences of u_0; and find A, B and C.

20. By splitting up the fraction of the form

$$\frac{u_x}{(x^2 - a^2)(x^2 - b^2)(x^2 - c^2)}$$

into partial fractions, show how to arrive at u_x in terms of known values of the function of which x occupies the central position.

21. If $u_x = Au_0 + B\Delta u_0 + C\Delta^2 u_{-1} + \dots$, i.e. a general expression for u_x in terms of central differences, prove by expressing all differences in terms of advancing differences of u_0 that

$$u_x = u_0 + x\Delta u_0 + x_2\Delta^2 u_{-1} + (x+1)_3 \Delta^3 u_{-1} + \dots,$$

obtaining the general term in the expansion.

CHAPTER VI

INVERSE INTERPOLATION

1. When performing direct interpolation, values of y corresponding to various values of the argument x are given and we are required to find a value of the entry y corresponding to a value of x intermediate between the given values. If it is required to obtain an interpolated value of the *argument* corresponding to an intermediate value of the *entry*, the process adopted is called inverse interpolation. In other words, for direct interpolation we assume a curve $y = u_x$ passing through the points (x, y) and estimate the value of y corresponding to some intermediate value x': for inverse interpolation we have a similar curve but are required to find a value of x corresponding to a value y'.

For certain functions we may obtain the result easily. If $y = \sin x$, then $x = \sin^{-1} y$; if $y = x^3$, then $x = y^{\frac{1}{3}}$; if $y = a^x$, then $x = \log y / \log a$. The required values of x can be calculated immediately in these examples.

On the other hand, if the data are simply corresponding numerical values of x and y, all that we can write down is a formula such as Newton's or Stirling's: we must then endeavour to obtain a value for x by solving an equation. For example

$$y = u_x = (1 + \Delta)^x u_0 = u_0 + x\Delta u_0 + x_2 \Delta^2 u_0 + x_3 \Delta^3 u_0 + \dots.$$

If second differences may be assumed constant we have a quadratic equation which can be solved at once. Should this assumption be inadmissible, then we are faced with an equation of higher degree than the second and the solution of such an equation may be very laborious. In these circumstances we resort to approximate methods of solution of the equation.

2. Before embarking on the various methods of obtaining the interpolated value of x corresponding to a given value of y, it is well to examine the underlying principle involved. This is best illustrated by means of an example.

Example 1.

Obtain a value for x when $u_x = 19$, given the following values:

x	0	1	2
u_x	0	1	20

We may write down at once

$$y = u_x = (1 + \Delta)^x u_0 = u_0 + x\Delta u_0 + x_2 \Delta^2 u_0;$$

i.e. $$19 = 0 + x + 18x_2 = x + 9(x^2 - x),$$

so that $$9x^2 - 8x - 19 = 0,$$

from which $$x = 1 \cdot 964 \ldots \text{ or } - 1 \cdot 075 \ldots.$$

But since we have to find an interpolated value of x corresponding to a value of y we may treat y as the argument and x as the entry. Let us write the data in the form

y	0	1	20
$x = v_y$	0	1	2

and apply the Lagrange formula to calculate v_{19} as if for direct interpolation.

We shall have

$$\frac{v_{19}}{19.18.(-1)} = \frac{1}{18.1.(-19)} + \frac{2}{(-1).20.19}$$

or $$v_{19} = 2 \cdot 8.$$

It will be seen therefore that there are two distinct sets of results. By adopting the first method x has the values $1 \cdot 964\ldots$ or $- 1 \cdot 075\ldots$ and by adopting the second method x has the unique value $2 \cdot 8$. It remains to examine the reasons for the difference and to ascertain which result is more likely to approximate to the true interpolated value or values.

In the first method it will be apparent that we have taken a curve of the form $y = a + bx + cx^2$—a parabolic curve—and have obtained values of x corresponding to $y = 19$. This gives two values of x, one on each side of the vertex of the parabola. In applying the Lagrange formula inversely we have assumed that x is a parabolic function of y and have given y a particular value (19) in the equation $x = \alpha + \beta y + \gamma y^2$. If we substitute the value of y corresponding to each value of x from the data, it is easily seen that $\alpha = 0$, $\beta = 398/380$ and $\gamma = -18/380$. The Lagrange equation is therefore $190x = 199y - 9y^2$.

Now if the two curves
$$y = 9x^2 - 8x$$
and
$$x = \frac{199}{190}y - \frac{9}{190}y^2$$
be plotted on the same graph, it will be seen that they take different shapes, thus:

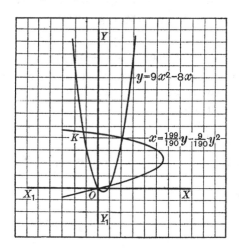

Fig. 13.

On the curve $y = 9x^2 - 8x$ the abscissae of the points whose ordinates are 19 are 1·96... and $-$ 1·07..., whereas on the other curve there is only one point for which the ordinate is 19, namely the point (2·8, 19). Unless therefore the two curves obtained from the data, (i) by treating x as the argument and (ii) by treating y as the argument, intersect at the required interpolated value, as for example at K in the above figure, the two methods are bound to give different results.

The question whether the Newton equation or the inverse interpolation method will give an answer more nearly to the true value can only be decided by a consideration of the data. For instance, if in this example there were reason to believe that for increasing positive values x and y increased together, it is more likely that the interpolated values of x when $y = 19$ would be 1·964... and $-$ 1·075... than the value $x = 2·8$.

3. The above example shows in a simple manner that the different processes of inverse interpolation may give different sets of results. We now proceed to a more general investigation of the problem.

The formulæ of direct interpolation are based on the properties of rational integral functions of the variable, and any formula which proceeds to nth differences gives exact results when applied to a rational integral function of the nth degree. By stopping short of nth differences the formula can, of course, be used to obtain approximate results, and the success of the interpolation depends on the magnitude of the terms omitted. Thus, if we use rth differences for a polynomial of the nth degree in x, the result is the exact value of terms up to and including the term in x^r. The terms beyond x^r are disregarded, and this can only be done legitimately if they are relatively unimportant.

In questions of direct interpolation there is only one value of y, i.e. of u_x, for a given value of x. There may be, however, more than one value of x for a given value of y. In fact, if y is a rational integral function of x, y is a rational function of x only when both functions are of the first degree. In other cases the inverse function may be an infinite series or an irrational function. For example, in the H^M Table of Mortality there is only one value of d_x for a given value of l_x (where l_x represents the number of persons attaining exact age x in any year of time, and d_x is the number of these who die before reaching age $x + 1$). In the neighbourhood of the peak of the death curve, however, there will be two values of l_x within a short range of interpolation for a given value of d_x.

For these reasons the subject of inverse interpolation is more troublesome than that of direct interpolation, although it should always be remembered that the conditions for good interpolation are the same for inverse interpolation as for direct. One principal condition is that within the range of interpolation there should be only one value of x corresponding to a given value of y.

Let us consider the equation in Example 1, namely

$$y = -8x + 9x^2,$$

where the range of interpolation is from 0 to 2. The first point to note is that the function is not a good subject for direct interpolation except when the formula is applied to its fullest extent—the second degree. The reason is that the last term is the predominating term throughout the greater part of the range.

In most instances, by altering the interval and reducing the range of interpolation, a function can be reduced to a good form for direct interpolation. Such a question as the following might be put:

Given the function $y = u_x = -8x + 9x^2$, for what intervals of x should u_x be tabulated so that in any interval an interpolated value of y can be obtained by first difference interpolation with an error less than, say, ·001?

Put
$$x = z/a;$$

then
$$u_x = v_z = -\frac{8z}{a} + \frac{9z^2}{a^2},$$

i.e.
$$a^2 v_z = -8az + 9z^2,$$
$$a^2 \Delta v_z = -8a + 18z + 9,$$

and
$$a^2 \Delta^2 v_z = 18,$$

so that
$$\Delta^2 v_z = 18/a^2.$$

Suppose v_z to be tabulated at unit intervals for values of z.

Then, for an interpolated value v_{z+t} between v_z and v_{z+1},
$$v_{z+t} = v_z + t\Delta v_z + \tfrac{1}{2}t\,(t-1)\,\Delta^2 v_z.$$

If we take $v_z + t\Delta v_z$ as the interpolated value, there is an error $\tfrac{1}{2}t\,(t-1)\,\Delta^2 v_z$ and the maximum numerical value of $\tfrac{1}{2}t\,(t-1)$ is $\tfrac{1}{8}$, being the value when t is $\tfrac{1}{2}$.

Therefore, by the conditions,
$$\tfrac{1}{2}t\,(t-1)\,\Delta^2 v_z < ·001,$$
$$\tfrac{1}{8}\Delta^2 v_z < ·001.$$

But $\Delta^2 v_z = 18/a^2$, $\quad \therefore \quad 18/8a^2 < ·001$;

i.e.
$$a^2 > 18000/8,$$

i.e.
$$> 2250,$$

or
$$a > \sqrt{2250},$$

and the most convenient value for a is 50.

We must therefore tabulate u_x at intervals of $\tfrac{1}{50}$ of unity, i.e. at intervals of ·02.

For example,
$$y = u_x = -8x + 9x^2.$$

x	z	$u_x = v_z$	Δv_z
1·10	55	2·0900	
			·2396
1·12	56	2·3296	
			·2468
1·14	57	2·5764	
			·2540
1·16	58	2·8304	
			·2612
1·18	59	3·0916	
			·2684
1·20	60	3·3600	

We may use this table for finding values of x corresponding to given values of u_x, and the interpolation is as legitimate as direct interpolation. While, however, direct interpolation to second differences is exact, inverse interpolation to second differences, while nearer the truth than first difference interpolation, is not exact.

4. Practical methods of inverse interpolation.

It is evident that the problem of inverse interpolation is the same as that of direct interpolation for unequal intervals. The methods of Lagrange or of divided differences could therefore be employed to obtain any intermediate value of x corresponding to a value of y, given a table of $y = u_x$, by the use of the inverse relation $x = v_y$. The labour involved in applying either of these methods is often prohibitive, and the methods usually adopted in practice are given below.

5. Successive approximation.

In the first place we obtain either by inspection or by a rough graph two values of x lying on either side of the required interpolated value. (For example, a value for x when y is zero in the function $y = x^2 - 4x + 2$—i.e. a solution of the equation $x^2 - 4x + 2 = 0$—lies between the values $x = 1$ and $x = 2$.) We then choose a suitable origin and unit of differencing so that if x be the interpolated value and lies between two successive values of the argument, x will be small compared with the unit of differencing.

Suppose that the required value lies between o and 1.

The method proceeds as follows:

$$u_x = u_0 + x\Delta u_0 + \tfrac{1}{2}x(x-1)\Delta^2 u_0 + \tfrac{1}{6}x(x-1)(x-2)\Delta^3 u_0 + \ldots.$$

Since x is small, a first approximation (α_1) will be obtained by neglecting terms involving second and higher differences of u_0.

$$\therefore\ u_x = u_0 + \alpha_1 \Delta u_0 \text{ approximately,}$$

i.e. $\quad\alpha_1 = (u_x - u_0)/\Delta u_0,\qquad$ first approximation.

Again, neglecting third and higher differences, we may write

$$u_x = u_0 + \alpha_2 \Delta u_0 + \tfrac{1}{2}\alpha_2(\alpha_1 - 1)\Delta^2 u_0,$$

where α_2 is a second approximation and is therefore not very different from α_1. This gives

$$\alpha_2 = \frac{u_x - u_0}{\Delta u_0 + \tfrac{1}{2}(\alpha_1 - 1)\Delta^2 u_0},\quad \text{second approximation.}$$

Similarly

$$\alpha_3 = \frac{u_x - u_0}{\Delta u_0 + \tfrac{1}{2}(\alpha_2 - 1)\Delta^2 u_0 + \tfrac{1}{6}(\alpha_2 - 1)(\alpha_2 - 2)\Delta^3 u_0},$$

$$\text{third approximation,}$$

and so on.

6. Elimination of third differences.

We have, as far as third differences, by expressing u_x in terms of $u_0, \Delta u_0, \ldots$,

$$u_x = u_0 + x\Delta u_0 + \tfrac{1}{2}x(x-1)\Delta^2 u_0 + \tfrac{1}{6}x(x-1)(x-2)\Delta^3 u_0.$$

Also, in terms of $u_1, \Delta u_1, \ldots$,

$$u_x = u_1 + (x-1)\Delta u_1 + \tfrac{1}{2}(x-1)(x-2)\Delta^2 u_1$$
$$+ \tfrac{1}{6}(x-1)(x-2)(x-3)\Delta^3 u_1.$$

If now we ignore the terms containing third differences and multiply both sides of the first equation by $3 - \alpha$ and both sides of the second equation by α (where α is an approximation to the required value, found by inspection or otherwise) and add, a new quadratic equation in x will be formed. The error involved in ignoring the third differences will be small, since

$$\tfrac{1}{6}x(x-1)(x-2)(3-\alpha)\Delta^3 u_0 + \tfrac{1}{6}\alpha(x-1)(x-2)(x-3)\Delta^3 u_1$$

will be small provided that $\Delta^3 u_0$ and $\Delta^3 u_1$ are not very different.

7. The following question is solved by both these methods.

Example 2.

Find the value of x for which y is 18,600, given

x	52	53	54	55	56
y	19,231	18,868	18,519	18,182	17,855

Changing the origin, the difference table is

x	y	Δy	$\Delta^2 y$	$\Delta^3 y$
0	19,231			
		-363		
1	18,868		14	
		-349		-2
2	18,519		12	
		-337		-2
3	18,182		10	
		-327		
4	17,855			

By the ordinary advancing difference formula

$$18{,}600 = 19{,}231 - 363x + \frac{14x\,(x-1)}{2!} - \frac{2x\,(x-1)\,(x-2)}{3!},$$

where the value of x is required corresponding to the value 18,600 of y.

(i) Successive approximation.

Since x is small, the first approximation will be

$$a_1 = \frac{19{,}231 - 18{,}600}{363} \quad \text{or} \quad 1{\cdot}7383\ldots.$$

Including the next term,

$$a_2 = \frac{631}{363 - 7\,(a_1 - 1)} \quad \text{or} \quad 1{\cdot}7634\ldots.$$

Similarly,

$$a_3 = \frac{631}{363 - 7\,(a_2 - 1) + \tfrac{1}{3}\,(a_2 - 1)\,(a_2 - 2)} \quad \text{or} \quad 1{\cdot}7646\ldots.$$

The required result is therefore $52 + 1{\cdot}7646\ldots = 53{\cdot}7646\ldots.$

(ii) Elimination of third differences.

We have

$$18{,}600 = u_x = (1 + \Delta)^x u_0 = 19{,}231 - 363x + 7x\,(x-1) - \tfrac{1}{3}x\,(x-1)\,(x-2)$$

and

$$18{,}600 = u_x = (1 + \Delta)^{x-1} u_1 = 18{,}868 - 349\,(x-1) + 6\,(x-1)\,(x-2)$$
$$- \tfrac{1}{3}\,(x-1)\,(x-2)\,(x-3).$$

By inspection a rough value of the interpolated value is $1{\cdot}75$, allowing for the change of origin.

If, therefore, we multiply the two equations by $(3 - 1·75)$ and $1·75$ respectively, and add, we may neglect the fourth term. The factors being $1·25$ and $1·75$ we can use 5 and 7: we thus obtain

$$12 \times 18{,}600 = 5\,[19{,}231 - 363x + 7x\,(x - 1)]$$
$$+ 7\,[18{,}868 - 349\,(x - 1) + 6\,(x - 1)\,(x - 2)]$$

or $223{,}200 = 230{,}758 - 4419x + 77x^2,$

i.e. $77x^2 - 4419x + 7558 = 0.$

Solving the quadratic, the value required is $x = 1·7646...$, which agrees with the value of a_3 in method (i) to four decimal places.

8. It is often convenient to employ a central difference formula as the basic equation, as in the following example.

Example 3.

Find the root of the equation $x^3 - 9x - 14 = 0$ which lies between 3 and 4. .

Let $y = x^3 - 9x - 14$. Then we have, by actual calculation,

x	3·0	3·2	3·4	3·6	3·8	4·0
y	− 14·000	− 10·032	− 5·296	·256	6·672	14·000

The difference table is

x	y	Δy	$\Delta^2 y$	$\Delta^3 y$
3·0	− 14·000			
		3·968		
3·2	− 10·032		·768	
		4·736		·048
3·4	− 5·296		·816	
		5·552		·048
3·6	·256		·864	
		6·416		·048
3·8	6·672		·912	
		7·328		
4·0	14·000			

Taking the origin at 3·6 and using Stirling's formula:

$$u_x = u_0 + x\,\frac{\Delta u_0 + \Delta u_{-1}}{2} + \frac{x^2}{2}\,\Delta^2 u_{-1} + \frac{x\,(x^2 - 1)}{6}\,\frac{\Delta^3 u_{-1} + \Delta^3 u_{-2}}{2},$$

the interval of differencing being 0·2;

i.e. $0 = ·256 + 5·984x + ·432x^2 + ·008x\,(x^2 - 1).$

The cubic equation can be solved by successive approximation, or we can repeat Stirling's formula for the next value of u_x and adopt the alternative method outlined above.

If the first of these methods be adopted, it will be found that successive approximations to the value of x are $-\cdot04278$, $-\cdot042913$, $-\cdot042971$. From the last we obtain as the required solution

$$3\cdot6 - (\cdot042971 \times \cdot2) \text{ or } 3\cdot5914058,$$

which is correct to six decimal places, the seventh being nearer to 7. If we choose our origin at the point (x, y) and the value of the interpolated value is $x + a$, then, when a lies between $-\frac{1}{4}$ and $\frac{1}{4}$, it is advantageous to use Stirling's formula. If a lies between $\frac{1}{4}$ and $\frac{3}{4}$ Bessel's formula should be applied. (Whittaker and Robinson: *Interpolation*, p. 60.)

9. The method of successive approximation is probably the best method for ordinary use. If we want a result that can be obtained to the required degree of accuracy by taking out differences as far as $\Delta^3 u$, or if the curve is a cubic, the elimination method will give a satisfactory answer. The disadvantage of this process is that we obtain thereby one result only—a root of a quadratic—and that we cannot approach our interpolated value by steps as is done in the method of successive approximation. Moreover when fourth and higher differences are not negligible, the elimination method breaks down.

Another method of inverse interpolation can be employed when the function is of the form $Ax^3 + Bx^2 + Cx + D$. This method depends upon divided differences with "repeated arguments." It can be shown that if, in the general equation for u_x in terms of u_0 and the divided differences of u_0, we let all the arguments coincide, the rth divided difference becomes $\dfrac{1}{r!}\left[\dfrac{d}{dx}u_x\right]_{x=r}$. This enables a table of values to be built up by repetition of certain values of x. As the arithmetical work is certainly no less than that involved in other methods, and as this method is restricted in its application to comparatively simple rational integral functions, it would seem to be of little practical value. A concise account of the method will be found in Steffensen's *Interpolation*, pp. 84 *et seq.*

10. The general investigation of the accuracy of finite difference methods of approximation is a problem in direct interpolation, and has been dealt with previously. In dealing with the subject of successive approximation, however, it is of interest to include in the present chapter an elementary demonstration of the fact

that in certain circumstances a better interpolation can be obtained by neglecting higher differences than by retaining them.

For example, if we have a third difference curve, then

$$u_x = u_0 + x\Delta u_0 + x_2\Delta^2 u_0 + x_3\Delta^3 u_0 \text{ exactly.}$$

The error (α) in taking two terms is $x_2\Delta^2 u_0 + x_3\Delta^3 u_0$,

and (β) in taking three terms is $x_3\Delta^3 u_0$.

(α) may be expressed as

$$\frac{x\,(x-1)\,(x-2)}{6}\left[\frac{3}{x-2}\frac{\Delta^2 u_0}{\Delta^3 u_0} + 1\right]\Delta^3 u_0,$$

and (β) as

$$\frac{x\,(x-1)\,(x-2)}{6}\Delta^3 u_0.$$

Then, ignoring the sign of $\dfrac{x\,(x-1)\,(x-2)}{6}\Delta^3 u_0$, which will be the same for both (α) and (β), (α) will be less than (β) if

$$\frac{3}{x-2}\frac{\Delta^2 u_0}{\Delta^3 u_0}$$

is negative and less than 2.

In these circumstances the error made by retaining first differences only is less than that made in continuing to second differences.

As an illustration consider the function $x^3 + 5x + 50$.

It is easily seen that $u_0 = 50$; $\Delta u_0 = 6$; $\Delta^2 u_0 = 6$; $\Delta^3 u_0 = 6$. If x is $\frac{1}{4}$, for example, $\dfrac{3}{x-2}\dfrac{\Delta^2 u_0}{\Delta^3 u_0} = -3/1\frac{3}{4}$, which is negative and less than 2.

(α) is therefore less than (β).

This can be otherwise shown by finding the values of the errors.

$$u_{\frac{1}{4}} = 51\frac{17}{64} \text{ exactly.}$$

Also
$$u_{\frac{1}{4}} = (1 + \Delta)^{\frac{1}{4}} u_0$$
$$= u_0 + \frac{1}{4}\Delta u_0 - \frac{3}{32}\Delta^2 u_0 + \ldots,$$
$$u_0 + \frac{1}{4}\Delta u_0 = 51\frac{1}{2} = 51\frac{32}{64},$$
$$u_0 + \frac{1}{4}\Delta u_0 - \frac{3}{32}\Delta^2 u_0 = 50\frac{15}{16} = 50\frac{60}{64},$$
$$51\frac{32}{64} - 51\frac{17}{64} = \frac{15}{64} \qquad \ldots\ldots(\alpha),$$

and
$$51\frac{17}{64} - 50\frac{60}{64} = \frac{21}{64} \qquad \ldots\ldots(\beta).$$

(α) is less than (β), so that the approximation to first differences is better than that to second differences.

EXAMPLES 6

1. Given $u_1 = 0$, $u_2 = 112$, $u_3 = 287$, $u_5 = 612$, find u_4. Using u_1, u_2, u_3 and u_4, find a value for x when $u_x = 270$.

2. The following values of u_x are given: $u_{10} = 544$, $u_{15} = 1227$, $u_{20} = 1775$. Find, correct to one decimal place, the value of x for which $u_x = 1000$.

3. Having given $\log 1 = 0$, $\log 2 = \cdot30103$, $\log 3 = \cdot47712$ and $\log 4 = \cdot60206$, find the number whose logarithm is $\cdot30500$:

(i) by expressing $\log x$ in terms of $\log 1$ and its differences and solving for x;

(ii) by using Lagrange's formula applied inversely.

Explain the nature of the assumptions in each case.

4. Apply Lagrange's formula inversely to find to one decimal place the age for which the annuity-value is $13\cdot6$, given the following table:

Age x	30	35	40	45	50
Annuity-value at $4\frac{1}{2}$ per cent. a_x	15·9	14·9	14·1	13·3	12·5

5. $f(0) = 16\cdot35$, $f(5) = 14\cdot88$, $f(10) = 13\cdot59$, $f(15) = 12\cdot46$. Find x when $f(x) = 14\cdot00$.

6. Given the following table of $f(x)$:
$$f(0) = 217, \quad f(1) = 140, \quad f(2) = 23, \quad f(3) = -6,$$
find approximately the value of x for which the function is zero.

7. The following values of $f(x)$ are given:
$$f(10) = 1754, \quad f(15) = 2648, \quad f(20) = 3564.$$
Find, correct to one decimal place, the value of x for which $f(x) = 3000$.

8. Given four values of a function u_0, u_1, u_2, u_3, show how to calculate an approximate value for x from the equation
$$u_x = u_0 + x\Delta u_0 + \frac{x(x-1)}{2!}\Delta^2 u_0 + \frac{x(x-1)(x-2)}{3!}\Delta^3 u_0$$
by obtaining a quadratic equation in place of a cubic.

Use the method to find x when $u_x = 1\cdot05$, given $u_{1\cdot0} = 1\cdot0000$, $u_{1\cdot1} = 1\cdot0323$, $u_{1\cdot2} = 1\cdot0627$, $u_{1\cdot3} = 1\cdot0914$.

9. Given that $(1\cdot20)^3 = 1\cdot728$, $(1\cdot21)^3 = 1\cdot772$, $(1\cdot22)^3 = 1\cdot816$, $(1\cdot23)^3 = 1\cdot861$, $(1\cdot24)^3 = 1\cdot907$, explain carefully how to find the real root of the equation $x^3 + x - 3 = 0$ by a method of inverse interpolation. What method would you adopt in practice? Obtain a value for the root to four decimal places.

10. The following table is available:

Age x	44	45	46	47
a_x at $4\frac{1}{2}$ per cent.	13·40	13·16	12·93	12·68

Find, to two decimal places, the age corresponding to an annuity of 13·00.

11. Find, to two decimal places, the real root of the equation

$$x^3 + x - 5 = 0$$

by means of divided differences applied inversely, using the values of the expression when $x = 0, 1, 2$ and 3.

What is the reason for the poor result obtained in this case?

(The true solution is $x = 1\cdot516$ approximately.)

12. The equation $x^3 - 6x - 11 = 0$ has a root between 3 and 4. Obtain it by inverse interpolation correct to three places of decimals.

13. The formula for the value of an annuity-certain for n years at rate per cent. i is given by

$$a_{\overline{n}|} = \frac{1 - v^n}{i}, \text{ where } v = (1 + i)^{-1}.$$

Given the following table, obtain to three decimal places the rate per cent. for which $a_{\overline{20}|}$ is 14:

Rate per cent.	3	$3\frac{1}{2}$	4	$4\frac{1}{2}$
$a_{\overline{20}|}$	14·8775	14·2124	13·5903	13·0079

14. Solve the equation $x = 10 \log_{10} x$, given the following data:

Argument x ...	1·35	1·36	1·37	1·38
$\log x$	·1303	·1335	·1367	·1399

15. Apply Lagrange's formula (inversely) to find a root of the equation $u_x = 0$, when $u_{30} = -30$, $u_{34} = -13$, $u_{38} = 3$, $u_{42} = 18$.

CHAPTER VII

SUMMATION

1. Certain series whose law is apparent or of which a sufficient number of terms are given to enable the law to be assumed may be summed by the methods of finite differences.

By definition we have

$$f(a + h) - f(a) = \Delta f(a) = \phi(a), \text{ say,}$$
$$f(a + 2h) - f(a + h) = \Delta f(a + h), \text{ i.e. } \phi(a + h),$$
$$\ldots\ldots\ldots\ldots\ldots\ldots\ldots\ldots\ldots$$
$$f(a + nh) - f(a + \overline{n - 1}h) = \Delta f(a + \overline{n - 1}h), \text{ i.e. } \phi(a + \overline{n - 1}h);$$
$$\therefore \ f(a + nh) - f(a) = \phi(a) + \phi(a + h) + \ldots + \phi(a + \overline{n - 1}h).$$

If therefore $f(x)$ is the function whose first difference is $\phi(x)$ we can find the sum of any number of terms of the series whose general term is $\phi(x)$ in terms of values of $f(x)$, for any given interval of differencing.

Generally, the interval of differencing is unity and the first term of the algebraic series under consideration is $\phi(1)$. By putting a and h each $= 1$, the required relation then becomes

$$\sum_{1}^{n} \phi(x) = f(n + 1) - f(1).$$

2. Although any function of x can be differenced, there is only a limited number of functions which are the first differences of other functions. For example, if $\Delta x = 1$, then

$$\Delta x^2 = (x + 1)^2 - x^2 = 2x + 1;$$
$$\therefore \ \Delta x^2 - \Delta x = 2x,$$

or
$$\tfrac{1}{2}\Delta (x^2 - x) = x;$$
$$\therefore \ \tfrac{1}{2}(x^2 - x), \text{ or } \tfrac{1}{2}x(x - 1),$$

is the function whose first difference is x.

Again, it can be quite easily seen that, since $\Delta a^x = (a - 1) a^x$,

$$\Delta \left\{ \frac{a^x}{a - 1} \right\} = a^x.$$

Therefore $\dfrac{a^x}{a-1}$ is the function whose difference is a^x.

We can therefore find $\overset{n}{\underset{1}{\Sigma}} u_x$ by the above method if u_x is of the form kx or ka^x.

The relation $\Delta x^{(m)} = mx^{(m-1)}$ enables the sum of any series whose nth term can be expressed in the factorial notation to be summed immediately.

Example 1.

Sum to n terms the series whose xth term is $x\,(x-1)\,(x-2)$.

Now $x\,(x-1)\,(x-2) = x^{(3)}$,

and since $\Delta x^{(4)} = 4x^{(3)}$,

$$\overset{n}{\underset{1}{\Sigma}}\, x^{(3)} = \left[\tfrac{1}{4}x^{(4)}\right]_1^{n+1},$$

where $\left[f(x)\right]_1^{n+1}$ represents the process of substituting $n+1$ and 1 for x successively in $f(x)$ and deducting the second result from the first.

$$\therefore\ \overset{n}{\underset{1}{\Sigma}}\, x^{(3)} = \tfrac{1}{4}\left[(n+1)^{(4)} - 1^{(4)}\right]$$
$$= \tfrac{1}{4}\,(n+1)\,n\,(n-1)\,(n-2),$$

since the product of four successive terms of which 1 is the first includes 0 and is therefore obviously zero.

In the above example the law of the series is known. It often happens that, owing to the fact that a limited number of terms is given, the law of the series must be assumed.

Example 2.

Find the sum of n terms of the series $0, 10, 33, 77, 150, \dots$.

By taking out the differences it is seen that $\Delta u = 10$, $\Delta^2 u = 13$, and that the only two values of $\Delta^3 u$ available are each 8. We must assume therefore that $\Delta^3 u$ is constant.

We may adopt several different methods for the solution of the problem. Of the three following methods, the first is probably the best.

(i) $u_n = (1 + \Delta)^{n-1}\, u_1$ (if u_1 be the first term)
$$= u_1 + (n-1)\,\Delta u_1 + (n-1)_2\,\Delta^2 u_1 + (n-1)_3\,\Delta^3 u_1$$
$$= 0 + 10\,(n-1) + 13\,(n-1)_2 + 8\,(n-1)_3.$$

$$\therefore\ \overset{n}{\underset{1}{\Sigma}}\, u = \overset{n}{\underset{1}{\Sigma}}\, \{10\,(n-1) + 13\,(n-1)_2 + 8\,(n-1)_3\}.$$

Since $(n-1)_r = n_{r+1} - (n-1)_{r+1} = \Delta (n-1)_{r+1}$, it follows that

$$\sum_1^n (n-1)_r = \Big[(n-1)_{r+1}\Big]_1^{n+1} = n_{r+1}.$$

$$\therefore \sum_1^n u = 10n_2 + 13n_3 + 8n_4.$$

(ii) $\quad u_n = u_1 + (n-1)\Delta u_1 + (n-1)_2 \Delta^2 u_1 + (n-1)_3 \Delta^3 u_1$

$$= 0 + 10\frac{(n-1)^{(1)}}{1!} + 13\frac{(n-1)^{(2)}}{2!} + 8\frac{(n-1)^{(3)}}{3!},$$

adopting the factorial notation.

$$\therefore \sum_1^n u = 10\left[\frac{(n-1)^{(2)}}{2.1!}\right]_1^{n+1} + 13\left[\frac{(n-1)^{(3)}}{3.2!}\right]_1^{n+1} + 8\left[\frac{(n-1)^{(4)}}{4.3!}\right]_1^{n+1}$$

$$= 5n(n-1) + \tfrac{13}{6}n(n-1)(n-2) + \tfrac{1}{3}n(n-1)(n-2)(n-3),$$

the value of the function being zero when $n = 1$.

(iii) $u_n = 0 + 10(n-1) + 13(n-1)_2 + 8(n-1)_3$ as in (i)

$$= \tfrac{1}{6}(8n^3 - 9n^2 + 31n - 30).$$

$$\therefore \sum_1^n u = (8S_3 - 9S_2 + 31S_1 - 30n), \text{ where } S_1, S_2, S_3 \text{ are respec-}$$

tively the sums of the first, second, third powers of the first n natural numbers,

$$= \tfrac{1}{6}\left[\frac{8n^2(n+1)^2}{4} - \frac{9n(n+1)(2n+1)}{6} + \frac{31n(n+1)}{2} - 30n\right].$$

Each of these three results becomes $\tfrac{1}{6}n(n-1)(2n^2 + 3n + 16)$ on simplifying.

Note. If the unit of differencing does not happen to be unity care must be taken in applying the identity $\Delta x^{(m)} = mhx^{(m-1)}$. Here $x^{(m-1)}$ is the difference of the function $x^{(m)}/mh$, so that in summing a series whose xth term is, for example,

$$2x(2x-2)(2x-4)$$

we must divide $2x(2x-2)(2x-4)(2x-6)$ by $h = 2$ as well as by $m = 4$ before taking the limits $n+1$ and 1.

3. Since $\Delta x^{(-m)} = -mx^{(-m-1)}$ the series whose xth term is of the form $[x(x+1)(x+2)\dots(x+k)]^{-1}$ can be summed immediately.

Example 3.

Sum to n terms the series whose xth term is $\dfrac{1}{(x+1)(x+2)(x+3)}$.

$$\Delta\left\{\frac{1}{(x+1)(x+2)}\right\} = -2\frac{1}{(x+1)(x+2)(x+3)}.$$

$$\therefore \sum_{1}^{n} \frac{1}{(x+1)(x+2)(x+3)} = -\tfrac{1}{2}\left[\frac{1}{(x+1)(x+2)}\right]_{1}^{n+1}$$

$$= -\tfrac{1}{2}\left[\frac{1}{(n+2)(n+3)} - \frac{1}{2 \cdot 3}\right].$$

4. It is worthy of remark that the rules for the summation of series of these two types, as given in the textbooks on algebra, are precisely the same as the above. For example, for a series whose nth term is

$$(a+nb)\,(a+\overline{n+1}b)\,(a+\overline{n+2}b)\,\ldots\,(a+\overline{n+r-1}b),$$

the finite difference method is simply to write this in factorial form, with interval of differencing b, and then to proceed on the lines laid down, thus:

$$\sum_{1}^{n} u_n = \sum_{1}^{n} (a+\overline{n+r-1}b)^{(r)} = \left[\frac{(a+\overline{n+r-1}b)^{(r+1)}}{b\,(r+1)}\right]_{1}^{n+1}$$

$$= \frac{(a+\overline{n+rb})^{(r+1)} - (a+rb)^{(r+1)}}{b\,(r+1)}$$

$$= \frac{(a+\overline{n+rb})\,u_n}{b\,(r+1)} + \text{a constant}.$$

This, of course, produces the same result as is given by the algebraic rule: "Write down the nth term, affix the next factor at the end, divide by the number of factors thus increased and by the common difference, and add a constant" (see Hall and Knight, *Higher Algebra*, p. 314).

For the series whose nth term is the reciprocal of the one above the inverse factorial is used, and a similar result is obtained.

5. It sometimes happens that on taking out successive differences of a series a stage is reached where a particular set of differences forms a geometrical progression. In that event the series can be considered as consisting of two separate series, (i) a series whose general term is $a + bx + cx^2 + \ldots + kx^{n-1}$ (a rational integral function of x), and (ii) a geometrical progression.

Suppose, for example, that second differences are in geometrical progression with common ratio r. Then

$$u_x = a + bx + cr^x.$$

For $\qquad \Delta u_x = b + c\,(r - 1)\,r^x,$

and $\qquad \Delta^2 u_x = c\,(r - 1)^2\,r^x = kr^x,$

where $\qquad k = c\,(r - 1)^2.$

It follows that for nth differences

$$\Delta^n u_x = c\,(r - 1)^n r^x.$$

Example 4.

Sum to n terms the series $1, 6, 11, 18, 31, 58, 115, \ldots$.

The difference table is

Third differences are in G.P. with common ratio 2.

u_x	Δu_x	$\Delta^2 u_x$	$\Delta^3 u_x$
1			
	5		
6		0	
	5		2
11		2	
	7		4
18		6	
	13		8
31		14	
	27		16
58		30	
	57		
115			

Assume therefore that

$$u_x = a + bx^{(1)} + cx^{(2)} + d2^x,$$
$$\Delta u_x = b + 2cx^{(1)} + d2^x\,(2 - 1)$$
$$= b + 2cx^{(1)} + d2^x,$$
$$\Delta^2 u_x = 2c + d2^x,$$
$$\Delta^3 u_x = d2^x.$$

Inserting the differences for the value $x = 1$, we have

$$2 = \Delta^3 u_1 = 2d; \quad 0 = \Delta^2 u_1 = 2c + 2d;$$
$$5 = \Delta u_1 = b + 2c + 2d.$$

From these equations we find easily that

$$d = 1; \quad c = -1; \quad b = 5.$$

Putting $x = 1$ in $u_x = a + bx^{(1)} + cx^{(2)} + d2^x$, we have

$$1 = u_1 = a + b + 2d,$$

whence $\qquad a = 1 - b - 2d = -6;$

$$\therefore\ u_x = -6 + 5x^{(1)} - x^{(2)} + 2^x;$$

$$\therefore\ \sum_1^n u_x = \left[-6x^{(1)} + \frac{5x^{(2)}}{2} - \frac{x^{(3)}}{3} + \frac{2^x}{2 - 1} \right]_1^{n+1}$$

$$= -6\,(n + 1)^{(1)} + 6 + \frac{5\,(n + 1)^{(2)}}{2} - \frac{(n + 1)^{(3)}}{3} + 2^{n+1} - 2,$$

since all the factorials except $(n + 1)^{(1)}$ vanish for the lower limit.

This simplifies to

$$2^{n+1} - 2 - \frac{n}{6}\,(2n^2 - 15n + 19).$$

Alternatively, we may proceed thus:

$$\Delta^3 u_x = d2^x.$$

Deduct $d2^x$ from u_x and difference the function $u_x - d2^x$ in the usual way.

By giving x the values $1, 2, 3, 4$ in succession it is easily seen that $u_x - d2^x$ takes the values $-1, 2, 3, 2$ respectively. On forming a difference table we find that the leading differences are

$$\Delta(u_x - d2^x) = 3, \quad \Delta^2(u_x - d2^x) = -2.$$

Then $\qquad u_x = 2^x - 1 + 3(x-1)_1 - 2(x-1)_2,$

so that

$$\sum_1^n u_x = \left[2^x - (x-1)_1 + 3(x-1)_2 - 2(x-1)_3\right]_1^{n+1}$$

$$= 2^{n+1} - 2 - n_1 + 3n_2 - 2n_3,$$

which, on simplification, gives the same result as that above.

6. The form $u_x v_x$. Summation by parts.

When the general term of the series is the product of two functions of x and when the value of each of the summations $\sum\limits_1^n u_x$ and $\sum\limits_1^n v_x$ is known, a method known as "summation by parts" can be adopted.

We have $\quad \Delta(U_x V_x) = U_{x+1} V_{x+1} - U_x V_x$

$$= U_{x+1}(V_{x+1} - V_x) + V_x(U_{x+1} - U_x)$$

$$= U_{x+1}\Delta V_x + V_x\Delta U_x;$$

$$\therefore \quad V_x\Delta U_x = \Delta(U_x V_x) - U_{x+1}\Delta V_x;$$

$$\therefore \quad \sum_1^n [V_x\Delta U_x] = \left[U_x V_{x1}\right]_1^{n+1} - \sum_1^n [U_{x+1}\Delta V_x].$$

It follows that when the function $u_x v_x$ can be put in the form $V_x\Delta U_x$ the summation can be performed at once if $\sum\limits_1^n [U_{x+1}\Delta V_x]$ can be evaluated (but not otherwise).

Example 5.

Find the sum of the series $a + 2a^2 + 3a^3 + 4a^4 + \dots$ to n terms. The terms are successive values of the function $y = xa^x$, and since

$$\Delta\left(\frac{a^x}{a-1}\right) = a^x,$$

we may write x for V_x and $\dfrac{a^x}{a-1}$ for U_x in the relation above.

$$\therefore \sum_1^n [xa^x] = \sum_1^n \left[x\Delta \left(\frac{a^x}{a-1} \right) \right]$$

$$= \left[\frac{a^x}{a-1} x \right]_1^{n+1} - \sum_1^n \left[\frac{a^{x+1}}{a-1} \Delta x \right]$$

$$= \left[\frac{a^x}{a-1} x \right]_1^{n+1} - \sum_1^n \left[\frac{a^{x+1}}{a-1} \right], \text{ since } \Delta x = 1,$$

$$= \left[\frac{a^x}{a-1} x \right]_1^{n+1} - \left[\frac{a^{x+1}}{(a-1)^2} \right]_1^{n+1}$$

$$= (n+1)\frac{a^{n+1}}{a-1} - \frac{a}{a-1} - \frac{a^{n+2}}{(a-1)^2} + \frac{a^2}{(a-1)^2}.$$

The above method is laborious if the rational integral function of x is of higher degree than the first. If, for example, the function were $y = x^3 a^x$, the term corresponding to $U_{x+1}\Delta V_x$ would be $\frac{a^{x+1}}{a-1}\Delta x^3$ or $\frac{a^{x+1}}{a-1}(3x^2 + 3x + 1)$, and the formula would have to be applied separately to this expression, twice in succession, in order to obtain eventually a simple function of a^x.

7. The result in para. 1, namely, that $\sum_1^n \phi(x) = f(n+1) - f(1)$, where $\Delta f(x) = \phi(x)$, can be obtained by the use of the operator E.

We have $\qquad \sum_1^n \phi(x) = \phi(1) + \phi(2) + \dots + \phi(n)$

$$= (1 + E + E^2 + \dots + E^{n-1})\phi(1)$$

$$= \frac{E^n - 1}{E - 1}\phi(1)$$

$$= \frac{E^n - 1}{E - 1}(E - 1)f(1),$$

since $\qquad \phi(1) = \Delta f(1) = (E - 1)f(1).$

$$\therefore \sum_1^n \phi(x) = (E^n - 1)f(1)$$

$$= f(n+1) - f(1).$$

Thus the operator $\sum_1^n$ is equivalent to the operator $\frac{E^n - 1}{E - 1}$, and we may safely substitute $\frac{E^n - 1}{E - 1}$ for $\sum_1^n$ in any series of operations.

Again, since $E^n u_x = u_{x+n}$, the identity $\overset{n}{\underset{1}{\Sigma}} u_x = \dfrac{E^n - 1}{E - 1} u_x$ can be expressed as

$$\overset{n}{\underset{1}{\Sigma}} u_x = \frac{1}{E - 1} (u_{x+n} - u_x)$$

$$= \frac{1}{\Delta} (u_{x+n} - u_x)$$

$$= \Delta^{-1} (u_{x+n} - u_x).$$

The result $\overset{n}{\underset{1}{\Sigma}} \phi (x) = f (n + 1) - f (1)$ is sometimes written as

$$\overset{n}{\underset{1}{\Sigma}} \phi (x) = \Big[f (x) \Big]_1^{n+1},$$

or $$\overset{n}{\underset{1}{\Sigma}} \Delta f (x) = \Big[f (x) \Big]_1^{n+1},$$

as in the numerical example given in para. 2.

8. The relation between the operators Σ and Δ.

It has been seen that if
$$\Delta f (x) = \phi (x)$$
then $$f (x) = \Sigma \phi (x),$$
where the summation is performed between certain limits.

If therefore we omit the limits we may say that with certain reservations summation is the inverse process to differencing.

Consequently $\phi (x) = \Delta f (x) = \Delta \Sigma \phi (x),$

so that $$\Delta \Sigma \equiv 1,$$

i.e. $$\Sigma \equiv \frac{1}{\Delta} \equiv \Delta^{-1}.$$

Now although $\Delta \Sigma \equiv 1$ it does not follow that $\Sigma \Delta \equiv 1$, for we shall obtain the same result by differencing $f (x) + c$, where c is a constant, as by differencing $f (x)$ alone.

Thus $$\Delta [f (x) + c] = \phi (x);$$

$$\therefore\; f (x) + c = \Delta^{-1} \phi (x) = \Sigma \phi (x) = \Sigma \Delta f (x),$$

so that $$\Sigma \Delta \not\equiv 1.$$

The symbol Σ may be treated as the equivalent of the inverse symbol Δ^{-1} provided that it be remembered that Σ and Δ are not commutative, and that where we are not summing between limits an arbitrary constant must be inserted.

The process of summation in finite differences is similar to the corresponding process in integral calculus and the relations between the symbols are analogous to those existing between the symbols of differentiation and integration. As a result, finite difference summation is often referred to as integration. Σu_x is said to be the indefinite integral of u_x; $\overset{n}{\underset{1}{\Sigma}} u_x$ the definite integral; and a function that can be integrated, such as a^x, to be "immediately integrable."

9. Other uses of the symbol Σ.

One of the commonest functions in the theory of life contingencies is the expression obtained by multiplying l_x (the number attaining age x) by the interest factor v^x. This product is denoted by D_x, and the connection between certain functions dependent on D_x is indicated thus:

$$N_x = \Sigma D_x; \quad S_x = \Sigma N_x.$$

Here Σ denotes summation from age x to the end of the mortality table, it being understood that values beyond the end of the table are zero.

When Σ is used in this special sense,

$$\Sigma u_x = u_x + u_{x+1} + u_{x+2} + \dots \text{ to the end of the table};$$

$$\therefore \ \Delta\Sigma u_x = (u_{x+1} + u_{x+2} + u_{x+3} + \dots) - (u_x + u_{x+1} + u_{x+2} + \dots)$$

$$= -u_x,$$

so that here $\Delta\Sigma \equiv -1.$

In point of fact, the correct way of showing the relation between the functions D and N, etc., is

$$N_x = \overset{t=\infty}{\underset{t=0}{\Sigma}} D_{x+t},$$

where x is fixed and t is the variable.

In modern mathematical works it is now usual to use the notations $\overset{\infty}{\underset{t=0}{\Sigma}}$, $\overset{n}{\underset{t=a}{\Sigma}}$ etc., where the variable t is specified for the lower limit only. The still shorter form $\overset{b}{\underset{a}{\Sigma}}$ is often used where there is no doubt about the variable.

Again, in algebraic series, Σ is often used loosely to indicate the sum of the first x terms of a series, thus:

$$\Sigma u_x = u_1 + u_2 + \ldots + u_x;$$

$$\therefore \quad \Delta\Sigma u_x = (u_1 + u_2 + \ldots + u_{x+1}) - (u_1 + u_2 + \ldots + u_x)$$

$$= u_{x+1}$$

$$= E u_x,$$

whence $\Delta\Sigma \equiv E$.

On the other hand, if Σ is specially defined so that Σu_x indicates a summation beginning with u_1 and ending with the last term preceding u_x, then

$$\Sigma u_x = u_1 + u_2 + u_3 + \ldots + u_{x-1};$$

$$\therefore \quad \Delta\Sigma u_x = (u_1 + u_2 + u_3 + \ldots + u_x) - (u_1 + u_2 + u_3 + \ldots + u_{x-1})$$

$$= u_x.$$

In these circumstances therefore $\Delta\Sigma \equiv 1$.

These illustrations serve to show that great care must be exercised in introducing Σ into any formula. The sense in which it is to be used should be clearly defined in every instance: the safest course is always to state the limits where possible.

10. Application of the relation between Σ and Δ.

By treating the operator Σ as equivalent to Δ^{-1}, the method of separation of symbols can be employed for the solution of problems. For example, a convenient formula for the evaluation of $\Sigma a^x u_x$ can be evolved by which the necessity for the continued application of summation by parts can be obviated.

Example 6.

Prove that

$$\Sigma a^x u_x = \frac{a^x}{a-1}\left\{1 - \frac{a\Delta}{a-1} + \frac{a^2\Delta^2}{(a-1)^2} - \frac{a^3\Delta^3}{(a-1)^3} + \ldots\right\} u_x + a \text{ constant.}$$

Now

$$E^p a^x u_x = a^{x+p} u_{x+p} = a^x (aE)^p u_x$$

and

$$\Sigma a^x u_x = \Delta^{-1} a^x u_x + c$$

$$= (E-1)^{-1} a^x u_x + c.$$

Let $\quad \phi(E) \equiv A_0 + A_1 E + A_2 E^2 + \ldots + A_r E^r + \ldots$

Then the $(r+1)$th term in $\phi(E) a^x u_x$ is $A_r E^r a^x u_x$.

I.e.
$$A_r a^{x+r} u_{x+r} = a^x A_r a^r u_{x+r}$$
$$= a^x A_r a^r E^r u_x$$
$$= a^x A_r (aE)^r u_x;$$
$$\therefore \; \phi(E) a^x u_x = a^x \phi(aE) u_x,$$

so that if $\phi(E)$ is the operation $(E-1)^{-1}$

$$(E-1)^{-1} a^x u_x = a^x (aE-1)^{-1} u_x + c;$$
$$\therefore \; \Sigma a^x u_x = a^x (aE-1)^{-1} u_x + c$$
$$= a^x (a + a\Delta - 1)^{-1} u_x + c$$
$$= a^x (a-1)^{-1} \left[1 + \frac{a\Delta}{a-1}\right]^{-1} u_x + c$$
$$= \frac{a^x}{a-1}\left[1 - \frac{a\Delta}{a-1} + \frac{a^2\Delta^2}{(a-1)^2} - \dots\right] u_x + c.$$

Example 7.

Apply the above formula to evaluate $\Sigma 3^x (x^3 + x^2 + x + 1)$.

$$\Delta u_x = \Delta(x^3 + x^2 + x + 1) = 3x^2 + 5x + 3,$$
$$\Delta^2 u_x = \Delta^2(x^3 + x^2 + x + 1) = 6x + 8,$$

and
$$\Delta^3 u_x = \Delta^3(x^3 + x^2 + x + 1) = 6;$$

$$\therefore \; \Sigma 3^x (x^3 + x^2 + x + 1)$$

$$= \frac{3^x}{3-1}\left\{u_x - \frac{3}{(3-1)}\Delta u_x + \frac{3^2}{(3-1)^2}\Delta^2 u_x - \frac{3^3}{(3-1)^3}\Delta^3 u_x\right\} + c$$

$$= \frac{3^x}{2}[x^3 + x^2 + x + 1 - \tfrac{3}{2}(3x^2 + 5x + 3) + \tfrac{9}{4}(6x+8) - \tfrac{27}{8}.6] + c$$

$$= \frac{3^x}{8}[4x^3 - 14x^2 + 28x - 23] + c.$$

It is often of advantage to set out the rational integral function in factorial notation; the successive differences can then be obtained with little difficulty.

Thus, by the method given in Chapter II, para. 23,

$$x^3 + x^2 + x + 1 = x^{(3)} + 4x^{(2)} + 3x^{(1)} + 1,$$

so that
$$\Delta u_x = 3x^{(2)} + 8x^{(1)} + 3,$$
$$\Delta^2 u_x = 6x^{(1)} + 8,$$
$$\Delta^3 u_x = 6,$$

and, by adopting the formula for $\Sigma a^x u_x$, we have easily that

$$\Sigma 3^x (x^3 + x^2 + x + 1) = \frac{3^x}{8}(4x^{(3)} - 2x^{(2)} + 18x^{(1)} - 23) + c.$$

To express $4x^{(3)} - 2x^{(2)} + 18x^{(1)} - 23$ in the form

$$ax^3 + bx^2 + cx + d,$$

we use the method of detached coefficients applied inversely:

2	4	$-$ 2	18	$-$ 23
	0	8	$-$ 10	
1	4	$-$ 10	28	
	0	4		
0	4	$-$ 14		
	0			
	4			

Hence

$$\Sigma 3^x (x^3 + x^2 + x + 1) = \frac{3^x}{8} (4x^3 - 14x^2 + 28x - 23) + c,$$

as before.

11. Series in general.

Certain series can be summed by purely algebraic methods only: others can be summed by algebra or by finite differences. For example, binomial, exponential and logarithmic series depend upon algebraic theorems, and algebraic methods should therefore be employed to find the sums of such series. As has been shown above, series whose nth terms can be expressed as rational integral functions of n can be summed by finite difference methods. Arithmetical and geometrical progressions (and series dependent thereon) can also be summed by finite differences, but for these algebraic processes are preferable.

There remain a few other types of series to which either algebra or finite difference methods can be applied.

Example 8.

Evaluate

$$\sum_1^n \frac{2x + 3}{x(x + 1)} 3^{-x}.$$

$$u_x = \frac{2x + 3}{x(x + 1)} \frac{1}{3^x} = \left\{ \frac{3}{x} - \frac{1}{x + 1} \right\} \frac{1}{3^x}$$

$$= \frac{3}{x} \frac{1}{3^x} - \frac{3}{x + 1} \frac{1}{3^{x+1}}$$

$$= - 3\Delta \left[\frac{1}{x} \frac{1}{3^x} \right];$$

$$\therefore \sum_{1}^{n} u_x = 3\left[-\frac{1}{x}\frac{1}{3^x} \right]_{1}^{n+1}$$

$$= 1 - \frac{1}{n+1}\frac{1}{3^n}.$$

Example 9.

Show that the general term of the recurring series

$$u_0 + u_1 x + u_2 x^2 + \ldots + u_r x^r + \ldots,$$

for which the scale of relation is $1 - px - qx^2$, is $Aa^n + Bb^n$, where a, b are functions of p, q and A, B are constants.

Since $1 - px - qx^2$ is the scale of relation,

$$u_n - pu_{n-1} - qu_{n-2} = 0;$$

i.e. $$u_n - pE^{-1}u_n - qE^{-2}u_n = 0,$$

or $$(1 - pE^{-1} - qE^{-2})u_n = 0.$$

Therefore $$(1 - aE^{-1})(1 - bE^{-1})u_n = 0$$

if $$a + b = p \quad \text{and} \quad ab = -q.$$

This will be true if either

$$(1 - aE^{-1})u_n \quad \text{or} \quad (1 - bE^{-1})u_n = 0,$$

i.e. if $$u_n - au_{n-1} \quad \text{or} \quad u_n - bu_{n-1} = 0.$$

Now if $$u_n - au_{n-1} = 0,$$

then $$u_n = au_{n-1},$$

and the series is a geometrical progression with common ratio a. The general term of the "a" series is therefore Aa^n.

Similarly the general term of the "b" series is Bb^n, where A and B are constants. But if a new series be formed by the addition of these two progressions the relationship will hold good for this new series. In other words the most general solution is

$$u_n = Aa^n + Bb^n,$$

where we may give A and B any values, but a and b must satisfy the equations $$a + b = p \quad \text{and} \quad ab = -q.$$

12. If we expand u_x by a finite difference formula, we can find the sum of a number of consecutive values of u_x by integrating both sides of the identity.

For example

$$u_x = u_0 + x\Delta u_0 + x_2\Delta^2 u_0 + x_3\Delta^3 u_0 + \ldots$$

$$= u_0 + x^{(1)}\Delta u_0 + \frac{x^{(2)}}{2!}\Delta^2 u_0 + \frac{x^{(3)}}{3!}\Delta^3 u_0 + \ldots,$$

as in Example 2 (ii).

$$\therefore \; \Sigma u_x = c + x^{(1)} u_0 + \tfrac{1}{2} x^{(2)} \Delta u_0 + \tfrac{1}{6} x^{(3)} \Delta^2 u_0 + \dots.$$

If the limits be 1 and n, we have

$$\sum_{1}^{n} u_x = \left[x^{(1)} u_0 + \tfrac{1}{2} x^{(2)} \Delta u_0 + \tfrac{1}{6} x^{(3)} \Delta^2 u_0 + \dots \right]_1^{n+1},$$

which can be evaluated in the usual way.

Example 10.

If fourth and higher differences are ignored, prove that the sum of n successive terms of a function, of which u_0 is the central term, is

$$n u_0 + \tfrac{1}{24} (n^3 - n) \Delta^2 u_{-1},$$

where n is odd.

Since u_0 is the central term, it will be convenient to use a central difference formula.

Gauss's forward formula gives

$$u_x = u_0 + x \Delta u_0 + \tfrac{1}{2} x (x - 1) \Delta^2 u_{-1} + \tfrac{1}{6} (x + 1) x (x - 1) \Delta^3 u_{-1}$$
$$= u_0 + x^{(1)} \Delta u_0 + \tfrac{1}{2} x^{(2)} \Delta^2 u_{-1} + \tfrac{1}{6} (x + 1)^{(3)} \Delta^3 u_{-1};$$
$$\therefore \; \Sigma u_x = C + x u_0 + \tfrac{1}{2} x^{(2)} \Delta u_0 + \tfrac{1}{6} x^{(3)} \Delta^2 u_{-1} + \tfrac{1}{24} (x + 1)^{(4)} \Delta^3 u_{-1}.$$

On summation between the limits $- \tfrac{1}{2} (n - 1)$ and $\tfrac{1}{2} (n - 1)$ the coefficients of Δu_0 and $\Delta^3 u_{-1}$ will cancel, and we shall have

$$\sum_{-\frac{1}{2}(n-1)}^{\frac{1}{2}(n-1)} u_x = \left[C + x u_0 + \tfrac{1}{2} x^{(2)} \Delta u_0 + \tfrac{1}{6} x^{(3)} \Delta^2 u_{-1} + \tfrac{1}{24} (x + 1)^{(4)} \Delta^3 u_{-1} \right]_{-\frac{1}{2}(n+1)}^{\frac{1}{2}(n+1)}$$

$$= u_0 \left[\frac{n + 1}{2} - \left(- \frac{n + 1}{2} \right) \right]$$

$$\quad + \tfrac{1}{6} \left[\frac{n + 1}{2} \cdot \frac{n}{2} \cdot \frac{n - 1}{2} - \left(- \frac{n + 1}{2} \cdot \frac{n}{2} \cdot \frac{n - 1}{2} \right) \right] \Delta^2 u_{-1}$$

$$= n u_0 + \tfrac{1}{24} (n^3 - n) \Delta^2 u_{-1}.$$

EXAMPLES 7

Sum the following series:

1. $7, 14, 19, 22, 23, 22, \dots$ to n terms.

2. $2, 12, 36, 80, 150, 252, \dots$ to n terms.

3. $10, 9, 7, 4, 0, 5, \dots$ to 30 terms.

4. $5, 10, 17, 28, 47, 82, \dots$ to 20 terms.

5. $10, 23, 60, 169, 494, \dots$ to n terms.

6. $1, 2, 4, 8, 17, 40, 104, \dots$ to n terms.

7. $1, 0, -1, 0, 7, 28, 79, \dots$ to $2k$ terms.

8. $10, 14, 10, 6, \dots$ to n terms.

9. $125, 343, 729, 1331, 2197, \dots$ to n terms.

10. $1, 0, 1, 8, 29, 80, 193, \dots$ to 17 terms.

Use the methods of finite differences to sum to n terms the series whose xth terms are

11. $(x + 3)(x + 4)(x + 5)$.   12. $x(x + 2)(x + 4)$.

13. $(3x - 2)(3x + 1)(3x + 4)$.   14. $x(x + 1)(x + 3)$.

15. $x(x + 1)(x + 3)(x + 4)$.   16. $(2x + 3)(2x + 5)(2x + 7)(2x + 9)$.

17. $\dfrac{1}{(x + 3)(x + 4)}$.   18. $\dfrac{1}{(x + 1)(x + 3)}$.

19. $\dfrac{x}{(x + 2)(x + 3)(x + 4)}$.   20. $\dfrac{1}{(3x - 2)(3x + 1)(3x + 4)}$.

21. $\dfrac{x + 3}{x(x + 1)(x + 2)}$.

22. Sum to n terms $2.4.8.14 + 4.6.10.16 + 6.8.12.18 + \dots$.

23. Obtain the general term of the series

$$\frac{3}{1.4.10} + \frac{5}{4.7.13} + \frac{7}{7.10.16} + \dots$$

and find the sum to n terms and to infinity.

24. Find $\sum_{1}^{n} u_x$, where $u_x = x(x + 2)(x + 5)$.

25. The two series $6, 24, 60, 120, \dots$ and $0, 0, 0, 6, 24, 60, 120, \dots$ are given. Find the sum of n terms of each of the two series. Compare the results and explain the difference.

26. Sum the series $1, 5, 17, 53, 161, \dots$ to n terms.

27. Evaluate $\Delta^{-1}(x^2 a^x)$.

28. Show that $\Delta(x!) = x(x!)$ and hence sum to n terms the series

$$1 + 3.2! + 7.3! + 13.4! + 21.5! + \dots.$$

29. Find $\sum_{1}^{n} u_x$, where $u_x = (3x - 1)(3x + 2)(3x + 5)(3x + 8)$.

30. Sum to n terms $1.3^2 + 3.5^2 + 5.7^2 + 7.9^2 + \ldots$.

31. Obtain the formula

$$\sum_{a}^{a+n-1} u_x = nu_a + n_2\Delta u_a + n_3\Delta^2 u_a + \ldots$$

and use the formula to find the sum of n terms of the series

$$-8,\ -5,\ 0,\ 14,\ 44,\ \ldots.$$

32. Prove that $\sum_{1}^{n} (x^2 + 1).x! = n.(n+1)!$

33. Sum to n terms the series whose xth terms are (i) $x^2 (3x + 2)$; (ii) $2^x (x^3 + x)$ by finite integration.

34. Evaluate $\sum_{1}^{n} \left\{ \dfrac{x.4^x}{(x+1)(x+2)} \right\}$.

35. Sum to infinity $\dfrac{1}{2.6.10} + \dfrac{1}{4.8.12} + \dfrac{1}{6.10.14} + \ldots$.

36. Find the sum of n terms of the series

$$1^2 + \frac{3^2}{2} + \frac{5^2}{2^2} + \frac{7^2}{2^3} + \ldots.$$

37. Obtain the indefinite integral of $(2x - 1) 3^x$.

38. Show that the series 10, 24, 61, 163, 452, 1290, 3759 can be split up into two other series. Find the two series and hence sum the original series to n terms.

39. Prove that $\Delta^{-1}[u_x v_x] = u_x \Delta^{-1}v_x - \Delta^{-1}[\Delta u_x \Delta^{-1}v_{x+1}]$ and apply this formula to find the sum of the first n terms of the series whose rth term is $(r+1)x^{r-1}$.

40. Evaluate $\quad \Delta^{-1}\left\{ \dfrac{(x+1)}{x(x+2)(x+3)(x+4)} \right\}$.

41. Find the sum of the squares of the first n natural numbers by the method of finite integration.

42. Sum to n terms $\dfrac{3}{2.5.8} + \dfrac{5}{5.8.11} + \dfrac{7}{8.11.14} + \ldots$.

43. Find the sum of the infinite series $\dfrac{1.3}{2} + \dfrac{3.5}{2^2} + \dfrac{5.7}{2^3} + \ldots$.

44. Find the sum of n terms of the series

$$2.2 + 7.4 + 14.8 + 23.16 + 34.32 + \ldots.$$

45. Prove that $\sum_0^{n-1} u_r x^r = \dfrac{u_0 - x^n u_n}{1 - x} + \dfrac{x}{(1-x)^2}(\Delta u_0 - x^n \Delta u_n)$

$$+ \dfrac{x^2}{(1-x)^3}(\Delta^2 u_0 - x^n \Delta^2 u_n) + \ldots.$$

Apply this formula to find the sum of the first n terms of the series whose rth term is $r(r+1)x^{r-1}$.

46. Evaluate $\Delta^{-1}\left[2^x \cdot x \cdot \dfrac{x!}{(2x+1)!}\right]$.

47. Use the method of finite integration to obtain the sum of n terms of the series $1.3^3 + 3.5^3 + 5.7^3 + \ldots$.

48. Find the function whose first difference is $ax^3 + bx^2 + cx + d$.

49. Prove that $1^r + 2^r x + 3^r x^2 + \ldots$ is a recurring series, and find its scale of relation.

50. If u_n is the nth term of the series $1, 2, 3, 5, 8, 13, \ldots$ in which each term after the second is the sum of the two preceding terms, prove by the process of mathematical induction or otherwise that

$$u_n{}^2 - u_{n-1}u_{n+1} = (-1)^n.$$

CHAPTER VIII

MISCELLANEOUS THEOREMS

1. In this chapter it is proposed to treat of certain propositions and applications of finite difference methods which are not essential to a first reading of the subject and which may conveniently be dealt with at a later stage. Some of the theorems are developments of familiar processes: others are alternative methods of approach for the solution of problems involving the principles of finite differences.

2. Differences of zero.

If in the identical relation

$$\Delta^n x^m = (E - 1)^n x^m$$

$$= (x + n)^m - n (x + n - 1)^m + n_2 (x + n - 2)^m - \dots$$

we put $x = 0$, we obtain

$$[\Delta^n x^m]_{x=0} = n^m - n (n - 1)^m + n_2 (n - 2)^m - \dots.$$

By continued application of this formula we can obtain values of $\Delta^n x^m$ when $x = 0$ for all integral values of n and m.

For example, if $m = 3$,

$$[\Delta x^3]_{x=0} = 1^3 = 1,$$

$$[\Delta^2 x^3]_{x=0} = 2^3 - 2 \cdot 1^3 = 6,$$

$$[\Delta^3 x^3]_{x=0} = 3^3 - 3 \cdot 2^3 + 3 \cdot 1^3 = 6.$$

The values of $[\Delta^n x^m]_{x=0}$ are known as "differences of zero," and in accordance with this definition the expression is often written as $\Delta^n o^m$.

It is evident that a table of values of differences of zero can be constructed if we can obtain a relation between corresponding values of $\Delta^n o^m$.

We have from the above

$$\Delta^n o^m = n^m - n\,(n-1)^m + n_2\,(n-2)^m - \dots$$
$$= n\,[n^{m-1} - (n-1)_1\,(n-1)^{m-1} + (n-1)_2\,(n-2)^{m-1} - \dots]$$
$$= n\,[(1+n-1)^{m-1} - (n-1)_1\,(1+n-2)^{m-1}$$
$$\qquad\qquad + (n-1)_2\,(1+n-3)^{m-1} - \dots]$$
$$= n\,[(E-1)^{n-1}\,x^{m-1}]_{x=1}$$
$$= n\Delta^{n-1}\,1^{m-1}$$
$$= n\Delta^{n-1}\,Eo^{m-1}$$
$$= n\Delta^{n-1}\,(1+\Delta)\,o^{m-1}$$
$$= n\,(\Delta^{n-1}o^{m-1} + \Delta^n o^{m-1}).$$

Again, since

$$\Delta^n o^m = n\Delta^{n-1}\,1^{m-1}$$
$$= n\,(n-1)\,\Delta^{n-2}\,2^{m-2}$$
$$\dots\dots\dots\dots\dots\dots\dots$$
$$= n\,(n-1)\dots(n-r+1)\,\Delta^{n-r}\,r^{m-r}$$
$$\dots\dots\dots\dots\dots\dots\dots,$$

we have, when $n = m$,

$$\Delta^n o^n = n\,(n-1)\dots 2\Delta\,(n-1)^1$$
$$= n\,(n-1)\dots 2.1\,n^0$$
$$= n!,$$

whence $\qquad\Delta^{n+r}o^n = 0,$

i.e. $\qquad\Delta^n o^m = 0,$ when $n > m$.

We can now build up a table of differences of zero by continued application of the above relation.

The table is

m	Δo^m	$\Delta^2 o^m$	$\Delta^3 o^m$	$\Delta^4 o^m$	$\Delta^5 o^m$	$\Delta^6 o^m$
1	1	0				
2	1	2	0			
3	1	6	6	0		
4	1	14	36	24	0	
5	1	30	150	240	120	0
6	1	62	540	1560	1800	720

and so on.

An alternative method for obtaining the relation

$$\Delta^n o^m = n \left(\Delta^{n-1} o^{m-1} + \Delta^n o^{m-1} \right),$$

depending upon the formula for the nth difference of the compound function $u_x v_x$, is given below (para. 4).

3. An interesting application of the use of the differences of zero for the calculation of the coefficients in an expansion is as follows.

The fundamental formula

$$u_x = u_0 + x\Delta u_0 + x_2 \Delta^2 u_0 + x_3 \Delta^3 u_0 + \ldots$$

can be written as

$$u_x = u_0 + x\Delta u_0 + \frac{x^{(2)}}{2!} \Delta^2 u_0 + \frac{x^{(3)}}{3!} \Delta^3 u_0 + \ldots.$$

$$\therefore \quad x^m = o^m + x\Delta o^m + \frac{x^{(2)}}{2!} \Delta^2 o^m + \frac{x^{(3)}}{3!} \Delta^3 o^m + \ldots.$$

By use of the relation

$$\Delta^n o^m = n \left(\Delta^n o^{m-1} + \Delta^{n-1} o^{m-1} \right), \text{ i.e. } \frac{\Delta^n o^m}{n!} = \frac{n\Delta^n o^{m-1}}{n!} + \frac{\Delta^{n-1} o^{m-1}}{(n-1)!},$$

a table of the coefficients in the expansion of x^m in terms of successive values of the factorial $x^{(k)}$ can be written down in a similar manner to that given above.

4. The compound function $u_x v_x$.

We can adapt the principle of separation of symbols to the evaluation of such expressions as $\Delta^n u_x v_x$ by a simple extension of the process of differencing.

Let $\Delta_1, E_1, \Sigma_1, \ldots$ denote operations on u_x alone and $\Delta_2, E_2, \Sigma_2, \ldots$ operations on v_x alone.

Then
$$\Delta u_x v_x = u_{x+1} v_{x+1} - u_x v_x$$
$$= E_1 u_x . E_2 v_x - u_x v_x$$
$$= (E_1 E_2 - 1) u_x v_x.$$
$$\therefore \quad \Delta^n u_x v_x = (E_1 E_2 - 1)^n u_x v_x.$$

By expressing $E_1 E_2$ in terms of Δ_1 and Δ_2 we are enabled to obtain expressions for the expansion of $\Delta^n u_x v_x$.

First, if $n = 1$, we have

$$\Delta u_x v_x = [(1 + \Delta_1)(1 + \Delta_2) - 1] u_x v_x$$
$$= (\Delta_1 + \Delta_2 + \Delta_1 \Delta_2) u_x v_x$$
$$= (\Delta_1 + \Delta_2 E_1) u_x v_x$$
$$= \Delta_1 u_x v_x + \Delta_2 E_1 u_x v_x$$
$$= v_x \Delta_1 u_x + E_1 u_x . \Delta_2 v_x$$
$$= v_x \Delta_1 u_x + u_{x+1} \Delta_2 v_x,$$

or, dropping the suffixes,

$$= v_x \Delta u_x + u_{x+1} \Delta v_x,$$

which is otherwise evident.

Again,

$$\Delta^n u_x v_x = (\Delta_1 + E_1 \Delta_2)^n u_x v_x$$
$$= (\Delta_1^n + n\Delta_1^{n-1} E_1 \Delta_2 + n_2 \Delta_1^{n-2} E_1^2 \Delta_2^2 + \ldots) u_x v_x,$$

which is easily seen to be

$$v_x \Delta^n u_x + n\Delta v_x \Delta^{n-1} u_{x+1} + n_2 \Delta^2 v_x \Delta^{n-2} u_{x+2} + \ldots.$$

If in the above expression we put $u_x = x^{m-1}$ and $v_x = x$, we have

$$\Delta^n (x^{m-1}.x) = x\Delta^n x^{m-1} + n\Delta^{n-1} (x+1)^{m-1}.$$

Let $x = 0$; then

$$\Delta^n 0^m = n\Delta^{n-1} 1^{m-1} = n\Delta^{n-1} E 0^{m-1} = n (\Delta^{n-1} 0^{m-1} + \Delta^n 0^{m-1}),$$

which is the relation proved in para. 2.

5. The following is a further illustration of the application of the above method.

Example 1.

Prove that

$$\Sigma^n (u_x v_x) = u_x \Sigma^n v_x - n\Delta u_x \Sigma^{n+1} v_{x+1} + (n+1)_2 \Delta^2 u_x \Sigma^{n+2} v_{x+2}$$
$$- (n+2)_3 \Delta^3 u_x \Sigma^{n+3} v_{x+3} + \ldots.$$

Now $$\Delta u_x v_x = [\Delta_2 + \Delta_1 (1 + \Delta_2)] u_x v_x.$$

$$\therefore \; \Sigma^n \equiv \Delta^{-n} \equiv [\Delta_2 + \Delta_1 (1 + \Delta_2)]^{-n} \equiv \Delta_2^{-n} (1 + \Delta_1 \Delta_2^{-1} E_2)^{-n}.$$

$$\therefore \; \Sigma^n u_x v_x = \Delta_2^{-n} [1 - n\Delta_1 \Delta_2^{-1} E_2 + (n+1)_2 \Delta_1^2 \Delta_2^{-2} E_2^2$$
$$- (n+2)_3 \Delta_1^3 \Delta_2^{-3} E_2^3 + \ldots] u_x v_x$$
$$= u_x \Sigma^n v_x - n\Delta u_x \Sigma^{n+1} v_{x+1} + (n+1)_2 \Delta^2 u_x \Sigma^{n+2} v_{x+2}$$
$$- (n+2)_3 \Delta^3 u_x \Sigma^{n+3} v_{x+3} + \ldots.$$

Note. If $n = 1$ we have

$$\Sigma u_x v_x = \Delta_2^{-1} \left(1 + \Delta_1 \Delta_2^{-1} E_2\right)^{-1} u_x v_x$$

$$= \Delta_2^{-1} \left(1 - \frac{\Delta_1 \Delta_2^{-1} E_2}{1 + \Delta_1 \Delta_2^{-1} E_2}\right) u_x v_x$$

$$= \left(\Delta_2^{-1} - \frac{\Delta_1 \Delta_2^{-1} E_2}{\Delta_2 + \Delta_1 E_2}\right) u_x v_x$$

$$= \left(\Delta_2^{-1} - \frac{\Delta_1 \Delta_2^{-1} E_2}{E_1 E_2 - 1}\right) u_x v_x$$

$$= u_x \Sigma v_x - \Delta^{-1} \left(\Delta u_x \Sigma v_{x+1}\right)$$

$$= u_x \Sigma v_{x+1} - \Sigma \left(\Delta u_x \Sigma v_{x+1}\right),$$

the ordinary formula for summation by parts.

6. Functions of two variables.

In Chapter II it was stated that, when x and y are independent variables, $u_{xy}, f(x,y), \ldots$ represent functions which assume different values according to the values of x and y. For example, the function $x^2 + 2xy + y^2 + x + 3y$, in which x and y both vary, may be written shortly as u_{xy}. If, further, y is a function of x, we may reduce u_{xy} to the form v_x and thus obtain a function depending on x alone.

Now suppose that x takes the value $x + h$ while y remains constant, and that y takes the value $y + k$ while x remains constant. Then the new value of the function is dependent on $x + h$ and $y + k$. It is not necessary for both x and y to vary: x may become $x + h$ while y remains constant or vice versa. This type of function is conveniently represented by the slightly different notation $f(x:y)$ or $u_{x:y}$.

If the values of the function proceed by equidistant intervals, we have the following scheme:

$u_{x:y}$	$u_{x+h:y}$	$u_{x+2h:y}$	$u_{x+3h:y}$	$\ldots$
$u_{x:y+k}$	$u_{x+h:y+k}$	$u_{x+2h:y+k}$	$u_{x+3h:y+k}$	$\ldots$
$u_{x:y+2k}$	$u_{x+h:y+2k}$	$u_{x+2h:y+2k}$	$u_{x+3h:y+2k}$	$\ldots$
$u_{x:y+3k}$	$u_{x+h:y+3k}$	$u_{x+2h:y+3k}$	$u_{x+3h:y+3k}$	$\ldots$
$\vdots$	$\vdots$	$\vdots$	$\vdots$	

or, if our origin be (o, o) and $h = k = 1$,

$u_{0:0}$	$u_{1:0}$	$u_{2:0}$	$u_{3:0}$	$\cdots$
$u_{0:1}$	$u_{1:1}$	$u_{2:1}$	$u_{3:1}$	$\cdots$
$u_{0:2}$	$u_{1:2}$	$u_{2:2}$	$u_{3:2}$	$\cdots$
$\vdots$	$\vdots$	$\vdots$	$\vdots$	

7. If we are to apply the processes of finite differences as hitherto defined we must distinguish between an increase in the value of x and an increase in the value of y. We therefore write E_x to denote the operation of increasing the value of x by a unit difference while y remains constant, and E_y similarly for y while x remains constant.

That is, $\quad E_x u_{0:0} = u_{1:0}$ and $E_y u_{0:0} = u_{0:1}$,

so that $\quad \Delta_x u_{0:0} = u_{1:0} - u_{0:0}$ and $\Delta_y u_{0:0} = u_{0:1} - u_{0:0}$.

Again, $\Delta_x \Delta_y u_{0:0} = \Delta_x (\Delta_y u_{0:0})$

$$= \Delta_x (u_{0:1} - u_{0:0})$$

$$= \Delta_x u_{0:1} - \Delta_x u_{0:0}$$

$$= u_{1:1} - u_{0:1} - u_{1:0} + u_{0:0},$$

and $\quad \Delta_x{}^2 \Delta_y u_{0:0} = \Delta_x{}^2 (u_{0:1} - u_{0:0})$

$$= \Delta_x{}^2 u_{0:1} - \Delta_x{}^2 u_{0:0}$$

$$= (u_{2:1} - 2u_{1:1} + u_{0:1}) - (u_{2:0} - 2u_{1:0} + u_{0:0}).$$

The general formula corresponding to the advancing difference formula for one independent variable is

$$u_{m:n} = (1 + \Delta_x)^m (1 + \Delta_y)^n u_{0:0}$$

$$= (1 + m\Delta_x + m_2\Delta_x{}^2 + \ldots)(1 + n\Delta_y + n_2\Delta_y{}^2 + \ldots) u_{0:0}$$

$$= (1 + m\Delta_x + m_2\Delta_x{}^2 + m_3\Delta_x{}^3 + \ldots$$

$$+ n\Delta_y + mn\Delta_x\Delta_y + m_2 n\Delta_x{}^2\Delta_y + \ldots$$

$$+ n_2\Delta_y{}^2 + mn_2\Delta_x\Delta_y{}^2 + \ldots$$

$$+ n_3\Delta_y{}^3 + \ldots) u_{0:0}$$

$$= u_{0:0} + (m\Delta_x + n\Delta_y) u_{0:0} + (m_2\Delta_x{}^2 + mn\Delta_x\Delta_y + n_2\Delta_y{}^2) u_{0:0}$$

$$+ (m_3\Delta_x{}^3 + m_2 n\Delta_x{}^2\Delta_y + mn_2\Delta_x\Delta_y{}^2 + n_3\Delta_y{}^3) u_{0:0} + \ldots.$$

8. Application of the formula.

Example 2.

Given the following table of values of $u_{x:y}$, estimate the value of $u_{23:17}$.

x	$y = 15$	$y = 20$	$y = 25$
20	5·947	4·418	3·547
25	6·046	4·530	
30	6·144		

Here the interval of differencing is 5. Changing the origin to the point (0, 0) and the unit to 1, the data are given for the points (0, 0), (1, 0), (2, 0); (0, 1), (0, 2); (1, 1). The value required is $u_{\cdot 6:\cdot 4}$.

Differencing downwards for values of $\Delta_x u_{0:0}$, etc., we have

$$\Delta_x u_{0:0} = \cdot 099; \quad \Delta_x^2 u_{0:0} = -\cdot 001.$$

Differencing across for values of $\Delta_y u_{0:0}$, etc.,

$$\Delta_y u_{0:0} = -1\cdot 529; \quad \Delta_y^2 u_{0:0} = \cdot 658.$$

Also $\Delta_x \Delta_y u_{0:0} = u_{1:1} - u_{0:1} - u_{1:0} + u_{0:0} = \cdot 013.$

$$\therefore \ u_{\cdot 6:\cdot 4} = (1 + \cdot 6\Delta_x - \cdot 12\Delta_x^2 \ldots)(1 + \cdot 4\Delta_y - \cdot 12\Delta_y^2 \ldots)u_{0:0}$$
$$= (1 + \cdot 6\Delta_x + \cdot 4\Delta_y - \cdot 12\Delta_x^2 + \cdot 24\Delta_x\Delta_y - \cdot 12\Delta_y^2)u_{0:0}$$
$$= 5\cdot 319.$$

9. While for most purposes the formula advanced above is probably as convenient as any that can be devised, special circumstances may arise in which other methods may be more suitable. Where the intervals are not equidistant we may apply either a method of divided differences or one of various adaptations of Lagrange's formula depending upon the number of points given. If, for example, four values of $u_{x:y}$ are given, namely $u_{\alpha:a}$; $u_{\alpha:b}$; $u_{\beta:a}$; $u_{\beta:b}$, then it is quite easy to show that

$$u_{x:y} = u_{\alpha:a} \frac{(x - \beta)(y - b)}{(\alpha - \beta)(a - b)} + u_{\alpha:b} \frac{(x - \beta)(y - a)}{(\alpha - \beta)(b - a)}$$
$$+ u_{\beta:b} \frac{(x - \alpha)(y - a)}{(\beta - \alpha)(b - a)} + u_{\beta:a} \frac{(x - \alpha)(y - b)}{(\beta - \alpha)(a - b)}.$$

If more than four values are given the formula becomes unwieldy. It is seldom necessary to interpolate except between equidistant values of the function, and in that event a form of advancing or central difference series is preferable.

Two-variable functions are of great frequency in actuarial work. Tables of annuity-values ($a_{x:y}$) depending upon joint lives are often available for quinquennial values only of x and y, and when values at ages other than those tabulated are required recourse must be had to methods of interpolation. Although the formulae given above are of general application special methods can be found to meet the requirements of the problem to be solved.

For example, if quinquennial values of $a_{x:y}$ are available, and if the two ages concerned are such that their sum is a multiple of 5, we may choose our origin and interval of differencing so that $x + y = 1$. We have then, from the general formula for $u_{x:y}$,

$$u_{x:1-x} = u_{0:0} + [x\Delta_x + (1-x)\Delta_y + \tfrac{1}{2}x(x-1)(\Delta_x^2 - 2\Delta_x\Delta_y + \Delta_y^2)]u_{0:0};$$

i.e.

$$u_{x:1-x} = u_{0:1} + x(u_{1:0} - u_{0:1}) + \tfrac{1}{2}x(x-1)(u_{2:0} - 2u_{1:1} + u_{0:2}).$$

Again, if $x + y = 2$, this formula becomes

$$u_{x:2-x} = \tfrac{1}{2}x(x-1)u_{2:0} - x(x-2)u_{1:1} + \tfrac{1}{2}(x-1)(x-2)u_{0:2},$$

or, on changing the origin,

$$u_{x:-x} = \tfrac{1}{2}(x-1)(x-2)u_{0:0} - x(x-2)u_{1:-1} + \tfrac{1}{2}x(x-1)u_{2:-2},$$

for which the data required are $u_{0:0}$, $u_{1:-1}$ and $u_{2:-2}$. The problem is thus reduced to a single variable interpolation.

This second formula is very useful in practice. As a rule we can choose our data within wide limits, and it has been found that with certain functions the three-term formula gives as good approximations to the true results as do formulae involving higher orders of differences (see Spencer, *J.I.A.* vol. XL, pp. 293–301).

The general second difference formula of which the above is a particular example is

$$u_{x:rx} = mu_{0:0} + nu_{1:r} + pu_{2:2r},$$

and in the note referred to above, Spencer gives a table showing the application of this formula according as r takes the values 0, 1, − 1 or 2.

Another form of the formula for an interpolated value of $u_{x:y}$ when four values are given is $u_{x:y} = \xi(\eta u_{0:0} + yu_{0:1}) + x(\eta u_{1:0} + yu_{1:1})$, where x and y are both less than unity and $x + \xi = y + \eta = 1$. The second difference formula can be written as

$$u_{x:y} = \{1 - (k_1\delta_x^2 + k_2\delta_y^2)\}\{\xi(\eta u_{0:0} + yu_{0:1}) + x(\eta u_{1:0} + yu_{1:1})\},$$

where $\delta_x^2 u$ and $\delta_y^2 u$ are second central differences with respect to x and y respectively and k_1 and k_2 are constants depending upon the values of x and y (Buchanan, *T.F.A.* vol. x, pp. 329, 330).

Example 3.

Values of the joint-life annuity $a_{x:y}$ for quinquennial ages being available, find a value for $a_{44:51}$.

(i) Take the origin at $(40 : 50)$; then if the interval of differencing be 5 years, $(44 : 51)$ will be represented by $(\cdot8 : \cdot2)$ and $x + y = 1$.

$$u_{x:1-x} = u_{0:1} + x\,(u_{1:0} - u_{0:1}) + \tfrac{1}{2}x\,(x - 1)\,(u_{2:0} - 2u_{1:1} + u_{0:2}).$$

The data required are

$$
\begin{aligned}
a_{40:50} &= 10\cdot894 & a_{40:55} &= 9\cdot796 & a_{40:60} &= 8\cdot553\\
a_{45:50} &= 10\cdot591 & a_{45:55} &= 9\cdot583\\
a_{50:50} &= 10\cdot059
\end{aligned}
$$

Then
$$
\begin{aligned}
u_{\cdot8:\cdot2} &= 9\cdot796 + \cdot8\,(10\cdot591 - 9\cdot796)\\
&\quad + \tfrac{1}{2}\,\cdot8\,(-\,\cdot2)\,(10\cdot059 - 19\cdot166 + 8\cdot553)\\
&= 9\cdot796 + \cdot6360 + \cdot0443\\
&= 10\cdot476.
\end{aligned}
$$

(ii) Take the origin at $(40 : 45)$ so that $(44 : 51)$ will be $(\cdot8 : 1\cdot2)$ and $x + y = 2$.

$$u_{x:2-x} = \tfrac{1}{2}\,(x - 1)\,(x - 2)\,u_{0:2} - x\,(x - 2)\,u_{1:1} + \tfrac{1}{2}x\,(x - 1)\,u_{2:0}.$$

The three values required are

$$
\begin{aligned}
a_{40:55} &= 9\cdot796,\\
a_{45:50} &= 10\cdot591,\\
a_{50:45} &= 10\cdot591.
\end{aligned}
$$

$$
\begin{aligned}
u_{\cdot8:1\cdot2} &= \tfrac{1}{2}\,(-\,\cdot2)\,(-\,1\cdot2)\,9\cdot796 - \cdot8\,(-\,1\cdot2)\,10\cdot591 + \tfrac{1}{2}\,(\cdot8)\,(-\,\cdot2)\,10\cdot591\\
&= 10\cdot496.
\end{aligned}
$$

If nine values surrounding the point $(44 : 51)$ be taken and a Lagrange formula for these nine values be used, the value for $a_{44:51}$ becomes $10\cdot475$.

This nine-point formula is a safe formula for occasional interpolation, and by its use the risk and labour attaching to the calculation of differences may be avoided. The formula is used centrally, the area of interpolation being as shown in the diagram. The ordinary single-variable Lagrange interpolation formula is used to interpolate for x in each column, and the formula is used again to interpolate for y from the three calculated values.

10. The above example shows that different degrees of accuracy may be obtained by choosing different sets of data on which to work. The general theory follows the same lines as that for single-variable interpolation. It will be remembered that the ordinary advancing difference formula may be applied to the expansion of u_x in terms of the differences of u_x on the assumption that $y = u_x$ is a rational integral function of x. In these circumstances we may represent the function graphically, and the successive values of x and y will be points on the plane curve $y = u_x$. When we are considering a function of two variables x and y we assume similarly that we may represent $z = u_{x:y}$ as a surface. Now in Chapter VI (para. 10) it was proved that the effect of including higher differences in the expansion for u_x does not necessarily give better results than if they are neglected. In the same way it may be shown that by choosing more points on which to work we may produce a result farther from the true value z on the surface $z = u_{x:y}$ than we should obtain by relying on fewer data.

With regular data the formulae with x, y in the central area of the given points are usually preferable. In the space for which x, y are both positive and less than $\frac{1}{2}$, a simple central difference formula is

$$u_{x:y} = u_{0:0} + \tfrac{1}{2}x\,(u_{1:0} - u_{-1:0}) + \tfrac{1}{2}y\,(u_{0:1} - u_{0:-1}).$$

This is based on five points.

This formula and the six-point formula consisting of the same terms with the addition of

$$\tfrac{1}{2}x^2\,(u_{1:0} - 2u_{0:0} + u_{1:0}) + \tfrac{1}{2}y^2\,(u_{0:1} - 2u_{0:0} + u_{0:-1})$$
$$+ xy\,(u_{1:1} + u_{0:0} - u_{1:0} - u_{0:1})$$

are probably the most useful interpolation formulae for ordinary actuarial purposes (Todhunter, *J.I.A.* vol. LIII, p. 89).

11. Central difference formulae: Fraser's diagrams.

No demonstration of central difference formulae would be complete without reference to Fraser's graphic method. In this method the ordinary differences of a function of x are combined with the relation $(x + 1)_r = x_r + x_{r-1}$ in diagrammatic form so that by adopting certain conventions any finite difference formula can be written down immediately (Fraser, *J.I.A.* vol. XLIII, pp. 235 *et seq.*).

We have $(x + t + 1)_r = (x + t)_r + (x + t)_{r-1},$

or $(x + t + 1)_r - (x + t)_r = (x + t)_{r-1}.$

A relation similar to the fundamental finite difference identity

$u_{x+h} - u_x = \Delta u_x$ exists therefore between these coefficients. If we carry the analogy still further we can construct a table of values of $(x + t)_r$ corresponding to a difference table.

The two tables are set down thus:

u_{-2} $(x + 3)_4$

    Δu_{-2} $(x + 2)_3$

u_{-1} $\Delta^2 u_{-2}$ $(x + 1)_2$ $(x + 2)_4$

   Δu_{-1} $\Delta^3 u_{-2}$ x_1 $(x + 1)_3$

u_0 $\Delta^2 u_{-1}$ $\Delta^4 u_{-2}$ x_2 $(x + 1)_4$

   Δu_0 $\Delta^3 u_{-1}$ $(x - 1)_1$ x_3

u_1 $\Delta^2 u_0$ $(x - 1)_2$ x_4

   Δu_1 $(x - 1)_3$

u_2 $(x - 1)_4$

If now these two tables be combined, we have the following scheme:

$$
\begin{array}{c}
u_{-2}-(x+2)_1 \\
(x+1)_0 \\
u_{-1}-(x+1)_1 \\
x_0 \\
u_0 \longrightarrow x_1 \\
(x-1)_0 \\
u_1-(x-1)_1 \\
(x-2)_0 \\
u_2-(x-2)_1
\end{array}
\qquad
\begin{array}{c}
\Delta u_{-2}-(x+2)_2 \\
\Delta u_{-1}-(x+1)_2 \\
\Delta u_0 \longrightarrow x_2 \\
\Delta u_1-(x-1)_2
\end{array}
\qquad
\begin{array}{c}
\Delta^2 u_{-3}-(x+3)_3 \\
\Delta^2 u_{-2}-(x+2)_3 \\
\Delta^2 u_{-1}-(x+1)_3 \\
\Delta^2 u_0 \longrightarrow x_3
\end{array}
\qquad
\begin{array}{c}
\Delta^3 u_{-3} \\
\Delta^3 u_{-2} \\
\Delta^3 u_{-1}
\end{array}
$$

where for any one of the hexagons we may write in general

$$
\begin{array}{c}
\Delta^r u_{-t} \longrightarrow (x+t)_{r+1} \\
(x+t-1)_r \qquad\qquad \Delta^{r+1} u_{-t} \\
\Delta^r u_{-t+1} - (x+t-1)_{r+1}
\end{array}
$$

Now

$$(x + t - 1)_r \Delta^r u_{-t} + (x + t)_{r+1} \Delta^{r+1} u_{-t} - (x + t - 1)_{r+1} \Delta^{r+1} u_{-t}$$

$$- (x + t - 1)_r \Delta^r u_{-t+1}$$

$$= (x + t - 1)_r \left[\Delta^r u_{-t} - \Delta^r u_{-t+1}\right] + \Delta^{r+1} u_{-t} \left[(x + t)_{r+1}\right.$$
$$\left. - (x + t - 1)_{r+1}\right]$$
$$= (x + t - 1)_r \left[- \Delta^{r+1} u_{-t}\right] + \Delta^{r+1} u_{-t} (x + t - 1)_r$$
$$= 0.$$

A relation is therefore established between the constituents of the various hexagons. If we make the following assumptions: (i) the oblique lines denote multiplication and the horizontal lines addition; (ii) a line taken in a clockwise direction gives the product a positive sign, and in the opposite direction a negative sign, we can say that the sum of the operations performed in travelling round any hexagon is zero. It follows easily that the sum of the operations in travelling round any closed circuit is also zero.

It is evident from a consideration of the diagram that if we travel from any value of $(x + t)_k$ to any difference $\Delta^m u_n$ the result will be the same whatever route be taken. For example, from $(x - 1)_0$ through $u_0, x_1, \Delta u_0, x_2$ to $\Delta^2 u_0$ and back along $(x - 1)_2, \Delta u_1, (x - 2)_1,$ $u_2, (x - 2)_0, u_1$ to $(x - 1)_0$ again enables the following identity to be established:

$$(x - 1)_0 u_0 + x_1 \Delta u_0 + x_2 \Delta^2 u_0 - (x - 1)_2 \Delta^2 u_0 - (x - 2)_1 \Delta u_1$$
$$- (x - 2)_0 u_2 + (x - 2)_0 u_1 - (x - 1)_0 u_1 = 0.$$

Re-writing this, we have

$$u_0 + x \Delta u_0 + \tfrac{1}{2} x (x - 1) \Delta^2 u_0 - \tfrac{1}{2} (x - 1) (x - 2) \Delta^2 u_0$$
$$- (x - 2) \Delta u_1 - u_2 + u_1 - u_1 = 0,$$

or

$$u_0 + x \Delta u_0 + \tfrac{1}{2} x (x - 1) \Delta^2 u_0 = u_2 + (x - 2) \Delta u_1$$
$$+ \tfrac{1}{2} (x - 2) (x - 1) \Delta^2 u_0.$$

Exactly the same result will be obtained by proceeding along an alternative route

$$(x - 1)_0, u_0, x_1, \Delta u_0, x_2, \Delta^2 u_0$$

and back through

$$(x - 1)_2, \Delta u_1, (x - 1)_1, u_1, (x - 1)_0.$$

The identity will be

$$(x - 1)_0 u_0 + x \Delta u_0 + x_2 \Delta^2 u_0 - (x - 1)_2 \Delta^2 u_0 - (x - 1)_1 \Delta u_1$$
$$- (x - 1)_0 u_1 = 0,$$

or $\quad u_0 + x\Delta u_0 + \tfrac{1}{2}x\,(x-1)\,\Delta^2 u_0 = \tfrac{1}{2}\,(x-1)\,(x-2)\,\Delta^2 u_0$

$$+ (x-1)\,\Delta u_1 + u_1;$$

i.e. $\qquad = \tfrac{1}{2}\,(x-1)\,(x-2)\,\Delta^2 u_0 + (x-2)\,\Delta u_1 + u_2,$

the same result as before.

12. Application of the hexagon diagram.

The above example gives a formula for u_2 in terms of u_0, Δu_0, $\Delta^2 u_0$ and Δu_1, and if we put $x = 2$ we have a well-known identity. A similar process will give a formula for u_n, and since we may take various routes a number of different expansions of u_n will arise, all giving exact expressions for u_n. It should be further observed that when an nth difference has been reached by travelling along the upper route the terms other than u_n in the lower route will be zero, and it follows that by travelling round any circuit we obtain expressions involving an initial term u_n and terms of lower degree than n. This is seen to be so by considering $\Delta^n u_0$: all the coefficients along the lower route will contain $(x - n)$ as a factor and will therefore vanish when $x = n$.

We have therefore from the diagram the following expansions:

(i) $u_n = u_0 + n_1\Delta u_0 + n_2\Delta^2 u_0 + n_3\Delta^3 u_0 + \dots$ (Newton's formula).

(ii) $u_n = u_0 + n_1\Delta u_0 + n_2\Delta^2 u_{-1} + (n+1)_3\,\Delta^3 u_{-1}$

$\qquad + (n+1)_4\,\Delta^4 u_{-2} + \dots$ (Gauss's forward formula).

(iii) $u_n = u_0 + n_1\Delta u_{-1} + (n+1)_2\,\Delta^2 u_{-1} + (n+1)_3\,\Delta^3 u_{-2} + \dots$

$\qquad\qquad\qquad\qquad\qquad$ (Gauss's backward formula).

(iv) $u_n = u_1 + (n-1)_1\,\Delta u_0 + n_2\Delta^2 u_0 + n_3\Delta^3 u_{-1}$

$\qquad + (n+1)_4\,\Delta^4 u_{-2} + \dots$

The mean of (ii) and (iii) gives Stirling's formula, and the mean of (iii) and (iv) can be arranged to give either Bessel's or Everett's form.

13. Further applications of the calculus of operations.

It has already been shown when considering the common operations of finite differences, Δu, Eu, Σu, that the symbols denoting the operations can, within limits, be treated as obeying the ordinary algebraic laws. By omitting the function u the various processes can be applied to the operators alone, with a resultant simplification of procedure. It will be seen later that the method can be adapted to the needs of the infinitesimal calculus, but before that stage is reached it is proposed to demonstrate the use of the method in other operations connected with finite differences.

14. The operator ∇.

In Chapter V attention was drawn to certain symbols of operation which may be considered as supplementary to the Δ and E which are the basic operators in finite differences. These symbols —namely δ and μ—may also be assumed to follow the normal algebraic laws (with the usual limitations), and the method of separation of symbols may be applied to them equally with Δ, E and Σ. A further symbol has been introduced connecting u_x with the next lower value u_{x-1} instead of with the more usual value u_{x+1}. This symbol is ∇, and ∇u_x is defined as $u_x - u_{x-1}$.

Corresponding to $\Delta u_x = (E - 1)\, u_x,$

we have therefore $\nabla u_x = (1 - E^{-1})\, u_x.$

Thus, for example,

$$\nabla^n u_x = (1 - E^{-1})^n u_x$$
$$= u_x - n u_{x-1} + n_2 u_{x-2} - n_3 u_{x-3} + \dots.$$

In addition to the familiar

$$\Delta x^{(m)} = m x^{(m-1)},$$

there is a similar relation

$$\nabla x^{(-m)} = m x^{(-m+1)},$$

where $x^{(-m)} \equiv (-1)^m (-x)^{(m)}$ and not the inverse factorial defined on p. 39; and if we denote the product

$$x \left(x + \tfrac{1}{2}n - 1\right)\left(x + \tfrac{1}{2}n - 2\right) \dots \left(x - \tfrac{1}{2}n + 1\right)$$

by $x^{[n]}$ it is easy to show that

$$\delta x^{[m]} = m x^{[m-1]}$$

(Steffensen, Interpolation, pp. 8, 9).

No new principle is involved in dealing with these further symbols of operation; their introduction simply enables us to develop expansions and to write down formulae for interpolation with an economy of labour.

15. "Summation n."

An interesting example of the development of a series of operations by the method of separation of symbols occurs in the theory of graduation. One of the objects of graduation is to obtain a smooth series of numbers instead of the rough series given by the actual data. A method for the solution of the problem consists in replacing each term of the series by the arithmetic mean of the n successive terms of which the given term is the central term. The operation of summing these successive terms is generally denoted by $[n]$ ("summation n").

For example $[5]\, u_0 = u_{-2} + u_{-1} + u_0 + u_1 + u_2,$

$$[n]\, u_0 = u_{-\frac{n-1}{2}} + u_{-\frac{n-3}{2}} + \ldots + u_{\frac{n-3}{2}} + u_{\frac{n-1}{2}}.$$

Consider a simple summation: $[3]\, u_0$.

By definition $[3]\, u_0 = u_{-1} + u_0 + u_1,$

and if we write v_0 for $[3]\, u_0$ we may operate again on v_0 to obtain $[3]\, v_0$.

In that event we shall have

$$[3]\, v_0 = [3]\, u_{-1} + [3]\, u_0 + [3]\, u_1$$
$$= u_{-2} + 2u_{-1} + 3u_0 + 2u_1 + u_2$$
$$= u_0 + (u_{-1} + u_0 + u_1) + (u_{-2} + u_{-1} + u_0 + u_1 + u_2)$$
$$= [1]\, u_0 + [3]\, u_0 + [5]\, u_0.$$

If therefore we denote the double operation $[3]\,[3]\, u_0$ by $[3]^2 u_0$, we have the symbolic identity

$$[3]^2 \equiv [1] + [3] + [5].$$

Similarly $[5]^2 \equiv [1] + [3] + [5] + [7] + [9],$

and $[n]^2 \equiv [1] + [3] + [5] + [7] + \ldots + [2n - 1],$

where n is odd.

The identity between $[3]^2$ and $[1] + [3] + [5]$ can be seen at once by writing down the terms in diagrammatic form:

$$[3]^2 u_0 = [3]\, u_{-1} + [3]\, u_0 + [3]\, u_1$$

$$= \begin{array}{l} u_{-2} + u_{-1} + u_0 \\ \quad + u_{-1} + u_0 + u_1 \\ \qquad + u_0 + u_1 + u_2 \end{array}$$

$$= \begin{array}{l} u_{-2} + u_{-1} + u_0 + u_1 + u_2 \\ \quad + u_{-1} + u_0 + u_1 \\ \qquad + u_0 \end{array}$$

$$= [5]\, u_0 + [3]\, u_0 + [1]\, u_0 . \qquad \text{(Fraser.)}$$

16. We can express $[n]$ in terms of the ordinary finite difference symbols thus:

For a simple value of n, say 3,

$$[3]\, u_0 = u_{-1} + u_0 + u_1 = 3u_0 + u_{-1} - 2u_0 + u_1$$

$$= 3u_0 + \Delta^2 u_{-1}$$

$$= (3 + \delta^2)\, u_0,$$

where δ^2 is the symbol denoting the second central difference.

Generally $[n] \equiv n + \dfrac{n^3 - n}{24} \delta^2 +$ terms in δ^4 and higher differences if these exist. (Cf. Chap. VII, Ex. 10.)

The relations above are on the assumption that n is odd. If n be even we must find a meaning for the summation symbol.

By analogy $[2]\, u_0$ is the sum of two values of u whose suffixes are such that their sum is zero and their difference unity.

I.e. $\qquad\qquad [2]\, u_0 = u_{-\frac{1}{2}} + u_{\frac{1}{2}}.$

Hence $\qquad\qquad [2]^2\, u_0 = \{[1] + [3]\}\, u_0$

$$= (4 + \delta^2)\, u_0,$$

so that $\qquad\qquad [2] \equiv 2\,(1 + \tfrac{1}{4}\delta^2)^{\frac{1}{2}}$

$$\equiv 2\,(1 + \tfrac{1}{8}\delta^2 - \tfrac{1}{128}\delta^4 + \ldots),$$

which is otherwise obtained by expressing $u_{-\frac{1}{2}} + u_{\frac{1}{2}}$ in terms of central differences. This agrees with

$$[n] \equiv n + \frac{n^3 - n}{24} \delta^2$$

as far as third differences.

The meaning of $[n]$ when n is even is now evident, and we need no longer restrict the values of n to odd integers. Thus the formula

$$[n]\, u_0 = u_{-\frac{n-1}{2}} + u_{-\frac{n-3}{2}} + \ldots + u_{\frac{n-3}{2}} + u_{\frac{n-1}{2}}$$

applies for any integral value of n whether odd or even.

17. By means of the relations already proved we may develop an unlimited number of formulae involving $[n]$, $[m]$, etc.

Example 4.

Prove that $10\,[1] - 3\,[3] \equiv 2\,[3] - [5]$ as far as third differences.

$$\{10\,[1] - 3\,[3]\}\, u_0 = 10u_0 - 3\left(3u_0 + \tfrac{24}{24}\delta^2 u_0\right)$$
$$= u_0 - 3\delta^2 u_0.$$

Also $\quad \{2\,[3] - [5]\}\, u_0 = 2\left(3u_0 + \tfrac{24}{24}\delta^2 u_0\right) - \left(5u_0 + \tfrac{120}{24}\delta^2 u_0\right)$

$$= u_0 - 3\delta^2 u_0.$$

Example 5.

Given $[5]\, u_{-1}$, $[5]\, u_0$, $[5]\, u_1$, find u_0, fourth and higher differences being neglected.

By Stirling's formula,

$$u_x = u_0 + x\,\frac{\Delta u_{-1} + \Delta u_0}{2} + \frac{x^2}{2}\Delta^2 u_{-1} + \frac{x(x^2-1)}{6}\,\frac{\Delta^3 u_{-1} + \Delta^3 u_{-2}}{2} + \ldots,$$

$$u_{-x} = u_0 - x\,\frac{\Delta u_{-1} + \Delta u_0}{2} + \frac{x^2}{2}\Delta^2 u_{-1} - \frac{x(x^2-1)}{6}\,\frac{\Delta^3 u_{-1} + \Delta^3 u_{-2}}{2} + \ldots.$$

$$\therefore \quad u_x + u_{-x} = 2u_0 + x^2\Delta^2 u_{-1}.$$

$$\therefore \quad [5]\, u_0 = u_{-2} + u_{-1} + u_0 + u_1 + u_2 = (u_2 + u_{-2}) + (u_1 + u_{-1}) + u_0$$
$$= 5u_0 + 5\Delta^2 u_{-1}.$$

Similarly $\quad [5]\, u_{-1} + [5]\, u_1 = 10u_0 + 135\Delta^2 u_{-1}.$

Eliminating $\Delta^2 u_{-1}$, we have

$$125u_0 = \{27\,[5]\, u_0 - [5]\, u_{-1} - [5]\, u_1\}.$$

An interesting note by Mr D. C. Fraser on the properties of the operator $[n]$ occurs in the *Actuarial Students' Magazine*, No. 3 (Edinburgh, 1930). Here the general form for $[n]\, u_0$ is given by Mr Fraser as

$$\frac{E^{\frac{n}{2}} - E^{-\frac{n}{2}}}{E^{\frac{1}{2}} - E^{-\frac{1}{2}}}\, u_0,$$

and the proof of the identity $[3]^2 \equiv [1] + [3] + [5]$ is made to depend on the development of the operator E. Thus:

$$[3]^2 u_0 = \frac{E^{\frac{3}{2}} - E^{-\frac{3}{2}}}{E^{\frac{1}{2}} - E^{-\frac{1}{2}}} [3]\, u_0$$

$$= \frac{E^{\frac{3}{2}} - E^{-\frac{3}{2}}}{E^{\frac{1}{2}} - E^{-\frac{1}{2}}} (u_{-1} + u_0 + u_1)$$

$$= \frac{(E^{\frac{3}{2}} - E^{-\frac{3}{2}})(E^{-1} + E^0 + E^1)}{E^{\frac{1}{2}} - E^{-\frac{1}{2}}} u_0$$

$$= \frac{(E^{\frac{1}{2}} - E^{-\frac{1}{2}}) + (E^{\frac{3}{2}} - E^{-\frac{3}{2}}) + (E^{\frac{5}{2}} - E^{-\frac{5}{2}})}{E^{\frac{1}{2}} - E^{-\frac{1}{2}}} u_0$$

$$= [1]\, u_0 + [3]\, u_0 + [5]\, u_0.$$

The general formula for $[n]^2 u_0$ can be proved in the same manner.

Many further examples of the use of $[n]$ will be found in various papers in the *Journal of the Institute of Actuaries*. For simple extensions of the method see particularly Hardy, *J.I.A.* vol. XXXII, p. 371 and Todhunter, *ib.* p. 378, and for generalizations, Lidstone, *J.I.A.* vol. LV, p. 177 and Aitken, *J.I.A.* vol. LX, p. 339.

EXAMPLES 8

1. Show that $\Delta^m x^n = 0$ or $n!$ according as $m >$ or $= n$.

Hence prove that if n and r are positive integers
$$n^r - n_1 (n-1)^r + n_2 (n-2)^r - n_3 (n-3)^r + \ldots = 0 \text{ or } n!$$
according as $r <$ or $= n$.

2. Use differences of zero to find $(2 \cdot 75)^3$ and $(- \tfrac{1}{4})^3$.

3. Prove that $\Delta^n 0^{n+1} = \tfrac{1}{2} n (n+1) \Delta^n 0^n$.

4. Prove the identity
$$\Delta^m 0^n + n\Delta^m 0^{n-1} + n_2\Delta^m 0^{n-2} + \ldots + \frac{n!}{(n-m)!} = \frac{\Delta^{m+1} 0^{n+1}}{m+1}.$$

5. Show that $(n+1) \Delta^n 0^n = 2 [\Delta^{n-1} 0^n + \Delta^n 0^n]$.

6. If $\delta u, \delta^2 u, \delta^3 u, \ldots$ represent differences for intervals of $1/m$ and $\Delta u, \Delta^2 u, \Delta^3 u, \ldots$ differences for unit intervals, then if fifth differences are constant, prove that
$$\delta^4 u_0 = \frac{\Delta^4 0^4}{4!} \cdot \frac{\Delta^4 u_0}{m^4} - \frac{10m\Delta^4 0^4 - \Delta^4 0^5}{5!} \cdot \frac{\Delta^5 u_0}{m^5}.$$

7. Show that $f(E^n) 0^m = n^m f(E) 0^m$.

8. If x be any quantity less than unity, prove that the limit of the series $1^n + 2^n x + 3^n x^2 + \ldots$ to infinity

$$= \frac{1}{(1-x)^2}\left\{\Delta o^n + \frac{x}{1-x}\Delta^2 o^n + \left(\frac{x}{1-x}\right)^2 \Delta^3 o^n + \ldots\right\}.$$

9. Prove that

$$\Sigma u_x v_x = u_{x-1}\Sigma v_x - \Delta u_{x-2}\,\Sigma^2 v_x + \Delta^2 u_{x-3}\,\Sigma^3 v_x - \ldots.$$

10. Given

$$u_{20:15} = 6\cdot004 \qquad u_{20:20} = 4\cdot304 \qquad u_{20:25} = 3\cdot325$$
$$u_{25:15} = 6\cdot029 \qquad u_{25:20} = 4\cdot346$$
$$u_{30:15} = 6\cdot075$$

find $u_{23:17}$ as accurately as possible.

11. Obtain a Lagrange formula for $u_{x:y}$, given $u_{0:0}$, $u_{1:0}$, $u_{0:1}$, $u_{1:1}$.

12. Show that if $u_{0:1} = u_{1:0}$ and $u_{0:2} = u_{2:0}$, then

$$u_{x:y} = u_{0:0} + (x+y)\left[\Delta_x + \frac{x+y-1}{2}\Delta_x^2\right]u_{0:0} + xy\left[u_{1:1} - u_{2:0}\right].$$

13. $a_{40:45} = 13\cdot133 \qquad a_{40:50} = 12\cdot450 \qquad a_{45:40} = 12\cdot880$
$$a_{50:40} = 11\cdot898 \qquad a_{45:45} = 12\cdot432$$

Find $a_{42:43}$.

14. Given the following premiums for endowment assurances, obtain as accurately as possible the premium for age 23, term 17 years:

Premiums

Age	Term 15 years	Term 20 years	Term 25 years
20	5·947	4·418	3·547
25	6·046	4·530	
30	6·144		

15. Find $u_{27:34}$, given

$$u_{20:20} = 3\cdot1000 \qquad u_{25:30} = 3\cdot6875$$
$$u_{20:25} = 3\cdot2625 \qquad u_{25:35} = 3\cdot9542$$
$$u_{20:30} = 3\cdot5042 \qquad u_{30:30} = 3\cdot9333$$
$$u_{20:35} = 3\cdot8458 \qquad u_{30:35} = 4\cdot1417$$
$$u_{25:25} = 3\cdot5000 \qquad u_{35:35} = 4\cdot5500$$

16. The following values of $f(x, y)$ are given:

$$f(35, 55) = 10\cdot020, \quad f(35, 50) = 11\cdot196, \quad f(35, 45) = 12\cdot019,$$
$$f(40, 55) = 9\cdot796, \quad f(40, 50) = 10\cdot894, \quad f(40, 45) = 11\cdot641,$$
$$f(45, 55) = 9\cdot583, \quad f(45, 50) = 10\cdot591, \quad f(45, 45) = 11\cdot243.$$

(i) Using only six of the above values, find $f(42, 52)$.

(ii) Making use of all the data, calculate $f(44, 51)$.

17. Prove that $\Delta\,(u_x v_x w_x)$ can be expressed in either of the two following forms:

(a) $u_{x+1} v_{x+1} \Delta w_x + u_{x+1} w_x \Delta v_x + v_x w_x \Delta u_x$.

(b) $\Delta u_x \Delta v_x \Delta w_x + u_x v_x \Delta w_x$ + two similar terms
$\qquad\qquad + u_x \Delta v_x \Delta w_x$ + two similar terms.

18. If $\qquad \nabla f(x) = f(x) - f(x-1)$,

prove that

$$\nabla^n f(x) = f(x) - n_1 f(x-1) + n_2 f(x-2) - \dots + (-1)^n f(x-n).$$

19. Prove that

$$E^x u_0 = [1 + x\nabla + (x+1)_2 \nabla^2 + (x+2)_3 \nabla^3 + \dots + (x+n)_{n+1} \nabla^{n+1} + \dots] u_0.$$

20. If $\qquad x^{[n]} = x\,(x + \tfrac{1}{2}n - 1)^{(n-1)}$,

prove that $\quad x^{[2n]} = x^2\,(x^2 - 1^2)\,(x^2 - 2^2) \dots (x^2 - \overline{n-1}^2)$

and $\qquad x^{[2n+1]} = x\,(x^2 - \tfrac{1}{4})\,(x^2 - \tfrac{9}{4}) \dots [x^2 - \tfrac{1}{4}(2n-1)^2]$.

21. Show that

$$f(x) = f(0) + \frac{x^{[1]}}{1!}\,\delta f(0) + \frac{x^{[2]}}{2!}\,\delta^2 f(0) + \dots + \frac{x^{[n]}}{n!}\,\delta^n f(0) + \dots,$$

where $x^{[n]}$ has the same meaning as in Question 20, and

$$\delta f(x) = f(x + \tfrac{1}{2}) - f(x - \tfrac{1}{2}).$$

22. Prove that $\quad \{2\,[3] - [5]\}\,u_0 = u_0 - 3\Delta^2 u_{-1}$ approximately.

23. Obtain the approximate formula

$$125 u_0 = [5]^3 \{u_0 + \Delta u_{-2} - \Delta u_1\}. \qquad \text{(Woolhouse.)}$$

24. Prove that $\quad [n]^2 - [m]^2 \equiv \{[n] - [m]\}\,\{[n] + [m]\}$.

25. One of Hardy's graduation formulae is

$$\frac{[4]\,[5]\,[6]}{120}\,\{u_0 + (\Delta u_{-2} - \Delta u_1)\} = u_0.$$

Prove that this is approximately true.

26. Express $\{[3] + [5] - [7]\}\,u_0$ in terms of $u_{-3}, u_{-1}, u_0, u_1, u_3$, and hence prove that

$$\frac{[5]\,[13]}{65}\,\{[3] + [5] - [7]\}\,u_0 \text{ reproduces } u_0 \text{ to third differences.}$$

27. If $w_n = [5]\,u_n$, prove King's formula:

$$u_0 = \cdot 2 w_0 - \cdot 008 \Delta^2 w_{-1},$$

fourth and higher differences being neglected.

CHAPTER IX

FUNCTIONS AND LIMITS

1. In Chapter II a function was defined as a varying expression depending for its value on the values of one or more dependent variables. Certain simple functions have occurred in the problems of finite differences: before proceeding to a consideration of the infinitesimal calculus, it will be necessary, however, to investigate more closely the different classes of functions and their properties.

2. Algebraic functions.

A form of function which will already be familiar to the student, both in algebra and in finite differences, is a rational integral function of the nth degree in x.

A function $y = f(x)$ is an *algebraic function* of x if it is the root of an equation of the form

$$\alpha + \beta y + \gamma y^2 + \ldots + \kappa y^n + \ldots = 0,$$

where the coefficients α, β, γ, ... κ, ... are rational integral functions of x. In such cases y will usually have more than one value for any given value of x. y is then called a multiple-valued function of x. A simple example is $y^2 + 2\alpha y + \beta = 0$, where α, β are functions of x: for any value of x, y may have either of the values

$$- \alpha \pm (\alpha^2 - \beta)^{\frac{1}{2}}.$$

In the majority of examples that will occur subsequently the algebraic functions involved will be defined by simple forms of equations (e.g.

$$ax + by + c = 0; \quad y^2 - 4ax = 0; \quad x^2 + y^2 = r^2),$$

and it will generally be unnecessary to consider the multiple-valued function $Ay^n + By^{n-1} + \ldots = 0$.

The relation between a function of x and its argument may be expressed in one of two different forms. Consider for example the function y defined by $y = f(x) = a + bx + cx^2 + dx^3 = 0$. For any value of x the value of y becomes evident by simple substitution. Where this is so, y is said to be an *explicit* function of x. On the other hand, if the relation connecting x and y is of the form $\phi(x, y) = a + bxy + cx^2y + dy^3 = 0$, we cannot find y by an immediate substitution of a value of x. A further process is necessary—in this example the solution of a cubic equation in y— before the value or values of y can be obtained. $\phi(x, y) = 0$ defines an *implicit* function of x and y. It should be noted that plane curves can be represented either by an explicit function of one variable, $y = f(x)$; or by an implicit function of two variables defined by $\phi(x, y) = 0$. Similarly, an explicit function of two variables, $z = f(x, y)$ and an implicit function of three variables defined by $\phi(x, y, z) = 0$ represent surfaces in three-dimensional geometry.

A familiar type of rational integral function to which reference has already been made (Chap. II, p. 60) is a homogeneous function.

$f(x, y, z, ...)$ is a homogeneous function of the nth degree in $x, y, z, ...$ if, when the variables $x, y, z, ...$ are replaced by $\lambda x, \lambda y, \lambda z, ...$ respectively, the resulting function is $\lambda^n f(x, y, z, ...)$. A simple example is

$$L(x^3 + y^3 + z^3) + M(x^2y + y^2z + z^2x + xy^2 + yz^2 + zx^2)$$
$$+ Nxyz;$$

this is a homogeneous function of the third degree in x, y and z.

3. Transcendental functions.

Any function that is not an algebraic function is called a *transcendental function*. Examples that occur at once are the trigonometrical ratios $\sin x$, $\cos x$, etc., and the exponential and logarithmic functions e^x, $\log x$. Since c^x is also an exponential function, $y = f(x) = a + bc^x$ is a transcendental function. The forms $a + bc^x$ and $a + bx + kc^x$ are of frequent occurrence in actuarial processes.

4. Rates.

Suppose that successive values of a function y and its argument x are given by the table

x	a	b	c	d	...
y	a'	b'	c'	d'	...

For the first interval, $\Delta x = b - a$, and $\Delta y = b' - a'$: for the second interval $\Delta x = c - b$, $\Delta y = c' - b'$, ... and so on. If for every interval, whatever the values of a, b, c, d, ..., $\Delta y/\Delta x$ is constant, then y is said to vary at a *constant rate* with respect to x.

It is evident that this constant variation will occur only in a limited number of instances. A well-known example is that of uniform motion in a straight line. If x represents time-intervals and y distance-intervals, the ratio $\Delta y/\Delta x$ represents the speed of the moving body, and if this ratio is constant, the body is said to be moving uniformly or at a constant rate.

More commonly, rates will be variable and the successive values of $\Delta y/\Delta x$ will not be equal. We can, however, assign a meaning to $\Delta y/\Delta x$ by considering each interval separately. For example, giving numerical values to x and y, uniform variation is illustrated by

$$
\begin{array}{ccccc}
x & 1 & 2 & 3 & 4 & \cdots \\
y & 5 & 10 & 15 & 20 & \cdots
\end{array}
$$

for $\Delta y/\Delta x = 5 = $ constant.

On the other hand, if corresponding values of x and y are

$$
\begin{array}{ccccc}
x & 1 & 2 & 3 & 4 & \cdots \\
y & 5 & 12 & 30 & 60 & \cdots
\end{array}
$$

$\Delta y/\Delta x$ takes the values 7, 18, 30, ... for successive intervals, and is variable. If, however, we were to consider the range 1 to 4 for x, we could say that over this range of values of x, y increases from 5 to 60, and that the average rate of increase of y over this range $= (60 - 5)/(4 - 1) = 55/3$.

We are led therefore to the following definition:

Given corresponding increments h and k in the values of x and y for the function $y = f(x)$, the average rate of variation of y with x is the uniform rate which would give an increment k in the value of y for the increment h in x.

5. The average rate of variation over an interval has been illustrated above by a body moving with variable speed. This is the speed over an interval of time, and its meaning can easily be appreciated. Another conception of the term " speed " is that of speed at a particular moment of time. Suppose that the distance travelled by a moving body varies with the square of the time that has elapsed since the beginning of the motion, so that $s = t^2$. The average speed over an interval Δt will be

$$\frac{(t + \Delta t)^2 - t^2}{(t + \Delta t) - t} \quad \text{or} \quad 2t + \Delta t.$$

Giving Δt the values 1, $\cdot 1$, $\cdot 01$, $\cdot 001$, $\ldots$ we may construct the following table:

Interval	t to $t + 1$	t to $t + \cdot 1$	t to $t + \cdot 01$	t to $t + \cdot 001$ ...
Average speed over interval	$2t + 1$	$2t + \cdot 1$	$2t + \cdot 01$	$2t + \cdot 001$ ...

Now the average speed over an interval tends to become more nearly equal to the speed at the beginning of the interval as the interval is reduced. The average speed over the interval tends to the value $2t$, and this must therefore be the value of the speed at the beginning of the interval.

More generally, the average rate of variation over an interval tends to the rate of change at a particular point (the beginning of the interval) as the interval is reduced.

It should be noted that although the value of

$$\frac{(t + \Delta t)^2 - t^2}{(t + \Delta t) - t}$$

tends to $2t$ as Δt is reduced, we cannot put $\Delta t = 0$ at once, for we then obtain $\frac{0}{0}$ which is meaningless in algebra. (This is what might be expected, for the average speed over a non-existent interval has no meaning.)

Suppose now that for the function $y = f(x)$ we take two successive values of the argument, namely, x and $x + h$. Then the average rate of variation of $f(x)$ in the interval x to $x + h$ will be

$$\frac{f(x + h) - f(x)}{(x + h) - x} = \frac{f(x + h) - f(x)}{h},$$

which tends to the rate of change of $f(x)$ at the point x as h is reduced. This rate of change is therefore the *limiting value* of the average rate of change as h tends to zero, and we must reach this limiting value by a process other than by direct substitution of $h = 0$ in the algebraic expression.

6. Certain limiting values may be illustrated by the application of the methods of elementary geometry.

Example 1.

Let A be a fixed point on a plane curve and let B_1AC_1 be any straight line drawn through A cutting the curve again at B_1. Let B_1 move down the curve towards A so that the secant takes up the successive positions

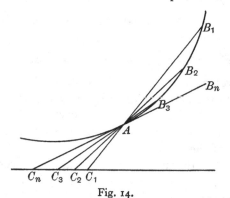

Fig. 14.

$B_2AC_2, B_3AC_3, \ldots$. Then the lengths of the secants cut off by the curve, namely $B_1A, B_2A, B_3A, \ldots$, become successively smaller. When, however, the two points BA virtually coincide, the secant approaches the position B_nAC_n, the tangent to the curve at the point A. In other words, the tangent B_nAC_n is the limiting position of the secant B_rAC_r as B moves along the curve to A.

Example 2.

Prove that $\sin\theta < \theta < \tan\theta$.

Let KOA be the angle $\theta\left(<\dfrac{\pi}{2}\right)$.

Draw a circle with OA as radius and let AB be a chord of the circle. Draw AT, BT, the tangents to the circle at A and B respectively, meeting at T. Then evidently the chord $AB < \text{arc } AB < AT + TB$;

i.e. $HA < \text{arc } AK < AT$.

$\therefore \quad \dfrac{HA}{OA} < \dfrac{\text{arc } AK}{\text{radius } OA} < \dfrac{AT}{OA}$,

or $\sin\theta < \theta < \tan\theta$.

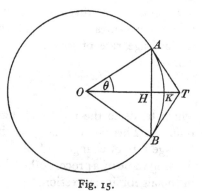

Fig. 15.

From these inequalities we have

$$1 < \frac{\theta}{\sin \theta} < \frac{1}{\cos \theta};$$

i.e. $$1 > \frac{\sin \theta}{\theta} > \cos \theta.$$

Therefore $\frac{\sin \theta}{\theta}$ lies between 1 and $\cos \theta$. In the limiting case when θ is zero, $\cos \theta$ is 1. (See Chapter 1, para. 11.)

Therefore when θ approaches the limit zero, $\frac{\sin \theta}{\theta}$ has 1 as its limiting value.

7. Continuous functions.

Before proceeding further to the consideration of limits and limiting values it is necessary to distinguish between those functions which vary continuously between two values of the argument and those which do not.

If we wished to plot the curve of the function $y = x^2$ for all real values of x, we could give x certain values, and by substituting these values in the equation $y = x^2$ we could obtain the corresponding values of y. It would be necessary to plot only a limited number of points (x, y) and by drawing a smooth curve through these points the graph of the function $y = x^2$ would result. Suppose, however, that a limitation were imposed upon the values of x, namely, that x

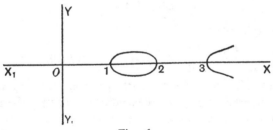

Fig. 16.

should always be a positive integer. The graphical representation of the values of x and y would be a series of isolated points, and a curve could not be drawn between any two successive values of (x, y).

Again, consider the function $y^2 = (x - 1)(x - 2)(x - 3)$. If y is to be real we have the following conditions (1) x must not be less than 1; (2) x must not lie between the values $x = 2$ and $x = 3$. This second condition shows that while x may have any value between 1 and 2 and any value greater than 3, for real values of y, there is no value of y corresponding to values of x between 2 and 3. y is said to be discontinuous between the values $x = 2$ and $x = 3$, and the curve will take the above shape (Fig. 16).

A type of function which, for a certain value of the variable, ceases to be continuous is $y = 1/x$. If x be zero, the function takes the form $1/0$ which is, strictly speaking, meaningless. As, however, $1/x$ becomes successively greater on decreasing x, it is possible to make $1/x$ greater than any finite value, by making x sufficiently small. The function is then said to "tend to infinity" or to "increase indefinitely" as x tends to zero.

8. Limits.

We are now in a position to give a clearer definition of what is meant by a limit. A simple definition is as follows:

If $y = f(x)$ and y tends continuously towards a certain value l, and can be made to differ as little as we please from that value by making x approach some fixed value a, then l is said to be the limiting value of $f(x)$ as x tends to the value a.

This may be expressed shortly as

$$\underset{x \to a}{\text{Lt}} \ f(x) = l.$$

For example, we have

$$\underset{h \to 0}{\text{Lt}} \ \frac{f(x + h) - f(x)}{h} = 2x \ \text{when} \ f(x) = x^2.$$

This definition is not sufficiently precise, and may prove inadequate in certain instances. Consider for example the following illustration.

The curve $y = \dfrac{\sin x}{x}$ is represented geometrically (see Fig. 17).

For large values of x the curve becomes indistinguishable from the axis of x and the value of y tends to zero, notwithstanding that, however large x may be, y may be always increasing numerically. It is obvious that the phrase "tends continuously towards a certain value *l*" does not mean "constantly increases (or decreases) to the value *l*."

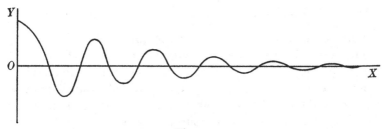

Fig. 17.

Now take the curve $y = \sin x$.

Here y does not tend to a limit as x becomes indefinitely great. It might be claimed, however, that y (i.e. $\sin x$) tends to unity for sufficiently large values of x. If this were countered by the argument that for a very large value of x, $\sin x$ was, say, $\frac{1}{2}$, the reply might be that the value of x was not sufficiently large, and that by

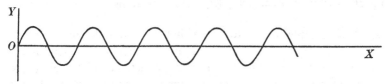

Fig. 18.

taking a larger value of x, $\sin x$ would differ from unity by as little as we pleased. The rejoinder to this would be that by taking a still larger value of x, $\sin x$ could be made to differ from $\frac{1}{2}$, or zero, or $-\frac{1}{2}$, etc. by as little as we pleased; and so on.

By the statement that $\underset{x \to \infty}{\mathrm{Lt}} \dfrac{\sin x}{x}$ is zero and that $\dfrac{\sin x}{x}$ can be made to differ from zero by as little as we please, we imply that, given a number, say, ·01, we must be able to find a value of x such that, *for all greater values of x,* $\dfrac{\sin x}{x}$ will differ from zero by less than ·01. In other words, the whole of the graph of $y = \dfrac{\sin x}{x}$ after this point will be contained within the two ordinates $y = ·01$ and $y = -·01$. Similarly, if the number ·001 were chosen, a value of

x must be found such that for all greater values of x, the graph will be contained in the limits $y = \cdot 001$ and $y = - \cdot 001$.

It is clear that the graph of $y = \dfrac{\sin x}{x}$ would satisfy such a series of tests, but that the graph of $y = \sin x$ would not.

This leads directly to the more rigorous definition of a limit:

Let $f(x)$ be a function such that x lies between two fixed values a and b (i.e. $a \leqslant x \leqslant b$) and let x' be any value of x satisfying these conditions. Then if l be a number such that corresponding to an arbitrary positive number ϵ, a positive number η can be found such that $f(x)$ differs from l by less than ϵ whenever $x - x' < \eta$, then l is said to be the limit of $f(x)$ as $x \to x'$.

It should be emphasized that the limit of $f(x)$ as $x \to a$ is not defined as a value of $f(x)$, and in particular is not necessarily equal to $f(a)$. It is a quantity quite distinct from the values of $f(x)$ although it is defined by means of these values in the neighbourhood of $x = a$. As a rule, the limit of $f(x)$ as $x \to a$ is required in circumstances in which $f(a)$ has no meaning.

9. It is a simple matter to prove that the algebraic sum, product or quotient of the limits of any finite number of functions is the limit of the sum, product or quotient respectively of the functions, provided that, when considering quotients, the limit of the divisor is not zero. The definition of a limit and these corollaries form the basis of the infinitesimal calculus.

The following elementary examples are typical of the methods employed in the evaluation of limits.

Example 3.

Find
$$\operatorname*{Lt}_{x \to a} \frac{x^3 - a^3}{x - a}.$$

We may not put $x = a$ immediately, for in that event the divisor will be zero and we shall arrive at the form $\frac{0}{0}$. If we divide throughout by $x - a$ the function becomes $x^2 + ax + a^2$ and if we let $x \to a$ in this expression we obtain $3a^2$. This is the limit when $x \to a$ of $\dfrac{x^3 - a^3}{x - a}$. Although it should be proved that a positive number η can be found such that $\dfrac{x^3 - a^3}{x - a} - 3a^2$ is less than any arbitrary number ϵ whenever

$x - a < \eta$, it may be taken for granted that this criterion holds in all the examples that will be dealt with subsequently, and that we may proceed straight to the limit as above.

Example 4.

Find $\underset{n \to \infty}{\text{Lt}} \left[\dfrac{1}{n^4} \Sigma n^3 \right]$ where n is a positive integer.

$$\Sigma n^3 = 1^3 + 2^3 + 3^3 + \ldots + n^3 = \frac{n^2 (n + 1)^2}{4} = \frac{n^2 + 2n^3 + n^4}{4}.$$

$$\therefore \quad \frac{1}{n} \Sigma n^3 = \frac{1}{4} \left[\frac{1}{n^2} + \frac{2}{n} + 1 \right] = \frac{1}{4n^2} + \frac{1}{2n} + \frac{1}{4}.$$

$$\therefore \quad \underset{n \to \infty}{\text{Lt}} \frac{1}{n^4} \Sigma n^3 = \underset{n \to \infty}{\text{Lt}} \frac{1}{4n^2} + \underset{n \to \infty}{\text{Lt}} \frac{1}{2n} + \underset{n \to \infty}{\text{Lt}} \frac{1}{4}$$

by the proposition above

$$= 0 + 0 + \tfrac{1}{4}$$
$$= \tfrac{1}{4}.$$

Example 5.

Show that $\qquad \underset{x \to 1}{\text{Lt}} \dfrac{x^6 - 5x + 4}{x^3 - 2x + 1} = 1.$

If we put $x = 1$ immediately we obtain the form $\frac{0}{0}$. As in Example 3, we could divide numerator and denominator by $x - 1$ and then find the limit. An alternative method is as follows:

Put $x = 1 + h$; then the function becomes a function of h instead of a function of x and we have to find the limit of the new function when $h \to 0$.

$$\frac{x^6 - 5x + 4}{x^3 - 2x + 1} = \frac{(1 + h)^6 - 5(1 + h) + 4}{(1 + h)^3 - 2(1 + h) + 1}$$

$$= \frac{1 + 6h + 15h^2 + \ldots - 5 - 5h + 4}{1 + 3h + 3h^2 + h^3 - 2 - 2h + 1}$$

$$= \frac{h + 15h^2 + \ldots}{h + 3h^2 + \ldots}$$

$$= \frac{1 + 15h + \ldots}{1 + 3h + \ldots}$$

and the limit of this expression when $h \to 0$ is 1.

10. Limit of a sequence.

Let $u_1 + u_2 + u_3 + u_4 + \ldots$ represent a sequence of numbers (real or imaginary). Then if successive values of u tend to be smaller and smaller the sum of the series may tend to approximate more and more to some fixed number. For example, the series

$$1 + \tfrac{1}{2} + (\tfrac{1}{2})^2 + (\tfrac{1}{2})^3 + \ldots + (\tfrac{1}{2})^{n-1} = [1 - (\tfrac{1}{2})^n]/(1 - \tfrac{1}{2}) = 2 - (\tfrac{1}{2})^{n-1},$$

so that the sum to n terms differs from 2 by the small quantity $(\tfrac{1}{2})^{n-1}$.

The larger the value of n, the more nearly the sum to n terms is equal to 2; the sum $\to 2$ as $n \to \infty$.

A series of a different type is

$$1 + 2 + 3 + 4 + \ldots + n.$$

The sum to n terms is $\tfrac{1}{2}n\,(n + 1)$, and there is no fixed number to which the sum of the series tends: if n be very large $\tfrac{1}{2}n\,(n + 1)$ is very large.

In the first example the limit of the sequence as n increases indefinitely is said to be 2, and the series is said to be *convergent*. In the second example there is no limit to the sum of the series, and the series is said to be *divergent*.

The definition of the limit of a sequence is as follows:

If $u_1, u_2, u_3, \ldots u_n, \ldots$ be an unending sequence of real or imaginary numbers, and if a number l exists such that corresponding to every positive number ϵ (however small) a number k can be found such that u_n differs from l by less than ϵ for all values of $n > k$, the sequence $u_1, u_2, u_3, \ldots u_n, \ldots$ is said to tend to the limit l as $n \to \infty$.

The limits of algebraic and other expansions are of the utmost importance in mathematical work, and while it is beyond the present scope to examine fully the convergence or otherwise of even the more important series, reference to them is essential for the proper understanding of the calculus.

11. $\dfrac{(x + h)^n - x^n}{h}$.

If n be a positive integer, this expression becomes

$$\tfrac{1}{h}\,[n_1 h x^{n-1} + n_2 h^2 x^{n-2} + n_3 h^3 x^{n-3} + \ldots + h^n]$$
$$= n_1 x^{n-1} + n_2 h x^{n-2} + n_3 h^2 x^{n-3} + \ldots + h^{n-1},$$

which evidently tends to $n x^{n-1}$ when $h \to 0$.

Suppose, however, that n be other than a positive integer. Then there will not be a limited number of terms, and we have

$$\mathop{\mathrm{Lt}}_{h \to 0} \frac{(x+h)^n - x^n}{h} = \mathop{\mathrm{Lt}}_{h \to 0} x^n \left[\frac{\left(1 + \dfrac{h}{x}\right)^n - 1}{h} \right]$$

$$= \mathop{\mathrm{Lt}}_{h \to 0} \frac{x^n}{h} \left[n_1 \left(\frac{h}{x}\right) + n_2 \left(\frac{h}{x}\right)^2 + n_3 \left(\frac{h}{x}\right)^3 + \ldots \right].$$

This involves a *double limit,* for the number of terms inside the bracket is not finite, and we are not entitled to assume that the limit of the sum of the terms is equal to the sum of the limits of the terms.

The investigation of a double limit requires further mathematical analysis, and the consideration of the limit of the above expression when n is not a positive integer will be deferred to a later chapter.

12. $\left(1 + \dfrac{1}{n}\right)^n.$

For all values of n it may be shown that

$$\mathop{\mathrm{Lt}}_{n \to \infty} \left(1 + \frac{1}{n}\right)^n$$

lies between

$$1 + 1 + \frac{1}{2!} + \frac{1}{3!} + \ldots + \frac{1}{n!}$$

and
$$1 + 1 + \frac{1}{2!} + \frac{1}{3!} + \ldots + \frac{1}{n!} + \frac{1}{n.n!}.$$

The expression

$$\mathop{\mathrm{Lt}}_{n \to \infty} \left(1 + \frac{1}{n}\right)^n$$

is denoted by e, so that

$$e = 1 + 1 + \frac{1}{2!} + \frac{1}{3!} + \ldots + \frac{1}{n!} + R,$$

where
$$R < \frac{1}{n.n!}.$$

Since, however,
$$\mathop{\mathrm{Lt}}_{n \to \infty} \frac{1}{n.n!}$$

is zero, e may be considered as the sum of the infinite series

$$1 + 1 + \frac{1}{2!} + \frac{1}{3!} + \ldots + \frac{1}{n!} + \ldots.$$

Again it may be shown that

$$\underset{n \to \infty}{\mathrm{Lt}} \left(\mathrm{I} + \frac{x}{n}\right)^n > \mathrm{I} + x + \frac{x^2}{2!} + \frac{x^3}{3!} + \ldots + \frac{x^n}{n!},$$

but
$$< \mathrm{I} + x + \frac{x^2}{2!} + \frac{x^3}{3!} + \ldots + \frac{x^n}{n!} + \frac{x^{n+1}}{(n + \mathrm{I} - x)\,n!},$$

and that
$$e^x = \underset{n \to \infty}{\mathrm{Lt}} \left(\mathrm{I} + \frac{x}{n}\right)^n = \mathrm{I} + x + \frac{x^2}{2!} + \frac{x^3}{3!} + \ldots + \frac{x^n}{n!} + \ldots,$$

if x is not zero.

In the inequalities above put $x = \mathrm{I}$.

Then
$$e^x > \mathrm{I} + x \quad \text{and} \quad < \mathrm{I} + x + \frac{x^2}{(2 - x)},$$

$$\therefore \quad e^x - \mathrm{I} > x \quad \text{and} \quad < x + \frac{x^2}{2 - x},$$

i.e.
$$\frac{e^x - \mathrm{I}}{x} > \mathrm{I} \quad \text{and} \quad < \mathrm{I} + \frac{x}{2 - x},$$

so that if x be positive $\underset{x \to 0}{\mathrm{Lt}} \dfrac{e^x - \mathrm{I}}{x} = \mathrm{I}$.

If x is negative we can replace x by $- y$ and obtain

$$\underset{x \to 0}{\mathrm{Lt}} \frac{e^x - \mathrm{I}}{x} = \underset{y \to 0}{\mathrm{Lt}} \frac{e^{-y} - \mathrm{I}}{- y} = \underset{y \to 0}{\mathrm{Lt}} \frac{\mathrm{I}}{e^y} \cdot \frac{e^y - \mathrm{I}}{y} = \mathrm{I}.$$

13. We may now proceed to a more formal definition of a continuous function.

(i) For continuity at a particular value of x, say at $x = a$, $f(a)$ must be a finite number (not infinity) and $\underset{x \to a}{\mathrm{Lt}} f(x)$ must be equal to $f(a)$.

(ii) $f(x)$ is continuous for a given range from $x = a$ to $x = b$ if it is continuous for every value of x between a and b, i.e. for all values of x such that $a \leqslant x \leqslant b$.

(It should be noted that $\underset{x \to a}{\mathrm{Lt}} f(x)$ must equal $f(a)$ whether x approaches a from the right or from the left.)

If the criterion (i) does not hold for the point whose abscissa is a, then the function is said to be discontinuous at the point.

For example, let $y = \mathrm{I}/x$, and let x pass through all values between $x = - \mathrm{I}$ and $x = \mathrm{I}$. Then at one point intermediate between -1 and $+1$, namely where $x = 0$, y takes the value $1/0$, which is not a finite number. The function is therefore discontinuous at the point $x = 0$ (cf. para. 7 above).

14. Asymptotes.

Consider the curve $\qquad y = \dfrac{x^2}{(x-1)^2}$.

Here y tends to infinity as $x \to 1$, and since we may write the equation as $y = \dfrac{1}{[1 - 1/x]^2}$, y tends to the value 1 when x tends to infinity in either direction.

The curve is of the following shape.

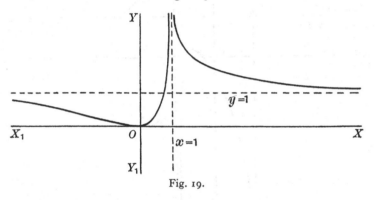

Fig. 19.

Discontinuities in the value of y when $x = 1$ and of x when $y = 1$ are apparent. It will be seen that the curve gradually approaches indefinitely near to the straight lines $x = 1$ and $y = 1$ but does not actually meet them at any finite distance from the origin.

Such lines are called *asymptotes* to the curve.

Example 6.

Find the asymptotes to the curve $y = \dfrac{(3x-1)(x-2)}{(x-3)(x+3)}$.

The equation of the curve may be written

$$y = 3 + \frac{29 - 7x}{(x-3)(x+3)} = 3 + \frac{4}{3(x-3)} + \frac{25}{3(x+3)}.$$

Then if x tend to infinity in either direction, the curve approaches the straight line $y = 3$. Hence $y = 3$ is an asymptote.

Further, if x is positive and greater than 29/7, the value of y is less than 3. Therefore, on the right the curve approaches $y = 3$ from underneath. If x is negative, on the left the curve approaches $y = 3$ from above.

Again, from the second form of the equation to the curve, it will be seen that $x = 3$ and $x = -3$ are asymptotes to the curve, since the curve gradually approaches these straight lines but does not meet them at a finite distance from the origin.

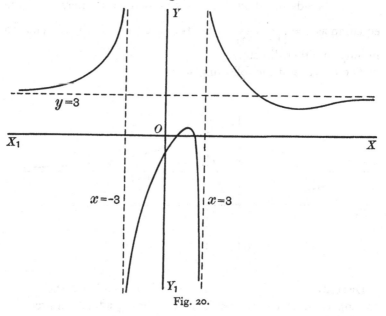

Fig. 20.

EXAMPLES 9

1. Find $\displaystyle \operatorname*{Lt}_{x \to a} \frac{x^p - a^p}{x^q - a^q}$ where p and q are positive integers.

2. Obtain $\displaystyle \sum_{r=1}^{r=n} \frac{r^2}{n^2}$ and hence show that the limit of the sum when $n \to \infty$ is finite.

3. Evaluate $\displaystyle \operatorname*{Lt}_{x \to 0} \frac{a^x - 1 - x \log a}{x^2}$.

4. Prove that $\displaystyle \operatorname*{Lt}_{\theta \to 0} \frac{\sin r\theta}{\theta} = r$.

5. Find the limiting value of
$$\sqrt{x^4 + ax^2 + bx + c} - \sqrt{x^4 + kx^2 + mx + n}$$
when n is indefinitely increased.

6. Prove that $1 > \cos\theta > 1 - \tfrac{1}{2}\theta^2$.

7. Show that $\underset{x\to 0}{\text{Lt}}\ x\log x = 0$ and hence find the limit of $\sin x \log x$ as $x \to 0$.

Find the following limiting values:

8. $\underset{x\to\infty}{\text{Lt}}\ \{x\sqrt{x^2+a^2} - \sqrt{x^4+a^4}\}$.

9. $\underset{x\to b}{\text{Lt}}\ \dfrac{(2x + b)^{\frac{1}{2}} - (3x)^{\frac{1}{2}}}{(x + 3b)^{\frac{1}{2}} - 2\,(x)^{\frac{1}{2}}}$.

10. $\underset{x\to\infty}{\text{Lt}}\ \sqrt{x}\,(\sqrt{x + 1} - \sqrt{x})$.

11. $\underset{x\to 1}{\text{Lt}}\ \dfrac{x^{\frac{3}{2}} - 1 + (x - 1)^{\frac{3}{2}}}{(x^2 - 1)^{\frac{3}{2}} - x + 1}$.

12. $\underset{x\to 0}{\text{Lt}}\ \dfrac{e^{ax} - e^{bx}}{a^{ex} - b^{ex}}$.

13. $\underset{x\to 0}{\text{Lt}}\ \tan m\theta \cot n\theta$.

14. $\underset{x\to 0}{\text{Lt}}\ x^x$.

15. $\underset{x\to a}{\text{Lt}}\ \dfrac{(3x - a)^{\frac{1}{2}} - (x + a)^{\frac{1}{2}}}{x - a}$.

16. $\underset{y\to 0}{\text{Lt}}\ \dfrac{\log(1 + y + y^2)}{y^2(1 - 2y)}$.

17. $\underset{n\to\infty}{\text{Lt}}\ \left[\left(1 + \dfrac{1}{n}\right)^n - \left(1 + \dfrac{1}{n}\right)\right]^{-n}$.

18. Show that $\dfrac{1 \cdot 3 \cdot 5 \ldots 2n - 1}{2 \cdot 4 \cdot 6 \ldots 2n} < \dfrac{2 \cdot 4 \cdot 6 \ldots 2n}{3 \cdot 5 \cdot 7 \ldots 2n + 1}$

and that $\dfrac{3 \cdot 5 \cdot 7 \ldots 2n + 1}{2 \cdot 4 \cdot 6 \ldots 2n} > \dfrac{4 \cdot 6 \cdot 8 \ldots 2n + 2}{3 \cdot 5 \cdot 7 \ldots 2n + 1}$.

19. From the inequalities in Question 18 prove that
$$\underset{n\to\infty}{\text{Lt}}\ \dfrac{1 \cdot 3 \cdot 5 \ldots 2n - 1}{2 \cdot 4 \cdot 6 \ldots 2n} = 0$$

and
$$\underset{n\to\infty}{\text{Lt}}\ \dfrac{3 \cdot 5 \cdot 7 \ldots 2n + 1}{2 \cdot 4 \cdot 6 \ldots 2n} = \infty .$$

Prove also that the limit when $n \to \infty$ of the product of these two functions lies between $\tfrac{1}{2}$ and 1.

20. Evaluate $\underset{n\to\infty}{\text{Lt}}\ n\left[1 - \log\left(1 + \dfrac{1}{n}\right)^{n-1}\right]$.

CHAPTER X

DIFFERENTIAL CALCULUS

DEFINITIONS; STANDARD FORMS; SUCCESSIVE DIFFERENTIATION

1. We have seen in the previous chapter that if $y = f(x)$ be a continuous function of x, the average rate of change of y with x is

$$\frac{f(x+h) - f(x)}{h},$$

or $\Delta y / \Delta x$, where $\Delta x = h$.

The limit of this function when the interval tends to zero (which we may call the rate of change) is called the differential coefficient of y with respect to x. If we denote this result by Dy, we have

$$Dy = \operatorname*{Lt}_{\Delta x \to 0} \Delta y / \Delta x = \operatorname*{Lt}_{h \to 0} \frac{f(x+h) - f(x)}{h},$$

and we are said to have "differentiated y with respect to x."

The usual notation for the differential coefficient is $\frac{dy}{dx}$, where $\frac{d}{dx}$ is an operator analogous to Δ, E, Σ, ... in finite differences. For convenience in working alternative methods of denoting $\frac{dy}{dx}$ are used. For example,

$$y', \dot{y}, Dy; \quad f'(x), Df(x), \frac{d}{dx} f(x),$$

represent the same result.

It should be noted that, although $\Delta y / \Delta x$ is the result of the division of a definite quantity Δy by another definite quantity Δx, $\frac{dy}{dx}$ represents an operation performed on the function y, the operator being $\frac{d}{dx}$. At this stage neither dy nor dx should be considered to have a separate meaning.

The differential coefficient of y with respect to x is sometimes called the "first derivative" or the "first derived function" of y with respect to x.

2. Before proceeding to examine the values of the differential coefficients of various functions, it will be of advantage to consider the geometrical interpretation of the operation of differentiation.

Let B_1AB represent the continuous curve $y = f(x)$ and let the coordinates of a point A on the curve be (x, y) or $\{x, f(x)\}$. Let B be a near point on the curve whose coordinates are $\{x + h, f(x + h)\}$.

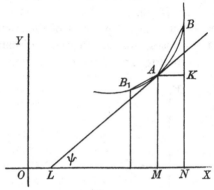

Fig. 21.

Then it is evident from the figure that, if θ be the angle BAK,

$$\tan \theta = BK/AK = \frac{BN - NK}{MN} = \frac{BN - MA}{ON - OM}$$

$$= \frac{f(x + h) - f(x)}{h}.$$

Now as the point B moves along the curve so as ultimately to coincide with the point A, the secant BA takes up the position of the tangent AL to the curve (see Ex. 1 of Chapter IX). The angle θ then becomes the angle ψ which the tangent AL makes with the axis of x.

But the limit of $\dfrac{f(x + h) - f(x)}{h}$ when B coincides with A is the limit of this expression as $h \to 0$.

Also $\qquad \underset{h \to 0}{\mathrm{Lt}} \dfrac{f(x + h) - f(x)}{h} = \dfrac{d}{dx} f(x).$

Therefore $\qquad \dfrac{d}{dx} f(x) = \tan \psi$

= the tangent of the angle that the tangent to the curve $y = f(x)$
at the point (x, y) makes with the x-axis.

The tangent to a curve at any point measures the slope or gradient of the curve at that point. The differential coefficient of y with respect to x is often referred to as the gradient of the curve $y = f(x)$ at the point (x, y).

It may happen that near the point A of the curve the curve is continuous as x increases, but that there is a discontinuity in the other direction—as in Fig. 22. If we were to consider the effect

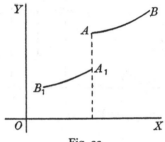

Fig. 22.

of allowing the point B_1 to approach A_1—the x coordinate of which is the same as that of the point A—the value of the differential coefficient would be different from that found by assuming B to coincide with A.

For this reason it is probably better to define the differential coefficient thus:

If $f(x)$ be a continuous function of x and if $\underset{h \to 0}{\mathrm{Lt}} \dfrac{f(x+h) - f(x)}{h}$ is equal to $\underset{h \to 0}{\mathrm{Lt}} \dfrac{f(x) - f(x-h)}{h}$, then either of these limits is called the differential coefficient of y with respect to x.

Another method of obtaining $\dfrac{dy}{dx}$ (when it exists) is to consider two points

$$B_1 \quad \{(x - h),\ f(x - h)\}$$

and $\qquad B \quad \{(x + h),\ f(x + h)\}$

which approach A simultaneously. By reference to Fig. 21 it will be seen that

$$\tan \psi = \frac{dy}{dx} = \operatorname*{Lt}_{h \to 0} \frac{f(x+h) - f(x-h)}{2h}.$$

This form is of advantage when the evaluation of

$$f(x+h) - f(x-h)$$

is simpler than the evaluation of $f(x+h) - f(x)$.

3. The following propositions are of general application:

(i) If a is any constant, then $\frac{da}{dx} = 0$.

This is obvious, since there can be no rate of change of a constant quantity.

(ii) $\frac{d}{dx} af(x) = a \frac{d}{dx} f(x)$, where a is a constant.

$$\frac{d}{dx} af(x) = \operatorname*{Lt}_{h \to 0} \frac{af(x+h) - af(x)}{h}$$

$$= a \operatorname*{Lt}_{h \to 0} \frac{f(x+h) - f(x)}{h}$$

$$= a \frac{d}{dx} f(x).$$

(iii) If $\qquad y = f(x) + \phi(x) + \psi(x) + \dots,$

then $\qquad \dfrac{dy}{dx} = \dfrac{d}{dx} f(x) + \dfrac{d}{dx} \phi(x) + \dfrac{d}{dx} \psi(x) + \dots.$

Since $\qquad y = f(x) + \phi(x) + \psi(x) + \dots,$

$$\Delta y = \Delta f(x) + \Delta \phi(x) + \Delta \psi(x) + \dots.$$

$$\therefore \frac{\Delta y}{\Delta x} = \frac{\Delta f(x)}{\Delta x} + \frac{\Delta \phi(x)}{\Delta x} + \frac{\Delta \psi(x)}{\Delta x} + \dots.$$

In the limit $\Delta x \to 0$, we have

$$\frac{dy}{dx} = \frac{d}{dx} f(x) + \frac{d}{dx} \phi(x) + \frac{d}{dx} \psi(x) + \dots.$$

(iv) If $y = uv$, where u, v are both functions of x, then

$$\frac{dy}{dx} = u \frac{dv}{dx} + v \frac{du}{dx}.$$

$$\Delta y = \Delta (uv)$$
$$= (u + \Delta u) (v + \Delta v) - uv$$
$$= u\Delta v + v\Delta u + \Delta u\Delta v.$$
$$\therefore \quad \frac{\Delta y}{\Delta x} = u \frac{\Delta v}{\Delta x} + v \frac{\Delta u}{\Delta x} + \Delta u \frac{\Delta v}{\Delta x}$$
$$= (u + \Delta u) \frac{\Delta v}{\Delta x} + v \frac{\Delta u}{\Delta x}.$$

Therefore since in the limit $\Delta x \to 0$, $u + \Delta u$ will become u,

$$\frac{dy}{dx} = u \frac{dv}{dx} + v \frac{du}{dx}.$$

A slightly different proof follows from the relation established in para. 4 of Chapter VIII:

$$\Delta y = \Delta u_x v_x = v_x \Delta u_x + u_{x+\Delta x} \Delta v_x \text{ (where the interval of differencing is } \Delta x).$$

$$\therefore \quad \frac{\Delta y}{\Delta x} = v_x \frac{\Delta u_x}{\Delta x} + u_{x+\Delta x} \frac{\Delta v_x}{\Delta x},$$

so that when $\Delta x \to 0$ we have

$$\frac{dy}{dx} = v \frac{du}{dx} + u \frac{dv}{dx},$$

which is the same formula as the above.

As a corollary we have, by successive applications of (iv),

$$\frac{d}{dx} uvw \ldots = uv \ldots \frac{dw}{dx} + vw \ldots \frac{du}{dx} + uw \ldots \frac{dv}{dx} + \ldots.$$

(v) If $y = \dfrac{u}{v}$, then $\dfrac{dy}{dx} = \left\{ \dfrac{v\dfrac{du}{dx} - u\dfrac{dv}{dx}}{v^2} \right\}.$

Now $\qquad \Delta y = \Delta \left(\dfrac{u}{v} \right) = \dfrac{u + \Delta u}{v + \Delta v} - \dfrac{u}{v}$

$$= \frac{(u + \Delta u) v - (v + \Delta v) u}{v (v + \Delta v)}$$

$$= \frac{v\Delta u - u\Delta v}{v (v + \Delta v)}.$$

$$\therefore \frac{\Delta y}{\Delta x} = \frac{v\dfrac{\Delta u}{\Delta x} - u\dfrac{\Delta v}{\Delta x}}{v\,(v + \Delta v)}.$$

I.e.
$$\frac{dy}{dx} = \frac{v\dfrac{du}{dx} - u\dfrac{dv}{dx}}{v^2}$$

when $\Delta x \to 0$.

Putting $u = 1$, we have

$$\frac{d}{dx}\frac{1}{v} = -\frac{1}{v^2}\frac{dv}{dx}.$$

(vi) If y is a function of x and z is a function of y, then

$$\frac{dz}{dx} = \frac{dz}{dy}\cdot\frac{dy}{dx}.$$

Since
$$\frac{\Delta z}{\Delta x} = \frac{\Delta z}{\Delta y}\cdot\frac{\Delta y}{\Delta x},$$

$$\frac{dz}{dx} = \frac{dz}{dy}\cdot\frac{dy}{dx}$$

when $\Delta x \to 0$.

It follows that

$$\frac{dz}{dt} = \frac{dz}{dy}\cdot\frac{dy}{dx}\cdot\frac{dx}{du}\cdot\frac{du}{dv} \cdots \frac{dr}{ds}\cdot\frac{ds}{dt},$$

where s is a function of t, r a function of s, etc.

(vii)
$$\frac{dy}{dx} = \frac{1}{\dfrac{dx}{dy}}.$$

We have
$$\frac{\Delta y}{\Delta x} = \frac{1}{\dfrac{\Delta x}{\Delta y}}.$$

$\therefore$ If $\dfrac{\Delta x}{\Delta y}$ be not equal to zero,

$$\frac{dy}{dx} = \frac{1}{\dfrac{dx}{dy}}.$$

Note. If more than one value of y correspond to a given value of x (e.g. if $y = \sin^{-1} x$), and/or more than one value of z to a given value of y, then in taking the changes in value Δx, Δy, Δz we must keep them consistent in assuming that $\dfrac{\Delta z}{\Delta x} = \dfrac{\Delta z}{\Delta y} \cdot \dfrac{\Delta y}{\Delta x}$, or that

$$\frac{\Delta y}{\Delta x} = \frac{1}{\dfrac{\Delta x}{\Delta y}}.$$

4. Standard forms: Algebraic.

We will now proceed to obtain the differential coefficients of some standard functions.

(i) $y = x^n$.

(a) n a positive integer.

This follows directly from the proof on page 144 where it was shown that

$$\underset{h \to 0}{\mathrm{Lt}}\ \frac{(x + h)^n - x^n}{h} = nx^{n-1}.$$

(b) n a positive fraction.

Let $n = \dfrac{p}{q}$ where p, q are positive integers.

Then
$$y = x^n = x^{p/q}.$$

$$\therefore\ y^q = x^p = z, \text{ say.}$$

We have
$$\left. \begin{aligned} \frac{dz}{dx} &= px^{p-1} \\[2mm] \frac{dz}{dy} &= qy^{q-1} \end{aligned} \right\} \quad \text{from } (a) \text{ above.}$$

and

But
$$\frac{dy}{dx} = \frac{dy}{dz} \cdot \frac{dz}{dx} = \frac{1}{\dfrac{dz}{dy}} \cdot \frac{dz}{dx}$$

$$= \frac{px^{p-1}}{qy^{q-1}} = \frac{p}{q} \cdot \frac{x^p}{y^q} \cdot \frac{y}{x}$$

$$= \frac{p}{q} \cdot \frac{y}{x} = \frac{p}{q} \cdot x^{\frac{p}{q}-1}$$

$$= nx^{n-1}.$$

(c) *n* negative.

Let $n = -m$ where m is positive (integral or fractional).

$$y = x^n = x^{-m} = \frac{1}{x^m}.$$

$$\therefore\ x^m y = 1,$$

and
$$\frac{d}{dx}(x^m y) = mx^{m-1}y + x^m \frac{dy}{dx},$$

since *m* is positive.

But $x^m y = 1 = $ constant.

$$\therefore\ \frac{d}{dx}(x^m y) = 0.$$

$$\therefore\ mx^{m-1}y + x^m \frac{dy}{dx} = 0.$$

$$\therefore\ \frac{dy}{dx} = -\frac{mx^{m-1}y}{x^m} = -\frac{my}{x}$$

$$= nx^{n-1}.$$

I.e. $\dfrac{dx^n}{dx} = nx^{n-1}$ for all values of *n* positive or negative, integral or fractional.

For example,
$$\frac{d}{dx}x^5 = 5x^4,$$

$$\frac{d}{dx}x^{-5} = -5x^{-6},$$

$$\frac{d}{dx}x^{\frac{1}{5}} = \tfrac{1}{5}x^{-\frac{4}{5}},$$

$$\frac{d}{dx}x^{-\frac{1}{5}} = -\tfrac{1}{5}x^{-\frac{6}{5}}.$$

(ii) $y = e^x$.

$$\frac{d}{dx}e^x = \operatorname*{Lt}_{h\to 0}\frac{e^{x+h} - e^x}{h} = e^x \operatorname*{Lt}_{h\to 0}\frac{e^h - 1}{h}$$

$$= e^x, \text{ since } \operatorname*{Lt}_{h\to 0}\frac{e^h - 1}{h} = 1 \quad (p.\ 146).$$

Corollary:
$$\frac{da^x}{dx} = a^x \log_e a.$$

For $\quad a^x = e^{x \log a}$ and $\dfrac{da^x}{dx} = \dfrac{de^{x \log a}}{dx} = \dfrac{de^{x \log a}}{d(x \log a)} \cdot \dfrac{d(x \log a)}{dx}$

$$= e^{x \log a} . \log a = a^x \log a.$$

(iii) $y = \log_e x.$

$$\frac{d}{dx} \log_e x = \underset{h \to 0}{Lt} \frac{\log (x + h) - \log x}{h}$$

$$= \underset{h \to 0}{Lt} \frac{\log x + \log \left(1 + \dfrac{h}{x}\right) - \log x}{h}$$

$$= \underset{h \to 0}{Lt} \frac{\log \left(1 + \dfrac{h}{x}\right)}{h}.$$

Now put $\dfrac{h}{x} = \dfrac{1}{k}$ so that if $x \neq 0$, $\underset{h \to 0}{Lt}$ is the same as $\underset{k \to \infty}{Lt}$.

Then

$$\underset{h \to 0}{Lt} \frac{\log \left(1 + \dfrac{h}{x}\right)}{h} = \underset{k \to \infty}{Lt} \left\{\frac{k}{x} \log \left(1 + \frac{1}{k}\right)\right\} = \frac{1}{x} \underset{k \to \infty}{Lt} \left\{k \log \left(1 + \frac{1}{k}\right)\right\}$$

$$= \frac{1}{x} \underset{k \to \infty}{Lt} \left\{\log \left(1 + \frac{1}{k}\right)^k\right\} = \frac{1}{x} \log \left\{\underset{k \to \infty}{Lt} \left(1 + \frac{1}{k}\right)^k\right\}$$

$$= \frac{1}{x} \log e = \frac{1}{x}.$$

Corollary: $\dfrac{d}{dx} \log_a x = \dfrac{1}{\log_e a} \cdot \dfrac{1}{x}.$

5. Standard forms: Trigonometrical.

(i) $y = \sin x.$

For the differentiation of $\sin x$ we adopt the alternative form

$$\frac{d}{dx} f(x) = \underset{h \to 0}{Lt} \frac{f(x + h) - f(x - h)}{2h}.$$

Then $\dfrac{d}{dx} \sin x = \underset{h \to 0}{Lt} \dfrac{\sin (x + h) - \sin (x - h)}{2h}$

$$= \underset{h \to 0}{Lt} \frac{2 \cos x \sin h}{2h} \qquad (\text{p. 14})$$

$$= \cos x \underset{h \to 0}{Lt} \frac{\sin h}{h}$$

$$= \cos x, \text{ since } \underset{h \to 0}{Lt} \frac{\sin h}{h} = 1 \quad \cdot(\text{p. 139}).$$

Similarly $\qquad \dfrac{d}{dx} \cos x = - \sin x.$

(ii) $y = \tan x.$

$$\frac{dy}{dx} = \operatorname*{Lt}_{h \to 0} \frac{\tan (x + h) - \tan (x - h)}{2h}$$

$$= \operatorname*{Lt}_{h \to 0} \frac{\sin (x + h) \cos (x - h) - \cos (x + h) \sin (x - h)}{2h \cos (x + h) \cos (x - h)}$$

$$= \operatorname*{Lt}_{h \to 0} \frac{\sin 2h}{2h} \cdot \frac{1}{\cos (x + h) \cos (x - h)}$$

$$= \frac{1}{\cos^2 x} = \sec^2 x.$$

Similarly $\qquad \dfrac{d}{dx} \cot x = - \operatorname{cosec}^2 x.$

(iii) $y = \sin^{-1} x.$

If $\qquad y = \sin^{-1} x,$ then $\sin y = x.$

Therefore, differentiating both sides with respect to x,

$$\cos y \frac{dy}{dx} = \frac{dx}{dx} = 1,$$

and $\qquad \dfrac{dy}{dx} = \dfrac{1}{\cos y} = \dfrac{1}{\sqrt{1 - x^2}}.$

In the same manner it may be proved that

$$\frac{d}{dx} \cos^{-1} x = - \frac{1}{\sqrt{1 - x^2}} \quad \text{and} \quad \frac{d}{dx} \tan^{-1} x = \frac{1}{1 + x^2}.$$

6. Miscellaneous examples of differentiation.

Example 1.

Differentiate with respect to x:

$$(a)\ \sqrt{a^2 - x^2}, \qquad (b)\ \frac{1}{\sqrt{a^2 - x^2}}, \qquad (c)\ \frac{x}{\sqrt{a^2 - x^2}}.$$

$$(a)\ \frac{d}{dx} \sqrt{a^2 - x^2} = \frac{d (a^2 - x^2)^{\frac{1}{2}}}{d (a^2 - x^2)} \cdot \frac{d (a^2 - x^2)}{dx}$$

$$= \tfrac{1}{2} (a^2 - x^2)^{-\frac{1}{2}} \cdot (- 2x)$$

$$= - \frac{x}{\sqrt{a^2 - x^2}}.$$

$$(b) \quad \frac{d}{dx} \frac{1}{\sqrt{a^2 - x^2}} = \frac{d (a^2 - x^2)^{-\frac{1}{2}}}{d (a^2 - x^2)} \cdot \frac{d (a^2 - x^2)}{dx}$$

$$= - \tfrac{1}{2} (a^2 - x^2)^{-\frac{3}{2}} \cdot (- 2x) = x (a^2 - x^2)^{-\frac{3}{2}}.$$

$$(c) \quad \frac{d}{dx} \frac{x}{\sqrt{a^2 - x^2}} = x \cdot \frac{d}{dx} \frac{1}{\sqrt{a^2 - x^2}} + \frac{1}{\sqrt{a^2 - x^2}} \cdot \frac{dx}{dx}$$

$$= x \cdot \frac{x}{(a^2 - x^2)^{\frac{3}{2}}} + \frac{1}{\sqrt{a^2 - x^2}} \cdot 1$$

$$= \frac{x^2 + a^2 - x^2}{(a^2 - x^2)^{\frac{3}{2}}} = \frac{a^2}{(a^2 - x^2)^{\frac{3}{2}}}.$$

Example 2.

Find $\dfrac{dy}{dx}$ where $y = \dfrac{2x + 5}{x^2 - 3x + 2}$.

The differentiation can be performed at once by treating y as the quotient of two functions of x, thus:

$$\frac{dy}{dx} = \frac{(x^2 - 3x + 2) \frac{d}{dx} (2x + 5) - (2x + 5) \frac{d}{dx} (x^2 - 3x + 2)}{(x^2 - 3x + 2)^2}$$

$$= \frac{2 (x^2 - 3x + 2) - (2x + 5) (2x - 3)}{(x^2 - 3x + 2)^2}$$

$$= \frac{- 2x^2 - 10x + 19}{(x^2 - 3x + 2)^2},$$

or, alternatively, we can split $\dfrac{2x + 5}{x^2 - 3x + 2}$ into partial fractions and differentiate each fraction separately;

$$\frac{dy}{dx} = \frac{d}{dx} \cdot \frac{2x + 5}{x^2 - 3x + 2} = \frac{d}{dx} \cdot \frac{2x + 5}{(x - 1) (x - 2)}$$

$$= \frac{d}{dx} \left(\frac{9}{x - 2} - \frac{7}{x - 1} \right) = - \frac{9}{(x - 2)^2} + \frac{7}{(x - 1)^2}$$

$$= \frac{- 9x^2 + 18x - 9 + 7x^2 - 28x + 28}{(x - 2)^2 (x - 1)^2}$$

$$= \frac{- 2x^2 - 10x + 19}{(x^2 - 3x + 2)^2}, \text{ as before.}$$

Example 3.

$$y = b^{c^x}. \quad \text{Find } \frac{dy}{dx}.$$

For this type of function it is useful to employ the process known as *logarithmic differentiation.* Here we take logarithms of both sides of the equation before differentiating and write

$$\log y = c^x \log b.$$

Let

$$z = \log y.$$

Then

$$\frac{dz}{dx} = \frac{dx}{dy} \cdot \frac{dy}{dx} = \frac{d(\log y)}{dy} \cdot \frac{dy}{dx} = \frac{1}{y} \cdot \frac{dy}{dx}.$$

Also

$$\frac{d}{dx}(c^x \log b) = c^x \log c \log b.$$

$$\therefore \frac{1}{y} \frac{dy}{dx} = c^x \log c \log b.$$

$$\therefore \frac{dy}{dx} = y c^x \log c \log b = b^{c^x} c^x \log c \log b.$$

Example 4.

Differentiate $\tan^{-1} \dfrac{1}{\sqrt{x^2 - 1}}$ with respect to x.

$$\frac{dy}{dx} = \frac{d \tan^{-1}(x^2-1)^{-\frac{1}{2}}}{d(x^2-1)^{-\frac{1}{2}}} \cdot \frac{d(x^2-1)^{-\frac{1}{2}}}{d(x^2-1)} \cdot \frac{d(x^2-1)}{dx}$$

$$= \frac{1}{1 + \dfrac{1}{x^2-1}} \cdot -\tfrac{1}{2}(x^2-1)^{-\frac{3}{2}} \cdot 2x$$

$$= -\frac{1}{x\sqrt{x^2-1}}.$$

Example 5.

Find $\dfrac{dy}{dx}$ where $y = x^x + x^{\frac{1}{x}}$.

It is important to note that $\dfrac{d}{dx} x^n = n x^{n-1}$ only where n is *a constant,* and it is therefore incorrect to state that $\dfrac{d}{dx} x^x = x \cdot x^{x-1}$. To obtain $\dfrac{d}{dx} x^x$ we must employ the method of logarithmic differentiation. Moreover, y is the sum of two functions of x, and if we are to employ this method we must differentiate each of the functions separately. It would be incorrect to take logarithms of each side of the equality as it stands, for if $y = u + v$ then $\log y \neq \log u + \log v$.

Let $\qquad y = x^x + x^{\frac{1}{x}} = u + v.$

Then $\qquad \log u = x \log x$ and $\log v = \dfrac{1}{x} \log x.$

$$\dfrac{1}{u}\dfrac{du}{dx} = x \cdot \dfrac{1}{x} + \log x = 1 + \log x.$$

$$\therefore \ \dfrac{du}{dx} = x^x (1 + \log x);$$

similarly $\qquad \dfrac{1}{v}\dfrac{dv}{dx} = \dfrac{1}{x} \cdot \dfrac{1}{x} + \log x \cdot - \dfrac{1}{x^2} = \dfrac{1}{x^2}(1 - \log x).$

$$\therefore \ \dfrac{dv}{dx} = x^{\frac{1}{x}} \cdot \dfrac{1}{x^2}(1 - \log x).$$

$$\therefore \ \dfrac{dy}{dx} = x^x (1 + \log x) + x^{\frac{1}{x}} \dfrac{(1 - \log x)}{x^2}.$$

Example 6.

Differentiate $x \sin x$ with respect to $\tan x$.

$$\dfrac{d(x\sin x)}{d\tan x} = \dfrac{d(x\sin x)}{dx} \cdot \dfrac{dx}{d\tan x}$$

$$= \dfrac{\dfrac{d(x\sin x)}{dx}}{\dfrac{d\tan x}{dx}} = \dfrac{x\cos x + \sin x}{\sec^2 x} = x\cos^3 x + \sin x \cos^2 x.$$

7. Successive differentiation.

If we differentiate dy/dx with respect to x we obtain a new function which is called the second differential coefficient of y with respect to x. By analogy with the symbolic notation adopted in finite differences, we write

$$\dfrac{d}{dx}\dfrac{dy}{dx} \quad \text{as} \quad \dfrac{d^2y}{dx^2},$$

where, it should be remembered, the independent variable is still x and not x^2. Similarly, the third differential coefficient of y with respect to x is $\dfrac{d^3y}{dx^3}$, and if y is differentiated n times with respect to x, the nth differential coefficient is $\dfrac{d^ny}{dx^n}$. In the alternative notation we have

$$D^2y, D^3y, \dots D^ny,$$
$$f''(x), f'''(x), \dots f^{(n)}(x).$$

A notation frequently employed for the nth derivative is y_n.

8. Successive differential coefficients of many simple functions can be found by an inductive process.

Example 7.

Find $\dfrac{d^n}{dx^n} \log x$.

$$y = \log x; \quad y_1 = 1/x; \quad y_2 = (-1).1/x^2;$$
$$y_3 = (-1)(-2).1/x^3; \quad y_4 = (-1)(-2)(-3).1/x^4;$$

and so on.

Therefore by induction $y_n = (-1)^{n-1} \dfrac{(n-1)!}{x^n}$.

Example 8.

$$y = (2x + 5)/(x^2 - 3x + 2). \text{ Find } y_n.$$

It is imperative where higher differential coefficients than the first are required to use the second method given in Example 2 of para. 6, and to express y in partial fractions before differentiating.

$$y = \frac{9}{x-2} - \frac{7}{x-1},$$

$$y_1 = -\frac{9 \cdot 1}{(x-2)^2} + \frac{7 \cdot 1}{(x-1)^2},$$

$$y_2 = \frac{9 \cdot 1 \cdot 2}{(x-2)^3} - \frac{7 \cdot 1 \cdot 2}{(x-1)^3},$$

$$y_3 = -\frac{9 \cdot 1 \cdot 2 \cdot 3}{(x-2)^4} + \frac{7 \cdot 1 \cdot 2 \cdot 3}{(x-1)^4},$$

$$\cdots\cdots\cdots\cdots\cdots\cdots$$

$$\therefore \ y_n = (-1)^n \, n! \left[\frac{9}{(x-2)^{n+1}} - \frac{7}{(x-1)^{n+1}} \right].$$

Example 9.

Show that if y be a rational integral function of the nth degree in x, then the nth differential coefficient of y with respect to x is constant.

If
$$y = a + bx + cx^2 + \ldots + kx^n,$$
$$y_1 = b + 2cx + \ldots + knx^{n-1},$$
$$y_2 = 2c + \ldots + kn(n-1)x^{n-2},$$

$$\cdots\cdots\cdots\cdots\cdots\cdots\cdots\cdots,$$

and each time that we differentiate we lower the degree of the function by unity. Hence after n differentiations we shall lower the degree of the function by n.

$$\therefore \ y_n = kn(n-1)(n-2)\ldots(n-\overline{n-1})x^{n-n}$$
$$= kn! \text{ which is constant.}$$

If we denote $\frac{d^n y}{dx^n}$ by $D^n y$ we may write $D^m x^m = m!$, which is analogous to $\Delta^m x^{(m)} = m!$

9. Leibnitz's Theorem.

In Chapter VIII, para. 4, we discussed the compound function $y = u_x v_x$ and the expansion resulting from differencing this function n times. The method of obtaining $\Delta^n u_x v_x$ was to introduce the symbols Δ_1 and Δ_2 (representing the operation of differencing u_x and v_x separately) and then to expand the resulting function by the method of separation of symbols.

In an exactly similar way we may find $\frac{d^n}{dx^n}(uv)$, where u and v are functions of x, by using the alternative notation D for $\frac{d}{dx}$.

Let D_1 and D_2 represent the operations of differentiating u and v respectively, where D_1 operates only on u and its successive differential coefficients and D_2 operates only on v and its successive differential coefficients.

Then
$$Duv = uDv + vDu$$
$$= D_1(uv) + D_2(uv).$$
$$\therefore D \equiv D_1 + D_2,$$

so that

$$D^n \equiv (D_1 + D_2)^n$$
$$\equiv D_1{}^n + n_1 D_1{}^{n-1} D_2 + n_2 D_1{}^{n-2} D_2{}^2 + \dots + n_r D_1{}^{n-r} D_2{}^r + \dots + D_2{}^n.$$

But $D_1{}^{n-r} D_2{}^r (uv) = \dfrac{d^{n-r}}{dx^{n-r}} u \cdot \dfrac{d^r}{dx^r} v.$

$$\therefore \frac{d^n y}{dx^n} = D^n(uv) = \frac{d^n u}{dx^n} v + n_1 \frac{d^{n-1} u}{dx^{n-1}} \cdot \frac{dv}{dx} + n_2 \frac{d^{n-2} u}{dx^{n-2}} \cdot \frac{d^2 v}{dx^2} + \dots$$
$$+ n_r \frac{d^{n-r} u}{dx^{n-r}} \cdot \frac{d^r v}{dx^r} + \dots + u \frac{d^n v}{dx^n}.$$

This is Leibnitz's Theorem for the successive differentiation of the product of two functions of x.

10. Application of Leibnitz's Theorem.

Example 10.

If $y = x^2 e^x$ find $\dfrac{d^n y}{dx^n}$.

In the general expansion above let $x^2 = v$ and $e^x = u$

Then
$$v = x^2, \qquad\qquad u = e^x,$$

$$\frac{dv}{dx} = 2x, \qquad\qquad \frac{du}{dx} = e^x,$$

$$\frac{d^2 v}{dx^2} = 2, \qquad\qquad \frac{d^2 u}{dx^2} = e^x.$$

$\dfrac{d^3 v}{dx^3}$ and higher derivatives are zero.

$$\therefore \frac{d^n}{dx^n}(x^2 e^x) = x^2 e^x + n.2x.e^x + \frac{n(n-1)}{2}.2e^x$$

$$= e^x (x^2 + 2nx + n^2 - n).$$

Example 11.

If
$$y = \log\{(x-1)^{\frac{1}{2}} + (x+1)^{\frac{1}{2}}\}$$

prove that
$$(x^2 - 1)\frac{d^2 y}{dx^2} + x\frac{dy}{dx} = 0$$

and that
$$(x^2 - 1)\frac{d^{n+2}y}{dx^{n+2}} + (2n+1)x\frac{d^{n+1}y}{dx^{n+1}} + n^2\frac{d^n y}{dx^n} = 0.$$

$$y = \log\{(x-1)^{\frac{1}{2}} + (x+1)^{\frac{1}{2}}\}.$$

$$\therefore \frac{dy}{dx} = \frac{1}{(x-1)^{\frac{1}{2}} + (x+1)^{\frac{1}{2}}}.\{\tfrac{1}{2}(x-1)^{-\frac{1}{2}} + \tfrac{1}{2}(x+1)^{-\frac{1}{2}}\} = \tfrac{1}{2}(x^2-1)^{-\frac{1}{2}}.$$

$$\therefore \frac{d^2 y}{dx^2} = \frac{d}{dx}\{\tfrac{1}{2}(x^2-1)^{-\frac{1}{2}}\} = -\tfrac{1}{2}x(x^2-1)^{-\frac{3}{2}}.$$

$$\therefore (x^2 - 1)\frac{d^2 y}{dx^2} + x\frac{dy}{dx} = 0;$$

Differentiate each of the products $(x^2 - 1)\dfrac{d^2 y}{dx^2}$ and $x\dfrac{dy}{dx}$ n times by Leibnitz's Theorem.

Then
$$(x^2 - 1)y_{n+2} + n.2x.y_{n+1} + \frac{n(n-1)}{2}.2.y_n$$

$$+ x.y_{n+1} + ny_n = 0;$$

i.e.
$$(x^2 - 1)y_{n+2} + (2n+1)xy_{n+1} + n^2 y_n = 0.$$

11. We will conclude this chapter with some miscellaneous examples of differentiation.

Example 12.

If y, z are both functions of x and if $y^2 + z^2 = k^2$ prove that

$$y \cdot \frac{d}{dx}\left(\frac{y}{k}\right) + \frac{d}{dx}\left(\frac{z^2}{k}\right) = \frac{z}{k} \cdot \frac{dz}{dx}.$$

$$y \cdot \frac{d}{dx}\left(\frac{y}{k}\right) + \frac{d}{dx}\left(\frac{z^2}{k}\right) = y \cdot \frac{d}{dx} \frac{y}{\sqrt{y^2 + z^2}} + \frac{d}{dx} \frac{z^2}{\sqrt{y^2 + z^2}}$$

$$= y \cdot \left[\frac{\frac{dy}{dx}\sqrt{y^2 + z^2} - \dfrac{y\left\{y\frac{dy}{dx} + z\frac{dz}{dx}\right\}}{\sqrt{y^2 + z^2}}}{(y^2 + z^2)}\right] + \frac{2z\frac{dz}{dx}\sqrt{y^2 + z^2} - \dfrac{z^2\left\{y\frac{dy}{dx} + z\frac{dz}{dx}\right\}}{\sqrt{y^2 + z^2}}}{(y^2 + z^2)}$$

$$= \frac{1}{(y^2 + z^2)^{\frac{3}{2}}} \left[y\frac{dy}{dx}(y^2 + z^2) - y^2\left(y\frac{dy}{dx} + z\frac{dz}{dx}\right) + 2z\frac{dz}{dx}(y^2 + z^2)\right.$$

$$\left. - z^2\left(y\frac{dy}{dx} + z\frac{dz}{dx}\right)\right]$$

which simplifies to

$$\frac{1}{(y^2 + z^2)^{\frac{3}{2}}} \left\{z\frac{dz}{dx}(y^2 + z^2)\right\} = \frac{z}{k} \cdot \frac{dz}{dx}.$$

Example 13.

Prove that if n be a positive integer, and a and b have any values, then

$$(a + b)(a + b - 1) \ldots (a + b - n + 1)$$

$$= \sum_{p=1}^{p=n}\left[\frac{n!}{p!q!}a(a - 1)\ldots(a - p + 1) . b(b - 1) \ldots (b - q + 1)\right]$$

where $p + q = n$.   (Vandermonde's Theorem.)

Now $D^n(uv) = \sum\left[\frac{n!}{p!q!}D^p(u)D^q(v)\right]$ by Leibnitz's Theorem.

Let $u = x^a$ and $v = x^b$ so that $uv = x^{a+b}$. Then

$$(a + b)(a + b - 1) \ldots (a + b - n + 1)x^{a+b-n}$$

$$= \sum\left[\frac{n!}{p!q!}a(a - 1)\ldots(a - p + 1)x^{a-p} . b(b - 1) \ldots (b - q + 1)x^{b-q}\right]$$

$$= \sum\left[\frac{n!}{p!q!}a(a - 1)\ldots(a - p + 1) . b(b - 1) \ldots (b - q + 1)x^{a+b-p-q}\right].$$

Since $p + q = n$ we may divide through by x^{a+b-n} and the proposition is proved.

Example 14.

If $y = f(x)$ obtain $\dfrac{d^2x}{dy^2}$ and $\dfrac{d^3x}{dy^3}$ in terms of $\dfrac{dy}{dx}, \dfrac{d^2y}{dx^2}$ and $\dfrac{d^3y}{dx^3}$.

Let y_1, y_2, y_3 stand for $\dfrac{dy}{dx}, \dfrac{d^2y}{dx^2}, \dfrac{d^3y}{dx^3}$ respectively.

(i) $$\frac{dx}{dy} = \frac{1}{y_1}.$$

(ii) $$\frac{d^2x}{dy^2} = \frac{d}{dy}\left(\frac{dx}{dy}\right) = \frac{d}{dy}\left(\frac{1}{y_1}\right) = \frac{d}{dx} \cdot \frac{1}{y_1} \cdot \frac{dx}{dy}$$

$$= -\frac{1}{y_1{}^2} \cdot y_2 \cdot \frac{1}{y_1} = -\frac{y_2}{y_1{}^3}.$$

(iii) $$\frac{d^3x}{dy^3} = \frac{d}{dy}\left(\frac{d^2x}{dy^2}\right) = \frac{d}{dx}\left(-\frac{y_2}{y_1{}^3}\right)\frac{dx}{dy}$$

$$= -\frac{y_3 y_1{}^3 - 3y_1{}^2 y_2{}^2}{y_1{}^6} \cdot \frac{1}{y_1}$$

$$= \frac{3y_2{}^2 - y_1 y_3}{y_1{}^5}.$$

EXAMPLES 10

1. If y represent the number of gallons of water in a leaking tank and x the number of hours since the tank was full, what does $\dfrac{dy}{dx}$ represent, and is it positive or negative?

2. Let x denote the annual expenditure, and y the annual receipts of a trading company. If $\dfrac{dy}{dx}$ be positive, and $\dfrac{d^2y}{dx^2}$ be negative for a given value of x, what inference would you draw? What additional statement could you make if you also knew whether $\dfrac{dy}{dx}$ were greater or less than unity?

3. Prove that, when b tends to a, the limit of $\dfrac{(b^{\frac{1}{2}} - a^{\frac{1}{2}})}{b - a}$ is $\frac{1}{2}a$ and deduce the differential coefficient of $\sqrt{x}$.

4. If a body in motion moves a distance of s feet in t seconds what are the meanings of $\dfrac{ds}{dt}$ and $\dfrac{d^2s}{dt^2}$?

5. Find from first principles the first differential coefficients with respect to x of $x \sqrt{a^2 - x^2}$ and $e^{x \log x}$.

6. (i) Give a geometrical interpretation of the differential coefficient of a function of x with respect to x.

(ii) Find, from first principles,

$$\frac{d}{dx}(x^5); \quad \frac{d}{dx}(ax + b)^n; \quad \frac{d}{dx}(x^x).$$

Differentiate with respect to x:—

7. $(a + bx)^n$; a^{nx}; $\sqrt{a^2 + x^2}$; $\log \dfrac{x}{a^x}$.

8. $(x + 1/x)^2$; $x^m (1 - x)^n$; $x^m e^x$; $x^n \log x$.

9. $\log_x a$; $\log x^{x^2}$; 10^{10^x}; $\dfrac{\log x}{x}$.

10. $\sin^2 x$; $\sin 2x$; $\cos^3 x$; $x^2 \sec x$.

11. $\sin^{-1} x^2$; $\sqrt{x \sin x}$; $\tan x \tan 2x$.

12. $x \cos^{-1} x$; $x^2 \tan^{-1} x$; $\sin x (\tan^{-1} x)^2$.

13. $(5 + 4x)^{\log x}$; $\dfrac{x^m}{(1 - \sqrt{1 - x^2})^m}$; $\log (\log x)$.

14. $a^x + x^a$; $x^x + (1 - x^2)^m$; x^{x^n}.

15. $\tan^{-1} \dfrac{3x}{1 + 4x}$; $x \sqrt{x} \sqrt{\cos^{-1} x}$.

16. If $$y = x \sqrt{x^2 + a^2} + a^2 \log (x + \sqrt{x^2 + a^2}),$$

prove that $$\frac{dy}{dx} = 2 \sqrt{x^2 + a^2}.$$

17. Show that the result of differentiating the expression

$$\frac{x + 1}{(x - 1)(x - 2)}$$

as it stands and differentiating the same expression when split up into partial fractions is the same.

18. Find $\dfrac{dy}{dx}$ given $y = x^y$.

19. Differentiate $\log \dfrac{xe}{e^x - 1}$ with respect to x.

20. A ladder, AB, 13 feet long, rests against a vertical wall, having its lower extremity B distant 5 feet from the wall. If B be made to slide outwards from the wall at the rate of $1\frac{1}{2}$ feet per second, find at what rate the upper end A will begin to slide down the wall.

21. Find $\dfrac{dy}{dx}$:

(i) $y = \dfrac{x\sqrt{x^2 - 4a^2}}{\sqrt{x^2 - a^2}}$; (ii) $e^y = \dfrac{(a + bx^n)^{\frac{1}{2}} - a^{\frac{1}{2}}}{(bx^n)^{\frac{1}{2}}}$.

22. If S_n equals the sum of a G.P. to n terms, of which r is the common ratio, prove that $(r - 1)\dfrac{dS_n}{dr} = (n - 1)S_n - nS_{n-1}$.

23. $y = \log \tan^{-1}\left\{\dfrac{2x^2 + a}{2ax^2 - 1}\right\}$. Find $\dfrac{dy}{dx}$.

24. (i) Find $\dfrac{dy}{dx}$ where $y = x^{e^x}$.

(ii) Find $\dfrac{dy}{dx}$ where $y = x\log\dfrac{y}{1 + x}$.

25. Prove that if $x + \sqrt{a^2 - y^2} = a\log\dfrac{a + \sqrt{a^2 - y^2}}{y}$ then
$$\frac{dy}{dx} = -\frac{y}{\sqrt{a^2 - y^2}}.$$

26. Differentiate $x^{(\log x)^2}$ with respect to $\log x$.

27. Differentiate $\tan^{-1}\left\{\dfrac{\sqrt{1 + x^2} - 1}{x}\right\}$ with regard to $\tan^{-1} x$.

28. If $t = \tan\dfrac{x}{2}$ differentiate the following with regard to t: $\sin x$; $\cos x$; $\sec^2 x$; x. Express the results in terms of t.

29. Differentiate $\log\sqrt[3]{\dfrac{a^3 + a^2x + ax^2 + x^3}{a^2 + ax + x^2}}$ with respect to x.

30. Differentiate $\log_{10} x$ with respect to x^2 and
$$\frac{(1 + x^2)^{\frac{1}{2}} + (1 - x^2)^{\frac{1}{2}}}{(1 + x^2)^{\frac{1}{2}} - (1 - x^2)^{\frac{1}{2}}}$$
with respect to $(1 - x^4)^{\frac{1}{2}}$.

31. If $\sqrt{1 - x^2} + \sqrt{1 - y^2} = a(x - y)$, prove that $\dfrac{dy}{dx} = \sqrt{\dfrac{1 - y^2}{1 - x^2}}$.

32. Differentiate $\log \dfrac{e^x + \sqrt{e^{2x} - a^2}}{e^x - \sqrt{e^{2x} - a^2}}$ with respect to x.

33. Find $\dfrac{dy}{dx}$ where $y\,(y^2 + x^2) = x + y$.

34. Differentiate (i) $\log \sin x$; (ii) $\tan^{-1}\left\{\dfrac{4x\,(1 - x^2)}{1 - 6x^2 + x^4}\right\}$.

35. Determine the coefficients $a_0,\, a_1,\, a_2,\, \ldots a_n$, so that

$$\frac{d}{dx}\left[\frac{a_0 x^n + a_1 x^{n-1} + a_2 x^{n-2} + \ldots + a_n}{e^x}\right] \text{ shall equal } \frac{x^n}{e^x}.$$

36. Differentiate $\tan^{-1} (\sin a/x + \cos a/x)$ with respect to x.

37. If $y^2 = a^2 x^2 + c$, differentiate with respect to x the functions (i) $\log (ax + y)$; (ii) xy, and express the results in terms of y.

38. $x = e^{\tan^{-1} z}$, where $z = (y - x^2)/x^2$. Find $\dfrac{dy}{dx}$.

39. Differentiate e^{ax} with respect to (i) x; (ii) e^x; (iii) x^x.

40. If $u_1,\, v_1,\, u_2,\, v_2$ represent functions of x show that

$$\frac{d}{dx}\left[\frac{u_1 u_2}{v_1 v_2}\right] = \frac{u_1 u_2}{v_1 v_2}\left\{\left[\frac{1}{u_1}\frac{du_1}{dx} - \frac{1}{v_1}\frac{dv_1}{dx}\right] + \left[\frac{1}{u_2}\frac{du_2}{dx} - \frac{1}{v_2}\frac{dv_2}{dx}\right]\right\}.$$

41. Find $\dfrac{d^3 y}{dx^3}$ when

$$\text{(i) } y = \frac{ax + b}{cx + d}; \qquad \text{(ii) } y = \frac{\log x}{x}.$$

42. If $y = \sin (\log x)$, prove that $x^2 \dfrac{d^2 y}{dx^2} + x \dfrac{dy}{dx} + y = 0$.

43. If $y = ax \cos \left[\dfrac{n}{x} + b\right]$, show that $x^4 \dfrac{d^2 y}{dx^2} + n^2 y = 0$.

44. Find the second differential coefficient of $x\,(x - 4)$ with regard to $\log x$.

45. Show that the equation $\dfrac{d^2 y}{dx^2} - 2m \dfrac{dy}{dx} + m^2 y = e^x$ is satisfied by

$$y = (A + Bx)\,e^{mx} + \frac{e^x}{(m - 1)^2}.$$

46. If $y = a + x \log y$, prove that, when $x = 0$, $y_1 = \log a$ and find y_2.

47. If $y = (x + \sqrt{x^2 + 1})^n$, prove that $(x^2 + 1)\dfrac{d^2 y}{dx^2} + x\dfrac{dy}{dx} - n^2 y = 0$.

48. If
$$A = a \cos (x + k) + b \sin (x + k),$$
$$B = a \sin (x + k) - b \cos (x + k),$$

show that
$$- \frac{d^2 A}{dB^2} = \frac{B^2 + A^2}{A^3}.$$

49. If $y = \dfrac{3x + 4}{5x + 6}$, prove that $\dfrac{d^2 y}{dx^2} \cdot \dfrac{d^3 y}{dx^3} = \dfrac{1}{2} \dfrac{dy}{dx} \cdot \dfrac{d^4 y}{dx^4}$.

50. $y = x \log \dfrac{x}{a + bx}$. Find the value of $x^3 \dfrac{d^2 y}{dx^2} - \left(y - x \dfrac{dy}{dx} \right)^2$.

51. Find the nth differential coefficient of $\dfrac{px + q}{(x - a)(x - b)(x - c)}$.

52. Find the nth differential coefficient of $x (x + 1)(x^2 - 3x + 2)^{-1}$.

53. Find $\dfrac{d^n y}{dx^n}$, where $y = \dfrac{(x - a)(x - b)}{(x - c)(x - d)}$.

54. Find $\dfrac{d^4 y}{dx^4}$ if $y = \dfrac{1}{(2x + 1)(1 - x)}$.

55. If $y = (x^2 - 1)^n$, prove

(a) $(x^2 - 1) \dfrac{dy}{dx} = 2nxy$;

(b) $(x^2 - 1) \dfrac{d^{n+2} y}{dx^{n+2}} + 2x \dfrac{d^{n+1} y}{dx^{n+1}} - n (n + 1) \dfrac{d^n y}{dx^n} = 0.$

56. If $y + A (x + \sqrt{x^2 - 1})^m + B (x - \sqrt{x^2 - 1})^m$, prove that
$$(x^2 - 1) \frac{d^2 y}{dx^2} + x \frac{dy}{dx} - m^2 y = 0,$$

and that
$$(x^2 - 1) \frac{d^{n+2} y}{dx^{n+2}} + (2n + 1) x \frac{d^{n+1} y}{dx^{n+1}} + (n^2 - m^2) \frac{d^n y}{dx^n} = 0.$$

57. Find $\dfrac{d^n y}{dx^n}$, where y equals

(i) $x^2 \log x \quad (n > 3)$;   (ii) $\dfrac{6x^3 + 5x^2 - 7}{3x^2 - 2x - 1}$.

58. Prove that $\dfrac{d^n}{dx^n} (e^{ax} u_x) = e^{ax} \left\{ \dfrac{d}{dx} + a \right\}^n u_x$.

59. If $y = e^{ax} [a^2 x^2 - 2nax + n (n + 1)]$, find $\dfrac{d^n y}{dx^n}$.

60. Find the nth differential coefficient of $\dfrac{1}{(x - a)^2 (x - b)}$.

61. If $y = x^n (\log x)^2$, prove that $x^2 \dfrac{d^{n+2} y}{dx^{n+2}} + x \dfrac{d^{n+1} y}{dx^{n+1}} = 2 (n!)$.

62. If $y = \sin(a \sin^{-1} x)$, show that

   (i) $(1 - x^2) \dfrac{d^2 y}{dx^2} - x \dfrac{dy}{dx} + a^2 y = 0$;

   (ii) $(1 - x^2) \dfrac{d^{n+2} y}{dx^{n+2}} - (2n + 1) x \dfrac{d^{n+1} y}{dx^{n+1}} + (a^2 - n^2) \dfrac{d^n y}{dx^n} = 0$.

63. If $y = \dfrac{\sin^{-1} x}{(1 - x^2)^{\frac{1}{2}}}$, prove that $(1 - x^2) \dfrac{dy}{dx} = xy + 1$; and if y_n denotes the nth differential coefficient of y, prove that, when $x = 0$, $y_n = (n - 1)^2 y_{n-2}$.

64. Prove that, if $x + y = 1$,

$$\frac{d^n}{dx^n}(x^n y^n) = n! \left[y^n - (n_1)^2 y^{n-1} x + (n_2)^2 y^{n-2} x^2 - \ldots \right].$$

65. Prove that, if $y = e^{\tan^{-1} x}$,

$$(1 + x^2) \frac{d^{n+1} y}{dx^{n+1}} = (1 - 2nx) \frac{d^n y}{dx^n} - n(n - 1) \frac{d^{n-1} y}{dx^{n-1}}.$$

66. If $u = \sin(m \tan^{-1} x)$, prove that

$$\frac{d^2 u}{dx^2}(1 + x^2)^2 + \frac{du}{dx}(2x + 2x^3) + m^2 u = 0,$$

and thence, by use of Leibnitz's Theorem, show that, if A_n denote the value of $\dfrac{d^n u}{dx^n}$ when x is put equal to zero,

$$A_{n+2} + (2n^2 + m^2) A_n + n(n - 1)^2 (n - 2) A_{n-2} = 0.$$

67. Prove that, if $\sin^{-1} y = a + b \sin^{-1} x$, then, when x is zero, $y_{n+2} = (n^2 - b^2) y_n$.

68. $y = x e^x \log x$. Prove that

$$x(y_4 - 4y_3 + 6y_2 - 4y_1 + y) = -2(y_3 - 3y_2 + 3y_1 - y).$$

69. If $y^3 + 3x^2 y + 1 = 0$, prove that $(x^2 + y^2)^3 \dfrac{dy}{dx} + 2(x^2 - y^2) = 0$.

70. If $u = k s^x g^{c^x}$, show that the ratio between $\dfrac{d^2 u}{dx^2}$ and u can be expressed in the form $p + qc^x + rc^{2x}$, and find p, q and r.

71. Differentiate:

   (i) $\sin^{-1}(\operatorname{cosec} \theta \sqrt{\cos 2\theta})$;   (ii) $\tan^{-1} \dfrac{x}{1 + (1 + x^2)^{\frac{1}{2}}}$.

72. Prove that $\left(\dfrac{d}{dx}\right)^n (e^{ax} x^r) = \left(\dfrac{a}{x}\right)^{n-r} \left(\dfrac{d}{dx}\right)^r (e^{ax} x^n)$.

73. Differentiate with respect to x:
$$\tan^{-1}\left[\frac{3\tan x - \tan^3 x}{1 - 3\tan^2 x}\right].$$

74. In the curve $b^2 y = \frac{1}{3}x^3 - ax^2$, find the coordinates of the points at which the tangent to the curve is parallel to the axis of x.

75. The equation to a curve is $4x^2 + 9y^2 + 16x - 18y - 11 = 0$. Find the points on the graph of the curve where the tangent is (i) parallel, (ii) perpendicular to the axis of x.

76. If $ax^2 + 2hxy + by^2 + 2gx + 2fy + c = 0$, show that
$$(hx + by + f)^3 \frac{d^2 y}{dx^2}$$
is constant.

77. $y = \tan^{-1}\left[(e^x + 1)/(e^x - 1)\right]^{\frac{1}{2}}$. Prove that
$$y_3 = y\,(1 + 12y_1^2)\,(1 + 4y_1^2).$$

78. If $y = (\sqrt{x} - 1)\,e^{\sqrt{x}}$, show that $2x\dfrac{d^2 y}{dx^2} = \frac{1}{2}y + \dfrac{dy}{dx}$.

79. If $y = \dfrac{ax + b}{Ax + B}$ and $z = \dfrac{ay + b}{Ay + B}$, show that
$$\frac{z'''}{z'} - \frac{3}{2}\left(\frac{z''}{z'}\right)^2 = \frac{y'''}{y'} - \frac{3}{2}\left(\frac{y''}{y'}\right)^2 = 0,$$
where accents denote differentiations with respect to x.

80. Prove by induction that $\dfrac{d^n}{dx^n}\,(x^{n-1}\log x) = \dfrac{(n-1)!}{x}$.

CHAPTER XI

EXPANSIONS

1. It has been shown in earlier chapters that, provided certain conditions hold, we can expand $f(x+h)$ in terms of $f(x)$ and the successive differences of $f(x)$. The ordinary advancing difference formula, for equidistant intervals, is

$$f(x+h) = (1+\Delta)^h f(x)$$
$$= f(x) + h\Delta f(x) + h_2\Delta^2 f(x) + h_3\Delta^3 f(x) + \ldots,$$

and this is a series involving ascending powers of h.

It is often necessary to express the function $f(x+h)$ in a series of ascending powers of h and of the successive differential co-efficients of $f(x)$. Although the required series will be of similar form to the above, the conditions governing the differential expansions are far more stringent than those governing the finite difference expansion. In finite differences we are given certain data, and in order to apply our formulae we assume in the first instance that the data follow simple laws. It is generally sufficient to assume that the given values are corresponding values of x and y in the rational integral function $y = f(x)$, or in some equally straightforward function such as $y = ab^x$. This is particularly so when considering actuarial functions, where the process of interpolation would be rendered impossible if some such assumptions were not made at the outset.

Now it was shown in the last chapter that the function $y = f(x)$ could have a unique differential coefficient at the point $x = a$ only if y were finite and continuous at that point. As a result we must be careful in dealing with expansions involving differential coefficients that the conditions of continuity hold.

2. Rolle's Theorem.

Before proceeding to obtain the general expansion of $f(x+h)$ in terms of $f(x)$ and its derivatives it will be necessary to consider some simple theorems connected with the first and second differential coefficients of the function. The first of these theorems is Rolle's Theorem, which states that

If $f(x)$ and $f'(x)$ $\left(\text{i.e. } \dfrac{d}{dx} f(x)\right)$ are continuous over the range $x = a$ to $x = b$, and if $f(x) = 0$ when $x = a$ and when $x = b$, then for at least one value of x between a and b, $f'(x)$ will be zero.

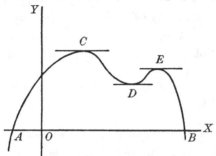

Fig. 23.

The proof is as follows:

Since $f(a) = f(b) = 0$, $f(x)$ cannot always be increasing or decreasing. Hence for at least one value between $x = a$ and $x = b$ there will be a change from an increase to a decrease or vice versa. For the particular value of x for which this is so, $f'(x)$ must be zero, which proves the proposition.

That the theorem is self-evident may be seen from the above diagram (Fig. 23).

If the curve represents the continuous function $y = f(x)$ and if $y = f(x) = 0$ for the values $x = a$ and $x = b$ (i.e. at the points A and B), then at the points C, D, E the tangents to the curve are parallel to the x-axis. That is, at these points $f'(x)$ is zero.

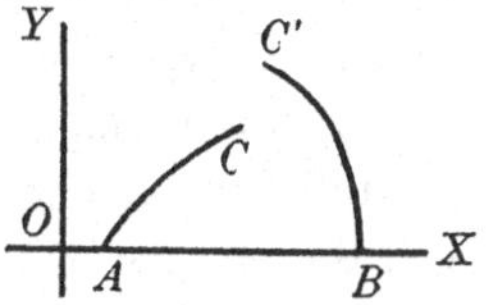

It should be noted that $f(x)$ must be continuous within the given range. If there be a discontinuity such as at the points C

Fig. 24.

and C' in Fig. 24, there is no unique differential coefficient; consequently the theorem does not apply and $f'(x)$ is not necessarily zero in the range.

Since difficulties may arise in dealing with multiple-valued functions, it is advisable to restrict the above proof to single-valued functions of x.

3. Mean Value Theorem.

As before, let $f(x)$ and $f'(x)$ be continuous in the range $x = a$ to $x = b$ and let $m = \dfrac{f(b) - f(a)}{b - a}$, so that

$$f(b) - f(a) - m(b - a) = 0.$$

Replace b by x in the left-hand side of this expression and let

$$\phi(x) = f(x) - f(a) - m(x - a).$$

Then obviously $\phi(a) = 0$ and we have shown that $\phi(b) = 0$.

Therefore Rolle's Theorem holds, since $f(x)$ and $f'(x)$ are continuous in the given range.

Hence $\phi'(x)$ will be zero for at least one value of x (x_1 say) between a and b.

But $\qquad \phi(x) = f(x) - f(a) - m(x - a).$

Therefore $\phi'(x) = f'(x) - m$ on differentiating.

Hence since $\phi'(x_1) = 0$, then $f'(x_1) = m$.

Therefore $\qquad \dfrac{f(b) - f(a)}{b - a} = f'(x_1).$

This is the Mean Value Theorem, and may be stated thus:

If $f(x)$ and $f'(x)$ are continuous in the range $x = a$ to $x = b$, then there is at least one value of x (x_1 say) between $x = a$ and $x = b$ such that $\dfrac{f(b) - f(a)}{b - a} = f'(x_1).$

This is equivalent to saying that if $y = f(x)$ is a continuous curve between the values A ($x = a$) and B ($x = b$), then there is at least one value of x, (x_1), where $a \leqslant x \leqslant b$, for which the tangent to the curve is parallel to the chord AB. That

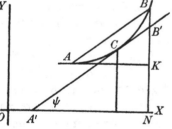

Fig. 25.

is, if the tangent at this point C make an angle ψ with the x-axis,

$$\tan \psi = \frac{B'N}{A'N} = \frac{BK}{AK} = \frac{f(b) - f(a)}{b - a}.$$

A more convenient form may be obtained for the result of this theorem. Since x_1 lies between a and b we may write

$$x_1 = a + \theta_1 (b - a),$$

where θ_1 is a positive proper fraction.

The mean value theorem becomes therefore

$$\frac{f(b) - f(a)}{b - a} = f'[a + \theta_1(b - a)],$$

or if $b - a = h$, so that $b = a + h$, then

$$f(a + h) - f(a) = hf'(a + \theta_1 h);$$

i.e. $\qquad\qquad f(a + h) = f(a) + hf'(a + \theta_1 h).$

4. We may extend the mean value theorem to include higher derivatives of $f(x)$, thus:

If $f(x)$, $f'(x)$ and $f''(x)$ are continuous in the range $x = a$ to $x = b$, then there is at least one value x_2 between $x = a$ and $x = b$ such that

$$f(b) = f(a) + (b - a)f'(a) + \tfrac{1}{2}(b - a)^2 f''(x_2).$$

Let $\qquad p = \dfrac{f(b) - f(a) - (b - a)f'(a)}{\tfrac{1}{2}(b - a)^2},$

and let $\quad \phi(x) = f(x) - f(a) - (x - a)f'(a) - \tfrac{1}{2}(x - a)^2 p.$

Then $\phi(a) = 0$ and $\phi(b) = 0$; and $\phi(x)$ satisfies the conditions of Rolle's Theorem.

Therefore for a value x_1 say between $x = a$ and $x = b$, $\phi'(x_1) = 0$.

But $\qquad\qquad \phi'(x) = f'(x) - f'(a) - (x - a)p,$

and this vanishes for the values a and x_1.

Therefore $\phi''(x) = 0$ for some value of x (x_2 say) between a and x_1, i.e. between a and b.

But $\qquad\qquad \phi''(x) = f''(x) - p.$

Hence since $\phi''(x_2) = 0$, then $p = f''(x_2)$.

$$\therefore \quad f(b) - f(a) - (b - a)f'(a) = \tfrac{1}{2}(b - a)^2 f''(x_2).$$

If as before we put $x_2 = a + \theta_2(b - a)$ and $b - a = h$, we have

$$f(b) = f(a) + hf'(a) + \tfrac{1}{2}h^2 f''(a + \theta_2 h).$$

5. Taylor's Theorem.

It is evident that we can extend the above process as long as the successive differential coefficients are continuous throughout the given range, and can thus obtain expressions for $f(b)$ in terms of $f(a)$ and its higher derivatives.

F

Consider the general case, where all the derivatives are continuous:

Let

$$q = \frac{f(b) - \left[f(a) + (b-a)f'(a) + \frac{(b-a)^2}{2!}f''(a) + \dots + \frac{(b-a)^{n-1}}{(n-1)!}f^{(n-1)}(a)\right]}{(b-a)^n}$$

and let

$$\phi(x) = f(b) - f(x) - (b-x)f'(x) - \frac{(b-x)^2}{2!}f''(x) - \dots$$

$$- \frac{(b-x)^{n-1}}{(n-1)!}f^{(n-1)}(x) - (b-x)^n q.$$

As before $\phi(a)$, $\phi(b)$ are both zero. Since $\phi(x)$, $\phi'(x)$ are continuous, $\phi'(x)$ is zero for a value x_1 in the given range.

But by differentiation

$$\phi'(x) = - \frac{(b-x)^{n-1}}{(n-1)!}f^{(n)}(x) + n(b-x)^{n-1}q,$$

all the remaining terms in the expression for $\phi(x)$ vanishing on differentiation.

$$\therefore \quad - \frac{(b-x_1)^{n-1}}{(n-1)!}f^{(n)}(x_1) + n(b-x_1)^{n-1}q = 0.$$

$$\therefore \quad q = \frac{f^{(n)}(x_1)}{n!} \quad \text{since } b \neq x_1.$$

If $x_1 = a + \theta(b-a)$ and $b - a = h$ we see that

$$f(b) = f(a) + hf'(a) + \frac{h^2}{2!}f''(a) + \dots$$

$$+ \frac{h^{n-1}}{(n-1)!}f^{(n-1)}(a) + \frac{h^n}{n!}f^{(n)}(a + \theta h).$$

An expansion for $f(x+h)$ in terms of $f(x)$ and ascending powers of h is at once evident. Replace b by $x + h$ and write x for a so that $b - a = (x + h) - x = h$ as before.

Then

$$f(x+h) = f(x) + hf'(x) + \frac{h^2}{2!}f''(x) + \frac{h^3}{3!}f'''(x) + \dots$$

$$+ \frac{h^{n-1}}{(n-1)!}f^{(n-1)}(x) + \frac{h^n}{n!}f^{(n)}(x + \theta h).$$

This is Taylor's Theorem.

If in the above expansion we put $x = 0$ we have

$$f(h) = f(0) + hf'(0) + \frac{h^2}{2!}f''(0) + \frac{h^3}{3!}f'''(0) + \dots$$

$$+ \frac{h^{n-1}}{(n-1)!}f^{(n-1)}(0) + \frac{h^n}{n!}f^{(n)}(\theta h),$$

or putting x for h

$$f(x) = f(0) + xf'(0) + \frac{x^2}{2!}f''(0) + \frac{x^3}{3!}f'''(0) + \dots$$

$$+ \frac{x^{n-1}}{(n-1)!}f^{(n-1)}(0) + \frac{x^n}{n!}f^{(n)}(\theta x).$$

In this form the expansion is known as Stirling's or Maclaurin's Theorem.

6. It will be noticed that the first n terms in Taylor's Theorem are of the form $\frac{h^r}{r!}f^{(r)}(x)$. The $(n+1)$th term is of the same form but involves a different value of the variable. This term is called the "remainder" term after n terms and is denoted by $R_n(x)$. If $\underset{n \to \infty}{\text{Lt}} R_n(x)$ is zero, then $f(x+h)$ can be expanded as an infinite series, and will be convergent. We may state therefore that if $f(x)$ and its successive differential coefficients are continuous within the given range, then

$$f(x) + hf'(x) + \frac{h^2}{2!}f''(x) + \dots + \frac{h^{n-1}}{(n-1)!}f^{(n-1)}(x) + \dots$$

converges to the limit $f(x+h)$, provided that $\underset{n \to \infty}{\text{Lt}} R_n(x)$ is zero.

7. Other forms for $R_n(x)$.

The form $\frac{h^n}{n!}f^{(n)}(x + \theta h)$ is called Lagrange's form of the remainder after n terms.

If the denominator in the expression for q in paragraph 5 be $(b-a)^p$ instead of $(b-a)^n$ it can be shown that

$$R_n(x) = \frac{h^n(1-\theta)^{n-p}}{(n-1)!\,p}f^{(n)}(x + \theta h).$$

This is Schlömilch's form. The Lagrange form follows immediately by putting $p = n$. If we put $p = 1$ we obtain another form,

$$R_n(x) = \frac{h^n(1-\theta)^{n-1}}{(n-1)!} f^{(n)}(x+\theta h),$$

due to Cauchy.

8. Examples on the above theorems.

In obtaining expansions for various functions of x it is more convenient to use Maclaurin's form than to use Taylor's. Moreover, since the condition for a convergent series applies equally to both forms, it is strictly necessary to prove that $\underset{n\to\infty}{\text{Lt}} R_n(x)$, i.e.

$\underset{n\to\infty}{\text{Lt}} \dfrac{x^n}{n!} f^{(n)}(\theta x)$, is zero before assuming that an infinite series can represent the function. For example, on expanding $(1+x)^n$ by Maclaurin's Theorem different conditions arise according to the values of x and n, and a complete investigation of the convergency of the various series involves further mathematical analysis. In the examples that follow it will be assumed that $\underset{n\to\infty}{\text{Lt}} R_n(x)$ is zero and that the function in question is the sum of an infinite convergent series.

Example 1.

Expand $\log(1 + x + x^2)$ as far as the term involving x^3.

$f(x) = \log(1 + x + x^2)$, and $f(0) = 0$,

$$f'(x) = \frac{1+2x}{1+x+x^2}, \qquad f'(0) = 1,$$

$$f''(x) = \frac{1-2x-2x^2}{(1+x+x^2)^2} = \frac{-2}{(1+x+x^2)} + \frac{3}{(1+x+x^2)^2}, \qquad f''(0) = 1,$$

$$f'''(x) = \frac{2(1+2x)}{(1+x+x^2)^2} + \frac{-6(1+2x)}{(1+x+x^2)^3}, \qquad f'''(0) = -4.$$

By Maclaurin's Theorem:

$$f(x) = f(0) + xf'(0) + \frac{x^2}{2!} f''(0) + \frac{x^3}{3!} f'''(0) + \dots$$

$$\therefore \quad \log(1 + x + x^2) = x + \frac{x^2}{2} - \frac{2x^3}{3} + \dots$$

Notes on this example:

(i) The expansion is true only if x is numerically less than unity.

(ii) Since $1 + x + x^2 = (1 - x^3)/(1 - x)$, an alternative method would be to expand $\log (1 - x^3) - \log (1 - x)$ by algebra.

(iii) It is simpler to differentiate products than to differentiate quotients. We might write

$$f'(x) = \frac{1 + 2x}{1 + x + x^2}$$

as $\qquad (1 + x + x^2) f'(x) = 1 + 2x$, so that $f'(0) = 1$.

Differentiate:

$$(1 + x + x^2) f''(x) + (1 + 2x) f'(x) = 2, \qquad f''(0) = 1,$$
$$(1 + x + x^2) f'''(x) + 2 (1 + 2x) f''(x) + 2f'(x) = 0, \qquad f'''(0) = -4,$$

and so on.

(iv) For an expansion involving higher powers of x we may continue the differentiation in (iii) by applying Leibnitz's Theorem, or we may adopt other methods, as in Example 3 below.

Example 2.

Prove that if x is any positive quantity

$$(x + 2) \log (1 + x) > 2x.$$

Now if θ is a positive proper fraction,

$$f(x) = f(0) + xf'(0) + \tfrac{1}{2}x^2 f''(\theta x).$$

Let $\qquad f(x) = (x + 2) \log (1 + x) - 2x$, so that $f(0) = 0$.

Then $\qquad f'(x) = \log (1 + x) + \dfrac{x + 2}{1 + x} - 2, \qquad f'(0) = 0,$

and $\qquad f''(x) = \dfrac{1}{1 + x} - \dfrac{1}{(1 + x)^2} = \dfrac{x}{(1 + x)^2}.$

$$\therefore \ f(x) = \tfrac{1}{2}x^2 \frac{\theta x}{(1 + \theta x)^2}.$$

But for all positive values of x this is positive, since θ is a positive proper fraction.

$\therefore (x + 2) \log (1 + x) - 2x$ is positive when x is positive,

i.e. $\qquad\qquad (x + 2) \log (1 + x) > 2x.$

9. Formation of a differential equation.

This method can be employed with advantage for the expansion of certain functions without the use of the above series. It must be assumed that the given function $f(x)$ can be expanded in the form

$a_0 + a_1 x + a_2 x^2 + \ldots + a_r x^r + \ldots$, and if on differentiating $f(x)$ a simple relation between the coefficients is evident, we can obtain the required expansion. It should be noted that the first one or two terms of the expansion may have to be found by a different method, such as by substitution of numerical values on both sides of the identity.

Example 3.

Expand $\log(1 + x + x^2)$ in ascending powers of x. (Cf. Ex. 1, p. 180.)

Let
$$\log(1 + x + x^2) = a_0 + a_1 x + a_2 x^2 + a_3 x^3 + \ldots + a_r x^r + \ldots.$$
Then by differentiating,
$$\frac{1 + 2x}{1 + x + x^2} = a_1 + 2a_2 x + 3a_3 x^2 + \ldots + ra_r x^{r-1} + \ldots,$$
or $\quad 1 + 2x = (1 + x + x^2)(a_1 + 2a_2 x + 3a_3 x^2 + \ldots + ra_r x^{r-1} + \ldots).$

Equating coefficients of powers of x,
$$
\begin{aligned}
a_1 &= 1, & a_1 &= 1, \\
2a_2 + a_1 &= 2, & a_2 &= \tfrac{1}{2}, \\
3a_3 + 2a_2 + a_1 &= 0, & a_3 &= -\tfrac{2}{3}, \\
4a_4 + 3a_3 + 2a_2 &= 0, & a_4 &= \tfrac{1}{4}, \\
5a_5 + 4a_4 + 3a_3 &= 0, & a_5 &= \tfrac{1}{5},
\end{aligned}
$$
and so on, the law of formation of the coefficients being
$$ra_r + (r-1)a_{r-1} + (r-2)a_{r-2} = 0,$$
except for the first two terms.
$$\therefore \quad \log(1 + x + x^2) = x + \frac{x^2}{2} - \frac{2x^3}{3} + \frac{x^4}{4} + \frac{x^5}{5} \ldots,$$
since a_0 is obviously zero.

Example 4.

If $y = \log(1 + \sin x)$ obtain a relation between the first three differential coefficients of y with respect to x, and hence expand y in an ascending series of powers of x.

$$f(x) = y = \log(1 + \sin x), \qquad f'(x) = \frac{\cos x}{1 + \sin x},$$

$$f''(x) = -\frac{1}{1 + \sin x}, \qquad f'''(x) = \frac{\cos x}{(1 + \sin x)^2}.$$

$$\therefore \quad f'''(x) + f'(x)f''(x) = 0.$$

Let $\quad f(x) = a_0 + a_1 x + a_2 x^2 + a_3 x^3 + a_4 x^4 + a_5 x^5 + \ldots.$

Then $f'(x) = a_1 + 2a_2 x + 3a_3 x^2 + 4a_4 x^3 + 5a_5 x^4 + \dots,$

$\qquad f''(x) = 2a_2 + 6a_3 x + 12a_4 x^2 + 20a_5 x^3 + \dots,$

$\qquad f'''(x) = 6a_3 + 24a_4 x + 60a_5 x^2 + \dots.$

Now $\qquad\qquad f(0) = 0, \qquad$ or $\qquad a_0 = 0,$

$\qquad\qquad\qquad f'(0) = 1, \qquad$ giving $\quad a_1 = 1,$

$\qquad\qquad\qquad f''(0) = -1, \qquad$,, $\qquad a_2 = -\tfrac{1}{2},$

$\qquad\qquad\qquad f'''(0) = 1, \qquad$,, $\qquad a_3 = \tfrac{1}{6}.$

Since $f'''(x) + f'(x)f''(x) = 0$, we have, by multiplying together the expansions for $f'(x)$ and $f''(x)$ and equating coefficients of x,

$$4a_2{}^2 + 6a_1 a_3 = -24a_4, \quad \text{so that} \quad a_4 = -\tfrac{1}{12}.$$

Similarly, equating coefficients of x^2,

$$6a_2 a_3 + 12a_2 a_3 + 12a_1 a_4 = -60a_5 \quad \text{and} \quad a_5 = \tfrac{1}{24},$$

and so on.

$$\therefore \quad \log(1 + \sin x) = x - \frac{x^2}{2} + \frac{x^3}{6} - \frac{x^4}{12} + \frac{x^5}{24} \dots.$$

10. The series $\dfrac{x}{e^x - 1}$.

The coefficients in the expansion of $\dfrac{x}{e^x - 1}$ are of great importance in the higher branches of mathematics, and the method of obtaining the series in ascending powers of x is an excellent example of the application of the above principles.

Consider $\qquad \dfrac{x}{e^x - 1} + \dfrac{x}{2} = \dfrac{x}{2} \cdot \dfrac{e^x + 1}{e^x - 1}.$

Let $\quad \dfrac{x}{2} \cdot \dfrac{e^x + 1}{e^x - 1} = a_0 + a_1 x + a_2 x^2 + a_3 x^3 + a_4 x^4 + \dots.$

Change the sign of x: the left-hand side becomes

$$-\frac{x}{2} \cdot \frac{e^{-x} + 1}{e^{-x} - 1} \quad \text{or} \quad \frac{x}{2} \cdot \frac{e^x + 1}{e^x - 1}.$$

$$\therefore \quad \frac{x}{2} \cdot \frac{e^x + 1}{e^x - 1} = a_0 - a_1 x + a_2 x^2 - a_3 x^3 + a_4 x^4 - \dots.$$

Add: then on dividing both sides by 2, we have

$$\frac{x}{2} \cdot \frac{e^x + 1}{e^x - 1} = a_0 + a_2 x^2 + a_4 x^4 + \dots,$$

which shows that no odd powers of x occur in the expansion of

$$\frac{x}{2}\cdot\frac{e^x+1}{e^x-1}.$$

Let $$f(x) = \frac{x}{e^x-1} + \frac{x}{2} = \frac{x}{2}\cdot\frac{e^x+1}{e^x-1}.$$

Then $$e^x f(x) = f(x) + \tfrac{1}{2}x + \tfrac{1}{2}xe^x.$$

Differentiate with respect to x:

$$e^x[f(x) + f'(x)] = f'(x) + \tfrac{1}{2} + \tfrac{1}{2}e^x(1+x).$$

Similarly, on successive differentiation,

$$e^x[f''(x) + 2f'(x) + f(x)] = f''(x) + \tfrac{1}{2}e^x(2+x),$$

$$e^x[f'''(x) + 3f''(x) + 3f'(x) + f(x)] = f'''(x) + \tfrac{1}{2}e^x(3+x),$$

and the law of formation is evident.

Moreover, if we expand $f(x)$ by Maclaurin's Theorem, we have

$$f(x) = f(0) + xf'(0) + \frac{x^2}{2!}f''(0) + \frac{x^3}{3!}f'''(0) + \ldots,$$

and since there are no odd powers of x in the expansion of $f(x)$, it follows that

$$f'(0) = f'''(0) = f^{\mathrm{v}}(0) = \ldots = 0.$$

Now $e^x[f(x) + f'(x)] = f'(x) + \tfrac{1}{2} + \tfrac{1}{2}e^x(1+x)$,

so that, when $x = 0$,

$$f(0) = \tfrac{1}{2} + \tfrac{1}{2} = 1 \text{ since } f'(0) = 0.$$

Similarly, by substitution of $x = 0$ in the next equation but one, we obtain

$$e^0[f'''(0) + 3f''(0) + 3f'(0) + f(0)] = f'''(0) + \tfrac{1}{2}e^0(3+0),$$

and, remembering that $f'(0)$ and $f'''(0)$ are zero, we find that $f''(0) = \tfrac{1}{6}$.

Similarly, $f^{\mathrm{iv}}(0) = -\tfrac{1}{30}, f^{\mathrm{vi}}(0) = \tfrac{1}{42}, f^{\mathrm{viii}}(0) = -\tfrac{1}{30}, \ldots$

$$\therefore \frac{x}{e^x-1} + \frac{x}{2} = \frac{x}{2}\cdot\frac{e^x+1}{e^x-1} = 1 + \frac{1}{6}\cdot\frac{x^2}{2!} - \frac{1}{30}\cdot\frac{x^4}{4!} + \frac{1}{42}\cdot\frac{x^6}{6!} - \frac{1}{30}\cdot\frac{x^8}{8!} + \cdots$$

or $$\frac{x}{e^x-1} = 1 - \frac{x}{2} + \frac{1}{6}\cdot\frac{x^2}{2!} - \frac{1}{30}\cdot\frac{x^4}{4!} + \frac{1}{42}\cdot\frac{x^6}{6!} - \frac{1}{30}\cdot\frac{x^8}{8!} + \cdots.$$

The coefficients of x^2, x^4, x^6, x^8, ... are denoted by B_1, B_2, B_3, B_4, ...; these are called Bernouilli's Numbers.

We have, therefore, that

$$\frac{x}{e^x - 1} = 1 - \tfrac{1}{2}x + B_1 \frac{x^2}{2!} - B_2 \frac{x^4}{4!} + B_3 \frac{x^6}{6!} - B_4 \frac{x^8}{8!} + \dots.$$

The expansion of $\dfrac{x}{e^x - 1}$ may be obtained otherwise by assuming that

$$\frac{x}{e^x - 1} = a_0 + a_1 x + a_2 x^2 + \dots + a_r x^r + \dots,$$

i.e. that

$$x = \left(x + \frac{x^2}{2!} + \frac{x^3}{3!} + \dots \right)(a_0 + a_1 x + a_2 x^2 + \dots + a_r x^r + \dots),$$

and equating coefficients of powers of x on both sides of the identity.

11. Differentiation of a known series.

It can be shown that if an infinite series converges to a value $f(x)$ within a given range, then the series formed by differentiating each term of the original series is $f'(x)$, provided that the second series is convergent for all values of the variable within the given range.

It sometimes happens that the function whose expansion is required is the differential coefficient of a function whose expansion is known. By the application of the simple process of differentiating each term of the known expansion the required result is easily obtained.

Example 5.

If

$$\log(1 - x - x^2) = -u_1 x - \tfrac{1}{2}u_2 x^2 - \tfrac{1}{3}u_3 x^3 - \dots,$$

prove that

$$u_n = u_{n-1} + u_{n-2}.$$

$$\frac{d}{dx}\log(1 - x - x^2) = -\frac{1 + 2x}{1 - x - x^2}.$$

But

$$\frac{d}{dx}\log(1 - x - x^2) = -u_1 - u_2 x - u_3 x^2 - u_4 x^3 - \dots.$$

$$\therefore -\frac{1 + 2x}{1 - x - x^2} = -u_1 - u_2 x - u_3 x^2 - u_4 x^3 - \dots,$$

i.e. $\dfrac{1 + 2x}{1 - x - x^2}$ is the generating function of the series

$$u_1 + u_2 x + u_3 x^2 + \dots + u_{n-2} x^{n-3} + u_{n-1} x^{n-2} + u_n x^{n-1} + \dots.$$

$$\therefore u_n - u_{n-1} - u_{n-2} = 0, \quad \text{or} \quad u_n = u_{n-1} + u_{n-2},$$

which proves the proposition.

12. Trigonometrical series.

Let $\qquad f(x) = \sin x.$

Then $\qquad f'(x) = \cos x = \sin\left(x + \dfrac{\pi}{2}\right),$

$$f''(x) = \cos\left(x + \frac{\pi}{2}\right) = \sin\left(x + 2\frac{\pi}{2}\right),$$

$$\ldots\ldots\ldots\ldots$$

and the nth differential coefficient is $\sin\left(x + n\dfrac{\pi}{2}\right).$

$$\therefore\ f(0) = 0;\ \ f'(0) = \sin\frac{\pi}{2} = 1;\ \ f''(0) = \sin\frac{2\pi}{2} = 0;$$

$$f'''(0) = \sin\frac{3\pi}{2} = -1;\ \ f^{\text{iv}}(0) = \sin\frac{4\pi}{2} = 0,$$

and so on.

Even derivatives will obviously be zero, and odd derivatives $+1$ and -1 alternately.

Therefore by Maclaurin's Theorem,

$$\sin x = x - \frac{x^3}{3!} + \frac{x^5}{5!} - \frac{x^7}{7!} + \ldots,$$

and it is easy to show that the series is convergent for all values of x.

Similarly $\qquad \cos x = 1 - \dfrac{x^2}{2!} + \dfrac{x^4}{4!} - \dfrac{x^6}{6!} + \ldots.$

This result can be obtained by replacing $n\theta$ by α in the expansion for $\cos n\theta$ in Example 11, p. 17, and by then considering the limit of the expansion as $n \to \infty$. It will be seen, however, that by finding the limit $n \to \infty$ in the series

$$\cos\alpha = (\cos\alpha/n)^n - n_2(\cos\alpha/n)^{n-2}(\sin\alpha/n)^2 + n_4(\cos\alpha/n)^{n-4}(\sin\alpha/n)^4 - \ldots$$

a double limit is involved. It is therefore simpler to obtain the cosine and sine series by Maclaurin's Theorem as above.

The series for $\tan x$ does not take a simple form: the first few terms can be obtained by division of the sine series by the cosine series, or by Maclaurin's Theorem.

The series for the inverse functions $\sin^{-1} x$, $\cos^{-1} x$, $\tan^{-1} x$ are easily evaluated by the integration of $(1 - x^2)^{-\frac{1}{2}}$ and $(1 + x^2)^{-1}$.

13. If u_x be a rational integral function of x, the expansion for u_x in terms of advancing differences is

$$u_x = u_0 + x_1 \Delta u_0 + x_2 \Delta^2 u_0 + \dots + x_n \Delta^n u_0 + \dots,$$

or, in factorial notation,

$$u_x = u_0 + \frac{x^{(1)}}{1!} \Delta u_0 + \frac{x^{(2)}}{2!} \Delta^2 u_0 + \dots + \frac{x^{(n)}}{n!} \Delta^n u_0 + \dots.$$

We may compare this with the Maclaurin expansion for u_x:

$$u_x = u_0 + \frac{x}{1!} D u_0 + \frac{x^2}{2!} D^2 u_0 + \dots + \frac{x^n}{n!} D^n u_0 + \dots.$$

Separating the symbols,

$$u_x = \left(1 + \frac{x}{1!} D + \frac{x^2}{2!} D^2 + \frac{x^3}{3!} D^3 + \dots + \frac{x^n}{n!} D^n + \dots \right) u_0.$$

Now whatever the degree of the polynomial in x represented by u_x we may treat the expression in brackets as an infinite series, for higher derivatives than, say, the nth will vanish.

Consequently, we can express u_x shortly as $e^{xD} u_0$—a convenient form for relating finite differences to differential calculus.

$$\therefore \quad (1 + \Delta)^x u_0 = u_x = e^{xD} u_0,$$

or symbolically $$(1 + \Delta)^x \equiv e^{xD}.$$

This result is analogous to the important relation in the Theory of Compound Interest, $(1 + i)^n = e^{n\delta}$, where δ is the force of interest corresponding to a rate of interest i.

EXAMPLES 11

1. Prove that $e^{x+h} = e^x + h e^x + \dfrac{h^2}{2!} e^x + \dots$.

2. Find the expansion of $\log(1 + e^x)$ in ascending powers of x as far as the term containing x^4.

3. Expand $(1 + x)^x$ by Maclaurin's Theorem as far as the term containing x^4.

4. Prove that

$$\frac{f(x+h) + f(x-h)}{2} = f(x) + \frac{h^2}{2!} f''(x) + \frac{h^4}{4!} f^{\text{iv}}(x) + \dots.$$

5. If $u = f(x)$, show that

$$f\left(\frac{x}{2}\right) = u - \frac{x}{2}\frac{du}{dx} + \frac{1}{2!}\left(\frac{x}{2}\right)^2\frac{d^2u}{dx^2} - \frac{1}{3!}\left(\frac{x}{2}\right)^3\frac{d^3u}{dx^3} + \dots$$

6. Assuming that $\dfrac{x}{\log(1+x)}$ can be expanded in ascending powers of x, find the first four terms of the expansion.

7. Expand $f(x)$ in powers of x as far as the term containing x^6, given that $f(0) = 1$; $f'(0) = 2$; $f''(0) = 3$ and $f'''(x) = f(x)$.

8. Prove that the first three terms in the expansion of $\log\dfrac{xe^x}{e^x - 1}$ are $\frac{1}{2}x - \frac{1}{24}x^2 + \frac{1}{2880}x^4$.

9. By means of a differential equation find a series for $\tan^{-1} x$.

10. If $\tan y = 1 + x + x^2$, expand y in terms of x as far as the term involving x^3.

11. Prove that

$$f(mx) = f(x) + (m-1)xf'(x) + (m-1)^2\frac{x^2}{2!}f''(x)$$

$$+ (m-1)^3\frac{x^3}{3!}f'''(x) + \dots$$

12. Show that if $y = \log(1 + \sin x)$, then $\dfrac{d^3y}{dx^3} + \dfrac{dy}{dx}\cdot\dfrac{d^2y}{dx^2} = 0$. Use this formula to obtain the expansion

$$\log(1 + \sin x) = x - \frac{x^2}{2} + \frac{x^3}{6} - \frac{x^4}{12} + \frac{x^5}{24}\dots,$$

and find the coefficient of x^6.

13. $ay^3 = xy + a$. Apply Maclaurin's Theorem to expand y in ascending powers of x as far as the term involving x^3.

14. If $\log y = \log \sin x - x^2$, prove that

$$\frac{d^2y}{dx^2} + 4x\frac{dy}{dx} + (4x^2 + 3)y = 0.$$

Hence expand y in terms of x as far as the term in x^5.

15. Prove that

$$\log(1 - x + x^2) = -x + \frac{x^2}{2} + \frac{2x^3}{3} + \frac{x^4}{4} - \frac{x^5}{5} - \frac{x^6}{6} - \frac{x^7}{7} + \frac{x^8}{8}\dots.$$

16. If $\sin y = a_1 x + a_2 x^2 + \dots + a_n x^n + \dots$ where $\tan y = x$, prove that

$$(n^2 + 3n + 2)a_{n+2} + (2n^2 + 1)a_n + (n^2 - 3n + 2)a_{n-2} = 0.$$

17. Show that $e^{x\cos x} = 1 + x + \dfrac{x^2}{2} - \dfrac{x^3}{3} \ldots$, and find the coefficient of x^4.

18. Expand $\dfrac{\sqrt{1+x}}{(1-x)}$ in ascending powers of x by first forming a differential equation.

19. If $e^{\sin^{-1}x} = a_0 + a_1 x + a_2 x^2 + \ldots + a_r x^r + \ldots$, prove that
$$\frac{(n+2)\,a_{n+2}}{n} = \frac{na_n}{n+1}.$$

20. Expand $\dfrac{x}{e^x - 1}$ as far as the term involving x^6. Use the result to expand $\dfrac{1}{e^x + 1}$ to four terms.

21. Prove that if x is positive
$$x > \log(1 + x) > x - \tfrac{1}{2}x^2.$$

22. Find the expansion of $e^{-x^2}\sin px$ in ascending powers of x as far as the term involving x^5.

CHAPTER XII

MAXIMA AND MINIMA

1. In Chapter IX, para. 13, a definition was given of a function $f(x)$ which is continuous at the point $x = a$. A property of such a function which is of frequent application in the calculus is as follows:

If $f(x)$ is a continuous function throughout the range of values considered, then for values of x near the point $x = a$, $f(x)$ has the same sign as $f(a)$, provided that $f(a)$ is not zero.

This proposition is almost self-evident. Since, *for a continuous function*, $\underset{x \to a}{\mathrm{Lt}} f(x)$ is equal to $f(a)$, it follows from the definition of a limit that there is a range of values over which $f(x)$ differs from $f(a)$ by less than ϵ where ϵ may be as small as we please. For any value of ϵ numerically less than $f(a)$ the sign of $f(x)$ for values of x within the corresponding range will be the same as that of $f(a)$.

Now let $y = f(x)$ be a continuous function of x.

Then
$$\frac{dy}{dx} = \underset{\Delta x \to 0}{\mathrm{Lt}} \frac{\Delta y}{\Delta x},$$

so that $\dfrac{\Delta y}{\Delta x} = \dfrac{dy}{dx} + \epsilon$ where ϵ is a small quantity whose limit as $\Delta x \to 0$ is zero.

If $\dfrac{dy}{dx}$ is not zero, the sign of $\dfrac{dy}{dx}$ will be the same as that of $\dfrac{\Delta y}{\Delta x}$ provided that we take Δx small enough; if $\Delta x \to 0$, the sign of Δy will be the same as that of $\Delta x \dfrac{dy}{dx}$.

Consequently if Δx is positive but $\to 0$, Δy will have the same sign as $\dfrac{dy}{dx}$.

But
$$\Delta y = f(x + \Delta x) - f(x).$$

Therefore $f(x + \Delta x) - f(x)$ will have the same sign as $\dfrac{dy}{dx}$ if Δx is positive, but $\to 0$.

If Δx is positive, $x + \Delta x$ is greater than x; i.e. x is increasing: and if $\frac{dy}{dx}$ is positive $f(x + \Delta x)$ is greater than $f(x)$; i.e. y is increasing.

Therefore $f(x)$ increases as x increases if $\frac{dy}{dx}$ is positive, and decreases as x increases if $\frac{dy}{dx}$ is negative.

Similarly, if Δx is negative, so that x is decreasing, $f(x)$ decreases as x decreases if $\frac{dy}{dx}$ is positive, and increases as x decreases if $\frac{dy}{dx}$ is negative.

Values of $f(x)$ at which the function ceases to increase (decrease) and begins to decrease (increase) are called *turning values* or *critical values*.

2. Maxima and Minima.

At the points where the function $y = f(x)$ ceases to increase and begins to decrease y is generally said to have a *maximum value*: conversely where the function ceases· to decrease and begins to increase y is said to have a *minimum value*.

It should be noted that a maximum value need not necessarily be the greatest numerical value of the function, nor need a minimum value be the least. For example, in Fig. 26, there are maxima at the points A and C, and minima at B and D. The numerical value, however, of the ordinate at D is greater than that of the ordinate at A, although the function assumes a minimum value at D and a maximum value at A.

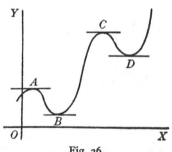

Fig. 26.

The following is a more correct definition of maximum and minimum values:

The function $y = f(x)$ has a maximum value at the point $x = a$, if $f(a)$ exceeds both $f(a + h)$ and $f(a - h)$ for all positive values of h less than a small finite quantity ϵ. Similarly, $f(x)$ has a minimum value when $x = a$, if $f(a)$ is less than both $f(a + h)$ and $f(a - h)$ for all positive values of h less than ϵ.

If therefore $f(a)$ is a maximum value of $y = f(x)$, (i) as x increases from $(a - h)$ to a, y increases and $\dfrac{dy}{dx}$ is positive; and (ii) as x increases from a to $(a + h)$, y decreases and $\dfrac{dy}{dx}$ is negative (para. 1). That is, as x increases $\dfrac{dy}{dx}$ changes from a positive to a negative value. The criterion for a maximum value at $x = a$ is therefore that $\dfrac{dy}{dx}$ changes sign from positive to negative as x passes through a. Conversely, for a minimum value $\dfrac{dy}{dx}$ changes from negative to positive.

Since a continuous function cannot change sign without passing through a zero value, we have that, for a critical value, $\dfrac{dy}{dx}$ must be zero provided that it be continuous.

If therefore $f(a)$ is a maximum or a minimum value of the function $y = f(x)$, and $f'(x)$ is continuous,

(i) $\left[\dfrac{dy}{dx}\right]_{x=a}$ must be zero;

(ii) $\dfrac{dy}{dx}$ must change from positive to negative for a maximum value;

(iii) $\dfrac{dy}{dx}$ must change from negative to positive for a minimum value.

Example 1.

Find the maximum and minimum values of
$$y = 4x^3 - 18x^2 + 24x + 11.$$

$$\frac{dy}{dx} = 12x^2 - 36x + 24.$$

We must equate $\dfrac{dy}{dx}$ to zero: this gives
$$12x^2 - 36x + 24 = 0,$$

i.e. $\qquad\qquad x^2 - 3x + 2 = 0,$

i.e. $\qquad\qquad x = 2 \text{ or } 1.$

These values of x give critical values to y.

To find which of these values gives a maximum and which a minimum we must proceed further.

Let $x = 2 - \Delta x$ and $2 + \Delta x$ in turn, where Δx is a small positive quantity.

(i) $\dfrac{dy}{dx} = (2 - \Delta x)^2 - 3 (2 - \Delta x) + 2$, when $x = 2 - \Delta x$,

$\qquad = 4 - 4\Delta x + (\Delta x)^2 - 6 + 3\Delta x + 2 = - \Delta x + (\Delta x)^2;$

(ii) $\dfrac{dy}{dx} = 4 + 4\Delta x + (\Delta x)^2 - 6 - 3\Delta x + 2 = \Delta x + (\Delta x)^2,$

when $x = 2 + \Delta x$.

Now since Δx is a small positive quantity,

$\qquad\qquad [- \Delta x + (\Delta x)^2]$ is negative

and $\qquad\qquad [\Delta x + (\Delta x)^2]$ is positive.

$\therefore \dfrac{dy}{dx}$ passes from negative to positive as x passes through the value 2.

$\therefore x = 2$ gives y a minimum value.

Similarly it may be shown that $x = 1$ gives y a maximum value.

The values required are therefore

$\qquad$ Maximum: $y = 4 \cdot 1^3 - 18 \cdot 1^2 + 24 \cdot 1 + 11 = 21.$

$\qquad$ Minimum: $y = 4 \cdot 2^3 - 18 \cdot 2^2 + 24 \cdot 2 + 11 = 19.$

3. An alternative method for determining the maximum or minimum values of a continuous function depends upon the rate of change of $\dfrac{dy}{dx}$. We have seen that if $f(a)$ is a maximum value, $\dfrac{dy}{dx}$ changes from positive as x passes through a. In other words $\dfrac{dy}{dx}$ is decreasing near the point, and consequently its differential coefficient, i.e. $\dfrac{d^2y}{dx^2}$, or $f''(x)$, must be negative. Therefore, by the proposition in para. 1, the sign of $f''(x)$ is the same as that of $f''(a)$ provided that $f''(a)$ is not zero.

We have therefore for a maximum value at the point $x = a$, $\dfrac{d^2y}{dx^2}$ must be negative: and conversely for a minimum value $\dfrac{d^2y}{dx^2}$ must be positive.

The test is easy to apply. For example, using the same function as in Ex. 1, we find that

$$\frac{d^2y}{dx^2} = \frac{d}{dx}\,12\,(x^2 - 3x + 2) = 12\,(2x - 3).$$

This is positive when $x = 2$ and negative when $x = 1$. Consequently $x = 2$ gives a minimum value and $x = 1$ a maximum (as above).

4. The tests for maximum and minimum values are quite straightforward and their application to simple problems presents little difficulty. The following examples are illustrative of the methods employed.

Example 2.

A window is in shape a rectangle with a semicircle covering the top. If the perimeter of the window be a fixed length p, find its maximum area.

We have first to choose an independent variable. Let BO, the radius of the semicircle, be x. Then since the perimeter of the figure is a fixed length p,

$$p = 2BC + CD + AKB$$
$$= 2BC + 2x + \pi x,$$

so that
$$BC = \frac{p - (2 + \pi)\,x}{2}.$$

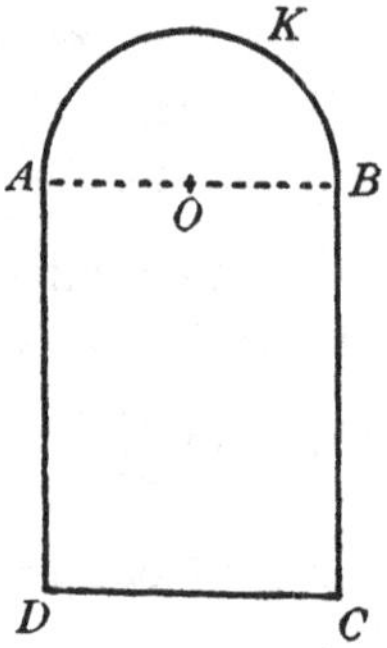

The area a will be [rectangle $ABCD$ + semicircle AKB],

i.e.
$$a = BC.CD + \tfrac{1}{2}\pi x^2$$
$$= \frac{p - (2 + \pi)\,x}{2}\,.2x + \tfrac{1}{2}\pi x^2$$
$$= xp - (2 + \pi)\,x^2 + \tfrac{1}{2}\pi x^2.$$
$$\therefore \frac{da}{dx} = p - 2x\,(2 + \pi) + \pi x.$$

Fig. 27.

For a maximum or minimum value $\dfrac{da}{dx} = 0$,

i.e.
$$x = \frac{p}{4 + \pi}.$$

It is evident that this will give a maximum value to a, for when $x = 0$ the area is zero. We need not therefore apply the second test.

Giving x the above value,

$$a = xp - (2 + \pi) x^2 + \tfrac{1}{2}\pi x^2$$

$$= \frac{p^2}{4 + \pi} - \frac{4 + \pi}{2} \cdot \frac{p^2}{(4 + \pi)^2} = \frac{p^2}{2 (4 + \pi)}.$$

Example 3.

Given $u_{-1} = -5$; $u_1 = -1$; $u_2 = 4$; $u_5 = 175$; find the maximum and minimum values of u_x.

Since four values of u_x are given we must assume that the function is a rational integral function of the third degree in x.

Let $\qquad\qquad y = u_x = a + bx + cx^2 + dx^3.$

Then $\qquad\qquad -5 = u_{-1} = a - b + c - d,$

$$-1 = u_1 = a + b + c + d,$$

$$4 = u_2 = a + 2b + 4c + 8d,$$

$$175 = u_5 = a + 5b + 25c + 125d.$$

Solving these equations we obtain easily that

$$a = 0; \quad b = 0; \quad c = -3; \quad d = 2.$$

$$\therefore \ y = -3x^2 + 2x^3.$$

For critical values $\dfrac{dy}{dx} = 0,$

i.e. $\qquad\qquad -6x + 6x^2 = 0,$

giving $\qquad\qquad x = 0 \text{ or } 1.$

Also $\qquad\qquad \dfrac{d^2y}{dx^2} = -6 + 12x.$

When $x = 0$, $\dfrac{d^2y}{dx^2}$ is negative, giving a maximum value;

$x = 1$, $\dfrac{d^2y}{dx^2}$ is positive, giving a minimum value.

Therefore maximum value of y is 0;

minimum value of y is -1.

Example 4.

A ladder is to be carried in a horizontal position round a corner formed by two streets a feet and b feet wide meeting at right angles. Prove that the length of the longest ladder that will pass round the corner without jamming is $(a^{\frac{2}{3}} + b^{\frac{2}{3}})^{\frac{3}{2}}$ feet.

In this example it is advisable to take as the variable the angle that the ladder makes with the wall of the street. Call this angle a. Let x be the distance across the corner. The longest ladder will of course be the shortest distance across the corner, and the problem reduces to one of finding the minimum value of x. Then

$$x = AB = AC + CB$$
$$= a \sec \alpha + b \csc \alpha,$$
$$\frac{dx}{d\alpha} = a \sec \alpha \tan \alpha - b \csc \alpha \cot \alpha;$$

i.e. for a maximum or minimum value,

$$a \sec \alpha \tan \alpha - b \csc \alpha \cot \alpha = 0,$$

or $$a \frac{\sin \alpha}{\cos^2 \alpha} - b \frac{\cos \alpha}{\sin^2 \alpha} = 0,$$

from which $$\tan \alpha = \frac{b^{\frac{1}{3}}}{a^{\frac{1}{3}}}.$$

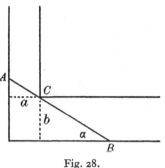

Fig. 28.

This evidently gives a minimum value to $a \sec \alpha + b \csc \alpha$, the maximum value being ∞.

$$\therefore \quad \sin \alpha = \frac{b^{\frac{1}{3}}}{(a^{\frac{2}{3}} + b^{\frac{2}{3}})^{\frac{1}{2}}}; \quad \cos \alpha = \frac{a^{\frac{1}{3}}}{(a^{\frac{2}{3}} + b^{\frac{2}{3}})^{\frac{1}{2}}},$$

and $$x = \frac{a}{\cos \alpha} + \frac{b}{\sin \alpha}$$
$$= (a^{\frac{2}{3}} + b^{\frac{2}{3}})^{\frac{3}{2}}$$

on simplifying.

5. Points of inflexion.

It has been seen above that, for a critical value at $x = a$, $f'(a) = 0$ and that in order to ascertain whether this value is a maximum or a minimum, recourse must be had to the change of sign of $f''(a)$, provided that $f''(a)$ is not zero. The question of what happens if $f''(a)$ is in fact zero now arises. Now $f''(a)$ will be zero if there is no rate of change of $f'(a)$. In that event the first differential coefficient will not increase (decrease) and then decrease (increase) as x passes through a, although $f'(x) = 0$ for the value $x = a$. $f'(x)$ will have the same sign for

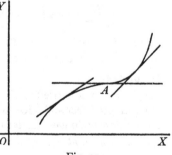

Fig. 29.

the value $x = a + h$ as for $x = a - h$ where h is small. There is therefore, as a rule, no maximum or minimum value at the point A, and A is said to be a *point of inflexion* on the curve.

In general there is a point of inflexion at $x = a$ if $f''(a)$ is zero: the exceptions depend upon the values of the higher derivatives.

Example 5.

Find the points of inflexion on the curve $y(1 + x^3) = 1$.

$$y = \frac{1}{1 + x^3},$$

$$\therefore \frac{dy}{dx} = \frac{-3x^2}{(1 + x^3)^2}.$$

Therefore for a critical value, $x = 0$.

But $$\frac{d^2y}{dx^2} = -3\left[\frac{2x}{(1 + x^3)^2} - \frac{6x^4}{(1 + x^3)^3}\right]$$

which is zero when $x = 0$ or $x = \sqrt[3]{\frac{1}{2}}$. There are therefore points of inflexion where $x = 0$ and $\sqrt[3]{\frac{1}{2}}$.

6. We have illustrated the critical values of the function $y = f(x)$ by reference to the geometry of the curve. The problem may also be considered analytically.

By the extension of the Mean Value Theorem (p. 177)

$$f(a + h) = f(a) + hf'(a) + \tfrac{1}{2}h^2f''(a + \theta_1 h),$$

and $$f(a - h) = f(a) - hf'(a) + \tfrac{1}{2}h^2f''(a - \theta_2 h),$$

where θ_1, θ_2 are positive proper fractions not necessarily equal.

Now for critical values $f'(a) = 0$.

Therefore $f(a + h) - f(a) = \tfrac{1}{2}h^2f''(a + \theta_1 h)$,

and $f(a - h) - f(a) = \tfrac{1}{2}h^2f''(a - \theta_2 h)$.

If h be made sufficiently small the right-hand side will have the same sign in both expressions. For a maximum value

$$f(a + h) - f(a) \text{ and } f(a - h) - f(a)$$

will both be negative. Therefore, since $\tfrac{1}{2}h^2$ is positive, the second differential coefficient must be negative. Similarly for a minimum value the second differential coefficient must be positive. If, however, $f''(a)$ is zero we must consider a further term: thus

$$f(a + h) = f(a) + hf'(a) + \frac{h^2}{2!}f''(a) + \frac{h^3}{3!}f'''(a + \theta_3 h),$$

$$f(a - h) = f(a) - hf'(a) + \frac{h^2}{2!}f''(a) - \frac{h^3}{3!}f'''(a - \theta_4 h),$$

which reduce to

$$f(a + h) - f(a) = \frac{h^3}{3!}f'''(a + \theta_3 h),$$

and $$f(a - h) - f(a) = -\frac{h^3}{3!}f'''(a - \theta_4 h).$$

It will be seen that here there can be no maximum or minimum value if $f'''(a)$ is not zero, for since the sign of the right-hand side can be made to depend upon the sign of $\frac{h^3}{3!}f'''(a)$, the signs of $f(a + h) - f(a)$ and $f(a - h) - f(a)$ will be different and there will be a point of inflexion.

We may carry this proof further. If $f'''(a)$ is zero, the condition for maxima and minima will depend upon the sign of $f^{\mathrm{iv}}(a)$—provided that $f^{\mathrm{iv}}(a)$ is not zero—and so on. In general, therefore, we may say that

For a maximum or minimum value the first derivative that does not vanish must be of an even order: if in that event the derivative is negative the critical value is a maximum and if positive a minimum. Otherwise there will be a point of inflexion.

It is worthy of note that if $f(x)$ is a continuous function, maximum and minimum values (if any) occur alternately.

Example 6.

Examine the critical values of $y = x^2 - 3x^3 + 3x^4 - x^5$.

$$y = x^2 - 3x^3 + 3x^4 - x^5.$$

$$\therefore \frac{dy}{dx} = 2x - 9x^2 + 12x^3 - 5x^4.$$

Equating this to zero we obtain the four values $x = 0, 1, 1, \frac{2}{5}$.

$$\frac{d^2y}{dx^2} = 2 - 18x + 36x^2 - 20x^3;$$

when $x = 0$, $\dfrac{d^2y}{dx^2} = 2$, giving a minimum value;

$\quad x = 1$, $\dfrac{d^2y}{dx^2} = 0$, which must be examined further;

$\quad x = \frac{2}{5}$, $\dfrac{d^2y}{dx^2} = -\cdot 72$, giving a maximum value.

Again $\qquad\qquad \dfrac{d^3y}{dx^3} = -18 + 72x - 60x^2$;

when $x = 1$, $\qquad \dfrac{d^3y}{dx^3} = -6$,

and since this is not zero $x = 1$ gives a point of inflexion.

7. In the above demonstrations it has been assumed that the functions concerned have a differential coefficient for all values of the
variable considered. There are, however, continuous functions which do
not have a definite derivative for
every value of the variable, although
they may have a maximum or minimum value at some point for which
there is no definite differential coefficient.

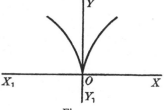

Fig. 30.

For example, there is a minimum value at the point $x = 0$ on
the curve

$$y = x^{\frac{2}{3}},$$

although there is no definite derivative at that point. When
$x = 0$, $\dfrac{dy}{dx}$ is infinite.

8. We will conclude this chapter with some miscellaneous applications of the above processes.

Example 7.

Find the maximum value of $(x - a)^2 (x - b)$.

$$y = (x - a)^2 (x - b),$$

$$\frac{dy}{dx} = 2 (x - a) (x - b) + (x - a)^2 = (x - a) (3x - 2b - a).$$

If $\dfrac{dy}{dx} = 0$, then $x = a$, or $\dfrac{a + 2b}{3}$;

$$\frac{d^2y}{dx^2} = 3x - 2b - a + 3(x - a) = 6x - 2b - 4a.$$

If $x = a$, $$\frac{d^2y}{dx^2} = 2a - 2b,$$

and if $x = \dfrac{a + 2b}{3}$, $$\frac{d^2y}{dx^2} = 2b - 2a.$$

We cannot therefore determine the sign of the second differential coefficient unless we know the relative magnitudes of a and b.

If $a > b$, $x = \dfrac{a + 2b}{3}$ gives y a maximum value,

$a < b$, $x = a$,,   ,,

$a = b$,   there is a point of inflexion for the value $x = a$.

The required values of $(x - a)^2(x - b)$ will be found by substitution of the values of x in the original expression.

Example 8.

Divide the number 21 into three parts a, b, c in continued proportion such that $3a + 6b + 4c$ may be a maximum.

Since a, b, c are in continued proportion, $a : b :: b : c$, so that we may write $a = bk$ and $b = ck$.

$$\therefore \quad a = ck^2.$$

But $$a + b + c = 21.$$

$$\therefore \quad (1 + k + k^2) c = 21 \quad \dotfill (i).$$

We have to find the maximum value of $3a + 6b + 4c$ or, in terms of c and k, of $(4 + 6k + 3k^2) c$.

Let $$(4 + 6k + 3k^2) c = z \dotfill (ii).$$

Then if there were one variable k, the necessary procedure would be to find the values of k which give $\dfrac{dz}{dk}$ a zero value. But c may vary as well as k, and if we differentiate z with respect to k a further differential coefficient, namely $\dfrac{dc}{dk}$, is involved. We can, however, make use of equation (i) and thus eliminate $\dfrac{dc}{dk}$ from our differential equations.

Differentiating equations (i) and (ii) respectively with respect to k,

$$(2k + 1) c + (1 + k + k^2) \frac{dc}{dk} = 0,$$

$$(6k + 6) c + (4 + 6k + 3k^2) \frac{dc}{dk} = \frac{dz}{dk} = 0$$

for a critical value.

Eliminating $\dfrac{dc}{dk}$, we obtain easily that

$$3k^2 + 2k - 2 = 0,$$

so that $k = \dfrac{-1 \pm \sqrt{7}}{3}$, the positive root giving a maximum value.

Substituting in (i) and simplifying,

$$c = 14 - \sqrt{7},$$

whence

$$a = 14 - 4\sqrt{7},$$

$$b = 5\sqrt{7} - 7,$$

and the required value of $3a + 6b + 4c$ becomes $56 + 14\sqrt{7}$.

(The minimum value, found from the value $k = \dfrac{-1 - \sqrt{7}}{3}$, is $56 - 14\sqrt{7}$).

Example 9.

Find the maximum value of $2(a - x)(x + \sqrt{x^2 + b^2})$ where x is real.

In certain circumstances it may happen that a simple and straight-forward method of obtaining maximum or minimum values can be evolved by reference to algebra or geometry.

For example, although by differentiating the above expression and equating the result to zero the required value can be obtained, a neater proof results from the use of a well-known algebraic property.

$$(a - x)^2 \text{ and } x^2 + b^2 \text{ are positive since } x \text{ is real.}$$

$$\therefore \quad (a - x)^2 + (x^2 + b^2) \not< 2\sqrt{(a - x)^2 (x^2 + b^2)},$$

i.e. $$\not< 2(a - x)\sqrt{x^2 + b^2},$$

i.e. $$a^2 - 2ax + x^2 + x^2 + b^2 \not< 2(a - x)\sqrt{x^2 + b^2},$$

or $$-2(a - x)x + a^2 + b^2 \not< 2(a - x)\sqrt{x^2 + b^2},$$

i.e. $$a^2 + b^2 \not< 2(a - x)(x + \sqrt{x^2 + b^2}).$$

In other words, $2(a - x)(x + \sqrt{x^2 + b^2})$ is not greater than $a^2 + b^2$, i.e. the maximum value of the expression is $a^2 + b^2$.

EXAMPLES 12

Find the maximum and minimum values, where such exist, of

1. $\dfrac{x}{(x^2 - 5x + 9)}$.

2. $\dfrac{x^3}{3} + ax^2 - 3a^2 x$.

3. $\dfrac{x^2 + x + 1}{x^2 - x + 1}$.

4. $x^2 (1 + x^2)^{-3}$.

5. $x^4 - 4x^2 + 73$.

6. $\dfrac{x^2 - 1}{(3 + x^2)^3}$.

7. $12x^5 - 45x^4 + 40x^3 + 6$.

8. $\dfrac{(x + a)(x + b)}{(x - a)(x - b)}$.

9. $x^3 - 5x^2 + 8x - 4$.

10. $ax + by$, where $xy = c^2$.

11. If $ux = a^2 + n^2 x^2$, find the value of x which gives u its smallest value.

12. Find the maxima and minima of $1 + 2 \sin \theta + 3 \cos^2 \theta$.

13. If $xy = 720$ find to one place of decimals the minimum value of $5x + 3y$.

14. Find the maximum value of $\dfrac{1}{x^x}$.

15. Show that $x^3 - 3x^2 + 6x + 3$ has neither a maximum nor a minimum value.

16. Find the minimum value of $9^x - 6x \log_e 3$.

17. Find the values of α and β in order that $x^6 + \alpha x^5 + \beta x^4$ may have a maximum value when $x = 2$ and a minimum value when $x = 3$.

18. $ABCD$ is a rectangular field; AB is 200 yards, BC is 100 yards. A man has to walk from A to C. He can walk at 5 miles an hour down the side AB, but directly he leaves the path AB and strikes across the grass he can only go at 3 miles an hour. Find which is his quickest route.

19. An open box is to be made on a square base with vertical sides out of a given quantity of cardboard of area c^2. What is the maximum volume of the box?

20. Into how many parts must the number ne be divided so that their continued product may be a maximum; n being a positive integer and e the base of the Napierian logarithms?

21. A rectangular piece of cardboard, sides a, b, has an equal square cut out of each corner. Find the side of the square so that the remainder may form a box of maximum volume.

22. Find the length of the shortest straight line which can be drawn through the point (a, b) terminated by the rectilinear axes.

23. A man is 2 miles from the nearest point A of a straight road, and he wishes to reach a point B on the road 4 miles from A. He can walk at 4 miles per hour until he reaches the road and at 5 miles per hour on the road. Find the least time in which he can reach B.

24. Find the maximum and minimum values of y regarded as a function of the variable x, where $ax^2 + 2hxy + by^2 + 2cx = 0$.

25. A fixed point is taken on a circle of radius r, and a chord is drawn from this point to any other point on the circle. The tangent to the circle at the second point is constructed and a perpendicular is dropped from the fixed point on to the tangent. Prove that the maximum area of the triangle formed by the chord, the tangent and the perpendicular is $3\sqrt{3}r^2/8$.

26. In a submarine telegraph cable the speed of signalling varies as $x^2 \log \dfrac{1}{x}$, where x is the ratio of the radius of the core to that of the covering. Show that the greatest speed is attained when this ratio is $1 : e^{\frac{1}{2}}$.

27. A person being in a boat a miles from the nearest point A of the beach wishes to reach as quickly as possible a point B which is b miles from A along the shore. The ratio of his rate of walking to his rate of rowing is λ. Find the distance from A at which he should land.

28. A wire of given length is cut into two portions which are bent into the shapes of a circle and a square respectively. Show that if the sum of the areas be the least possible the side of the square is twice the radius of the circle.

29. An open tank is to be constructed with a square base and vertical sides so as to contain a given quantity of water. Show that the expense of lining it with lead will be least if the depth is made half the width.

30. Find the least value of $ae^{\kappa x} + be^{-\kappa x}$.

31. Find the maximum area of the rectangle which can be drawn with its sides passing through the four corners of a given rectangle whose sides are a and b in length respectively.

32. A train passes a station X at a rate of 30 miles per hour. Its speed increases and at any point exceeds the speed at X by a quantity proportional to the time elapsed since leaving X. At the end of a minute it passes Y, 3840 feet from X. A second train passes X 8 seconds after

the first and travels at a uniform speed of 45 miles per hour. Find the minimum distance between the two trains at any time.

33. A function y is the sum of two functions of which the first varies as the cube of x and the second inversely as the square of x. The least value of y is 5 which occurs when $x = 1$. Find the complete expression of y as a function of x.

34. Trace the curve $y = \dfrac{x^2 + 1}{x^2 + x + 1}$, finding the maximum and minimum values of y.

35. Find the maximum and minimum values of $y = x + \dfrac{4}{x + 2}$. Illustrate your results by drawing a graph of the function.

36. If x be the independent variable find the maximum and minimum values of y given

$$y - 12 - x^4 (5x^2 + 6x - 15) = 0.$$

37. Explain how to discriminate between the maxima and minima values of $f(x)$, if

$$\frac{df(x)}{dx} = (x - a)^4 (x - b)^3 (x - c),$$

and a, b, c be in ascending order of magnitude.

38. Explain what is meant by a "point of inflexion" on a curve and show how to find the points of inflexion, if any, on the curve $y = f(x)$. Find the points of inflexion on the curve

$$y^2 = \frac{x^2}{a^2} (a^2 - x^2).$$

39. Draw a graph of the curve $y = e^{-x^2}$, and find the points of inflexion.

40. Find the points of inflexion on the curve $y = \dfrac{x^2}{1 + x^2}$ and illustrate by a diagram.

41. Prove that the triangle of maximum area inscribed in a circle is such that the tangents to the circle at the angular points are parallel to the opposite sides.

42. If $\dfrac{x^2}{a} + \dfrac{y^2}{b} = 1$, show that the maximum and minimum values of $x^2 + xy + y^2$ are the roots of the equation

$$4z^2 - 4z(a + b) + 3ab = 0.$$

43. $9y^2 + 6xy + 4x^2 - 24y - 8x + 4 = 0.$
Find the maximum and minimum values of y.

44. Given
$$\log_{10} e = \cdot 4343; \quad \log_{10} 2 = \cdot 3010; \quad \log_{10} 3 = \cdot 4771,$$
find the maximum and minimum values of
$$12 \left(\log_e x + 1\right) + x^2 - 10x.$$

45. Draw a rough sketch of a curve
$$y \left(2x^2 + 13x - 7\right) = 10x^2 + 30x,$$
and find the maximum and minimum values of y.

46. If $x^2 + y^2 = 1$, find the minimum value of $3x + 4y$.

47. Find the minimum value of
$$\frac{a^2 \cos^2 x + b^2 \sin^2 x}{\sin^2 x \cos^2 x}.$$

CHAPTER XIII

MISCELLANEOUS THEOREMS

1. Indeterminate forms.

It has been demonstrated in Chapter IX (para. 8) that the limit of $f(x)$ as $x \to a$ is frequently required although $f(a)$ itself has no meaning. Forms such as $\frac{0}{0}$ which result from the direct substitution of a for x in $f(x)$ are called *indeterminate forms*. To obtain $\underset{x \to a}{Lt} f(x)$, where $f(a)$ is an indeterminate form, we may resort to algebraic methods as previously shown, or we may adapt the processes of the differential calculus to the solution of the problem.

Let $\phi(x)$ and $\psi(x)$ be two functions of x continuous as far as the value $x = a$ and let $\phi(a) = 0 = \psi(a)$, so that $\frac{\phi(a)}{\psi(a)}$ is of the indeterminate form $\frac{0}{0}$.

Let $f(x) = \frac{\phi(x)}{\psi(x)}$. Write $a + h$ for x, so that $\underset{x \to a}{Lt}$ is the same as $\underset{h \to 0}{Lt}$.

Then $f(x) = \frac{\phi(x)}{\psi(x)} = \frac{\phi(a+h)}{\psi(a+h)} = \frac{\phi(a) + h\phi'(a + \theta_1 h)}{\psi(a) + h\psi'(a + \theta_2 h)}$.

But $\phi(a)$ and $\psi(a)$ are each zero.

Therefore $f(x) = \frac{\phi'(a + \theta_1 h)}{\psi'(a + \theta_2 h)}$ (dividing numerator and denominator by h).

Therefore $\underset{x \to a}{Lt} f(x) = \underset{h \to 0}{Lt} \frac{\phi(x)}{\psi(x)} = \frac{\phi'(a)}{\psi'(a)}$, since when $h \to 0$, $a + \theta_1 h$ and $a + \theta_2 h$ each $\to a$.

To obtain $\underset{x \to a}{Lt} f(x)$ when $f(a)$ is the indeterminate form $\frac{0}{0}$ we therefore differentiate numerator and denominator separately and put $x = a$ in the result.

If $\phi'(a)$ and $\psi'(a)$ are both zero (so that the form $\frac{0}{0}$ is again obtained) a further differentiation must be effected and *a* substituted for x in $\dfrac{\phi''(x)}{\psi''(x)}$; and so on if this be indeterminate.

2. The following examples are illustrative of the method.

Example 1.

Show that $\underset{x \to 1}{\mathrm{Lt}} \dfrac{x^6 - 5x + 4}{x^3 - 2x + 1}$ is 1 (cf. Ex. 5, p. 143).

$\dfrac{x^6 - 5x + 4}{x^3 - 2x + 1}$ takes the form $\dfrac{0}{0}$ when 1 is substituted for x.

$$\therefore \quad \underset{x \to 1}{\mathrm{Lt}} \frac{x^6 - 5x + 4}{x^3 - 2x + 1} = \underset{x \to 1}{\mathrm{Lt}} \frac{6x^5 - 5}{3x^2 - 2} = \frac{1}{1} = 1.$$

Example 2.

Find $\underset{\theta \to 0}{\mathrm{Lt}} \dfrac{\sin^{-1}\theta - \theta}{\theta^3}$.

$$\underset{\theta \to 0}{\mathrm{Lt}} \frac{\sin^{-1}\theta - \theta}{\theta^3} \qquad \text{form } \frac{0}{0}.$$

Differentiating numerator and denominator separately:

$$= \underset{\theta \to 0}{\mathrm{Lt}} \frac{\dfrac{1}{\sqrt{1 - \theta^2}} - 1}{3\theta^2} \qquad \text{form } \frac{0}{0}.$$

Differentiating again:
$$= \underset{\theta \to 0}{\mathrm{Lt}} \frac{\theta(1 - \theta^2)^{-\frac{3}{2}}}{6\theta}$$

$$= \underset{\theta \to 0}{\mathrm{Lt}} \frac{(1 - \theta^2)^{-\frac{3}{2}}}{6}, \text{ on dividing through by } \theta,$$

$$= \tfrac{1}{6}.$$

3. Other indeterminate forms: ∞/∞; $0 \times \infty$; $\infty - \infty$; 0^0; ∞^0; 1^∞.

In order to obtain the limits of functions which take these forms it is strictly necessary to consider each variation separately and to prove that we may in effect obtain the required limit by application of the calculus. It will be sufficient, however, simply to indicate the methods to be adopted for the solution of the problems.

(*a*) The form ∞/∞.

If $\underset{x \to a}{\mathrm{Lt}} \dfrac{\phi(x)}{\psi(x)}$ take the form $\dfrac{\infty}{\infty}$, it can be shown that, as for the form $\dfrac{0}{0}$,
$$\underset{x \to a}{\mathrm{Lt}} \frac{\phi(x)}{\psi(x)} = \underset{x \to a}{\mathrm{Lt}} \frac{\phi'(x)}{\psi'(x)}.$$

(For a proof of this theorem, see Gibson's *Elementary Treatise on the Calculus*, p. 420.)

(*b*) Form $0 \times \infty$.

Let $\underset{x \to a}{\mathrm{Lt}} \; \phi(x)\,\psi(x)$ take the form $0 \times \infty$, $(\phi(a) = 0; \psi(a) = \infty)$.

Then $\phi(x)\,\psi(x) = \dfrac{\phi(x)}{\dfrac{1}{\psi(x)}}$ which is of the form $\dfrac{0}{0}$, and the ordinary processes may be adopted.

(*c*) $\infty - \infty$; 0^0; ∞^0; 1^∞.

These forms are best treated by algebraic methods, e.g. by expanding certain series, by taking logarithms, etc. It is advisable not to adopt any standard methods for evaluation of limits in these examples, but to consider each one separately as it arises.

Example 3.

Evaluate $\underset{x \to \infty}{\mathrm{Lt}} \; x^n e^{-x}$, where n is a positive integer.

$$
\begin{aligned}
\underset{x \to \infty}{\mathrm{Lt}} \; x^n e^{-x} &= \underset{x \to \infty}{\mathrm{Lt}} \; \frac{x^n}{e^x} && \text{form } \frac{\infty}{\infty} \\
&= \underset{x \to \infty}{\mathrm{Lt}} \; \frac{n x^{n-1}}{e^x} && \text{''} \\
&= \underset{x \to \infty}{\mathrm{Lt}} \; \frac{n(n-1)\,x^{n-2}}{e^x} && \text{''} \\
&\qquad \dotsm\dotsm\dotsm\dotsm\dotsm \\
&= \underset{x \to \infty}{\mathrm{Lt}} \; \frac{n!}{e^x} \\
&= 0.
\end{aligned}
$$

Example 4.

Find $\underset{x \to 0}{\mathrm{Lt}} \; \left\{ \dfrac{1}{x} - \dfrac{1}{x^2} \log(1 + x) \right\}$.

$\underset{x \to 0}{\mathrm{Lt}} \; \left\{ \dfrac{1}{x} - \dfrac{1}{x^2} \log(1 + x) \right\}$ is of the form $\infty - \infty$.

$$
\begin{aligned}
\text{Write it as} \quad & \underset{x \to 0}{\mathrm{Lt}} \; \frac{x - \log(1 + x)}{x^2} && \text{form } \frac{0}{0} \\
&= \underset{x \to 0}{\mathrm{Lt}} \; \frac{1 - (1 + x)^{-1}}{2x} \\
&= \underset{x \to 0}{\mathrm{Lt}} \; \frac{(1 + x)^{-2}}{2} = \tfrac{1}{2}.
\end{aligned}
$$

Example 5.

$$\operatorname*{Lt}_{x \to 1} (1 - x^2)^{\frac{1}{\log (1-x)}}.$$

This takes the form 0^0 when 1 is substituted for x.

Let

$$y = (1 - x^2)^{\frac{1}{\log (1-x)}}.$$

Then

$$\log y = \frac{1}{\log (1 - x)} \log (1 - x^2).$$

$$\therefore \quad \operatorname*{Lt}_{x \to 1} \log y = \operatorname*{Lt}_{x \to 1} \frac{\log (1 - x^2)}{\log (1 - x)} \qquad \text{form } \frac{0}{0}$$

$$= \operatorname*{Lt}_{x \to 1} \frac{\dfrac{-2x}{1 - x^2}}{-\dfrac{1}{1 - x}},$$

which, on removing the common factor $\dfrac{1}{1 - x}$, is

$$\operatorname*{Lt}_{x \to 1} \frac{2x}{1 + x} = 1.$$

$$\therefore \quad \operatorname*{Lt}_{x \to 1} y = e.$$

Note. Care must be taken in applying the principles of the differential calculus to indeterminate forms to remember that

(i) the method holds only when the function takes an indeterminate form when a is substituted for x. Otherwise $\operatorname*{Lt}_{x \to a} \dfrac{\phi(x)}{\psi(x)}$ will not be $\operatorname*{Lt}_{x \to a} \dfrac{\phi'(x)}{\psi'(x)}$;

(ii) the differentiation is performed on the numerator and denominator separately. $\dfrac{\phi(x)}{\psi(x)}$ must not be differentiated as the quotient of two functions of x.

4. Partial differentiation.

If $f(x, y) = 0$ defines an implicit function of x and y, we may obtain $\dfrac{dy}{dx}$ by differentiating in the usual manner and then solving the resulting equation for $\dfrac{dy}{dx}$.

F

For example, if

$$x^2 + xy + y^2 = 0,$$

then

$$2x + y + xy' + 2yy' = 0,$$

and

$$y' = - (2x + y)/(x + 2y).$$

Where there are two or more independent variables an alternative method can be adopted which is often simpler in its application. This is the method known as partial differentiation.

Consider the function $f(x, y) = x^2 + xy + y^2$ where x and y are independent variables. Then if we differentiate $f(x, y)$ with respect to x keeping y constant, the result is said to be the partial differential coefficient of $f(x, y)$ with respect to x; similarly, on differentiating with respect to y keeping x constant, we obtain the partial differential coefficient of $f(x, y)$ with respect to y.

The usual notation is $\dfrac{\partial}{\partial x} f(x, y)$; $\dfrac{\partial}{\partial y} f(x, y)$ for partial derivatives with respect to x and y respectively.

In the above example $\dfrac{\partial f}{\partial x} = 2x + y$ and $\dfrac{\partial f}{\partial y} = x + 2y$.

Generally, if u be written for $f(x, y)$,

$$\frac{\partial u}{\partial x} = \underset{\Delta x \to 0}{\mathrm{Lt}} \frac{f(x + \Delta x, y) - f(x, y)}{\Delta x},$$

and

$$\frac{\partial u}{\partial y} = \underset{\Delta y \to 0}{\mathrm{Lt}} \frac{f(x, y + \Delta y) - f(x, y)}{\Delta y}.$$

5. To prove that, if x and y be functions of a third variable z, then

$$\frac{du}{dz} = \frac{\partial u}{\partial x} \frac{dx}{dz} + \frac{\partial u}{\partial y} \frac{dy}{dz}.$$

Let x, y, u become $x + \Delta x$, $y + \Delta y$, $u + \Delta u$ respectively when z becomes $z + \Delta z$.

Now if we let x vary while $y + \Delta y$ remains constant, we have, by the Mean Value Theorem,

$$f(x + \Delta x, y + \Delta y) = f(x, y + \Delta y) + \Delta x \frac{\partial}{\partial x} f(x + \theta_1 \Delta x, y + \Delta y).$$

Similarly,

$$f(x, y + \Delta y) = f(x, y) + \Delta y \frac{\partial}{\partial y} f(x, y + \theta_2 \Delta y).$$

Adding these two results and dividing by Δz, we obtain

$$\frac{\Delta u}{\Delta z} = \frac{f(x + \Delta x, y + \Delta y) - f(x, y)}{\Delta z}$$

$$= \frac{\Delta x}{\Delta z} \frac{\partial}{\partial x} f(x + \theta_1 \Delta x, y + \Delta y) + \frac{\Delta y}{\Delta z} \frac{\partial}{\partial y} f(x, y + \theta_2 \Delta y).$$

Taking the limit $\Delta z \to 0$, so that $\Delta u, \Delta x, \Delta y$ also $\to 0$,

$$\frac{\Delta u}{\Delta z}, \frac{\Delta x}{\Delta z}, \frac{\Delta y}{\Delta z} \quad \text{become} \quad \frac{du}{dz}, \frac{dx}{dz}, \frac{dy}{dz} \quad \text{respectively,}$$

$$\frac{\partial}{\partial x} f(x + \theta_1 \Delta x, y + \Delta y) \quad \text{becomes} \quad \frac{\partial}{\partial x} f(x, y), \text{ i.e. } \frac{\partial u}{\partial x},$$

and $\quad \dfrac{\partial}{\partial y} f(x, y + \theta_2 \Delta y) \quad$ becomes $\quad \dfrac{\partial}{\partial y} f(x, y)$, i.e. $\dfrac{\partial u}{\partial y}$.

$$\therefore \quad \frac{du}{dz} = \frac{\partial u}{\partial x} \frac{dx}{dz} + \frac{\partial u}{\partial y} \frac{dy}{dz}.$$

Corollary. If $z = x$, so that y is a function of x, and u, although expressed in terms of x and y, is a function of the single variable x,

then $\quad \dfrac{du}{dx} = \dfrac{\partial u}{\partial x} + \dfrac{\partial u}{\partial y} \dfrac{dy}{dx}$, since $\dfrac{dx}{dx} = 1$.

Suppose now that $u = f(x, y) = 0$; then

$$0 = \frac{\partial u}{\partial x} + \frac{\partial u}{\partial y} \frac{dy}{dx},$$

or $\quad \dfrac{dy}{dx} = -\dfrac{\partial u}{\partial x} \bigg/ \dfrac{\partial u}{\partial y}.$

This is a convenient formula for obtaining $\dfrac{dy}{dx}$ when y is an implicit function of x.

For example, if $\quad x^2 + xy + y^2 = 0$,

$$0 = (2x + y) + (x + 2y) \frac{dy}{dx}.$$

$$\therefore \quad \frac{dy}{dx} = -\frac{2x + y}{x + 2y} \quad \text{as before.}$$

6. A further investigation of the theory of partial differentiation involves detailed mathematical analysis. Two important theorems are, however, worthy of mention:

(i) Defining $\dfrac{\partial^2 u}{\partial x \partial y}$ as the operation $\dfrac{\partial}{\partial x}\left(\dfrac{\partial}{\partial y}\right)$, i.e. the process of partial differentiation of $\dfrac{\partial u}{\partial y}$ with respect to x, keeping y constant, it can be shown that

$$\frac{\partial^2 u}{\partial x \partial y} = \frac{\partial^2 u}{\partial y \partial x}.$$

In other words, the operations of differentiating partially with respect to x and y are commutative.

(ii) If $u = f(x, y)$ is a homogeneous function of the nth degree in x and y, then

$$x\frac{\partial u}{\partial x} + y\frac{\partial u}{\partial y} = nu \quad \text{(Euler's Theorem)}.$$

The proofs of these theorems are difficult, and it will be sufficient to verify that they are true by simple examples.

Example 6.

If $u = y^x$, show that $\dfrac{\partial^2 u}{\partial x \partial y} = \dfrac{\partial^2 u}{\partial y \partial x}$.

$$\frac{\partial u}{\partial y} = xy^{x-1}; \quad \frac{\partial^2 u}{\partial x \partial y} = \frac{\partial}{\partial x}\left(\frac{\partial u}{\partial y}\right) = y^{x-1} + xy^{x-1}\log y,$$

$$\frac{\partial u}{\partial x} = y^x \log y; \quad \frac{\partial^2 u}{\partial y \partial x} = \frac{\partial}{\partial y}\left(\frac{\partial u}{\partial x}\right) = xy^{x-1}\log y + y^x\frac{1}{y}$$

$$= xy^{x-1}\log y + y^{x-1},$$

which proves the proposition.

Example 7.

Show that Euler's Theorem for a homogeneous function of x and y holds for

$$ax^3 + by^3 + cx^2y + dxy^2.$$

It is required to prove that, if

$$u = ax^3 + by^3 + cx^2y + dxy^2,$$

then

$$x\frac{\partial u}{\partial x} + y\frac{\partial u}{\partial y} = 3u.$$

$$\frac{\partial u}{\partial x} = 3ax^2 + 2cxy + dy^2,$$

$$\frac{\partial u}{\partial y} = 3by^2 + cx^2 + 2dxy.$$

$$\therefore \ x\,\frac{\partial u}{\partial x} + y\,\frac{\partial u}{\partial y} = 3ax^3 + 2cx^2y + dxy^2 + 3by^3 + cx^2y + 2dxy^2$$
$$= 3u.$$

Euler's Theorem can be extended to any number of variables, so that, if u is a homogeneous function of x, y, z, ... of degree n,

$$x\,\frac{\partial u}{\partial x} + y\,\frac{\partial u}{\partial y} + z\,\frac{\partial u}{\partial z} + \ldots = nu.$$

7. Relation between the operators $\dfrac{d}{dx}$ and Δ.

It has been shown that, if u_x be a rational integral function of x, we may express u_x in the form $e^{xD}u_0$, where D denotes the operation of differentiation (Chap. XI, para. 13).

I.e. $\qquad\qquad E^x u_0 = e^{xD} u_0,$

or $\qquad\qquad\qquad E^x \equiv e^{xD}.$

If now $x = 1$ we have

$$E \equiv e^D \ \text{ or } \ 1 + \Delta \equiv e^D,$$

so that $\qquad\qquad D \equiv \log\,(1 + \Delta)$

$$\equiv \Delta - \frac{\Delta^2}{2} + \frac{\Delta^3}{3} - \frac{\Delta^4}{4} + \ldots,$$

$$D^2 \equiv \left[\Delta - \frac{\Delta^2}{2} + \frac{\Delta^3}{3} - \frac{\Delta^4}{4} + \ldots\right]^2$$

$$\equiv \Delta^2 - \Delta^3 + \tfrac{11}{12}\Delta^4 - \tfrac{5}{6}\Delta^5 + \ldots.$$

Similarly, $\qquad D^3 \equiv \Delta^3 - \tfrac{3}{2}\Delta^4 + \tfrac{7}{4}\Delta^5 - \ldots.$

We have therefore a convenient method for expressing the differential coefficients of a function of x in terms of the differences of the function.

Example 8.

μ_x (the force of mortality) $= -\dfrac{1}{l_x}\dfrac{dl_x}{dx}$, where l_x is the number of persons at exact age x in any year of time. Given the following table, find a value for μ_{50}.

Age ...	50	51	52	53
l_x	73,499	72,724	71,753	70,599

The difference table is

x	l_x	Δl_x	$\Delta^2 l_x$	$\Delta^3 l_x$
50	73,499			
		-775		
51	72,724		-196	
		-971		13
52	71,753		-183	
		-1154		
53	70,599			

$$\therefore \frac{dl_x}{dx} = \left(\Delta - \frac{\Delta^2}{2} + \frac{\Delta^3}{3}\right) l_x$$

$$= -775 + 98 + 4\cdot333\ldots, \quad \text{when } x = 50,$$

$$= -672\cdot667.$$

$$\therefore \mu_{50} = \left[-\frac{1}{l_x}\frac{dl_x}{dx}\right]_{x=50} = \frac{672\cdot667}{73,499} = \cdot00915\ldots.$$

8. We can easily express $\dfrac{du_x}{dx}$ in terms of central differences. For example, Stirling's formula is

$$u_x = u_0 + x\,\frac{\Delta u_0 + \Delta u_{-1}}{2} + \frac{x^2}{2!}\Delta^2 u_{-1} + \frac{x(x^2-1)}{3!}\,\frac{\Delta^3 u_{-1} + \Delta^3 u_{-2}}{2}\ldots.$$

Differentiating with respect to x:

$$\frac{du_x}{dx} = \frac{\Delta u_0 + \Delta u_{-1}}{2} + x\Delta^2 u_{-1} + \frac{3x^2-1}{6}\,\frac{\Delta^3 u_{-1} + \Delta^3 u_{-2}}{2} +\ldots.$$

$$\therefore \left(\frac{du_x}{dx}\right)_{x=0} = \frac{\Delta u_0 + \Delta u_{-1}}{2} - \frac{1}{12}[\Delta^3 u_{-1} + \Delta^3 u_{-2}]$$

as far as third differences

$$= \frac{u_1 - u_{-1}}{2} - \frac{1}{12}[u_2 - 3u_1 + 3u_0 - u_{-1} + u_1 - 3u_0 + 3u_{-1} - u_{-2}]$$

$$= \frac{2}{3}(u_1 - u_{-1}) - \frac{1}{12}(u_2 - u_{-2}) \quad \text{on simplifying.}$$

Changing the origin, we have

$$\frac{du_x}{dx} = \frac{2}{3}(u_{x+1} - u_{x-1}) - \frac{1}{12}(u_{x+2} - u_{x-2}).$$

A first approximation will evidently be

$$\frac{du_x}{dx} = \frac{u_{x+1} - u_{x-1}}{2},$$

or, if the unit of differencing be h,

$$= \frac{u_{x+h} - u_{x-h}}{2}.$$

9. Another formula, giving the differential coefficient in terms of differences of u_x, can be obtained from Bessel's formula.

$$u_x = \frac{u_0 + u_1}{2} + (x - \tfrac{1}{2}) \Delta u_0 + \frac{x(x-1)}{2!} \frac{\Delta^2 u_{-1} + \Delta^2 u_0}{2}$$

$$+ \frac{(x - \tfrac{1}{2}) x (x - 1)}{3!} \Delta^3 u_{-1} + \dots.$$

Changing x to $x + \tfrac{1}{2}$,

$$u_{x+\frac{1}{2}} = \frac{u_0 + u_1}{2} + x \Delta u_0 + \frac{(x + \tfrac{1}{2})(x - \tfrac{1}{2})}{2!} \frac{\Delta^2 u_{-1} + \Delta^2 u_0}{2}$$

$$+ \frac{x (x + \tfrac{1}{2})(x - \tfrac{1}{2})}{3!} \Delta^3 u_{-1} + \dots.$$

Differentiating:

$$\frac{d}{dx} u_{x+\frac{1}{2}} = \Delta u_0 + x \frac{\Delta^2 u_{-1} + \Delta^2 u_0}{2} + \left(\frac{x^2}{2} - \frac{1}{24}\right) \Delta^3 u_{-1} + \dots.$$

If $x = 0$, $\qquad$ $\dfrac{d}{dx} u_{\frac{1}{2}} = \Delta u_0 - \dfrac{\Delta^3 u_{-1}}{24} + \dots.$

Changing the origin to $x - \tfrac{1}{2}$ we have the approximation

$$\frac{d}{dx} u_x = \Delta u_{x-\frac{1}{2}} - \frac{\Delta^3 u_{x-\frac{3}{2}}}{24} + \dots.$$

An interesting discussion on the calculation of the values of differential coefficients of a function by means of selected values of the variable will be found in $T.F.A.$ vol. IX, pp. 238 et $seq.$ (G. J. Lidstone). By means of prepared tables of coefficients Mr Lidstone evolves formulae for the values of the successive differential coefficients, using both advancing differences and central differences. In addition, alternative processes are given for the values of the derivatives when the intervals are unequal.

10. Osculatory interpolation.

It may happen that we know the values of u_x at intervals of a unit, and that we wish to calculate a complete table of values with smaller intervals. For example it is a common practice to calculate every fifth value in a life-table, and to complete the table by interpolation: here the unit interval for the preliminary calculations is five years.

If we decide to use a third difference formula then every interpolation involves four of the given values. For the interval 0 to 1 the best course is to base the formula on the four values u_{-1}, u_0, u_1, u_2, thus giving equal weight to values on either side of the interval. An appropriate formula is Bessel's formula, namely,

$$u_x = \tfrac{1}{2}(u_0 + u_1) + (x - \tfrac{1}{2})\Delta u_0 + \frac{x(x-1)}{2!}\frac{\Delta^2 u_0 + \Delta^2 u_{-1}}{2}$$

$$+ \frac{(x - \tfrac{1}{2})x(x-1)}{3!}\Delta^3 u_{-1} \quad \ldots\ldots\text{(i)}.$$

This is the formula for the interval 0 to 1. For the interval 1 to 2 we should use the corresponding formula based on the four given values u_0, u_1, u_2, u_3.

Thus for the two intervals 0 to 1 and 1 to 2, the two interpolation curves have a common ordinate when $x = 1$; they may not necessarily have a common tangent. Two neighbouring interpolation curves will usually cut one another at the point of junction, and while there will be a smooth run of values within each unit interval the values will not run smoothly with those in the next interval.

We are led therefore to enquire whether we can find a series of curves of interpolation which shall have common tangents as well as common ordinates at the points of junction. Such curves are said to have *contact of the first order* at the points where they join, and the necessary condition for this contact is evidently that u_x and $\dfrac{du_x}{dx}$ must have the same values at these points on the one curve as on the other.

The interpolation curve given by Bessel's formula (i) for the interval 0 to 1 was based on the conditions that it should have u_{-1}, u_0, u_1, u_2 as ordinates. We retain the condition that u_0 and u_1

should be ordinates and abandon the condition that u_{-1} and u_2 should be ordinates. Instead, we shall stipulate that the differential coefficients of u_x when $x = 0$ and when $x = 1$ have known values. To fix these values we shall proceed as follows:

The interpolation curves for the two intervals -1 to 0 and 0 to 1 are to have the same tangent when $x = 0$ as the curve of second degree which has u_{-1}, u_0 and u_1 for ordinates. The equation to this curve may be written

$$F_x(-1, 0, 1) = \tfrac{1}{2}(u_0 + u_1) + (x - \tfrac{1}{2})\Delta u_0 + \tfrac{1}{2}x(x - 1)\Delta^2 u_{-1} \ldots\text{(ii)}.$$

The interpolation curves for the two intervals 0 to 1 and 1 to 2 are to have the same tangent when $x = 1$ as the curve of the second degree which has u_0, u_1 and u_2 for ordinates. In a similar manner to the above the equation to this curve may be written

$$F_x(0, 1, 2) = \tfrac{1}{2}(u_0 + u_1) + (x - \tfrac{1}{2})\Delta u_0 + \tfrac{1}{2}x(x - 1)\Delta^2 u_0 \ldots\text{(iii)}.$$

It will be noticed that the forms that we have chosen for the equations (ii) and (iii) differ only in the last term.

Differentiating (ii),

$$F_x'(-1, 0, 1) = \Delta u_0 + (x - \tfrac{1}{2})\Delta^2 u_{-1},$$

so that $\qquad F_0'(-1, 0, 1) = \Delta u_0 - \tfrac{1}{2}\Delta^2 u_{-1} \qquad \ldots\ldots\text{(iv)}.$

Differentiating (iii),

$$F_x'(0, 1, 2) = \Delta u_0 + (x - \tfrac{1}{2})\Delta^2 u_0,$$

and $\qquad F_1'(0, 1, 2) = \Delta u_0 + \tfrac{1}{2}\Delta^2 u_0 \qquad \ldots\ldots\text{(v)}.$

The values of $F_0'(-1, 0, 1)$ and $F_1'(0, 1, 2)$ in (iv) and (v) are to be values of the differential coefficients of the required interpolation curve for the interval 0 to 1.

Let v_x be that curve, so that its ordinates when $x = -1, 0, 1, 2$ form the basis for an ordinary interpolation formula of the third degree:

$$v_x = \tfrac{1}{2}(v_0 + v_1) + (x - \tfrac{1}{2})\Delta v_0 + \frac{x(x-1)}{2!}\frac{\Delta^2 v_0 + \Delta^2 v_{-1}}{2}$$

$$+ \frac{(x - \tfrac{1}{2})x(x-1)}{3!}\Delta^3 v_{-1} \quad\ldots\ldots\text{(vi)}.$$

The tangents to this curve are given by the equation

$$v_x' = \Delta v_0 + (x - \tfrac{1}{2})\frac{\Delta^2 v_0 + \Delta^2 v_{-1}}{2} + \frac{3x^2 - 3x + \tfrac{1}{2}}{6}\Delta^3 v_{-1} \ldots\text{(vii)}.$$

The conditions to be satisfied are:

$$v_0 = u_0,$$

$$v_1 = u_1,$$

$$v_0' = F_0'(-1, 0, 1) = \Delta u_0 - \tfrac{1}{2}\Delta^2 u_{-1},$$

$$v_1' = F_1'(0, 1, 2) = \Delta u_0 + \tfrac{1}{2}\Delta^2 u_0 \qquad \ldots\ldots\text{(viii)}.$$

We have at once $\tfrac{1}{2}(v_0 + v_1) = \tfrac{1}{2}(u_0 + u_1)$, and $\Delta v_0 = \Delta u_0$; these determine the first and second terms in (vi).

From (vii), $\quad v_0' = \Delta v_0 - \dfrac{1}{2}\dfrac{\Delta^2 v_0 + \Delta^2 v_{-1}}{2} + \dfrac{1}{12}\Delta^3 v_{-1},$

$$v_1' = \Delta v_0 + \dfrac{1}{2}\dfrac{\Delta^2 v_0 + \Delta^2 v_{-1}}{2} + \dfrac{1}{12}\Delta^3 v_{-1},$$

and therefore $\quad v_0' + v_1' = 2\Delta v_0 + \tfrac{1}{6}\Delta^3 v_{-1},$

$$v_1' - v_0' = \tfrac{1}{2}(\Delta^2 v_0 + \Delta^2 v_{-1}).$$

But, from (viii),

$$v_0' + v_1' = 2\Delta u_0 + \tfrac{1}{2}\Delta^3 u_{-1},$$

$$v_1' - v_0' = \tfrac{1}{2}(\Delta^2 u_0 + \Delta^2 u_{-1}).$$

Comparing the two expressions for $v_0' + v_1'$ we have at once

$$\Delta^3 v_{-1} = 3\Delta^3 u_{-1} \text{ (since } \Delta v_0 = \Delta u_0),$$

and from the two expressions for $v_1' - v_0'$

$$\tfrac{1}{2}(\Delta^2 v_0 + \Delta^2 v_{-1}) = \tfrac{1}{2}(\Delta^2 u_0 + \Delta^2 u_{-1}).$$

We have now found the values of all four terms of the formula (vi), and we can write the formula in terms of u's as follows:

$$v_x = \tfrac{1}{2}(u_0 + u_1) + (x - \tfrac{1}{2})\Delta u_0 + \frac{x(x-1)}{2}\frac{\Delta^2 u_0 + \Delta^2 u_{-1}}{2}$$

$$+ \frac{x(x-1)(x-\tfrac{1}{2})}{2}\Delta^3 u_{-1} \ldots\ldots\text{(ix)}.$$

This result is a formula of *osculatory interpolation*, and differs from the ordinary central difference formula (i) only in the last term.

The difference is

$$v_x - u_x = \frac{x(x-1)(x-\tfrac{1}{2})}{3}\Delta^3 u_{-1} = \frac{x(x-1)(2x-1)}{6}\Delta^3 u_{-1}.$$

11. The problem of osculatory interpolation has been discussed by many eminent actuarial authorities in the past. The method was devised by Dr Sprague (see *J.I.A.* vol. XXII, p. 270) and was subsequently developed by Mr George King and Dr Buchanan. An elementary demonstration of the method, depending upon advancing differences, is given by Mr King in the Supplement to the 75th Annual Report of the Registrar-General. Dr Buchanan has given an alternative method based on Everett's formula (*J.I.A.* vol. XLII, pp. 369–94) and in the appendix to his paper there appears a simple demonstration of the formulae by Mr G. J. Lidstone.

The proof in para. 10 above is due to Mr D. C. Fraser, and depends on Bessel's formula. The ordinary interpolation formula ending with the term $\Delta^3 u_{-1}$ can be written in many different forms, all giving identical results, and the addition of the expression $\dfrac{x (x - 1) (2x - 1)}{6} \Delta^3 u_{-1}$ produces an osculatory formula.

Suppose, for example, that we take the descending difference formula

$$u_x = u_{-1} + (x + 1) \Delta u_{-1} + \frac{x (x + 1)}{2} \Delta^2 u_{-1} + \frac{x (x^2 - 1)}{6} \Delta^3 u_{-1}.$$

Adding the term $\dfrac{x (x - 1) (2x - 1)}{6} \Delta^3 u_{-1}$ we have

$$v_x = u_{-1} + (x + 1) \Delta u_{-1} + x (x + 1) \Delta^2 u_{-1}$$
$$+ \left\{ \frac{x (x^2 - 1)}{2} + \frac{x (x - 1) (2x - 1)}{6} \right\} \Delta^3 u_{-1}$$
$$= u_0 + x \Delta u_{-1} + \frac{x (x + 1)}{2} \Delta^2 u_{-1} + \frac{x^2 (x - 1)}{2} \Delta^3 u_{-1},$$

which is the form obtained by Mr Lidstone in the appendix to Dr Buchanan's paper.

An interesting Note on the application of a graphic method to formulae of osculatory interpolation appears in the *Actuarial Students' Magazine*, No. 3 (Edinburgh, 1930). By treating osculatory interpolation as a particular case of divided differences, Mr Fraser shows that a diagram similar to the hexagon diagram for ordinary differences (Chap. VIII, para. 11) can be employed to obtain the various forms of osculatory interpolation formulae.

EXAMPLES 13

1. Obtain the limit when $n \to \infty$ of $\dfrac{x^n}{n!}$, where x is finite.

2. Evaluate $\underset{x \to 0}{\text{Lt}} \; x \log x$.

Find the following limits:

3. $\underset{x \to 1}{\text{Lt}} \dfrac{2x^3 - 3x^2 + 1}{3x^5 - 5x^3 + 2}$.

4. $\underset{x \to 0}{\text{Lt}} \dfrac{a^x - 1}{b^x - 1}$.

5. $\underset{x \to 1}{\text{Lt}} \dfrac{x^m - 1}{x^n - 1}$.

6. $\underset{x \to a}{\text{Lt}} \, [x^{\frac{1}{2}} - a^{\frac{1}{2}} + (x - a)^{\frac{1}{2}}] \, (x^2 - a^2)^{-\frac{1}{2}}$.

7. $\underset{x \to 1}{\text{Lt}} \dfrac{1 - x + \log x}{1 - (2x - x^2)^{\frac{1}{2}}}$.

8. $\underset{x \to a}{\text{Lt}} \dfrac{x - a + \sqrt{x^m - a^m}}{\sqrt{x^n - a^n}}$.

9. $\underset{x \to 0}{\text{Lt}} \dfrac{xe^x - \log (1 + x)}{x^2}$.

10. $\underset{x \to 0}{\text{Lt}} \, (1 + x^3)^{\frac{1}{x^3}}$.

11. $\underset{x \to 0}{\text{Lt}} \, (\log x)^{\log (1 - x)}$.

12. $\underset{x \to 0}{\text{Lt}} \dfrac{(1 + x)^{\frac{1}{n}} - 1}{x}$.

13. $\underset{x \to \infty}{\text{Lt}} \, x \, (a^{\frac{1}{x}} - 1)$.

14. $\underset{x \to 0}{\text{Lt}} \dfrac{(1 + x)^{\frac{1}{x}} - e + \frac{1}{2}ex}{x^2}$.

15. $\underset{x \to 0}{\text{Lt}} \, (x \log x)^x$.

16. $\underset{x \to 0}{\text{Lt}} \dfrac{e^x + e^{-x} + 2 \sin x - 4x}{x^5}$.

17. $\underset{x \to 0}{\text{Lt}} \dfrac{\sin^{-1} x - x}{x^3 \cos x}$.

18. An arithmetical and a geometrical progression have each the same first and last terms, a and b, and the same number of terms. If the sums of their terms are s_1 and s_2 respectively, find the limiting value of $\dfrac{s_1}{s_2}$ when the number of terms is indefinitely increased.

19. Prove that the limit of $\left(2 - \dfrac{x}{a}\right)^{\tan \frac{\pi x}{2a}}$ as x tends to a is $e^{\frac{2}{\pi}}$.

20. a and p are positive integers. Find
$$\underset{x \to 0}{\text{Lt}} \dfrac{(a + p)^x - a^x}{x^p}.$$

21. Determine a, b, c so that, as θ tends to zero, the function
$$\dfrac{\theta (a + b \cos \theta) - c \sin \theta}{\theta^5}$$
shall tend to the limit unity.

22. If $x = r \cos \theta$ and $y = r \sin \theta$, prove that
$$\frac{\partial x}{\partial r} = \frac{\partial r}{\partial x} = \cos \theta.$$

Find the value of $x \dfrac{\partial u}{\partial x} + y \dfrac{\partial u}{\partial y}$, given:

23. $u = \sin^{-1} \dfrac{\sqrt{x} - \sqrt{y}}{\sqrt{x} + \sqrt{y}}$.

24. $u = \sin^{-1} \dfrac{x}{y} + \tan^{-1} \dfrac{y}{x}$.

25. $u = x^3 \log \dfrac{\sqrt[3]{y} - \sqrt[3]{x}}{\sqrt[3]{y} + \sqrt[3]{x}}$.

26. $u = \dfrac{x^{\frac{1}{4}} + y^{\frac{1}{4}}}{x^{\frac{1}{5}} + y^{\frac{1}{5}}}$.

27. Show that $\dfrac{\partial^2 u}{\partial x \, \partial y} = \dfrac{\partial^2 u}{\partial y \, \partial x}$, where
$$u = \log (x^2 + y^2) - \log xy.$$

28. Find $\dfrac{dy}{dx}$, given $x^3 + y^3 + 3xy = 0$.

29. Prove that, if $x^3 + y^3 + 3xyz = u$, then
$$x \frac{\partial u}{\partial x} + y \frac{\partial u}{\partial y} + z \frac{\partial u}{\partial z} = 3u.$$

30. If $ue^v = x$, find the value of
$$x \frac{\partial u}{\partial x} + y \frac{\partial u}{\partial y}.$$

31. Prove that $\dfrac{du_x}{dx} = \dfrac{u_{x+m} - u_{x-m}}{2m}$ approximately.

Give a geometrical interpretation of this approximation.

32. Prove that the differential coefficient of $f(n)$ with respect to n is approximately equal to
$$\tfrac{2}{3} \{f(n+1) - f(n-1)\} - \tfrac{1}{12} \{f(n+2) - f(n-2)\}.$$

33. Find the first three differential coefficients of $\sqrt[3]{x}$, when $x = 50$, given the following cube roots:
$$\sqrt[3]{50} = 3 \cdot 6840; \quad \sqrt[3]{51} = 3 \cdot 7084; \quad \sqrt[3]{52} = 3 \cdot 7325; \quad \sqrt[3]{53} = 3 \cdot 7563;$$
$$\sqrt[3]{54} = 3 \cdot 7798; \quad \sqrt[3]{55} = 3 \cdot 8030; \quad \sqrt[3]{56} = 3 \cdot 8259.$$

34. $u_6 = 1 \cdot 556, \quad u_7 = 1 \cdot 690, \quad u_9 = 1 \cdot 908, \quad u_{12} = 2 \cdot 158$.

Find the value of $\dfrac{du_x}{dx}$, when $x = 8$, by using divided differences.

35. Prove that

$$\frac{du_x}{dx} = \frac{1}{h}(u_{x+h} - u_{x-h}) - \frac{1}{2h}(u_{x+2h} - u_{x-2h}) + \frac{1}{3h}(u_{x+3h} - u_{x-3h}) - \ldots.$$

36. The first differences of the first differential coefficient of $\log u_x$ are in geometrical progression. Determine the form of u_x.

37. Show that $\dfrac{d^3 f(x)}{dx^3} = \Delta^3 f(x - \tfrac{3}{2})$ approximately.

By considering the function $f(x) = a + bx + c^x$ and using the above relation, prove that $\log_e c = c^{\frac{1}{2}} - c^{-\frac{1}{2}}$ approximately, where c is a small quantity.

38. Given that $u_0 = 5$, $u_1 = 15$ and $u_2 = 57$, and that the value of $\dfrac{du_x}{dx}$ is 4 when $x = 0$ and 72 when $x = 2$, find the values of $\Delta^3 u_0$ and $\Delta^4 u_0$.

39. Show that $(1 + \log E)^r \, o^m = \dfrac{r!}{(r-m)!}$, when $r > m$.

40. If $\delta u_x = u_{x+\frac{1}{2}} - u_{x-\frac{1}{2}}$, prove that

$$\frac{du_x}{dx} = \delta u_x - \frac{1}{24}\delta^3 u_x + \frac{3}{640}\delta^5 u_x - \ldots.$$

CHAPTER XIV

INTEGRAL CALCULUS

DEFINITIONS AND STANDARD FORMS

1. If values of the continuous function $y = f(x)$ be given for equidistant intervals, and if $\phi(x)$ be a function such that

$$f(x + h) - f(x) = \phi(x),$$

then
$$\sum_{a}^{b} \phi(x) = f(a + nh) - f(a),$$

where
$$b = a + (n - 1)h \qquad \text{(p. 97)}.$$

This gives an expression for the sum of the values of $\phi(x)$ for values of x differing by the constant finite difference h. We may obtain in a similar manner the limit of the sum of the values of $\phi(x)$ when the difference h tends to zero.

Let
$$\phi(x) = \frac{df(x)}{dx} = \operatorname*{Lt}_{h \to 0} \frac{f(x + h) - f(x)}{h}.$$

Then we may write

$$\phi(a) = \frac{f(a + h) - f(a)}{h} + \eta_1,$$

where η_1 tends to zero as h tends to zero.

$$\therefore \ h\phi(a) = f(a + h) - f(a) + h\eta_1.$$

Similarly,

$$h\phi(a + h) = f(a + 2h) - f(a + h) + h\eta_2,$$
$$h\phi(a + 2h) = f(a + 3h) - f(a + 2h) + h\eta_3,$$

$$\dots\dots\dots\dots\dots\dots$$

$$h\phi(a + \overline{n - 1}h) = f(a + nh) - f(a + \overline{n - 1}h) + h\eta_n.$$

On summing:

$$h[\phi(a) + \phi(a + h) + \phi(a + 2h) + \dots + \phi(a + \overline{n - 1}h)]$$
$$= f(a + nh) - f(a) + h(\eta_1 + \eta_2 + \eta_3 + \dots + \eta_n).$$

If the n small quantities are all numerically less than η, then

$$h(\eta_1 + \eta_2 + \eta_3 + \dots + \eta_n) < hn\eta.$$

If now $b - a = nh$, so that the product of n and h is always finite, then the limit of $hn\eta$ as $h \to 0$ is zero.

$$\therefore \; \operatorname{Lt} h \left(\eta_1 + \eta_2 + \eta_3 + \dots + \eta_n\right) = 0, \quad \text{when } h \to 0.$$

I.e. $\underset{h \to 0}{\operatorname{Lt}} h \left[\phi (a) + \phi (a + h) + \phi (a + 2h) + \dots + \phi (a + \overline{n - 1}h)\right]$

$$= f (a + nh) - f (a)$$
$$= f (b) - f (a).$$

The limit

$$\underset{h \to 0}{\operatorname{Lt}} \; h \left[\phi (a) + \phi (a + h) + \phi (a + 2h) + \dots + \phi (a + \overline{n - 1}h)\right]$$

is denoted by the symbol $\displaystyle\int_a^b \phi (x) \, dx$ and is called the *definite integral* of $\phi (x)$ with respect to x, between the limits $x = a$ and $x = b$.

Corresponding to the symbol D for the operation of differentiation, the symbol I is sometimes used to denote integration with respect to a variable.

2. In finite differences we can find the sum $\displaystyle\overset{b}{\underset{a}{\Sigma}} F (x)$ only when we know (or can obtain) another function $f (x)$ such that $\Delta f (x) = F (x)$. Similarly we can evaluate $\displaystyle\int_a^b \phi (x) \, dx$ in general only if the differential coefficient of a known function $f (x)$ is $\phi (x)$. In other words, corresponding to the relations

$$\Delta f (x) = F (x),$$

and
$$f (x) = \Sigma F (x),$$

we have
$$Df (x) = \phi (x),$$

and
$$f (x) = I\phi (x).$$

Just as
$$\Delta \Sigma \equiv 1,$$

so
$$DI \equiv 1.$$

Again
$$\Delta \{f (x) + c\} = F (x),$$

where c is a constant independent of x, and

$$f (x) + c = \Sigma F (x).$$

Also
$$D \{f (x) + c\} = \phi (x).$$

$$\therefore \; f (x) + c = I\phi (x).$$

Therefore the process $IDf(x)$ does not reproduce $f(x)$ but $f(x) + c$, and I and D are not commutative.

It is evident that corresponding to $\Sigma \equiv \Delta^{-1}$ we have the analogous relation $I \equiv D^{-1}$, where it is to be remembered that

$$I\phi(x) = f(x) + c.$$

3. The primary consideration when obtaining the value of the integral $\int_a^b \phi(x)\, dx$ is the finding of a function $f(x)$ such that $\dfrac{df(x)}{dx} = \phi(x)$. Where we are not concerned with the summation, but only with the initial problem of determining this inverse function, we are said to integrate $\phi(x)$ with respect to x. In that event we find the *indefinite integral* and write the integral function as $\int \phi(x)\, dx$. In the same way as $\dfrac{d}{dx}$ represents the operation of finding the differential coefficient of a function of x with respect to x, so $\int dx$ represents the operation of finding the integral. The symbol $\int$ is meaningless by itself, and we must be careful always to associate with this symbol the dx which renders it intelligible.

In finite differences the number of functions which are immediately integrable is strictly limited: in the infinitesimal calculus a far larger number of functions exists such that, given $\phi(x)$, we can find $D^{-1}\phi(x)$. Every function of x is not integrable (in the calculus sense), and it is only by application of the known properties of the differential calculus that it is possible to evaluate $\int \phi(x)\, dx$.

4. Geometrical interpretation of an integral.

Before proceeding to investigate methods of integrating functions of x it is helpful to illustrate the meaning of definite integration by reference to geometry.

Let AB represent the continuous function $y = f(x)$, and let P_0, P_n be two points on the curve whose coordinates are $\{a, f(a)\}$ and $\{b, f(b)\}$ respectively, so that $OM_0 = a$ and $OM_n = b$. Divide $M_0 M_n$ into n equal parts each equal to h. Then $nh = b - a$. If we complete the set of inner rectangles $P_0 K_1 M_1 M_0$, $P_1 K_2 M_2 M_1$, ... $P_{n-1} K_n M_n M_{n-1}$ it is evident that the sum of these rectangles is slightly less than the area cut off by the curve, the ordinates $P_0 M_0$, $P_n M_n$ and the x-axis.

Again, if we complete the set of outer rectangles of which $Q_0 P_1 M_1 M_0$ is the first and $Q_{n-1} P_n M_n M_{n-1}$ is the last, the sum of

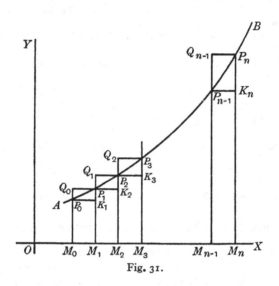

Fig. 31.

these outer rectangles will be slightly greater than the area of the curve $P_0 P_n M_n M_0$.

Now the difference between the set of outer and of inner rectangles is evidently the sum of the small rectangles $Q_0 P_0 K_1 P_1$, etc., and this sum is $h (P_n M_n - P_0 M_0)$, since the rectangles are all of base h. Since $P_n M_n - P_0 M_0$ is finite, the limit of $h (P_n M_n - P_0 M_0)$ as n tends to infinity is zero. In other words, as $h \to 0$ the difference between the area $P_0 P_n M_n M_0$ and the sum of the rectangles $P_0 K_1 M_1 M_0$, $P_1 K_2 M_2 M_1$, ... $P_{n-1} K_n M_n M_{n-1}$ tends to zero.

But $\quad P_0 K_1 M_1 M_0 = M_0 M_1 . P_0 M_0 = hf(a)$

$$P_1 K_2 M_2 M_1 = M_1 M_2 . P_1 M_1 = hf(a+h)$$

$$\cdots\cdots\cdots$$

$$P_{n-1} K_n M_n M_{n-1} = M_{n-1} M_n . P_{n-1} M_{n-1} = hf(a + \overline{n-1}h).$$

$$\therefore \text{ Area } P_0 P_n M_n M_0 = \underset{h \to 0}{\text{Lt }} h \overset{a+(n-1)h}{\underset{a}{\Sigma}} f(x) = \int_a^b f(x)\, dx$$

where $$b = a + nh.$$

We may therefore define the definite integral as the area of the curve $y = f(x)$ between the curve, the ordinates $x = a$, $x = b$ and the x-axis.

5. Alternatively we may proceed as follows:

Let PQ be the curve $y = f(x)$ and let the area $PHML$ be z. If H be the point (x, y), so that a small increase in the length OM,

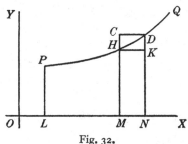

Fig. 32.

namely MN, may be denoted by Δx, then $DN = y + \Delta y$ and the area $PDNL = z + \Delta z$.

It is evident from Fig. 32 that the rectangle

$$CDNM = DN.MN = (y + \Delta y)\, \Delta x;$$

the area $$HDNM = \Delta z;$$

and the rectangle $$HKNM = y \Delta x.$$

$$\therefore \quad (y + \Delta y)\, \Delta x > \Delta z > y \Delta x,$$

or $$y + \Delta y > \Delta z / \Delta x > y,$$

when $\Delta x \to 0$, $y + \Delta y \to y$, since Δy tends to zero as Δx tends to zero.

Also $$\underset{\Delta x \to 0}{\text{Lt }} \frac{\Delta z}{\Delta x} = \frac{dz}{dx},$$

$$\therefore \quad y = \frac{dz}{dx},$$

and the area $z = \int y\, dx$.

The arguments in this paragraph and in para. 4 postulate a concave curve. Similar arguments apply to a convex curve. An ordinary curve having points of inflexion can be broken up into portions concave or convex as the case may be.

6. The definition of a definite integral enables us to represent in a convenient form the limits of the sums of certain series when the number of terms tends to infinity.

Example 1.

Obtain as a definite integral

$$\underset{n\to\infty}{\text{Lt}}\left[\frac{1}{\sqrt{n^2-1^2}}+\frac{1}{\sqrt{n^2-2^2}}+\dots+\frac{1}{\sqrt{n^2-(n-1)^2}}\right].$$

The expression in brackets may be written as

$$E=\frac{1}{n}\frac{1}{\sqrt{1-(1/n)^2}}+\frac{1}{n}\frac{1}{\sqrt{1-(2/n)^2}}+\dots+\frac{1}{n}\frac{1}{\sqrt{1-\{(n-1)/n\}^2}},$$

which is of the form

$$h\left[f(a)+f(a+h)+f(a+2h)+\dots+f(a+\overline{n-1}h)\right],$$

where $h=\dfrac{1}{n}$, $a=0$ and $f(x)$ is $\dfrac{1}{\sqrt{1-x^2}}$.

$$\therefore\quad\underset{n\to\infty}{\text{Lt}}\ E=\underset{h\to0}{\text{Lt}}\ E=\int_0^1\frac{1}{\sqrt{1-x^2}}\,dx.$$

7. Standard forms.

The two following theorems are almost self-evident:

(i) $\displaystyle\int a\,\phi(x)\,dx = a\int\phi(x)\,dx$, where a is independent of x.

(ii) $\displaystyle\int(u\pm v\pm w\pm\dots)\,dx=\int u\,dx\pm\int v\,dx\pm\int w\,dx\pm\dots,$

where $u, v, w, \dots$ are functions of x.

(i) follows directly from the fact that if $\phi(x)=\dfrac{df(x)}{dx}$,

then $$\frac{d\,af(x)}{dx}=a\,\frac{df(x)}{dx}=a\,\phi(x),$$

$$\therefore\quad\int a\,\phi(x)\,dx=af(x)=a\int\phi(x)\,dx.$$

(ii) $\quad \dfrac{d}{dx}\left(\displaystyle\int u\,dx \pm \int v\,dx \pm \int w\,dx \pm \ldots\right) = u \pm v \pm w \pm \ldots,$

$\therefore \displaystyle\int u\,dx \pm \int v\,dx \pm \int w\,dx \pm \ldots = \int (u \pm v \pm w \pm \ldots)\,dx.$

By the use of these theorems and the simpler standard results that have been obtained by direct differentiation of well-known forms, various integrals can be written down at once.

For example,

$$\frac{dx^{n+1}}{dx} = (n + 1)\,x^n \quad \text{or} \quad \frac{d}{dx}\frac{x^{n+1}}{n+1} = x^n,$$

$$\therefore \int x^n\,dx = \frac{x^{n+1}}{n+1} \qquad \ldots\ldots\text{(i)}.$$

Since $\dfrac{d}{dx}\left\{\dfrac{x^{n+1}}{n+1} + c\right\} = x^n$, where c is any constant, the indefinite integral $\displaystyle\int x^n\,dx$ is $\dfrac{x^{n+1}}{n+1} + c$. Strictly speaking, in evaluating indefinite integrals the arbitrary constant should always be added to the result. The constant of integration will be omitted in the following examples, but wherever there is an indefinite integral the presence of the constant is to be inferred.

$$\frac{d}{dx}\log x = \frac{1}{x},$$

$$\therefore \int \frac{dx}{x} = \log x \qquad \ldots\ldots\text{(ii)}.$$

From the two theorems above it is evident that

$$\int (ax^n + b)\,dx = a\int x^n\,dx + b\int dx$$

$$= a\,\frac{x^{n+1}}{n+1} + bx \qquad \ldots\ldots\text{(iii)},$$

unless n is -1,

and $\qquad \displaystyle\int \left(\frac{a}{x} + b\right)dx = a\int \frac{dx}{x} + b\int dx$

$$= a\log x + bx \qquad \ldots\ldots\text{(iv)}.$$

$$\frac{de^x}{dx} = e^x,$$

$$\therefore \int e^x dx = e^x \qquad \ldots\ldots(v).$$

$$\frac{d}{dx} \sin x = \cos x \quad \text{and} \quad \frac{d}{dx} \cos x = -\sin x,$$

$$\therefore \left. \begin{array}{l} \int \cos x \, dx = \sin x \\[2mm] \int \sin x \, dx = -\cos x \end{array} \right\} \qquad \ldots\ldots(vi).$$

$$\frac{d}{dx} \tan x = \sec^2 x \quad \text{and} \quad \frac{d}{dx} \cot x = -\csc^2 x,$$

$$\therefore \left. \begin{array}{l} \int \sec^2 x \, dx = \tan x \\[2mm] \int \csc^2 x \, dx = -\cot x \end{array} \right\} \qquad \ldots\ldots(vii).$$

$$\frac{d}{dx} \sin^{-1} x = \frac{1}{\sqrt{1-x^2}} \quad \text{and} \quad \frac{d}{dx} \cos^{-1} x = -\frac{1}{\sqrt{1-x^2}},$$

$$\therefore \int \frac{dx}{\sqrt{1-x^2}} = \sin^{-1} x \quad \text{or} \quad -\cos^{-1} x \qquad \ldots\ldots(viii).$$

These two apparently different results are the same, the difference being in the constant of integration. Let $\cos^{-1} x = \alpha$ so that $\cos \alpha = x$; then $\sin\left(n\frac{\pi}{2} - \alpha\right) = x$.

$$\therefore \quad \sin^{-1} x = n\frac{\pi}{2} - \alpha$$

$$= n\frac{\pi}{2} - \cos^{-1} x$$

$$= \text{constant} - \cos^{-1} x.$$

The above are the principal standard forms, and by the use of these forms in conjunction with methods which will be outlined later a large number of different forms of functions can be integrated (see Chapter xv).

8. Some simple functions that can be integrated directly from the standard forms are given below.

Example 2.

Find $\int \dfrac{dx}{x^2 + a^2}$.

If we differentiate $\tan^{-1} x$ we obtain $\dfrac{1}{x^2 + 1}$. Let us see the effect of differentiating $\tan^{-1} kx$.

$$\frac{d}{dx} \tan kx = \frac{d}{d(kx)} \tan^{-1} kx \frac{d(kx)}{dx}$$

$$= \frac{1}{1 + k^2 x^2} k.$$

This is almost in the form required if we replace k by $\dfrac{1}{a}$. Then

$$\frac{d}{dx} \tan^{-1} \frac{x}{a} = \frac{1}{1 + \dfrac{x^2}{a^2}} \frac{1}{a} = a \frac{1}{x^2 + a^2},$$

$$\therefore \quad \tan^{-1} \frac{x}{a} = \int a \frac{1}{x^2 + a^2} dx,$$

or

$$\int \frac{dx}{x^2 + a^2} = \frac{1}{a} \tan^{-1} \frac{x}{a}.$$

Example 3.

Find $\int \dfrac{dx}{x^2 - a^2}$.

We cannot immediately recognize $\dfrac{1}{x^2 - a^2}$ as the differential coefficient of a known function. If, however, we express $\dfrac{1}{x^2 - a^2}$ as

$$\frac{1}{2a} \left[\frac{1}{x - a} - \frac{1}{x + a} \right],$$

we see at once that each of the component fractions is the derivative of a logarithmic function of x.

$$\frac{d}{dx} \frac{1}{x - a} = \log(x - a),$$

$$\frac{d}{dx} \frac{1}{x + a} = \log(x + a);$$

$$\therefore \int \frac{dx}{x^2 - a^2} = \frac{1}{2a} \int \left(\frac{1}{x-a} - \frac{1}{x+a} \right) dx$$

$$= \frac{1}{2a} \left[\log (x-a) - \log (x+a) \right]$$

$$= \frac{1}{2a} \log \frac{x-a}{x+a}.$$

Similarly

$$\int \frac{dx}{a^2 - x^2} = \frac{1}{2a} \int \left(\frac{1}{a-x} + \frac{1}{a+x} \right) dx$$

$$= \frac{1}{2a} \left[- \log (a-x) + \log (a+x) \right]$$

$$= \frac{1}{2a} \log \frac{a+x}{a-x}.$$

Example 4.

Find $\int \sin n\theta\, d\theta$ and $\int \cos n\theta\, d\theta$.

$$\frac{d}{d\theta} \sin n\theta = \frac{d}{d(n\theta)} \sin n\theta \frac{d(n\theta)}{d\theta}$$

$$= \cos n\theta . n$$

$$= n \cos n\theta,$$

$$\therefore \int \cos n\theta\, d\theta = \frac{1}{n} \sin n\theta.$$

Similarly $\qquad \int \sin n\theta\, d\theta = -\frac{1}{n} \cos n\theta.$

Note: $\sin^n \theta$ and $\cos^n \theta$ are not immediately integrable. If, however, we express these functions in terms of multiple angles we can at once write down their integrals.

E.g. $\qquad \sin^2 \theta = \frac{1}{2} (1 - \cos 2\theta).$

$$\therefore \int \sin^2 \theta\, d\theta = \int \left(\frac{1}{2} - \frac{1}{2} \cos 2\theta \right) d\theta$$

$$= \frac{1}{2}\theta - \frac{1}{2}.\frac{1}{2} \sin 2\theta$$

$$= \frac{1}{2}\theta - \frac{1}{4} \sin 2\theta.$$

Again $\qquad \sin 3\theta = 3 \sin \theta - 4 \sin^3 \theta,$

$$\therefore \ \sin^3 \theta = \frac{3}{4} \sin \theta - \frac{1}{4} \sin 3\theta.$$

$$\therefore \int \sin^3 \theta\, d\theta = \int \left(\frac{3}{4} \sin \theta - \frac{1}{4} \sin 3\theta \right) d\theta$$

$$= -\frac{3}{4} \cos \theta + \frac{1}{12} \cos 3\theta,$$

and so on.

EXAMPLES 14

1. Denoting $\int u_x\, dx$ by Iu_x express the operator I in terms of the operator Δ and show that, as far as first differences,

$$I \equiv \Sigma + \frac{1}{2} - \frac{\Delta}{12}.$$

Integrate with respect to x:

2. $3x^n$; $\frac{1}{3}x^{-n}$; e^{2x}.

3. $(x^2 + a^2)^2$; $a + bx + cx^2$; $(x + 1)^3$.

4. $\sin x$; $\cos x$; $\operatorname{cosec}^2 x$.

5. a^x; $a^x + b$; $a^x + bx + c$.

6. $\sin 2x$; $\cos 3x$; $\sec^2 4x$.

7. $\dfrac{1}{x+1}$; $\dfrac{1}{(1-x)^2}$; $\dfrac{1}{(a+3x)^3}$.

8. $\dfrac{3x-2}{x^2}$; $\dfrac{ax^2+bx+c}{x^n}$.

9. $\dfrac{1}{(x+1)(x-1)}$; $\dfrac{x^2-x+1}{x(x^2+1)}$.

10. $\dfrac{a}{\sqrt{1-x^2}}$; $\dfrac{1}{\sqrt{1-a^2x^2}}$.

11. Express $\cos 3x$ in terms of powers of $\cos x$ and hence integrate $\cos^3 x$.

12. Integrate $\dfrac{(y-1)^2}{y^n}$ with respect to y and deduce $\displaystyle\int \dfrac{x^2\, dx}{(1+x)^n}$.

13. Express as a definite integral the limit when x is increased indefinitely of

$$\frac{1}{x} + \frac{1}{x+m} + \frac{1}{x+2m} + \ldots + \frac{1}{x+xm}.$$

14. Represent the sum of the series

$$\frac{n}{n^2+1^2} + \frac{n}{n^2+2^2} + \frac{n}{n^2+3^2} + \ldots + \frac{n}{2n^2},$$

when n is increased indefinitely, as a definite integral.

15. Express $\dfrac{1}{x(x-1)(x-2)}$ in partial fractions and hence integrate the function with respect to x.

16. Evaluate $\displaystyle\int \dfrac{(x^2 + x)\, dx}{(1-x)(1+x^2)}$.

17. Integrate $(1 + x)^{-1}(1 - x^2)^{-1}$ with respect to x.

18. Prove from first principles that

$$(a) \int_a^b e^{-x}\, dx = e^{-a} - e^{-b}; \quad (b) \int_a^b x^2\, dx = \tfrac{1}{3}(b^3 - a^3).$$

19. Prove by differentiation that $\log \left\{ \dfrac{(x + \sqrt{x^2 - a^2})}{a} \right\}$ is the integral of $\dfrac{\text{I}}{\sqrt{x^2 - a^2}}$.

20. Integrate

$$\text{(i)} \; 2 \sqrt{x} - \frac{\text{I}}{2x^2}; \quad \text{(ii)} \; \sqrt{x}\left(x^5 + \frac{3}{x}\right),$$

and verify the result by differentiation.

21. $v = \dfrac{ds}{dt}; \; f = \dfrac{dv}{dt}$ and $s = 0$ when $t = 0$.

    Prove that   (i) $v \; = u + ft$, where u is constant;

                   (ii) $s \; = ut + \frac{1}{2}ft^2 + $ a constant;

                   (iii) $2fs = v^2 - u^2$.

22. If $\dfrac{d^2 y}{dx^2}$ is constant, show that y is of the form $ax^2 + bx + c$.

23. $\dfrac{d^3 u_x}{dx^3} = e^x$. Find the form of u_x.

24. u and v are functions of t, viz. $\dfrac{du}{dt} = \sin t; \; \dfrac{dv}{dt} = \cos t$. Prove that a relation of the form $u^2 + v^2 - 2\alpha u - 2\beta v = \gamma$ exists, where α, β, γ are constants independent of t.

25. If $a^2 \dfrac{d^2 y}{dx^2} = a - x$, find y when $x = 2a$, any necessary constants being determined by the condition that when $x = a$, $\dfrac{dy}{dx} = 1$ and $y = a$.

26. If $u_x = A + Bc^x$ where A, B and c are constants and

$$u_x = -\frac{\text{I}}{l_x} \frac{dl_x}{dx},$$

find l_x in terms of x.

27. Find the value of $\displaystyle\int \left(\frac{du}{dt}\right)^2 dt$, where $u = \sin^{-1} t + k$.

28. Integrate

$$\frac{\text{I}}{2} \frac{d}{dx} \{\tan^{-1} x + \log \sqrt{1 + x} - \log \sqrt{1 - x}\}$$

with respect to x^4.

CHAPTER XV

MORE DIFFICULT INTEGRALS: INTEGRATION BY PARTS

1. Differentiation can be applied to any continuous function of x by the application of simple and straightforward principles. The inverse process of integration is at the best a tentative process and depends very largely on whether the function to be integrated can be recognized as the derivative of another function. It may happen that, although the function as it stands is not familiar as the differential coefficient of another function of the variable, it can be so transformed as to be immediately integrable. A simple example has been given in the previous chapter, where, knowing the standard form $\int (1 + x^2)^{-1}\, dx$, we can derive at once the integral of $(a^2 + x^2)^{-1}$ with respect to x.

The integration of more complicated functions is largely a matter of practice. There are, however, certain standard methods of attack, which, although they may not invariably produce the required result, can often be applied with success to the solution of the problems of integration.

2. The method of substitution.

Let us consider the problem that is denoted by $\int y\, dx$. In the first place, the dx shows that the independent variable is x. Secondly, y is a function of x such that if we know, or can find, z, another function of x, whose derivative with regard to x is y, then z is the required value.

Put shortly, if

$$\frac{dz}{dx} = y, \quad \text{then} \quad \int y\, dx = z.$$

A familiar example is

$$\frac{dx^{n+1}}{dx} = (n + 1)\, x^n,$$

or
$$\frac{d}{dx}\left\{\frac{1}{n+1}\,x^{n+1}\right\} = x^n,$$

so that if $y = x^n$, then

$$\int y\,dx = \frac{1}{n+1}\,x^{n+1}.$$

Suppose that y is a more complicated function of x, say $(a + bx)^n$. We do not immediately recognize $\int y\,dx$, and it is necessary to proceed further.

Let
$$z = a + bx.$$

Then
$$\frac{dz}{dx} = b,$$

and
$$\frac{dy}{dz} = \frac{dy}{dx}\frac{dx}{dz} = \frac{dy}{dx}\frac{1}{b}.$$

If therefore we replace the independent variable x by the new variable z, any differentiation with respect to x becomes a differentiation with respect to z by the simple process of dividing by the constant b.

The integral $\int y\,dx$ may therefore be written as $\int y\left[\frac{1}{b}\,dz\right]$, and, since $y = (a + bx)^n = z^n$,

$$\int y\,dx = \int (a + bx)^n\,dx = \int z^n\,dx$$

$$= \int z^n\left[\frac{1}{b}\,dz\right]$$

$$= \int \frac{1}{b}\,z^n\,dz$$

$$= \frac{1}{b}\frac{1}{n+1}\,z^{n+1}$$

$$= \frac{1}{b}\frac{1}{n+1}\,(a + bx)^{n+1}.$$

This is an example of the method of substitution.

Again, to evaluate $\int y\,dx$ where y is the function $\dfrac{\sin x}{1 + \cos x}$, let
$$z = \cos x.$$

Then $$\frac{dz}{dx} = -\sin x,$$

$$\therefore \quad \frac{dy}{dz} = \frac{dy}{dx}\frac{dx}{dz} = \frac{dy}{dx}\left[-\frac{1}{\sin x}\right].$$

Therefore, as above, $\int y\, dx$ becomes

$$\int\left[-\frac{1}{\sin x}\right] y\, dz;$$

i.e. $$\int\frac{\sin x}{1 + \cos x}\, dx = \int\frac{\sin x}{1 + \cos x}\left[-\frac{1}{\sin x}\right] dz$$

$$= \int\left[-\frac{1}{1 + \cos x}\right] dz$$

$$= \int -\frac{1}{1 + z}\, dz$$

$$= -\log(1 + z)$$

$$= -\log(1 + \cos x).$$

When applying the method of substitution it is customary to shorten the initial process. If the substitution is $z = \cos x$, we write, instead of

$$\frac{dz}{dx} = -\sin x,$$

the relation $$dz = -\sin x\, dx,$$

so that in the integral we may immediately replace dx by

$$\left[-\frac{1}{\sin x}\right] dz.$$

In general, if the substitution is $f(x) = \phi(y)$, instead of writing $f'(x) = \phi'(y)\dfrac{dy}{dx}$ we write immediately $f'(x)\, dx = \phi'(y)\, dy$. It will be observed that the process is to differentiate each function with regard to the variable in which it is expressed, x, y or z for example, and then to multiply by dx, dy or dz as the case may be. The expressions $f'(x)\, dx$, $\phi'(y)\, dy$, ... are termed *differentials* of $f(x)$, $\phi(y)$, ... respectively.

For the purpose of integration this procedure should be looked upon simply as a convenient means of passing from one variable to another, and not necessarily as a splitting up of the $\dfrac{dz}{dx}$ into two parts dz and dx.

We may consider the problem from another point of view. The definition of a definite integral is the limit of $h\Sigma\phi(x)$ between $x = a$ and $x = b - h$, as h tends to zero. Since h denotes a small increase in the value of the variable, we may equally well write the integral as

$$\underset{\Delta x \to 0}{\text{Lt}}\ \overset{x=b-\Delta x}{\underset{x=a}{\Sigma}}\ \phi(x).\Delta x = \underset{\Delta x \to 0}{\text{Lt}}\ [\phi(a)\,\Delta x + \phi(a + \Delta x)\,\Delta x + \ldots$$
$$+\ \phi(b - \Delta x)\,\Delta x],$$

or $\displaystyle\int_a^b \phi(x)\,dx$, where the Δx is the small increase in the value of x which tends to zero.

The method of substitution is then as follows. If, as in the second example above,

$$z = \cos x,$$

then
$$\Delta z = \cos(x + \Delta x) - \cos x$$
$$= -2\sin(x + \tfrac{1}{2}\Delta x)\sin\tfrac{1}{2}\Delta x.$$

Now
$$\underset{\Delta x \to 0}{\text{Lt}}\ -\sin(x + \tfrac{1}{2}\Delta x) = -\sin x,$$

and
$$\underset{\Delta x \to 0}{\text{Lt}}\ \frac{\sin\tfrac{1}{2}\Delta x}{\tfrac{1}{2}\Delta x} = 1,$$

$$\therefore\ \underset{\Delta z \to 0}{\text{Lt}}\ \phi(x)\,\Delta z = \underset{\Delta x \to 0}{\text{Lt}}\ \{-2\sin(x + \tfrac{1}{2}\Delta x)\sin\tfrac{1}{2}\Delta x . \phi(x)\}$$
$$= -2\sin x\ \underset{\Delta x \to 0}{\text{Lt}}\ \phi(x)\tfrac{1}{2}\Delta x$$
$$= -\sin x\ \underset{\Delta x \to 0}{\text{Lt}}\ \phi(x)\,\Delta x.$$

$$\therefore\ \underset{\Delta x \to 0}{\text{Lt}}\ \phi(x)\,\Delta x = \left[-\frac{1}{\sin x}\right]\underset{\Delta z \to 0}{\text{Lt}}\ \phi(x)\,\Delta z,$$

which gives the same result as that found above.

3. If $y = f(x)$, then $\phi(y) = \phi\{f(x)\}$, and if $f'(x)$ denote, as usual, the differential coefficient of $f(x)$ with respect to x, then

$$\phi(y)\frac{dy}{dx} = \phi\{f(x)\}f'(x);$$

i.e.
$$\phi(y)\,dy = \phi\{f(x)\}f'(x)\,dx,$$

so that
$$\int \phi(y)\,dy = \int \phi\{f(x)\}f'(x)\,dx.$$

Now on the right-hand side the integrand is the product of two functions, $\phi \{f(x)\}$ and $f'(x)$. If we associate $f'(x)$ with dx we have (i) a function of x, namely $\phi \{f(x)\}$, and (ii) $f'(x)\,dx$, which is a differential. It is evident therefore that if it is required to integrate an expression consisting of the product of two functions, one the differential of a known function $f(x)$ and the other a function of $f(x)$, the substitution $f(x) = y$ will reduce the integral to the simpler form $\int \phi(y)\,dy$.

It must be noted, however, that if the product is to be simplified in this manner, both conditions must be satisfied. The form of substitution is frequently determined by the recognition that the expression to be integrated contains $f'(x)\,dx$, the differential of $f(x)$.

For example, consider the integrals

$$\int \frac{x\,dx}{\sqrt{1+x^2}}; \quad \int \frac{x^3\,dx}{\sqrt{1+x^2}}; \quad \frac{\sqrt{1+x^2}}{x}\,dx.$$

These may be written

$$\int \frac{1}{\sqrt{1+x^2}}\,x\,dx; \quad \int \frac{x^2}{\sqrt{1+x^2}}\,x\,dx; \quad \int \frac{\sqrt{1+x^2}}{x^2}\,x\,dx,$$

and it is evident that each of the expressions consists of $x\,dx$ (the differential of $\frac{1}{2}x^2$) and a function of $\frac{1}{2}x^2$. The substitution of y for x^2 will therefore simplify the process of integration for all three examples. It will be observed that this substitution is suggested partly, if not wholly, by the presence of $x\,dx$.

Again, consider

$$\int \frac{dx}{\sqrt{1+x^2}}; \quad \int \frac{x^2\,dx}{\sqrt{1+x^2}}; \quad \int \frac{\sqrt{1+x^2}}{x^2}\,dx.$$

It will not help to write these in the form $\int \phi(x^2)\,dx$, as the required $x\,dx$ is absent. The substitution $y = x^2$ will not therefore simplify the integrals.

4. Further examples of substitution.

It does not follow that any integral can be evaluated by a simple substitution nor indeed that the simplest substitution is the best.

The examples given below are merely indicative of the methods to be employed: they are not necessarily of universal application.

Example 1.

$$\int \frac{x^2}{(a+bx)^n}\, dx. \quad (n \neq 1.)$$

The substitution is $\qquad z = a + bx.$

We have $\qquad dz = b\,dx$ and $x = \dfrac{z-a}{b}.$

$$I = \int \left(\frac{z-a}{b}\right)^2 \frac{1}{z^n}\frac{1}{b}\, dz$$

$$= \int \frac{z^2 - 2az + a^2}{z^n}\frac{1}{b^3}\, dz$$

$$= \frac{1}{b^3}\int \left(z^{2-n} - 2az^{1-n} + a^2 z^{-n}\right) dz$$

$$= \frac{1}{b^3}\left[\int z^{2-n}\, dz - 2a\int z^{1-n}\, dz + a^2\int z^{-n}\, dz\right]$$

$$= \frac{1}{b^3}\left[\frac{1}{3-n}z^{3-n} - 2a\frac{1}{2-n}z^{2-n} + a^2\frac{1}{1-n}z^{1-n}\right].$$

If n is a positive integer greater than 3, this result is more conveniently written as

$$-\frac{1}{b^3}\left[\frac{1}{(n-3)z^{n-3}} - \frac{2a}{(n-2)z^{n-2}} + \frac{a^2}{(n-1)z^{n-1}}\right],$$

where $\qquad z \equiv a + bx.$

The above method can be applied to any function of the form $\dfrac{x^m}{(a+bx)^n}$, where m is a positive integer. It is easily seen that the integral will be $\dfrac{1}{b^{m+1}}\int \dfrac{(z-a)^m}{z^n}\, dz$. By expanding the expression in brackets by the binomial theorem and integrating each term separately, the result follows.

Example 2.

$$\int \frac{2x\, dx}{1+x^2}.$$

The facts that $2x\,dx$ is the differential of x^2 and that the remainder of the integrand is a function of x^2 suggest the substitution $x^2 = y$, or, better, $1 + x^2 = y$.

Put, therefore, $z = 1 + x^2$, so that $dz = 2x\,dx$.
Then

$$I = \int \frac{2x\,dx}{1 + x^2} = \int \frac{dz}{1 + x^2} = \int \frac{dz}{z} = \log z = \log (1 + x^2).$$

This is an example of a general proposition. Where the numerator of a fraction is the derivative of the denominator, the required integral is the logarithm of the denominator.

In other words:

$$\int \frac{\frac{dy}{dx}}{y}\,dx = \log y.$$

For example,

$$\int \frac{-\sin x}{1 + \cos x}\,dx = \int \frac{\frac{d(1 + \cos x)}{dx}}{1 + \cos x}\,dx = \log (1 + \cos x).$$

$$\text{(Cf. para. 2 above.)}$$

Again, $$\int \cot x\,dx = \int \frac{\cos x}{\sin x}\,dx = \int \frac{\frac{d\sin x}{dx}}{\sin x}\,dx = \log \sin x.$$

Example 3.

$$\int \frac{d\theta}{\sin \theta}.$$

Now $$\sin \theta = \frac{2\tan \tfrac{1}{2}\theta}{1 + \tan^2 \tfrac{1}{2}\theta}. \qquad \text{(Chap. I, para. 16.)}$$

$$\therefore\ I = \int \frac{1 + \tan^2 \tfrac{1}{2}\theta}{2\tan \tfrac{1}{2}\theta}\,d\theta.$$

Put $$t = \tan \tfrac{1}{2}\theta,$$

$$dt = \tfrac{1}{2}\sec^2 \tfrac{1}{2}\theta\,d\theta = \tfrac{1}{2}(1 + \tan^2 \tfrac{1}{2}\theta)\,d\theta.$$

$$\therefore\ d\theta = \frac{2dt}{1 + \tan^2 \tfrac{1}{2}\theta}.$$

$$\therefore\ I = \int \frac{1 + \tan^2 \tfrac{1}{2}\theta}{2\tan \tfrac{1}{2}\theta}\ \frac{2dt}{1 + \tan^2 \tfrac{1}{2}\theta} = \int \frac{dt}{\tan \tfrac{1}{2}\theta} = \int \frac{dt}{t}$$

$$= \log t$$

$$= \log \tan \tfrac{1}{2}\theta.$$

Corollary:

$$\int \frac{d\theta}{\cos\theta} = \int \frac{d\theta}{\sin\left(\frac{1}{2}\pi - \theta\right)}$$

$$= -\log\tan\tfrac{1}{2}\left(\tfrac{1}{2}\pi - \theta\right)$$

$$= -\log\tan\left(\tfrac{1}{4}\pi - \tfrac{1}{2}\theta\right)$$

$$= -\log\frac{\tan\frac{1}{4}\pi - \tan\frac{1}{2}\theta}{1 + \tan\frac{1}{4}\pi\tan\frac{1}{2}\theta}$$

$$= -\log\frac{1 - \tan\frac{1}{2}\theta}{1 + \tan\frac{1}{2}\theta} \qquad \text{(since } \tan\tfrac{1}{4}\pi = 1\text{)}$$

$$= \log\frac{1 + \tan\frac{1}{2}\theta}{1 - \tan\frac{1}{2}\theta}.$$

Example 4.

$$\int \frac{dx}{\sqrt{x^2 + a^2}}.$$

Method (i). Put $x = a\tan\alpha$, so that $dx = a\sec^2\alpha\,d\alpha$.

$$I = \int \frac{1}{\sqrt{x^2 + a^2}}\, a\sec^2\alpha\,d\alpha$$

$$= \int \frac{1}{\sqrt{a^2\tan^2\alpha + a^2}}\, a\sec^2\alpha\,d\alpha$$

$$= \int \frac{1}{a\sqrt{\tan^2\alpha + 1}}\, a\sec^2\alpha\,d\alpha$$

$$= \int \sec\alpha\,d\alpha \qquad \text{(since } \tan^2\alpha + 1 = \sec^2\alpha\text{)}$$

$$= \int \frac{d\alpha}{\cos\alpha}$$

$$= \log\frac{1 + \tan\frac{1}{2}\alpha}{1 - \tan\frac{1}{2}\alpha} \qquad \text{(from Example 3 above),}$$

where $\qquad\qquad\qquad \tan\alpha = x/a.$

Method (ii). Put $\sqrt{x^2 + a^2} = z - x.$

Then $\qquad\qquad\qquad x^2 + a^2 = z^2 - 2zx + x^2,$

or $\qquad\qquad\qquad a^2 = z^2 - 2zx.$

$$\therefore\ 0 = 2z\,dz - 2z\,dx - 2x\,dz;$$

i.e. $\qquad\qquad\qquad dx = \frac{z - x}{z}\,dz.$

$$\therefore \ I = \int \frac{dx}{\sqrt{x^2 + a^2}} = \int \frac{1}{z - x} \frac{z - x}{z} \, dz = \int \frac{dz}{z}$$

$$= \log z$$

$$= \log (x + \sqrt{x^2 + a^2}).$$

This result is the same as that produced by the first method. For, if

$$x/a = \tan \alpha,$$

$$\log (x + \sqrt{x^2 + a^2}) = \log (a \tan \alpha + \sqrt{a^2 \tan^2 \alpha + a^2})$$

$$= \log a (\tan \alpha + \sec \alpha)$$

$$= \log a + \log \left\{ \frac{\sin \alpha}{\cos \alpha} + \frac{1}{\cos \alpha} \right\}$$

$$= \log a + \log \frac{\sin \alpha + 1}{\cos \alpha}$$

$$= \log a + \log \left\{ \frac{\dfrac{2 \tan \frac{1}{2}\alpha}{1 + \tan^2 \frac{1}{2}\alpha} + 1}{\dfrac{1 - \tan^2 \frac{1}{2}\alpha}{1 + \tan^2 \frac{1}{2}\alpha}} \right\}$$

$$= \log a + \log \frac{(1 + \tan \frac{1}{2}\alpha)^2}{1 - \tan^2 \frac{1}{2}\alpha}$$

$$= \log a + \log \frac{1 + \tan \frac{1}{2}\alpha}{1 - \tan \frac{1}{2}\alpha},$$

which is the solution given by Method (i), since $\log a$ is a constant, and the result of differentiating

$$\log \frac{1 + \tan \frac{1}{2}\alpha}{1 - \tan \frac{1}{2}\alpha} + \log a$$

is the same as that of differentiating

$$\log \frac{1 + \tan \frac{1}{2}\alpha}{1 - \tan \frac{1}{2}\alpha} + \text{any arbitrary constant.}$$

Method (iii). Put $x = 1/y$ in order to obtain an odd power of y outside the square root.

Then

$$dx = - (1/y^2) \, dy,$$

$$x^2 + a^2 = 1/y^2 + a^2 = (1 + a^2y^2)/y^2.$$

$$\therefore \int \frac{dx}{\sqrt{x^2 + a^2}} = \int \frac{y}{\sqrt{1 + a^2y^2}} \left(-\frac{1}{y^2} \right) dy$$

$$= \int \frac{- \, dy}{y \sqrt{1 + a^2y^2}}.$$

To eliminate the square root, put $1 + a^2 y^2 = z^2$.

$$\therefore \ 2a^2 y\, dy = 2z\, dz,$$

and
$$I = \int \frac{-z\, dz}{a^2 y^2 z} = \int \frac{-dz}{z^2 - 1},$$

since
$$y^2 = \frac{(z^2 - 1)}{a^2}.$$

On integrating and substituting, first for z in terms of y, and then for y in terms of x, we have

$$I = \tfrac{1}{2} \log \frac{\sqrt{x^2 + a^2} + x}{\sqrt{x^2 + a^2} - x},$$

which is easily seen to be $\log \left(\sqrt{x^2 + a^2} + x\right) - \log a$ on multiplying numerator and denominator of the fraction by $\sqrt{x^2 + a^2} + x$.

Corollaries:

(i) $\displaystyle \int \frac{dx}{\sqrt{x^2 - a^2}} = \log \left(x + \sqrt{x^2 - a^2}\right);$

(ii) $\displaystyle \int \frac{dx}{\sqrt{(x - a)(x - b)}} = \int \frac{dx}{\sqrt{x^2 - (a + b)x + ab}}$

$$= \int \frac{dx}{\sqrt{\{x - \tfrac{1}{2}(a + b)\}^2 - \{\tfrac{1}{2}(a - b)\}^2}}$$

$$= \log \{x - \tfrac{1}{2}(a + b) + \sqrt{(x - a)(x - b)}\}$$

$$= \log \tfrac{1}{2}\{(x - a) + (x - b) + 2\sqrt{(x - a)(x - b)}\}$$

$$= \log \left(\sqrt{x - a} + \sqrt{x - b}\right)^2 - \log 2$$

$$= 2 \log \left(\sqrt{x - a} + \sqrt{x - b}\right),$$

disregarding the constant of integration.

Example 5.

$$\int \frac{dx}{1 + x^3}.$$

$\dfrac{1}{1 + x^3}$ is not recognizable as the derivative of another function of x.
We proceed therefore to express it in partial fractions.

$$\frac{1}{1 + x^3} = \frac{1}{3} \frac{1}{1 + x} + \frac{1}{3} \frac{2 - x}{1 - x + x^2}.$$

$$\int \frac{dx}{1 + x} = \log (1 + x) \qquad \text{at once.}$$

$$\int \frac{2 - x}{1 - x + x^2}\, dx \qquad \text{needs further investigation.}$$

Now if the fraction were of the form

$$\frac{\dfrac{df(x)}{dx}}{f(x)},$$

the integral would be $\log f(x)$. Here

$$f(x) = 1 - x + x^2 \quad \text{and} \quad \frac{df(x)}{dx} = -1 + 2x,$$

which is not the numerator in the given integral. If, however, we express the numerator thus:

$$2 - x = -\tfrac{1}{2}(-1 + 2x) + \tfrac{3}{2},$$

the integral becomes

$$\int -\frac{1}{2}\left\{\frac{-1 + 2x}{1 - x + x^2}\right\} dx + \int \frac{3}{2}\frac{1}{1 - x + x^2} dx.$$

The first of these is $-\tfrac{1}{2}\log(1 - x + x^2)$, and the second may be written in the form

$$\int \frac{3}{2}\frac{1}{(x - \tfrac{1}{2})^2 + (\sqrt{3}/2)^2} dx.$$

This is of the form

$$\int \frac{3}{2}\frac{1}{x^2 + a^2} dx,$$

the integral of which is

$$\frac{3}{2}\left\{\frac{1}{a}\tan^{-1}\frac{x}{a}\right\}.$$

$$\therefore \int \frac{3}{2}\frac{1}{(x - \tfrac{1}{2})^2 + (\sqrt{3}/2)^2} dx = \frac{3}{2}\frac{1}{\sqrt{3}/2}\tan^{-1}\frac{x - \tfrac{1}{2}}{\sqrt{3}/2},$$

or

$$\sqrt{3}\tan\frac{2x - 1}{\sqrt{3}}.$$

The complete integral is, therefore,

$$\int \frac{dx}{1 + x^3} = \frac{1}{3}\int \frac{dx}{1 + x} - \frac{1}{3}\int \frac{1}{2}\frac{-1 + 2x}{1 - x + x^2} dx + \frac{1}{3}\int \frac{3}{2}\frac{1}{(x - \tfrac{1}{2})^2 + (\sqrt{3}/2)^2} dx$$

$$= \frac{1}{3}\log(1 + x) - \frac{1}{6}\log(1 - x + x^2) + \frac{1}{\sqrt{3}}\tan^{-1}\frac{2x - 1}{\sqrt{3}}.$$

Example 6.

$$\int \frac{x^n}{\sqrt{x^2 + a^2}} dx, \text{ where } n \text{ is an integer.}$$

From a consideration of the illustrative examples in para. 3 (p. 239), it will be seen that if n is a positive or negative odd integer, the integral can be simplified at once.

Let n be $2m + 1$. Then the integral becomes

$$\int \frac{(x^2)^m}{\sqrt{x^2 + a^2}} x\, dx,$$

and consists of the differential of $\frac{1}{2}x^2$, namely $x\, dx$, and a function of $\frac{1}{2}x^2$.

The substitution $\frac{1}{2}x^2 = y$, or, better, $x^2 + a^2 = y$, will therefore simplify the integral.

When n is even it will be found that, in expressions containing $\sqrt{x^2 \pm a^2}$, the substitution $x = 1/y$ has the effect of changing the index of the term outside the radical from an even number to an odd number.

Let n be $2m$. The integral becomes

$$\int \frac{x^{2m}}{\sqrt{x^2 + a^2}}\, dx.$$

Put $x = 1/y$, so that $dx = (- 1/y^2)\, dy$.

$$I = \int - \frac{1}{y^{2m}\, \sqrt{(1/y^2) + a^2}} \frac{1}{y^2}\, dy$$

$$= \int - \frac{1}{y^{2m+1}\, \sqrt{1 + a^2 y^2}}\, dy,$$

and the index of y^{2m+1} being an odd integer, the substitution $1 + a^2 y^2 = z^2$ will now be effective.

Corollary. Since

$$ax^2 + bx + c = a\left(x^2 + \frac{b}{a}x + \frac{c}{a}\right)$$

$$= a\left[\left(x + \frac{b}{2a}\right)^2 + \left(\frac{c}{a} - \frac{b^2}{4a^2}\right)\right],$$

which is of the form $a(x^2 + k^2)$, we may integrate by the above methods functions of the form

$$\frac{x^n}{\sqrt{ax^2 + bx + c}}.$$

5. Forms of integral which can be evaluated by the application of general methods are those involving irrational expressions of a simple linear or quadratic type.

Type (i).

$$\int \frac{dx}{(x + a)\, \sqrt{x + b}}.$$

Since the only consideration is the elimination of the radical, put $\sqrt{x + b} = z$, so that $x = z^2 - b$.

Then
$$dx = 2z\,dz,$$

i.e.
$$\frac{dx}{2\sqrt{x + b}} = \frac{dx}{2z} = dz,$$

and the integral becomes

$$\int \frac{2\,dz}{x + a} = \int \frac{2\,dz}{z^2 + a - b},$$

which is immediately integrable.

Corollary. The form

$$\int \frac{(x + a)\,dx}{(x + c)\,\sqrt{x + b}}$$

is evaluated by writing the integral as

$$\int \left[\frac{1}{\sqrt{x + b}} + \frac{a - c}{(x + c)\,\sqrt{x + b}} \right] dx.$$

The first integral is a standard form and the second is of Type (i) above.

Type (ii).

$$\int \frac{dx}{(x - k)\,\sqrt{a + 2bx + cx^2}} \qquad (c \text{ positive}).$$

Several methods are available here, the procedure depending upon the particular substitution adopted. We may consider either the quadratic function or the linear function as suitable for the substitution, but in neither case is the process immediately obvious.

(a) Let
$$\sqrt{a + 2bx + cx^2} = z - x\sqrt{c}.$$

Then
$$a + 2bx + cx^2 = z^2 - 2zx\sqrt{c} + cx^2,$$

or
$$a + 2bx = z^2 - 2zx\sqrt{c}.$$

$$\therefore \quad 2b\,dx = 2z\,dz - 2\sqrt{c}\,(z\,dx + x\,dz),$$

and
$$dx = \frac{z - x\sqrt{c}}{b + z\sqrt{c}}\,dz.$$

The integral is therefore

$$\int \frac{1}{(x-k)(z - x\sqrt{c})} \frac{z - x\sqrt{c}}{b + z\sqrt{c}}\, dz$$

$$= \int \frac{dz}{(b + z\sqrt{c})(x-k)},$$

and, since

$$a + 2bx = z^2 - 2zx\sqrt{c},$$

$$x = \frac{z^2 - a}{2(z\sqrt{c} + b)},$$

so that the integral takes the form

$$\int \frac{dz}{(b + z\sqrt{c})\left[\dfrac{z^2 - a}{2(z\sqrt{c} + b)} - k\right]}$$

$$= \int \frac{2dz}{z^2 - a - 2k(z\sqrt{c} + b)},$$

which is of the simple rational form

$$\int \frac{dz}{z^2 + Cz + D}.$$

(b) Let

$$x - k = \frac{1}{z}, \quad \text{or} \quad x = k + \frac{1}{z};$$

then

$$dx = -\frac{1}{z^2}\, dz.$$

$$\int \frac{dx}{(x-k)\sqrt{a + 2bx + cx^2}}$$

$$= \int -\frac{1}{z^2} \frac{1}{\dfrac{1}{z}\sqrt{\left\{a + 2b\left(k + \dfrac{1}{z}\right) + c\left(k + \dfrac{1}{z}\right)^2\right\}}}\, dz$$

$$= \int -\frac{1}{z^2} z \frac{1}{\dfrac{1}{z}\sqrt{Az^2 + Bz + C}}\, dz,$$

where $Az^2 + Bz + C \equiv (a + 2bk + ck^2) z^2 + 2k(b + c) z + c.$

$$\therefore \quad I = -\int \frac{dz}{\sqrt{Az^2 + Bz + C}},$$

which is immediately integrable.

For further information on the subject of these integrals the student is advised to read Williamson, *Integral Calculus*, chapter IV. Another general method will be found in Henry, *Calculus and Probability*, where the required substitution is obtained by putting one of the constituent functions of the expression equal to y^r. The index r is then determined so that the integral can be evaluated by known processes.

6. Integration by parts.

From the relation $\Delta u_x v_x = u_{x+1} \Delta v_x + v_x \Delta u_x$ a formula for the finite integration $\Sigma u_x v_x$ was obtained. Similarly, since

$$\frac{d}{dx}(uv) = u\frac{dv}{dx} + v\frac{du}{dx},$$

we may derive an expression for the integration of the product of two functions of x.

For, integrating both sides, we have

$$uv = \int u\frac{dv}{dx}\,dx + \int v\frac{du}{dx}\,dx,$$

or

$$\int u\frac{dv}{dx}\,dx = uv - \int v\frac{du}{dx}\,dx.$$

Replace u by U and let $\dfrac{dv}{dx} = V$, so that $v = \int V dx$.

Then

$$\int UV dx = U\int V dx - \int\left(\frac{dU}{dx}\int V dx\right)dx.$$

If therefore $\left[\dfrac{dU}{dx}\int V dx\right]$ is integrable we can at once find the value of $\int UV dx$.

In words the formula may be written thus:

The integral of the product of two functions of x = (the first function × integral of the second) − the integral of (the differential coefficient of the first × integral of the second).

A few simple examples will show the application of this process.

Example 7.

$$\int xe^x\,dx.$$

The point to consider at the outset is which of the two functions should be taken as " the first function " and which " the second." Take x as the first function; we are to differentiate the first function and the differentiation of x will produce a constant.

$$\int xe^x\,dx = x\int e^x\,dx - \int\left(\frac{dx}{dx}\int e^x\,dx\right)dx$$

$$= xe^x - \int e^x\,dx = xe^x - e^x.$$

Example 8.

$$\int x\log x\,dx.$$

We must choose $\log x$ as the function to be differentiated, for if we take x as the first function we shall have to find the integral of $\log x$—which is not apparent.

$$\int x\log x\,dx = \log x\int x\,dx - \int\left\{\frac{d\log x}{dx}\left(\int x\,dx\right)\right\}dx$$

$$= \log x\,\frac{x^2}{2} - \int\frac{1}{x}\frac{x^2}{2}\,dx$$

$$= \frac{x^2}{2}\log x - \int\frac{x}{2}\,dx$$

$$= \frac{x^2}{2}\log x - \frac{x^2}{4}.$$

7. The method of integration by parts is useful even where we have to integrate a *single* function of x. We may treat $f(x)$ as the product of two functions, one function being $f(x)$ and the other unity.

Example 9.

$$\int\tan^{-1}x\,dx.$$

Let the first function be $\tan^{-1}x$ and the second function 1.
Then

$$\int\tan^{-1}x\,dx = \int\tan^{-1}x\,.\,1\,dx$$

$$= \tan^{-1}x\int 1\,dx - \int\left\{\frac{d}{dx}(\tan^{-1}x)\int 1\,dx\right\}dx$$

$$= \tan^{-1}x\,.\,x - \int\frac{1}{1+x^2}x\,dx$$

$$= x\tan^{-1}x - \tfrac{1}{2}\log(1+x^2).$$

Example 10.

$$\int \sqrt{x^2 + a^2}\, dx.$$

As above

$$\int \sqrt{x^2 + a^2}\, dx = \int \sqrt{x^2 + a^2} \cdot 1\, dx$$

$$= \sqrt{x^2 + a^2} \int 1\, dx - \int \left\{ \frac{d}{dx} \sqrt{x^2 + a^2} \int 1\, dx \right\} dx$$

$$= \sqrt{x^2 + a^2} \cdot x - \int \frac{x}{\sqrt{x^2 + a^2}}\, x\, dx$$

$$= \sqrt{x^2 + a^2} \cdot x - \int \frac{x^2}{\sqrt{x^2 + a^2}}\, dx$$

$$= \sqrt{x^2 + a^2} \cdot x - \int \left\{ \frac{x^2 + a^2}{\sqrt{x^2 + a^2}} - \frac{a^2}{\sqrt{x^2 + a^2}} \right\} dx$$

$$= \sqrt{x^2 + a^2} \cdot x - \int \sqrt{x^2 + a^2}\, dx + \int \frac{a^2\, dx}{\sqrt{x^2 + a^2}}.$$

$$\therefore\ 2 \int \sqrt{x^2 + a^2}\, dx = x \sqrt{x^2 + a^2} + a^2 \int \frac{dx}{\sqrt{x^2 + a^2}}$$

$$= x \sqrt{x^2 + a^2} + a^2 \log (x + \sqrt{x^2 + a^2}).$$

$$\therefore\ \int \sqrt{x^2 + a^2}\, dx = \tfrac{1}{2} \{ x \sqrt{x^2 + a^2} + a^2 \log (x + \sqrt{x^2 + a^2}) \}.$$

This example is instructive in that the process of integration by parts does not immediately give the required result. When we have performed the necessary operations we are left with $\int \sqrt{x^2 + a^2}\, dx$ on both sides of the identity, and we have to clear the right-hand side of this integral before the answer is obtained.

A somewhat similar process is necessary in the evaluation of the following important integral involving trigonometrical functions.

Example 11.

$$\int e^x \sin x\, dx.$$

Here it is immaterial which function is chosen as the first function. Take e^x as the first function: then

$$\int e^x \sin x\,dx = e^x \int \sin x\,dx - \int \left\{\frac{de^x}{dx} \int \sin x\,dx\right\} dx$$

$$= - e^x \cos x + \int e^x \cos x\,dx.$$

This does not immediately give the required result. If, however, we consider $\int e^x \cos x\,dx$ and integrate by parts, we obtain a further equality which enables the integral to be evaluated.

$$\int e^x \cos x\,dx = e^x \int \cos x\,dx - \int \left\{\frac{de^x}{dx} \int \cos x\,dx\right\} dx$$

$$= e^x \sin x - \int e^x \sin x\,dx.$$

Let

$$\int e^x \sin x\,dx - S,$$

and

$$\int e^x \cos x\,dx = C.$$

Then

$$S = - e^x \cos x + C,$$

and

$$C = e^x \sin x - S,$$

or

$$S - C = - e^x \cos x,$$

$$S + C = e^x \sin x.$$

Hence

$$\int e^x \sin x\,dx = S = \tfrac{1}{2}e^x (\sin x - \cos x),$$

and

$$\int e^x \cos x\,dx = C = \tfrac{1}{2}e^x (\sin x + \cos x).$$

8. Reduction formulae.

It has been shown in the preceding paragraph that, in certain instances, integration by parts may not produce the required result immediately; another stage must be reached before the integration can be effected. It is often possible, however, to relate an integral to one or more integrals of similar form, so that by proceeding successively the original integral can eventually be obtained. If, for example, we are required to integrate u_n, where u_n is a function of x involving x^n and lower powers (n being a positive integer), it may be possible to relate the integral of the function to the integral of u_{n-1}. The formula connecting these integrals is called a "reduction formula." Reduction formulae are of importance in the integral calculus, and their use often leads to the evaluation of integrals which could not otherwise be obtained. For the purpose of illustration it is unnecessary to give more than a few elementary examples of the application of these formulae to indefinite integrals. It will be seen later (Chapter XVI) that the process may be adopted to greater advantage in considering problems involving definite integrals.

Example 12.

$$\int e^x x^n \, dx.$$

$$u_n = \int e^x x^n \, dx = x^n e^x - \int n x^{n-1} e^x \, dx$$

$$= x^n e^x - n u_{n-1}.$$

Similarly $\qquad u_{n-1} = x^{n-1} e^x - (n-1) u_{n-2},$

and so on.

The integral can therefore be made to depend upon the value of u_0,

i.e. on $\int e^x dx$.

Thus
$$\int e^x x^3 \, dx = x^3 e^x - 3 \int e^x x^2 \, dx,$$

$$\int e^x x^2 \, dx = x^2 e^x - 2 \int e^x x \, dx,$$

$$\int e^x x \, dx = x e^x - \int e^x dx$$

$$= x e^x - e^x.$$

$$\therefore \int e^x x^3 \, dx = x^3 e^x - 3 \left[x^2 e^x - 2 \left(x e^x - e^x \right) \right]$$

$$= e^x \left(x^3 - 3x^2 + 6x - 6 \right).$$

Example 13.

$$\int \tan^n \theta \, d\theta,$$

where n is odd.

$$\tan^n \theta = \tan^{n-2} \theta \tan^2 \theta = \tan^{n-2} \theta \left(\sec^2 \theta - 1 \right).$$

$$\therefore \int \tan^n \theta \, d\theta = \int \tan^{n-2} \theta \sec^2 \theta \, d\theta - \int \tan^{n-2} \theta \, d\theta.$$

To evaluate

$$\int \tan^{n-2} \theta \sec^2 \theta \, d\theta,$$

put $\qquad\qquad\qquad \tan \theta = z.$

Then
$$\sec^2 \theta \, d\theta = dz,$$

and
$$\int \tan^{n-2} \theta \sec^2 \theta \, d\theta = \int z^{n-2} dz = \frac{z^{n-1}}{n-1} = \frac{\tan^{n-1} \theta}{n-1}.$$

$$\therefore \ u_n = \frac{1}{n-1} \tan^{n-1} \theta - u_{n-2}$$

$$= \frac{1}{n-1} \tan^{n-1} \theta - \frac{1}{n-3} \tan^{n-3} \theta + \frac{1}{n-5} \tan^{n-5} \theta - \ldots,$$

where the last term is $(-1)^m \int \tan \theta \, d\theta$, since n is odd $(= 2m + 1)$, or

$$(-1)^{m+1} \log \cos \theta.$$

Many reduction formulae result from the differentiation of simple functions of the variable. It will be sufficient to give one example of the process.

Example 14.

Find a reduction formula for the evaluation of the integral

$$\int \frac{x^n}{\sqrt{1 + x^2}} \, dx,$$

where n is a positive integer.

We have identically

$$\frac{d}{dx} x^{n-1} \sqrt{1 + x^2} = (n-1) x^{n-2} \sqrt{1 + x^2} + \frac{x}{\sqrt{1 + x^2}} x^{n-1}$$

$$= \frac{(n-1) x^{n-2} (1 + x^2) + x^n}{\sqrt{1 + x^2}}$$

$$= \frac{(n-1) x^{n-2} + (n-1) x^n + x^n}{\sqrt{1 + x^2}}$$

$$= (n-1) \frac{x^{n-2}}{\sqrt{1 + x^2}} + \frac{n x^n}{\sqrt{1 + x^2}}.$$

By integration

$$x^{n-1} \sqrt{1 + x^2} = (n-1) \int \frac{x^{n-2} dx}{\sqrt{1 + x^2}} + n \int \frac{x^n dx}{\sqrt{1 + x^2}},$$

i.e.
$$u_n = \frac{1}{n} x^{n-1} \sqrt{1 + x^2} - \frac{n-1}{n} u_{n-2}.$$

By continuing the process we arrive at the forms

$$\int \frac{dx}{\sqrt{1 + x^2}} \ (n \text{ even}), \ \text{or} \ \int \frac{x \, dx}{\sqrt{1 + x^2}} \ (n \text{ odd}),$$

which are immediately integrable.

9. It is evident from the explanations above that the evaluation of an integral may depend on one or more of a number of different artifices. For complicated functions it may be necessary to resort to several alternatives before the solution can be found. Indeed, in many instances the integral may be no known function.

The following example is of a different type from those hitherto examined, and is given in order to show that certain obvious substitutions must be rejected as being unsuitable for the evaluation of the integral.

Example 15.

$$\int \frac{dy}{(1 - y^3)^{\frac{1}{3}}}.$$

Let

$$I = \int \frac{dy}{(1 - y^3)^{\frac{1}{3}}}.$$

(i) Put $1 - y^3 = z$, so that $y = (1 - z)^{\frac{1}{3}}$.

Then

$$- 3y^2 \, dy = dz.$$

$$I = \int - \frac{1}{3y^2} \frac{1}{z^{\frac{1}{3}}} \, dz = - \frac{1}{3} \int \frac{dz}{z^{\frac{1}{3}} (1 - z)^{\frac{2}{3}}},$$

which has produced a more complicated form.

(ii) Put $(1 - y^3)^{\frac{1}{3}} = z$, so that $y^3 = 1 - z^3$.

Then

$$\tfrac{1}{3} (1 - y^3)^{-\frac{2}{3}} (- 3y^2) \, dy = dz;$$

i.e.

$$- y^2 (1 - y^3)^{-\frac{2}{3}} \, dy = dz.$$

$$I = \int \frac{1}{z} \frac{- dz}{y^2 (1 - y^3)^{-\frac{2}{3}}} = \int \frac{- z \, dz}{(1 - z^3)^{\frac{2}{3}}},$$

which is not immediately integrable.

(iii) Trials (i) and (ii) fail because the integrand does not contain a term $y^2 dy$ which is the differential of $\tfrac{1}{3} y^3$. In dealing with functions of the form $\sqrt{a^2 + x^2}$ we have found that the substitution $x = 1/y$ changes the index of the term outside the radical, and this suggests that the above integral might be simplified by the substitution $y = 1/z$, so that

$$dy = (- 1/z^2)\, dz.$$

Carrying out this substitution, we obtain

$$I = - \int \frac{1}{z^2} \frac{dz}{(1 - 1/z^3)^{\frac{1}{3}}} = - \int \frac{dz}{z(z^3 - 1)^{\frac{1}{3}}} = - \int \frac{z^2\, dz}{z^3(z^3 - 1)^{\frac{1}{3}}}.$$

Since the integrand now consists of the two parts (i) $z^2\, dz$, the differential of $\frac{1}{3}z^3$, and (ii) $z^3(z^3 - 1)^{\frac{1}{3}}$, a function of $\frac{1}{3}z^3$, the required conditions are satisfied. The substitution $z^3 = x$ will therefore simplify the integral.

A better substitution, which will rationalize the denominator of the integrand, is $z^3 - 1 = x^3$: this substitution will not affect the above conditions.

Putting $z^3 - 1 = x^3$, we have $3z^2\, dz = 3x^2\, dx$, and

$$I = - \int \frac{x^2\, dx}{(x^3 + 1)\, x} = - \int \frac{x\, dx}{x^3 + 1}.$$

By expressing this in partial fractions, and employing the usual processes, the integral becomes

$$- \tfrac{1}{6} \log (1 - x + x^2) - \frac{1}{\sqrt{3}} \tan^{-1} \frac{(2x - 1)}{\sqrt{3}} + \log (1 + x),$$

where

$$x = (z^3 - 1)^{\frac{1}{3}}$$
$$= \frac{(1 - y^3)^{\frac{1}{3}}}{y}.$$

EXAMPLES 15

Integrate the following functions with respect to x:

1. $\dfrac{x^2}{(1 + x)^n}$; $\dfrac{x - 2}{x \sqrt{x}}$; $\dfrac{x + 1}{\sqrt{x + 2}}$.

2. $\dfrac{x + 1}{x^2 - 4x + 3}$; $\dfrac{3x^2 - 1}{x^2 - 3x + 2}$; $\dfrac{x^3}{\sqrt{x - 1}}$.

3. $\dfrac{x}{x^4 - a^4}$; $\dfrac{3x + 1}{(x - 1)^2 (x + 3)}$.

4. $\dfrac{\cos x}{3 + 4 \sin x}$; $\dfrac{8x}{4x^2 + 3}$; $\dfrac{e^x - \sin x}{e^x + \cos x}$.

5. $\dfrac{1}{\sqrt{2-x-x^2}}$; $\dfrac{1}{\sqrt{2+x+x^2}}$.

6. $\dfrac{\sin x}{\frac{1}{2}+\frac{1}{3}\cos x}$; $\dfrac{1}{1-x^3}$.

7. $\dfrac{x^2-1}{x^4+x^2+1}$; $\dfrac{x^2}{x^6-a^6}$.

8. $\dfrac{x}{\sqrt{1+x^2}}$; $\dfrac{3x+4}{4x^2+3}$.

9. $\sin 2x \cos 3x$; $\cos x \cos \frac{1}{2}x$.

10. $\dfrac{x^3}{\sqrt{a^2+x^2}}$; $\dfrac{1}{x\sqrt{1+x^n}}$.

11. Find the value of the integral of $\dfrac{1}{a+2bx+cx^2}$ according as $ac-b^2$ is of the form $-k^2$ or $+k^2$.

12. Evaluate $\displaystyle\int \dfrac{dx}{x^2\sqrt{2+x^2}}$.

13. Integrate with respect to x:

(i) $\dfrac{x}{y}$; (ii) $\dfrac{x^2}{y}$; (iii) $\dfrac{x^3}{y}$, where $y \equiv \sqrt{x^2-1}$.

14. Resolve $\dfrac{3x^2+x-2}{(x-1)^3(x+1)}$ into partial fractions and integrate it.

15. By using the known relations connecting $\sin x$ and $\cos x$ with t, where $t = \tan \frac{1}{2}x$, evaluate

$$\int \dfrac{dx}{\sin x}; \quad \int \dfrac{dx}{1+\cos x}; \quad \int \sec x \operatorname{cosec} x \, dx,$$

expressing the results in terms of t.

By using the formula for integration by parts, evaluate

16. $\displaystyle\int x \log x \, dx$; $\displaystyle\int e^{ax} x^2 \, dx$.   17. $\displaystyle\int x^2 e^x \, dx$; $\displaystyle\int x^2 \log x \, dx$.

18. $\displaystyle\int x \sin x \, dx$; $\displaystyle\int x^3 \cos x \, dx$.   19. $\displaystyle\int x \tan^{-1} x \, dx$; $\displaystyle\int \dfrac{xe^x}{(1+x)^2} \, dx$.

20. $\displaystyle\int e^{ax} \cos bx \, dx$.

F

Integrate the following functions with respect to x:

21. $\dfrac{1}{\sqrt{4x^2 - 7}}$.

22. $\sec x$.

23. $\dfrac{\log(1 - x)}{(1 - x)}$.

24. $\dfrac{\log(\log x)}{x}$.

25. $(a^2 + x^2)^{-\frac{5}{2}}$.

26. $(x + b)(x^2 + 2bx + c)^n$.

27. $\dfrac{1}{\sqrt{3x^2 + x + 8}}$.

28. $\dfrac{1}{1 + c^x}$.

29. $\dfrac{x + 1}{x^2 + x + 1}$.

30. $\dfrac{x}{\sqrt{5 + 2x + x^2}}$.

31. $\dfrac{1}{x(1 + x^3)}$.

32. $\dfrac{1}{41 + 9\cos x}$.

33. $\dfrac{1}{(1 + x)\sqrt{1 + x^2}}$.

34. $\dfrac{1}{x\sqrt{x^2 + 2x - 3}}$.

35. $\dfrac{1}{x\sqrt{2 + x - x^2}}$.

36. $\dfrac{\tan x}{a + b\tan^2 x}$.

37. $\sqrt{\dfrac{a + x}{a - x}}$.

38. $\dfrac{1}{\sqrt{x} + \sqrt{x + a}}$.

39. $\dfrac{\sin x}{4\cos x + 3\sin x}$.

40. $\dfrac{1}{a + b\cos^2 x}$.

41. Prove that

$$\int u\,\frac{d^2 v}{dx^2}\,dx = u\,\frac{dv}{dx} - v\,\frac{du}{dx} + \int v\,\frac{d^2 u}{dx^2}\,dx.$$

42. If y is a function of x whose integral is known show that the inverse function where x is regarded as a function of y can always be integrated. Apply this method to find:

(a) $\displaystyle\int \log y\,dy$, given that $\displaystyle\int e^x\,dx = e^x$;

(b) $\displaystyle\int \cos^{-1} y\,dy$, given that $\displaystyle\int \cos x\,dx = \sin x$.

43. Integrate $\dfrac{x^3}{(x^2 + 1)^3}$,

  (i) by the substitution $u = x^2 + 1$;
  (ii) by the substitution $x = \tan \theta$.

Explain the difference between the results.

44. If $\mu_x = -\dfrac{1}{l_x}\dfrac{dl_x}{dx}$ and is of the form $a + bx + mc^x$, show that l_x is of the form $ks^x w^{x^2} g^{c^x}$.

45. Integrate $\dfrac{x}{1 + x^4}$ with respect to x.

46. Evaluate $\displaystyle\int\dfrac{(x-1)^{\frac{1}{2}}\,dx}{x\,(x+1)^{\frac{1}{2}}}$.

47. If $a > b$, integrate $(a-x)^{-\frac{1}{2}}\,(b-x)^{-\frac{1}{2}}$ with respect to x.

48. Obtain by successive reduction
$$\int x^3\,(a^2 + x^2)^{-\frac{5}{2}}\,dx.$$

49. Find a formula of reduction for $\displaystyle\int e^{px}\,x^q\,dx$ and hence evaluate $\displaystyle\int x\,e^{qx}\,dx$.

50. By differentiating $\dfrac{x}{(x^2 - a^2)^{m-1}}$, find a formula of reduction for $\displaystyle\int\dfrac{dx}{(x^2 - a^2)^m}$.

Hence or otherwise evaluate $\displaystyle\int\dfrac{dx}{(x^2 - a^2)^2}$.

51. Evaluate $\displaystyle\int x^3\,(\log x)^2\,dx$.

52. Prove that
$$\int\cos^m x\,\sin nx\,dx = \frac{m}{m+n}\int\cos^{m-1} x\,\sin(n-1)\,x\,dx - \frac{\cos^m x\,\cos nx}{m+n}.$$

53. If
$$u_n = \int x^n\,\sqrt{2ax - x^2}\,dx,$$
show that
$$(n+2)\,u_n = (2n+1)\,au_{n-1} - x^{n-1}\,(2ax - x^2)^{\frac{3}{2}}.$$

Hence obtain
$$\int x\,\sqrt{2ax - x^2}\,dx.$$

54. Integrate $\dfrac{1}{\sin(x-a)\,\sin(x-b)}$ with respect to x.

55. Use the method of integration by parts to find $\displaystyle\int x^2\,\sin^{-1} x\,dx$.

56. Find $\displaystyle\int\dfrac{\sin 2\phi}{\sin^4\phi + \cos^4\phi}\,d\phi$.

57. Show that the substitution $u^2 = \dfrac{x - a}{\beta - x}$ renders the integral $\displaystyle\int \sqrt{(x - a)(\beta - x)}\, dx$ integrable. $(\beta > a.)$

Hence evaluate $\displaystyle\int \sqrt{(3 - x)(x - 2)}\, dx$.

58. If μ_x is in the form of

$$A + Bc^x \left(\log_e x + \frac{1}{\log_e c} \frac{1}{x} \right),$$

find an expression for l_x, where

$$\mu_x = -\frac{1}{l_x} \frac{dl_x}{dx}.$$

59. Show that the integral

$$\int \frac{dx}{x \sqrt{3x^2 + 2x + 1}}$$

is rationalized by the substitution

$$x = \frac{2(y + 1)}{y^2 - 3}.$$

By means of this substitution evaluate the integral.

60. Integrate $\operatorname{cosec} x$ with respect to x.

61. Find $\displaystyle\int \frac{15 - \cos 2x}{3 + \cos 2x}\, dx$.

By means of the substitutions indicated, evaluate the following integrals:

62. $\displaystyle\int \frac{x^3\, dx}{(x^2 + 1)^3}$.　　　Substitution $x = \tan \phi$.

63. $\displaystyle\int \frac{(x^4 - 1)\, dx}{x^2 \sqrt{x^4 + x^2 + 1}}$.　　　,,　　　$z = (x^4 + 1)/x^2$.

64. $\displaystyle\int \frac{(x^4 - 1)\, dx}{x^2 \sqrt{x^4 + x^2 + 1}}$.　　　,,　　　$z = x + 1/x$.

65. $\displaystyle\int \frac{dx}{x^5 (2 - x^3)^{\frac{5}{3}}}$.　　　,,　　　$z = (2 - x^3)/x^3$.

66. $\displaystyle\int \frac{(1 + 2x^{\frac{3}{4}})^{\frac{2}{3}}\, dx}{x^3}$.　　　,,　　　$2 + x^{-\frac{3}{4}} = z$.

67. $\int \dfrac{x\,dx}{\sqrt{1+x}+\sqrt[3]{1+x}}$. Substitution $x + 1 = z^6$.

68. $\int \dfrac{dx}{\sqrt{x+a}+\sqrt{x+b}}$.   ,, $2x + a + b = \tfrac{1}{2}(a-b)(t^2 + 1/t^2)$.

(Express the result as a function of t.)

69. $\int \dfrac{dx}{x\,(a + bx^n)^4}$.   Substitution $a + bx^n = zx^n$.

70. $\int \dfrac{x^7\,dx}{x^{12} - 1}$.   ,, $z = x^4$.

71. $\int \dfrac{d\phi}{2 + \cos \phi}$.   ,, $x = (1 + 2 \cos \phi)/(2 + \cos \phi)$.

CHAPTER XVI

DEFINITE INTEGRALS: AREAS: MISCELLANEOUS THEOREMS

1. The definite integral $\int_a^b \phi(x)\,dx$ has been defined thus: if $\frac{d}{dx} f(x) = \phi(x)$, then $\int_a^b \phi(x) = f(b) - f(a)$. In dealing with indefinite integrals the sole consideration is to obtain the function $f(x)$ which when differentiated will give $\phi(x)$. For definite integrals a further process is necessary, namely that of finding the values of $f(b)$ and $f(a)$. It should be noted that a definite integral will always be a function of a and b (the limits of the integration) and will not be a function of x, the independent variable.

The ordinary procedure follows similar lines to those adopted for summation in finite differences and the work is carried on thus:

Example 1.

Evaluate
$$\int_4^5 (x-3)^2\,dx.$$

$$
\begin{aligned}
\int_4^5 (x-3)^2\,dx &= \left[\frac{(x-3)^3}{3}\right]_4^5 \\
&= \frac{(5-3)^3}{3} - \frac{(4-3)^3}{3} \\
&= \frac{2^3}{3} - \frac{1^3}{3} = \frac{8}{3} - \frac{1}{3} = \frac{7}{3}.
\end{aligned}
$$

2. Before proceeding to a detailed investigation of the methods for the solution of problems involving definite integration there are certain simple theorems to be proved. These are of general application.

(i) $$\int_a^b \phi(x)\,dx = -\int_b^a \phi(x)\,dx.$$

If $$\frac{d}{dx} f(x) = \phi(x), \quad \text{then} \quad \int \phi(x) = f(x).$$

$$\therefore \quad \int_a^b \phi(x)\,dx = f(b) - f(a)$$
$$= -\,[f(a) - f(b)]$$
$$= -\int_b^a \phi(x)\,dx.$$

(ii) $\qquad \int_a^c \phi(x)\,dx = \int_a^b \phi(x)\,dx + \int_b^c \phi(x)\,dx.$

As before, if

$$\frac{d}{dx}f(x) = \phi(x), \quad \text{then} \quad \int \phi(x) = f(x).$$

$$\therefore \quad \int_a^c \phi(x)\,dx = f(c) - f(a)$$
$$= f(c) - f(b) + f(b) - f(a)$$
$$= \int_b^c \phi(x)\,dx + \int_a^b \phi(x)\,dx.$$

(iii) $\qquad \int_0^a \phi(x)\,dx = \int_0^a \phi(a - x)\,dx.$

This is an example of the change of limits brought about by the substitution of a different variable for the original variable x.

If $\qquad (a - x) = y \quad$ so that $\quad -dx = dy,$

then $\qquad \phi(a - x)\,dx = -\phi(y)\,dy.$

Also when $\qquad x = 0, \quad y = a,$

and when $\qquad x = a, \quad y = 0.$

$$\therefore \quad \int_0^a \phi(x)\,dx = \int_a^0 [-\phi(y)]\,dy = \int_0^a \phi(y)\,dy \quad \text{(i) (above)}$$
$$= \int_0^a \phi(a - x)\,dx.$$

It should be noted that if the upper limit is the independent variable, the integral is not a definite integral, but simply another form of the indefinite integral.

For example,

$$\int_a^x \phi(x)\,dx = f(x) - f(a)$$
$$= f(x) + \text{a constant}$$
$$= \int \phi(x)\,dx.$$

3. There is no new principle involved in the evaluation of definite integrals. Care must be taken, however, that if a substitution be made for the independent variable, the limits of integration are changed accordingly. This is particularly to be noted when the substitution turns an algebraic expression into a trigonometrical expression, or vice versa.

The following illustrative examples show the procedure to be employed.

Example 2.

$$\int_0^1 \frac{x^2}{(3x+2)^2}\, dx.$$

Put $3x + 2 = y$: then when $x = 0$, $y = 2$; and when $x = 1$, $y = 5$. Also $3dx = dy$.

The integral becomes

$$\int_2^5 \frac{\left(\dfrac{y-2}{3}\right)^2}{y^2}\frac{dy}{3}$$

$$= \frac{1}{27}\int_2^5 \frac{y^2 - 4y + 4}{y^2}\, dy$$

$$= \frac{1}{27}\int_2^5 \left(1 - \frac{4}{y} + \frac{4}{y^2}\right) dy$$

$$= \frac{1}{27}\left[y - 4\log y - \frac{4}{y}\right]_2^5$$

$$= \frac{1}{27}\left[\left(5 - 4\log 5 - \frac{4}{5}\right) - \left(2 - 4\log 2 - \frac{4}{2}\right)\right]$$

$$= \frac{1}{27}\left(3 - 4\log \frac{5}{2} + \frac{6}{5}\right) = \frac{1}{27}\left(\frac{21}{5} - 4\log \frac{5}{2}\right).$$

Example 3.

$$\int_0^a \frac{dx}{a^2 + x^2}.$$

$\int \dfrac{dx}{a^2 + x^2}$ is a standard form and its value is $\dfrac{1}{a}\tan^{-1}\dfrac{x}{a}$.

Therefore the definite integral

$$= \left[\frac{1}{a}\tan^{-1}\frac{x}{a}\right]_0^a$$

$$= \frac{1}{a}\tan^{-1} 1 - \frac{1}{a}\tan^{-1} 0$$

$$= \frac{1}{a}\cdot\frac{\pi}{4} - \frac{1}{a}\cdot 0 = \frac{\pi}{4a}.$$

There are two points to be noted when evaluating a definite integral for which the indefinite integral is an inverse trigonometrical function. They are

(1) In no circumstances can the result be expressed in degrees, since the ordinary rules for the differentiation and integration of trigonometrical functions hold only when the angles are measured in radians.

(2) The value of the definite integral is usually the smallest positive angle. If, for example, $\tan x$ is made to vary continuously from o to 1 and x commences at the value o, it will end at the value $\frac{\pi}{4}$: similarly if it commences at the value $n\pi$ it will end at the value $n\pi + \frac{\pi}{4}$.

The reasons for these restrictions will be more apparent when geometrical applications of definite integrals are considered. (See para. 6, later.)

Example 4.

$$\int_0^a \frac{dx}{(a^2 + x^2)^{\frac{3}{2}}}.$$

Let $x = a \tan \phi$; then $dx = a \sec^2 \phi \, d\phi$.

When $x = $ o, $\tan \phi = $ o and $\phi = $ o;

and when $x = a$, $\tan \phi = $ 1 and $\phi = \frac{\pi}{4}$.

Therefore the integral becomes

$$\int_0^{\frac{\pi}{4}} \frac{a \sec^2 \phi \, d\phi}{(a^2 \tan^2 \phi + a^2)^{\frac{3}{2}}}$$

$$\int_0^{\frac{\pi}{4}} \frac{a \sec^2 \phi \, d\phi}{a^3 \sec^3 \phi} = \int_0^{\frac{\pi}{4}} \frac{1}{a^2} \cos \phi \, d\phi$$

$$= \left[\frac{1}{a^2} \sin \phi \right]_0^{\frac{\pi}{4}} = \frac{1}{a^2} \left[\sin \frac{\pi}{4} - \sin \text{o} \right]$$

$$= \frac{1}{a^2} \left[\frac{1}{\sqrt{2}} - \text{o} \right]$$

$$= \frac{1}{a^2 \sqrt{2}}.$$

Note. The substitution $x = \frac{1}{y}$ will also simplify this integral.

Example 5.

$$\int_0^\pi \sin^2 x\,dx.$$

$$\int_0^\pi \sin^2 x\,dx = \int_0^\pi \tfrac{1}{2}.2\sin^2 x\,dx = \int_0^\pi \tfrac{1}{2}\left(1 - \cos 2x\right)dx$$

$$= \left[\tfrac{1}{2}\left(x - \tfrac{1}{2}\sin 2x\right)\right]_0^\pi = \tfrac{1}{2}\left[\pi - \tfrac{1}{2}\sin 2\pi - 0\right] = \tfrac{1}{2}\pi,$$

since $$\sin 2\pi = 0.$$

Example 6.

Prove that $$\int_0^{\frac{\pi}{2}} \sin^n x\,dx = \int_0^{\frac{\pi}{2}} \cos^n x\,dx.$$

From (iii) above (para. 2),

$$\int_0^a f(x)\,dx = \int_0^a f(a - x)\,dx$$

and $$\sin x = \cos\left(\frac{\pi}{2} - x\right).$$

$$\therefore \int_0^{\frac{\pi}{2}} \sin^n x\,dx = \int_0^{\frac{\pi}{2}} \sin^n\left(\frac{\pi}{2} - x\right)dx = \int_0^{\frac{\pi}{2}} \cos^n x\,dx.$$

Example 7.

Evaluate $$\int_0^{\frac{\pi}{2}} x \sin x\,dx.$$

The function $x \sin x$ is the product of two functions of x and we must integrate the expression by parts. We may obtain the indefinite integral by this method and insert the limits after the integration has been performed.

$$\int x \sin x\,dx = -x \cos x - \int(-\cos x)\,dx$$
$$= -x \cos x + \sin x.$$

$$\therefore \int_0^{\frac{\pi}{2}} x \sin x\,dx = \left[-x \cos x + \sin x\right]_0^{\frac{\pi}{2}}$$

$$= -\frac{\pi}{2}\cos\frac{\pi}{2} + \sin\frac{\pi}{2} - 0\cos 0 + \sin 0$$

$$= 0 + 1 - 0 + 0$$

$$= 1.$$

4. When the function whose definite integral is required is the product of two functions of the variable, we may proceed as above, or we may adopt a more specific formula for definite integration.

Let u_t and v_t be two functions of a variable t, and let a and b be two constants independent of t.

Then

$$\int u_t v_t \, dt = u_t \int v_t \, dt - \int \frac{du_t}{dt} \left(\int v_t dt \right) dt.$$

We may write $\int v_t dt$ as $\int_a^t v_k dk$; for if $\int v_t dt = V_t$ then

$$\int_a^t v_k dk = \left[V_k \right]_a^t = V_t - V_a$$

$$= \int v_t dt - \text{constant}$$

$$= \int v_t dt,$$

the constant being simply the constant of integration. (See para. 2.)

$$\therefore \int u_t v_t dt = u_t \int_a^t v_k dk - \int \frac{du_t}{dt} \left(\int_a^t v_k dk \right) dt.$$

$$\therefore \int_a^b u_t v_t dt = \left[u_t \int_a^t v_k dk - \int \frac{du_t}{dt} \left(\int_a^t v_k dk \right) dt \right]_a^b$$

$$= u_b \int_a^b v_k dk - u_a \int_a^a v_k dk - \int_a^b \frac{du_t}{dt} \left(\int_a^t v_k dk \right) dt$$

$$= u_b \int_a^b v_k dk - \int_a^b \frac{du_t}{dt} \left(\int_a^t v_k dk \right) dt,$$

since

$$\int_a^a v_k dk = V_a - V_a = 0.$$

Alternatively, since

$$- \int_t^b v_k dk = - (V_b - V_t) = V_t - \text{constant} = \int v_t dt,$$

we may obtain

$$\int_a^b u_t v_t dt = u_a \int_a^b v_k dk + \int_a^b \frac{du_t}{dt} \left(\int_t^b v_k dk \right) dt.$$

(See Actuarial Note, *J.I.A.* vol. XLIV, pp. 403-5.)

Applying the first of these formulae to the evaluation of the integral in Ex. 7, we have

$$\int_0^{\frac{\pi}{2}} x \sin x \, dx = \frac{\pi}{2} \int_0^{\frac{\pi}{2}} \sin x \, dx - \int_0^{\frac{\pi}{2}} \frac{dx}{dx} \left(\int_0^x \sin k \, dk \right) dx,$$

where the "u" function is x, and the "v" function is $\sin x$.
Now

$$\int_0^x \sin k \, dk = \left[-\cos k \right]_0^x = -\cos x + \cos 0 = -\cos x + 1.$$

$$\therefore \quad \int_0^{\frac{\pi}{2}} x \sin x \, dx = \frac{\pi}{2} \left[-\cos x \right]_0^{\frac{\pi}{2}} - \int_0^{\frac{\pi}{2}} (-\cos x + 1) \, dx$$

$$= \frac{\pi}{2} \left[-\cos \frac{\pi}{2} + \cos 0 \right] - \left[-\sin x + x \right]_0^{\frac{\pi}{2}}$$

$$= \frac{\pi}{2} \left[0 + 1 \right] - \left[-\sin \frac{\pi}{2} + \frac{\pi}{2} \right]$$

$$= \frac{\pi}{2} + \sin \frac{\pi}{2} - \frac{\pi}{2}$$

$$= \sin \frac{\pi}{2}$$

$$= 1, \text{ as before.}$$

5. The following examples are illustrative of the methods employed in the evaluation of certain types of integrals.

The value of the function $\frac{x^n}{e^x}$ when $x = 0$ is evidently zero (since $e^0 = 1$), and the limit of the function when $x \to \infty$ is also zero (see Ex. 3, Chap. XIII). These properties of the function enable the definite integral $\int_0^\infty x^n e^{-x} \, dx$ to be readily evaluated when n is a positive integer.
Thus

$$\int x^n e^{-x} \, dx = x^n (-e^{-x}) - \int \frac{dx^n}{dx} (-e^{-x}) \, dx$$

$$= -x^n e^{-x} + n \int x^{n-1} e^{-x} \, dx.$$

$$\therefore \int_0^\infty x^n e^{-x} dx = \left[-x^n e^{-x} \right]_0^\infty + n \int_0^\infty x^{n-1} e^{-x} dx$$

$$= n \int_0^\infty x^{n-1} e^{-x} dx \text{ since } \left[-x^n e^{-x} \right]_0^\infty \text{ is zero.}$$

Similarly

$$\int_0^\infty x^{n-1} e^{-x} dx = (n-1) \int_0^\infty x^{n-2} e^{-x} dx,$$

and so on.

$$\therefore \int_0^\infty x^n e^{-x} dx = n (n-1) (n-2) \ldots \int_0^\infty e^{-x} dx$$

$$= n (n-1) (n-2) \ldots \left[-e^{-x} \right]_0^\infty$$

$$\begin{cases} \underset{x \to \infty}{\text{Lt}} \ e^{-x} = \underset{x \to \infty}{\text{Lt}} \ \frac{1}{e^x} = 0 \\ \text{and} \ e^{-x} = 1 \ \text{when} \ x = 0. \end{cases}$$

$$\therefore \int_0^\infty x^n e^{-x} dx = n (n-1) (n-2) \ldots 1.$$

Again, consider the integral $\int_0^1 x^{n-1} (1-x)^{m-1} dx$, where m and n are positive and m is an integer. If we put $1 - x = z$, then $-dx = dz$. The new variable z takes the values 1 and 0 when x has the values 0 and 1 respectively, and the form of the integral is now $\int_1^0 - (1-z)^{n-1} z^{m-1} dz$.

This is the same as $\int_0^1 z^{m-1} (1-z)^{n-1} dz$.

Changing the variable to x—which does not alter the value of the integral—the integral becomes $\int_0^1 x^{m-1} (1-x)^{n-1} dx$.

To evaluate the integral we proceed in the usual manner.

$$\int x^{n-1} (1-x)^{m-1} dx = \frac{x^n}{n} (1-x)^{m-1} - \int \frac{d}{dx} (1-x)^{m-1} \frac{x^n}{n} dx$$

$$= \frac{x^n}{n} (1-x)^{m-1} + \int \frac{m-1}{n} x^n (1-x)^{m-2} dx$$

$$= \frac{x^n}{n} (1-x)^{m-1} + \frac{m-1}{n} \int x^n (1-x)^{m-2} dx.$$

The term $\dfrac{x^n}{n}(1-x)^{m-1}$ vanishes for limits $x=0$ and $x=1$.

$$\therefore \int_0^1 x^{n-1}(1-x)^{m-1}\,dx = \frac{m-1}{n}\int_0^1 x^n(1-x)^{m-2}\,dx$$

$$= \frac{m-1}{n}\frac{m-2}{n+1}\int_0^1 x^{n+1}(1-x)^{m-3}\,dx,$$

similarly.

$$\dots\dots\dots\dots$$

$$= \frac{(m-1)(m-2)\dots 2\cdot 1}{n(n+1)\dots(n+m-2)}\int_0^1 x^{m+n-2}\,dx$$

$$= \frac{(m-1)(m-2)\dots 2\cdot 1}{n(n+1)\dots(n+m-1)}.$$

The above integrals are of the utmost importance in the higher branches of mathematics. They are called Eulerian Integrals,

$$\int_0^1 x^{m-1}(1-x)^{n-1}\,dx$$

being the First Eulerian Integral and

$$\int_0^\infty x^n e^{-x}\,dx$$

the Second Eulerian Integral. The proofs above have been based on the assumption that the indices have particular values (e.g. in $\int_0^1 x^{m-1}(1-x)^{n-1}dx$, m is an integer). It can be proved, however, that the properties of the integrals are the same if certain of these restrictions are removed. The First Eulerian Integral $\int_0^1 x^{m-1}(1-x)^{n-1}dx$ is a function of the positive quantities m and n and is written as $\beta(m, n)$; the Second Eulerian Integral is a function of n alone and is written as $\Gamma(n+1)$. These functions are called Beta and Gamma functions respectively.

We have
$$\beta(m, n) = \int_0^1 x^{m-1}(1-x)^{n-1}\,dx$$

$$= \frac{(m-1)(m-2)\dots 2\cdot 1}{n(n+1)\dots(n+m-1)}$$

$$= \frac{(m-1)!\,(n-1)!}{(n+m-1)!},$$

if m and n are positive integers.

Also $\Gamma(n+1) = \int_0^\infty x^n e^{-x} dx = n(n-1) \ldots 3.2.1,$

which is $n!$ when n is a positive integer.

Hence $\beta(m, n) = \Gamma(m)\,\Gamma(n)/\Gamma(m, n) = \beta(n, m).$

6. Areas of curves.

It has been shown that the integral $\int_a^b \phi(x)\,dx$ represents the area of the curve $y = \phi(x)$ between the curve, the x-axis and the two ordinates $x = a$ and $x = b$. Every definite integral denotes an area, and provided that the function in question is integrable we can find areas of those parts of curves cut off by different straight lines and, in many instances, by other curves. In solving problems connected with areas it is always advisable to draw a rough graph of the curve: otherwise the true area required may not be apparent.

Example 8.

Find the area cut off by the curve $y^2 = 4x$, the x-axis and the ordinates $x = 0$ and $x = 4$.

The curve is the parabola LOK in the diagram, and the area required is that bounded by the curve OL and the straight lines OX, LM, i.e. the part OLM.

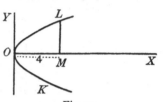

Fig. 33.

$$\text{Area} = \int_0^4 y\,dx$$

$$= \int_0^4 2\sqrt{x}\,dx, \qquad \text{since } y^2 = 4x$$

$$= 2 \int_0^4 x^{\frac{1}{2}}\,dx$$

$$= 2 \left[\frac{x^{\frac{3}{2}}}{\frac{3}{2}} \right]_0^4$$

$$= \tfrac{4}{3}[4^{\frac{3}{2}}] = 10\tfrac{2}{3}.$$

Note. Since the result represents an area, we should write $10\tfrac{2}{3}$ *square units* as our answer. In practice, the words "square units" are omitted, but it should not be forgotten that this qualification always exists. If, for example, squared paper were used and we chose an inch as our unit for x (along OX) and for y (along OY), the area OML would be $10\frac{2}{3}$ square inches.

Similarly, if the integral to be evaluated were

$$\int_0^1 \frac{dx}{\sqrt{1 - x^2}},$$

the area required would be

$$\left[\sin^{-1}x\right]_0^1 \quad \text{or} \quad (\sin^{-1}1 - \sin^{-1}0),$$

the value of which is $\frac{\pi}{2}$. The full result would be "$\frac{\pi}{2}$ square units" or "$\frac{1}{2}(3\cdot14159 \dots)$ square units," so that if our units were inches the area would be $1\cdot571$ square inches, correct to three decimal places.

Example 9.

Find the area of the loop of the curve $y^2 = x^4(x + 2)$.

For real values of the variables x cannot be less than -2. Also when $y = 0$, $x = 0$ or -2. Again for every value of x between 0 and -2

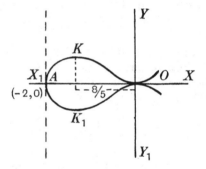

Fig. 34.

there will be two values of y, equal in magnitude and opposite in sign.

Also

$$\frac{dy}{dx} = \frac{d}{dx}(x^2 \sqrt{x + 2})$$

$$= \frac{x^2}{2\sqrt{x + 2}} + 2x \sqrt{x + 2}.$$

If this be equated to zero,

$$x^2 + 4x(x + 2) = 0;$$

i.e.

$$5x^2 + 8x = 0,$$

$$\therefore \quad x = 0 \text{ or } -8/5.$$

Of these $x = -8/5$ gives a maximum value to y, and K will be the highest point of the loop.

If we integrate y between the limits -2 and 0 we shall obtain the area cut off by the curve between the axes and the ordinate $x = -2$, i.e. the area OKA. The area of the whole loop $OKAK_1$ will be twice this area.

Therefore the area of the loop

$$= 2 \int_{-2}^{0} y \, dx = 2 \int_{-2}^{0} x^2 (x + 2)^{\frac{1}{2}} \, dx.$$

To evaluate the integral, let $(x + 2)^{\frac{1}{2}} = z$.

Then when $x = -2$, $z = 0$, and when $x = 0$, $z = \sqrt{2}$.

Also

$$\frac{dx}{2 (x + 2)^{\frac{1}{2}}} = dz.$$

The required area is therefore

$$2 \int_{0}^{\sqrt{2}} (z^2 - 2)^2 z . 2z \, dz$$

$$= 2 \int_{0}^{\sqrt{2}} (z^4 - 4z^2 + 4) 2z^2 \, dz$$

$$= 2 \int_{0}^{\sqrt{2}} (2z^6 - 8z^4 + 8z^2) \, dz$$

$$= 2 \left[\frac{2z^7}{7} - \frac{8z^5}{5} + \frac{8z^3}{3} \right]_{0}^{\sqrt{2}}$$

$$= 2 \left[\frac{2 . 2^{\frac{7}{2}}}{7} - \frac{8 . 2^{\frac{5}{2}}}{5} + \frac{8 . 2^{\frac{3}{2}}}{3} \right],$$

which simplifies to

$$\frac{256 \sqrt{2}}{105}.$$

Note. In the above figure the area AKO corresponds to the positive value of $\sqrt{x + 2}$, and the area $AK_1 O$ to the negative value. The area $= 2 \int_{-2}^{0} x^2 \sqrt{x + 2} \, dx$, where the $\sqrt{x + 2}$ means the positive value of the square root; there is therefore no ambiguity of sign when z is substituted for $\sqrt{x + 2}$.

Example 10.

Find the area between the curve $y^2 (1 - x) = x^3$ and its asymptote.

The straight line $x = 1$ is an asymptote to the curve. x cannot exceed 1 for real values of y, and the curve gradually approaches the straight line $x = 1$, meeting it only at an infinite distance from the origin.

We require therefore

$$2 \int_0^1 y \, dx = 2 \int_0^1 x^{\frac{3}{2}}/(1 - x)^{\frac{1}{2}} \, dx.$$

The substitution is $x = \sin^2 \theta$ and the integral becomes

$$2 \int_0^{\frac{\pi}{2}} 2 \sin^4 \theta \, d\theta.$$

Expressing $\sin^4 \theta$ in terms of multiple angles, we have for the area required

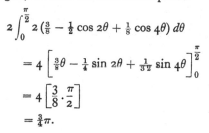

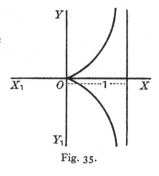

$$2 \int_0^{\frac{\pi}{2}} 2 \left(\tfrac{3}{8} - \tfrac{1}{2} \cos 2\theta + \tfrac{1}{8} \cos 4\theta \right) d\theta$$

$$= 4 \left[\tfrac{3}{8}\theta - \tfrac{1}{4} \sin 2\theta + \tfrac{1}{32} \sin 4\theta \right]_0^{\frac{\pi}{2}}$$

$$= 4 \left[\tfrac{3}{8} \cdot \tfrac{\pi}{2} \right]$$

$$= \tfrac{3}{4}\pi.$$

Fig. 35.

7. Differentiation under the integral sign.

There are various devices for evaluating definite integrals where the function to be integrated is of the form $f(x, k)$, k being independent of x. A method that can often be used to advantage depends upon the process of differentiating under the integral sign.

Let $u = \int_a^b f(x, k) \, dx$ where a and b are constants independent of k. Suppose that k be changed to $k + \Delta k$, so that u becomes $u + \Delta u$, x remaining unaltered.

Then $u + \Delta u = \int_a^b f(x, k + \Delta k) \, dx$

and $\Delta u = \int_a^b f(x, k + \Delta k) \, dx - \int_a^b f(x, k) \, dx$

$$= \int_a^b [f(x, k + \Delta k) - f(x, k)] \, dx,$$

$$\therefore \quad \frac{\Delta u}{\Delta k} = \int_a^b \frac{f(x, k + \Delta k) - f(x, k)}{\Delta k} \, dx.$$

But $\dfrac{f(x, k + \Delta k) - f(x, k)}{\Delta k} = \dfrac{df(x, k)}{dk} + \alpha,$

where α is a small quantity which vanishes in the limit as $\Delta k \to 0$;

$$\therefore \frac{\Delta u}{\Delta k} = \int_a^b \frac{df(x, k)}{dk}\, dx + \int_a^b \alpha\, dx.$$

When $\Delta k \to 0$ the second integral vanishes, for it cannot be numerically greater than $(b - a)\,\alpha_1$ (where α_1 is the greatest value of α), and α_1 ultimately vanishes.

Therefore when $\Delta k \to 0$ we shall have

$$\frac{du}{dk} = \operatorname*{Lt}_{\Delta k \to 0} \frac{\Delta u}{\Delta k} = \int_a^b \frac{df(x, k)}{dk}\, dx.$$

By successive differentiation it follows that

$$\frac{d^n u}{dk^n} = \int_a^b \frac{d^n f(x, k)}{dk^n}\, dx.$$

If a or b be infinite this proof will not hold, for then we cannot say that, when $\Delta k \to 0$, $(b - a)\,\alpha_1$ vanishes. A complete proof involves higher mathematical analysis and it will be sufficient to assume that in the examples dealt with in this chapter we may differentiate under the integral sign, even if one of the limits be infinite.

The following example is a practical application of the method.

Example 11.

We have

$$\int_0^1 x^{n-1}\, dx = \left[\frac{x^n}{n}\right]_0^1 = \frac{1}{n}.$$

Let $x = \dfrac{z}{a + z}$, where a and z are independent; then when $x = 0$, $z = 0$.

We may write the expression for x as

$$\frac{1}{1 + a/z},$$

so that when $x = 1$, $a/z = 0$ and z is infinite.

$$dx = d\left(\frac{z}{a + z}\right) = d\left(1 - \frac{a}{a + z}\right)$$

$$= \frac{a}{(a + z)^2}\, dz.$$

$$\therefore \int_0^1 x^{n-1}\, dx = \int_0^\infty \left(\frac{z}{a + z}\right)^{n-1} \frac{a}{(a + z)^2}\, dz$$

$$= \int_0^\infty \frac{a z^{n-1}}{(a + z)^{n+1}}\, dz.$$

But
$$\int_0^1 x^{n-1}dx = 1/n;$$

$$\therefore \int_0^\infty \frac{z^{n-1}}{(a+z)^{n+1}}\,dz = 1/an.$$

Since a is independent of z, we have

$$\frac{d}{da}\int_0^\infty \frac{z^{n-1}}{(a+z)^{n+1}}\,dz = \int_0^\infty \left[\frac{d}{da}\frac{z^{n-1}}{(a+z)^{n+1}}\right]dz = \int_0^\infty \frac{-(n+1)z^{n-1}}{(a+z)^{n+2}}\,dz.$$

Since
$$\int_0^\infty \frac{z^{n-1}}{(a+z)^{n+1}}\,dz = 1/an,$$

$$\frac{d}{da}\int_0^\infty \frac{z^{n-1}}{(a+z)^{n+1}}\,dz = \frac{d}{da}\left(\frac{1}{an}\right) = \frac{1}{n}\left(\frac{-1}{a^2}\right).$$

Also
$$\frac{d}{da}\int_0^\infty \frac{z^{n-1}}{(a+z)^{n+1}}\,dz = \int_0^\infty \frac{-(n+1)z^{n-1}}{(a+z)^{n+2}}\,dz,$$

$$\therefore \int_0^\infty \frac{-(n+1)z^{n-1}}{(a+z)^{n+2}}\,dz = \frac{1}{n}\left(\frac{-1}{a^2}\right),$$

i.e.
$$\int_0^\infty \frac{z^{n-1}}{(a+z)^{n+2}}\,dz = \frac{1}{n(n+1)}\frac{1}{a^2}.$$

From the known integral $\int_0^\infty \dfrac{z^{n-1}}{(a+z)^{n+1}}\,dz$ we have therefore obtained the integral $\int_0^\infty \dfrac{z^{n-1}}{(a+z)^{n+2}}\,dz.$

This process may be repeated, and we shall have

$$\int_0^\infty \frac{z^{n-1}}{(a+z)^{n+3}}\,dz = \frac{1.2}{n(n+1)(n+2)}\frac{1}{a^3},$$

$$\int_0^\infty \frac{z^{n-1}}{(a+z)^{n+4}}\,dz = \frac{1.2.3}{n(n+1)(n+2)(n+3)}\frac{1}{a^4},$$

so that generally

$$\int_0^\infty \frac{z^{n-1}}{(a+z)^{n+r}}\,dz = \frac{1.2.3\ldots(r-1)}{n(n+1)(n+2)\ldots(n+r-1)}\frac{1}{a^r}$$

$$= \frac{(r-1)!\,(n-1)!}{(n+r-1)!}\frac{1}{a^r},$$

if r and n are positive integers.

8. Double integrals.

The formula for integration by parts is

$$\int uv\,dx = u \int v\,dx - \int \left(u' \int v\,dx\right) dx.$$

If x be the function u the second term on the right-hand side is

$$\int \left(x' \int v\,dx\right) dx, \quad \text{i.e.} \quad \int \left(\int v\,dx\right) dx.$$

Omitting the brackets the term is $\iint v\,dx\,dx$. This is a form of double integral, and its meaning is simply that we must integrate v with respect to x, and then integrate the result also with respect to x.

Thus, since $\int xe^x\,dx = xe^x - e^x,$

$$\iint xe^x\,dx\,dx = \int (xe^x - e^x)\,dx = (xe^x - e^x) - e^x = xe^x - 2e^x.$$

A more general form of double integral is the form in which there are two independent variables. If v be a function of x and y, $\iint v\,dx\,dy$ denotes the process of integrating v with respect to x and then integrating the new function with respect to y.

In performing the integration with respect to x, y must be assumed constant, and similarly when integrating the result with respect to y, x must be assumed constant.

Example 12.

Evaluate $\iint (4x + 3y^2)\,dx\,dy.$

Since this is an abbreviated form of $\int \left[\int (4x + 3y^2)\,dx\right] dy$, we must first find $\int (4x + 3y^2)\,dx$, where y is assumed to be independent of x.

$$\int (4x + 3y^2)\,dx = 4\frac{x^2}{2} + 3xy^2 + a.$$

Again, $\int (2x^2 + 3xy^2 + a)\,dy = 2x^2y + xy^3 + ay + b;$

$$\therefore \iint (4x + 3y^2)\, dx\, dy = 2x^2 y + xy^3 + ay + b,$$

where a and b are arbitrary constants.

If we had been required to integrate $\iint (4x + 3y^2)\, dy\, dx$, we should have obtained, firstly,

$$\int (4x + 3y^2)\, dy = 4xy + y^3 + c,$$

and then

$$\int (4xy + y^3 + c)\, dx = 2x^2 y + xy^3 + cx + d,$$

where c and d are constants not necessarily the same as a and b above.

9. Suppose that, in the above example, we had had to evaluate the integral between limits, so that the problem read thus:

Find the value of $\displaystyle\int_1^2 \int_3^4 (4x + 3y^2)\, dx\, dy$.

Firstly,

$$\int_3^4 (4x + 3y^2)\, dx = \left[2x^2 + 3xy^2 \right]_3^4$$
$$= 2 \cdot 4^2 + 3 \cdot 4y^2 - 2 \cdot 3^2 - 3 \cdot 3y^2$$
$$= 14 + 3y^2.$$

Secondly,

$$\int_1^2 (14 + 3y^2)\, dy = \left[14y + y^3 \right]_1^2$$
$$= 14 \cdot 2 + 2^3 - 14 \cdot 1 - 1^3$$
$$= 21.$$

Now if the order of integration had been reversed, we should have had to evaluate $\displaystyle\int_3^4 \int_1^2 (4x + 3y^2)\, dy\, dx$.

In the usual manner,

$$\int_1^2 (4x + 3y^2)\, dy = \left[4xy + y^3 \right]_1^2$$
$$= 4 \cdot 2x + 2^3 - 4 \cdot 1x - 1^3$$
$$= 4x + 7.$$

$$\int_3^4 (4x + 7)\, dx = \left[2x^2 + 7x \right]_3^4$$
$$= 2 \cdot 4^2 + 7 \cdot 4 - 2 \cdot 3^2 - 7 \cdot 3$$
$$= 21, \text{ as before.}$$

This leads to the general proposition:
If x and y be independent, then

$$\int_a^\beta \int_a^b f(x, y)\, dx\, dy = \int_a^b \int_a^\beta f(x, y)\, dy\, dx,$$

provided that the limits of x and y are independent of each other, and that neither $f(x, y)$ nor its integrals become infinite for any values of x and y between the limits of integration.

The proof of this theorem is difficult, the most satisfactory demonstration depending on a double summation. It will be therefore taken for granted that the proposition holds within the limitations imposed. For a rigid proof of the proposition the student should consult any recognized textbook on more advanced Integral Calculus.

10. It should be noted that where one or more of the limits of a double integral is a function of either variable, we may not take the order of integration indifferently. A common form of double integral that occurs in mean value and probability problems is one in which one of the limits for integration involves one of the variables. The integral is of the type

$$\int_0^a \int_0^{a-x} f(x, y)\, dy\, dx,$$

where the result of integrating $f(x, y)$ with respect to y and inserting the limits produces a function of x. In these problems it is necessary to adhere strictly to the order of the integration.

Example 13.
Show that

$$\int_0^a \int_0^{a-x} (x^2 + y^2)\, dy\, dx \neq \int_0^{a-x} \int_0^a (x^2 + y^2)\, dx\, dy.$$

$$\int_0^a \int_0^{a-x} (x^2 + y^2)\, dy\, dx = \int_0^a \left[x^2 y + \tfrac{1}{3} y^3 \right]_0^{a-x} dx$$

$$= \int_0^a \left[x^2 (a - x) + \tfrac{1}{3} (a - x)^3 \right] dx$$

$$= \int_0^a \left(ax^2 - x^3 + \tfrac{1}{3} a^3 - a^2 x + ax^2 - \tfrac{1}{3} x^3 \right) dx$$

$$= \frac{1}{3} \int_0^a \left(a^3 - 3a^2 x + 6ax^2 - 4x^3 \right) dx$$

$$= \frac{1}{3} \left[a^3 x - \frac{3a^2 x^2}{2} + \frac{6ax^3}{3} - \frac{4x^4}{4} \right]_0^a$$

$$= \frac{1}{3} \left[a^4 - \frac{3a^4}{2} + \frac{6a^4}{3} - \frac{4a^4}{4} \right]$$

$$= \frac{a^4}{6}.$$

$$\int_0^{a-x} \int_0^a (x^2 + y^2) \, dx \, dy = \int_0^{a-x} \left[\tfrac{1}{3}x^3 + xy^2 \right]_0^a dy$$

$$= \int_0^{a-x} (\tfrac{1}{3}a^3 + ay^2) \, dy$$

$$= \left[\frac{a^3 y}{3} + \frac{ay^3}{3} \right]_0^{a-x}$$

$$= \frac{a}{3} [a^2 (a - x) + (a - x)^3],$$

which is a function of x and is obviously not equal to the constant quantity $\dfrac{a^4}{6}$.

EXAMPLES 16

1. Prove that

$$\int_a^b \phi(x) \, dx = h\phi \{a + \theta h\},$$

where $h = b - a$ and $0 < \theta < 1$.

Evaluate the following definite integrals:

2. $\displaystyle\int_0^n x^n \, dx$; $\displaystyle\int_1^5 (ax + bx^2) \, dx$.

3. $\displaystyle\int_0^k e^{-a^2 x} \, dx$; $\displaystyle\int_{-5}^5 \sqrt{x^{m+n}} \, dx$.

4. $\displaystyle\int_0^{\frac{\pi}{4}} \sin x \, dx$; $\displaystyle\int_0^1 \tan^{-1} x \, dx$.

5. $\displaystyle\int_{3\frac{1}{2}}^4 \frac{dx}{1 + 3x + 2x^2}$; $\displaystyle\int_0^1 \frac{1 - x + 2x^2}{1 + x + x^2} \, dx$.

6. $\displaystyle\int_1^2 \frac{dx}{x^3 (3 - x)}$; $\displaystyle\int_0^\pi \frac{dx}{2 - \cos x}$.

7. $\displaystyle\int_0^a \frac{dx}{\sqrt{x+a}+\sqrt{x}};\ \int_0^{\frac{\pi}{4}} \sin\theta \sec^2\theta\, d\theta.$

8. $\displaystyle\int_0^{\frac{\pi}{2}} \cos^4 x\, dx;\ \int_0^{\pi} \frac{dx}{17+8\cos x}.$

9. $\displaystyle\int_0^1 \frac{x^3}{(2x+1)^5}\, dx;\ \int_0^1 x^3 (1-x)^{\frac{5}{2}}\, dx.$

10. $\displaystyle\int_a^b x\log x\, dx;\ \int_{-\frac{\pi}{2}}^{\frac{\pi}{2}} e^x \cos x\, dx.$

11. $\displaystyle\int_0^{\frac{\pi}{2}} x^2 \sin x\, dx;\ \int_0^1 e^{-\frac{1}{2}x} x^2\, dx.$

12. Prove that
$$\int_0^{\frac{1}{2}} \frac{dx}{(1-2x^2)\sqrt{1-x^2}} = \tfrac{1}{2}\log(2+\sqrt{3}).$$

13. Use the substitution $x=\sec\theta$ to evaluate $\displaystyle\int_2^4 \frac{dx}{x(x^2-1)}.$

14. Prove that
$$\int_1^e x(\log x)^3\, dx = \frac{e^2+3}{8}.$$

15. If $b > (a+1)$, find the value of
$$\int_{a+1}^b (x-b)\log(x-a)\, dx.$$

16. Evaluate $\displaystyle\int_0^{\infty} \frac{dx}{(1+x^2)^3}.$

17. Prove that if a and b are positive and b is less than a
$$\int_0^{\pi} \frac{dx}{a+b\cos x} = \frac{\pi}{\sqrt{a^2-b^2}}.$$

18. Find $\displaystyle\int_0^{\frac{\pi}{4}} \tan^5 x\, dx.$

19. Integrate $\dfrac{e^x(1+x\log x)}{x}$ between the limits $x=1$ and $x=2$.

20. Prove that
$$\int_a^h u_t\left(\int_t^h v_t\, dt\right) dt = \int_a^h v_t\left(\int_a^t u_t\, dt\right) dt.$$

21. In the curve $y = x^2$ the abscissa from o to 2 is divided into n equal parts each of length $2/n$. Show that the area of the set of inner rectangles is

$$\frac{8}{3}\left[1 - \frac{3}{2n} + \frac{1}{2n^2}\right]$$

and that the area of the set of outer rectangles is

$$\frac{8}{3}\left[1 + \frac{3}{2n} + \frac{1}{2n^2}\right].$$

Putting $n = 10$, 100, 1000, 10,000, ... etc. obtain two series between which there is only one number and deduce that this number must be the area contained between the curve, the axis of x and the ordinate corresponding to the abscissa $x = 2$.

22. Prove directly from the definition of a definite integral as the limit of the sum of a series that

$$\int_0^a \sin nx \, dx = \frac{1}{n} - \frac{\cos na}{n}.$$

23. By evaluating $\int_0^1 (1 - x^2)^n \, dx$ in two different ways (n being a positive integer), prove that

$$1 - \frac{n}{3 \cdot 1!} + \frac{n(n-1)}{5 \cdot 2!} - \frac{n(n-1)(n-2)}{7 \cdot 3!} + \ldots = \frac{2^n \, n!}{3 \cdot 5 \cdot 7 \ldots (2n+1)}.$$

24. Evaluate $\int_1^2 \frac{(2 - 3x)}{x^3(2 + x)} \, dx$.

25. Prove that $\int_1^5 \frac{(x + 1) \, dx}{(x^2 - 6x + 13)^2} = \frac{1}{8}(\pi + 2)$.

26. Find $\int_0^1 \frac{x^2 + \frac{3}{4}}{2x^2 + x + \frac{5}{4}} \, dx$.

27. Prove that $\int_0^{\frac{\pi}{2}} \cos^3 x \sin 5x = \frac{1}{4}$.

28. Find the area enclosed between the curve $y^2 = 4ax$, the x-axis and the straight line $x = 9a$.

29. Find the area between the curve $y^2 = 4ax$, the x-axis and the ordinates $2ab$ and $2ac$.

30. Plot the curve $y^2 = x(x - 1)^2$ between $x = 0$ and $x = 3$ and find the area of the loop.

31. Find the area between the curve $y^2 = 4ax$ and the straight line $y = x$.

32. Draw a rough sketch of the curve $y^2 = x^4 (1 + x)$ between $x = 0$ and $x = -1$ and find the area of the loop.

33. Find the area between the axes of co-ordinates, the ordinate $y = 9$ and the curve $y = \frac{1}{2} (e^x + e^{-x})$.

34. Find the area of the loop of the curve $y^2 = x^3 + 3x^2$.

35. The equation of a curve is given by $y = \log x + \frac{1}{x}$. Find the area bounded by the axis of y, the curve, and the two abscissae whose lengths are 2 and 3.

36. Find the areas cut off between the axis of the co-ordinates, the ordinate $x = 3a$ and (1) the parabola $y^2 = ax$, (2) the circle $x^2 + y^2 = 4ax$. Hence find the area common to the two curves.

37. Trace the curve $xy^2 = 4 (2 - x)$ and find the area which lies between it and the y-axis.

38. Prove that the area of the loop of the curve $y^2 (a + x) = x^2 (a - x)$ is $2a^2 \left(1 - \frac{\pi}{4}\right)$.

39. Find the area included between the curves $y^2 - 4ax = 0$ and $x^2 - 4ay = 0$.

40. Find separately the two finite areas each bounded by the three curves: (a) $xy = 1$, (b) $y^2 = x$, (c) $x = 2$.

41. Given that

$$\int \frac{dx}{\sqrt{x^2 + a^2}} = \log (x + \sqrt{x^2 + a^2}),$$

deduce
$$\int (x^2 + a^2)^{-\frac{3}{2}} dx$$

by differentiation under the sign of integration.

42. Prove that
$$\frac{d}{dc} \left(\int_a^b f(x, c) \, dx \right) = \int_a^b \frac{df(x, c)}{dc} \, dx,$$

where the limits are independent of c.

Given
$$\int_0^\pi \frac{x \, dx}{1 + \cos a \sin x} = \frac{\pi a}{\sin a},$$

deduce the value of
$$\int_0^\pi \frac{x \, dx}{(1 + \cos a \sin x)^2}.$$

43. Prove that

$$\int_0^1 \frac{dx}{1 + 2x \cos \theta + x^2} = \frac{\theta}{2 \sin \theta},$$

where θ is independent of x.

44. Definite integrals may sometimes be obtained by differentiating under the sign of integration. Illustrate the process by finding the values of the definite integrals

$$\int_0^\infty x^n e^{-ax}\, dx; \quad \int_0^\infty \frac{\log(1 + a^2 x^2)}{1 + x^2}\, dx.$$

45. Given that the length of the arc of the curve $y = \phi(x)$ between the points whose abscissae are a and b is

$$\int_a^b \sqrt{1 + \left(\frac{dy}{dx}\right)^2}\, dx,$$

find the equation of the curve the arc of which beginning from $x = 0$ is always $\sqrt{2ax}$.

46. Show that a form of Maclaurin's series expressing $f(x)$ in terms of $f(0), f'(0), f''(0), \ldots$ can be obtained by repeatedly integrating by parts the integral

$$\frac{x^n}{(n-1)!} \int_0^1 (1 - t)^{n-1} f^{(n)}(xt)\, dt.$$

47. Evaluate $\quad \int_0^1 (x^4 + x^2 + 1)(x^2 + 1)^{-\frac{1}{2}}\, dx.$

48. Prove that, if $m > n$,

$$\int_0^1 \int_x^{\frac{1}{x}} x^{m-1} y^{n-1}\, dy\, dx = \frac{2}{m^2 - n^2}.$$

49. If x and y are independent variables, find $\int_0^x \sqrt{x^2 + y^2}\, dy$, and integrate the result with respect to x between the limits $x = 0$ and $x = 1$.

50. Evaluate $\quad \dfrac{\displaystyle\int_0^a \int_0^{a-x} \frac{1}{2}a(x + y)\, dy\, dx}{\displaystyle\int_0^a \int_0^{a-x} dy\, dx}.$

CHAPTER XVII

APPROXIMATE INTEGRATION

1. In order to obtain the area of a curve by the methods of the integral calculus as given in the preceding chapters two conditions must necessarily hold. These conditions are

  (i) the equation of the curve must be known; and in that event

  (ii) the function $y = u_x$ representing the equation of the curve must be integrable.

In the theory of life contingencies these conditions are rarely satisfied. Rates of mortality, marriage, etc. are generally obtained from actual observations and the functions derived from these rates are seldom capable of expression in the form of a mathematical expansion. For example, if l_x be the number of persons attaining exact age x in any year of time, the number living between ages x and $x + 1$ is given by

$$L_x = \int_0^1 l_{x+t} \, dt,$$

where x and t are independent.

Unless l_{x+t} follows some definite mathematical law, we cannot evaluate the integral by the methods hitherto employed. By making certain assumptions, however, we can obtain approximations to the value of the integral which are accurate enough for practical purposes.

Thus, if we expand l_{x+t} in terms of l_x and differences of l_x, we have

$$l_{x+t} = (1 + \Delta)^t l_x$$

$$= l_x + t \Delta l_x \qquad \text{to first differences.}$$

But $$\Delta l_x = l_{x+1} - l_x,$$

and $l_x - l_{x+1}$ is d_x, the number out of the l_x persons who die before reaching age $x + 1$.

$$\therefore \; L_x = \int_0^1 l_{x+t}\, dt$$

$$= \int_0^1 (l_x - t d_x)\, dt \quad \text{as far as first differences}$$

$$= \left[t l_x - \tfrac{1}{2} t^2 d_x \right]_0^1$$

$$= l_x - \tfrac{1}{2} d_x$$

$$= l_x - \tfrac{1}{2}\, (l_x - l_{x+1})$$

$$= \tfrac{1}{2}\, (l_x + l_{x+1}).$$

This is an approximate value of L_x on the assumption that l_{x+t} is a first difference function of l_x.

It is evident that a simple approximation to first differences will not be justifiable except in a limited number of instances: the construction of formulae for approximate integration will necessarily depend on the data available and on the degree of accuracy required.

2. Simpson's rule.

Suppose that we are given two values only of u_x and that we represent these two values by means of the points H and K whose co-ordinates are (a, u_a) and (b, u_b) respectively. Suppose also that we have sufficient information to justify our representing the function $y = u_x$ by a curve of small slope and small changes of slope, not affected by periodic changes.
An infinite number of such mathematical curves can be drawn to pass through H and K. The simplest curve passing through the points is a straight line, and for the purpose of interpolation there is usually no justification for adopting any formula other than a first difference formula, as was done for example in obtaining the approximation to L_x in the preceding paragraph. If

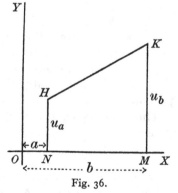

Fig. 36.

the straight line be drawn, the area cut off by the curve, the x-axis and the ordinates $x = a$ and $x = b$ will be that of the trapezium $HNMK$. The area of the trapezium is $\tfrac{1}{2}\, (u_a + u_b)\, (b - a)$.

Alternatively, this area is $\int_a^b u_x dx$.

An approximation to the integral is therefore $\frac{1}{2}(u_a + u_b)(b - a)$.

If $y = u_x = l_{x+t}$ and the limits b and a are 1 and 0 respectively, we have the approximation to $\int_0^1 l_{x+t}\, dt$ given above, namely

$$\frac{1}{2}(l_x + l_{x+1}).$$

Let us consider the effect on the approximation of introducing a third known value of u_x. In other words, suppose our data to be u_a, u_b, u_c. Then there is still an unlimited number of curves which can be drawn to pass through the three points H, K, L. The simplest of these curves will now no longer be a straight line, but will be a second difference curve. The form of this curve will be $y = A + Bx + Cx^2$, and since three points on the curve are given we are in possession of sufficient data to determine the coefficients A, B, C.

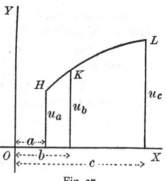

Fig. 37.

In practice the data will generally be available at equidistant intervals, and since we may choose our origin where we please, the problem is therefore reduced to one of finding the second difference curve which passes through the points $(0, u_0)$, $(1, u_1)$, $(2, u_2)$.

Having found the equation of the curve we can then find the area enclosed by the curve, the extreme ordinates and the x-axis, by integrating the function thus obtained between the limits 0 and 2.

Assume therefore that $y = u_x = a + bx + cx^2$ is the required equation.

Then, by substitution,

$$u_0 = a,$$
$$u_1 = a + b + c,$$
$$u_2 = a + 2b + 4c,$$

whence
$$a = u_0,$$
$$b = \tfrac{1}{2}(-u_2 + 4u_1 - 3u_0),$$
$$c = \tfrac{1}{2}(u_2 - 2u_1 + u_0).$$

Also
$$\int_0^2 u_x \, dx = \int_0^2 (a + bx + cx^2)\, dx$$
$$= \left[ax + \tfrac{1}{2}bx^2 + \tfrac{1}{3}cx^3 \right]_0^2$$
$$= 2a + 2b + \tfrac{8}{3}c$$
$$= \tfrac{1}{3}(u_0 + 4u_1 + u_2),$$

on substituting for a, b and c.

This is *Simpson's rule* for approximate integration.
We can obtain this formula by alternative methods.
For example, let
$$u_x = (1 + \Delta)^x u_0 = u_0 + x\Delta u_0 + \tfrac{1}{2}x(x-1)\Delta^2 u_0$$

as far as second differences.

Then
$$\int_0^2 u_x \, dx = \int_0^2 \{u_0 + x\Delta u_0 + \tfrac{1}{2}x(x-1)\Delta^2 u_0\}\, dx$$
$$= \int_0^2 \{u_0 + x(\Delta u_0 - \tfrac{1}{2}\Delta^2 u_0) + x^2 \tfrac{1}{2}\Delta^2 u_0\}\, dx$$
$$= \left[xu_0 + \tfrac{1}{2}x^2(\Delta u_0 - \tfrac{1}{2}\Delta^2 u_0) + \tfrac{1}{6}x^3\Delta^2 u_0 \right]_0^2$$
$$= 2u_0 + 2(\Delta u_0 - \tfrac{1}{2}\Delta^2 u_0) + \tfrac{4}{3}\Delta^2 u_0$$
$$= 2u_0 + 2\Delta u_0 + \tfrac{1}{3}\Delta^2 u_0,$$

and since
$$u_0 = u_0,$$
$$u_1 = u_0 + \Delta u_0,$$
$$u_2 = u_0 + 2\Delta u_0 + \Delta^2 u_0,$$

this reduces to $\tfrac{1}{3}(u_0 + 4u_1 + u_2)$ as before.

A third method is to assume that the integral can be expressed in the form
$$mu_0 + nu_1 + pu_2.$$

Then if $y = a + bx + cx^2$ we have eventually that
$$\int_0^2 u_x \, dx = 2a + 2b + \tfrac{8}{3}c,$$

as in the first method.

Substituting in the assumed expression for the integral:

$$ma + n(a + b + c) + p(a + 2b + 4c) = 2a + 2b + \tfrac{8}{3}c.$$

Whence, by equating coefficients of a, b, c and solving the resulting equations,

$$m = \tfrac{1}{3}; \quad n = \tfrac{4}{3}; \quad p = \tfrac{1}{3}.$$

3. Change of unit.

The formula $\int_0^2 u_x dx = \tfrac{1}{3}(u_0 + 4u_1 + u_2)$ is an approximate formula obtained by considering unit intervals. If we wish to transform the formula to a form in which the interval is changed to, say, n, then the given values of u_x will be u_0; u_n; u_{2n}. Our new variable is z, where $z = nx$.

$$\therefore \quad dz = n\,dx.$$

The new limits are evidently o and $2n$.

The formula is

$$\int_0^{2n} \frac{\mathrm{I}}{n} u_z dz = \tfrac{1}{3}(u_0 + 4u_n + u_{2n}),$$

i.e.

$$\int_0^{2n} u_z dz = \tfrac{1}{3}n(u_0 + 4u_n + u_{2n}),$$

or, on changing the variable to x,

$$\int_0^{2n} u_x dx = \tfrac{1}{3}n(u_0 + 4u_n + u_{2n}).$$

This principle is of universal application and any formula of approximate integration can immediately be transferred from unit intervals to $n$thly intervals and vice versa.

For example, the formula

$$\int_0^{10} u_x dx = 2\tfrac{1}{2}(u_1 + u_4 + u_6 + u_9)$$

becomes

$$\int_0^{20} u_x dx = 5(u_2 + u_8 + u_{12} + u_{18})$$

on doubling the interval;

and

$$\int_0^{10n} u_x dx = 2\tfrac{1}{2}n(u_n + u_{4n} + u_{6n} + u_{9n})$$

when the interval is n.

F

4. Change of origin.

Consider again Simpson's rule:

$$\int_0^2 u_x dx = \tfrac{1}{3}(u_0 + 4u_1 + u_2).$$

We have obtained a formula which gives in terms of u_0, u_1 and u_2 the area of the curve cut off by the ordinates $x = 0$ and $x = 2$. If we change the origin so that the point $(1, u_1)$ becomes the point $(0, v_0)$, as in Fig. 38, we shall have a formula of integration between the limits -1 and 1 in terms of v_{-1}, v_0 and v_1. The formula will be otherwise unaltered and we shall have found an approximation to the same area with reference to a new y-axis $O_1 Y_1$.

In its new form the formula becomes

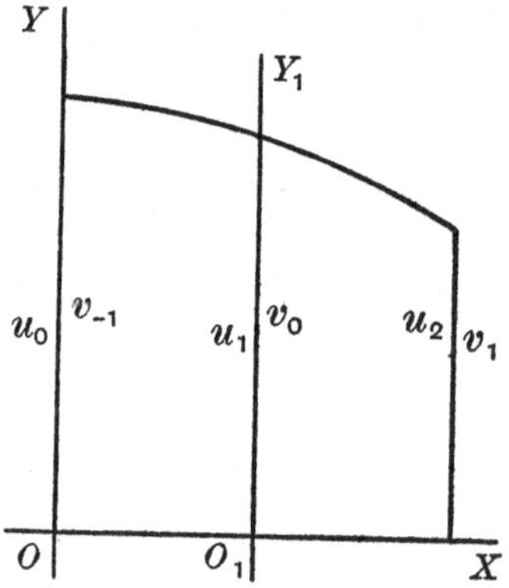

Fig. 38.

$$\int_{-1}^1 v_x dx = \tfrac{1}{3}(v_{-1} + 4v_0 + v_1),$$

or, changing back to u's,

$$\int_{-1}^1 u_x dx = \tfrac{1}{3}(u_{-1} + 4u_0 + u_1).$$

Now when it is desired to obtain an approximate integration formula it is evident that integration between -1 and 1 (or between $-n$ and n) involves much less labour than integration between 0 and 2 (or between 0 and $2n$). Thus, if

$$u_x = a + bx + cx^2,$$

then

$$u_0 = a,$$

$$u_{-1} = a - b + c,$$

$$u_1 = a + b + c,$$

and

$$\tfrac{1}{3}(u_{-1} + 4u_0 + u_1) = \tfrac{1}{3}\{4u_0 + (u_{-1} + u_1)\}$$
$$= \tfrac{1}{3}(4a + 2a + 2c)$$
$$= \tfrac{1}{3}(6a + 2c).$$

Also $\displaystyle\int_{-1}^{1} (a + bx + cx^2)\, dx = \left[ax + \tfrac{1}{2}bx^2 + \tfrac{1}{3}cx^3 \right]_{-1}^{1}$

$$= 2a + \tfrac{2}{3}c,$$

which proves the approximation.

Again, since in this form the coefficients of odd powers of x disappear in the definite integral and also in the paired terms u_t and u_{-t}, we could equally well employ as our assumed expansion for u_x the third difference function $a + bx + cx^2 + dx^3$.

We should have

$$4u_0 + (u_{-1} + u_1) = 4a + a - b + c - d + a + b + c + d = 6a + 2c$$

as before, and

$$ax + \tfrac{1}{2}bx^2 + \tfrac{1}{3}cx^3 + \tfrac{1}{4}dx^4 = 2a + \tfrac{2}{3}c.$$

This leads to the important fact that Simpson's rule is true to one more order of differences than was originally assumed, i.e. it is true to third differences.

For the above reasons, namely

(i) for simplicity in working;

(ii) to enable us to find the true order of differences to which the approximation is correct;

it is advisable to integrate between $-n$ and n in preference to any other limits.

This can always be done by a suitable change of limits; for example, integration between $\tfrac{1}{2}$ and 1 can be simplified to integration between say 2 and 4 by increasing the interval from $\tfrac{1}{2}$ to 2. Then, by changing the origin, a formula can be obtained for integration between -1 and 1. To express the formula in the required form the process can then be reversed.

Example 1.

Show that $\displaystyle\int_{1\cdot5}^{2\cdot5} v_x\, dx = \frac{1}{24}\,(v_1 + 22v_2 + v_3)$ approximately.

$$\int_{1\cdot5}^{2\cdot5} v_x\, dx = \frac{1}{2}\int_{3}^{5} u_x\, dx \text{ (if we double the interval).}$$

This will produce a formula in u_2; u_4; u_6.

In the first place we will obtain a formula for $\displaystyle\int_{-1}^{1} u_x\, dx$.

This formula will have to be of the form $mu_{-2} + nu_0 + pu_2$, since we have moved our origin to the point where x was originally 4.

Let $\qquad\qquad u_x = a + bx + cx^2 + dx^3.$

Then $\qquad\qquad u_0 = a,$

$$u_{-2} = a - 2b + 4c - 8d,$$

and $\qquad\qquad u_2 = a + 2b + 4c + 8d,$

so that

$$\tfrac{1}{24}(u_{-2} + 22u_0 + u_2) = \tfrac{1}{24}(22a + 2a + 8c) = a + \tfrac{1}{3}c.$$

$$\int_{-1}^{1} u_x\, dx = \left[ax + \tfrac{1}{2}bx^2 + \tfrac{1}{3}cx^3 + \tfrac{1}{4}dx^4 \right]_{-1}^{1} = 2a + \tfrac{2}{3}c.$$

$$\therefore\ \frac{1}{24}(u_{-2} + 22u_0 + u_2) = \frac{1}{2}\int_{-1}^{1} u_x\, dx.$$

Changing the origin back again to the original origin:

$$\frac{1}{24}(u_2 + 22u_4 + u_6) = \frac{1}{2}\int_{3}^{5} u_x\, dx.$$

$$\therefore\ \frac{1}{24}(v_1 + 22v_2 + v_3) = \int_{1\cdot5}^{2\cdot5} v_x\, dx.$$

Moreover, although only three values of v_x have been given (so that only second differences are known), the formula is true to at least third differences.

5. Some well-known approximate integration formulae.

(1) *Extension of Simpson's rule.*

We have $\qquad \int_{0}^{2} u_x\, dx = \tfrac{1}{3}(u_0 + 4u_1 + u_2).$

Therefore by changing the origin

$$\int_{2}^{4} u_x\, dx = \tfrac{1}{3}(u_2 + 4u_3 + u_4).$$

Similarly $\qquad \int_{4}^{6} u_x\, dx = \tfrac{1}{3}(u_4 + 4u_5 + u_6).$

$$\dotfill$$

In general, by addition,

$$\int_{0}^{2n} u_x\, dx = \tfrac{1}{3}(u_0 + 4u_1 + 2u_2 + 4u_3 + 2u_4 + \ldots + u_{2n}).$$

This is a formula for approximate integration used extensively in practical mathematics. In engineering problems, where the curve to be integrated has actually been sketched as the result of experiments, a small unit may be chosen and a large number of ordinates drawn. In that event the extended formula can be applied. This will in general give better results than the single formula

$$\int_0^{2n} u_x dx = \frac{n}{3} (u_0 + 4u_n + u_{2n}).$$

It should be noted that Simpson's rule, applied many times (as above), does not assume that a smooth curve can be drawn between all the points $u_0, u_1, \ldots u_{2n}$. The method of obtaining the formula has in fact been to draw a number of disjointed curves between u_0, u_1, u_2; u_2, u_3, u_4; $\ldots u_{2n-2}, u_{2n-1}, u_{2n}$, and the curve passing through three points such as u_0, u_1, u_2 will not as a rule pass through the next series u_3 and u_4.

(2) *The "three-eighths" rule.*

The following symmetrical formula can be derived by working on the above lines, when four consecutive points are given.

If the four points were u_0, u_1, u_2, u_3 we should obviously integrate between 0 and 3. Change the unit and origin so that we pass firstly to the limits 0 and 6 and secondly to the limits -3 and 3.

We require $\int_{-3}^3 u_x dx$, given u_{-3}, u_{-1}, u_1, u_3.

Let $$u_x = a + bx + cx^2 + dx^3,$$

so that $$u_{-1} + u_1 = 2 (a + c)$$

and $$u_{-3} + u_3 = 2 (a + 9c).$$

If $$\int_{-3}^3 u_x dx = m (u_{-1} + u_1) + n (u_{-3} + u_3),$$

we have

$$\left[ax + \tfrac{1}{2}bx^2 + \tfrac{1}{3}cx^3 + \tfrac{1}{4}dx^4 \right]_{-3}^3 = m (u_{-1} + u_1) + n (u_{-3} + u_3);$$

i.e. $$6a + 18c = m (u_{-1} + u_1) + n (u_{-3} + u_3)$$
$$= m (2a + 2c) + n (2a + 18c)$$
$$= a (2m + 2n) + c (2m + 18n),$$

from which, easily, $m = 18/8$ and $n = 6/8$.

$$\therefore \int_{-3}^{3} u_x\, dx = \tfrac{3}{8} \{6\,(u_{-1} + u_1) + 2\,(u_{-3} + u_3)\},$$

i.e. $$\int_{0}^{6} u_x\, dx = \tfrac{3}{8} \{6\,(u_2 + u_4) + 2\,(u_0 + u_6)\},$$

or $$\int_{0}^{3} u_x\, dx = \tfrac{3}{8} \{3\,(u_1 + u_2) + (u_0 + u_3)\}$$
$$= \tfrac{3}{8} (u_0 + 3u_1 + 3u_2 + u_3).$$

(3) *Weddle's rule.*

Suppose that seven equidistant ordinates are given. In order to reduce the algebra to a minimum, we integrate between limits − 3 and + 3, and write the assumed formula for u_x thus:

$$u_x = a + bx + \frac{cx^2}{2} + \frac{dx\,(x^2 - 1)}{6} + \frac{ex^2\,(x^2 - 1)}{24} + \frac{fx\,(x^2 - 1)\,(x^2 - 4)}{120}$$
$$+ \frac{gx^2\,(x^2 - 1)\,(x^2 - 4)}{720}.$$

This is Stirling's formula with the constants $a, b, c, \ldots g$ replacing the differences of u_x.

Then

$$\int_{-3}^{3} u_x\, dx = \left[ax + \frac{bx^2}{2} + \frac{cx^3}{6} + \frac{d}{6}\left(\frac{x^4}{4} - \frac{x^2}{2}\right) + \frac{e}{24}\left(\frac{x^5}{5} - \frac{x^3}{3}\right) \right.$$
$$\left. + \frac{f}{120}\left(\frac{x^6}{6} - \frac{5x^4}{4} + \frac{4x^2}{2}\right) + \frac{g}{720}\left(\frac{x^7}{7} - \frac{5x^5}{5} + \frac{4x^3}{3}\right) \right]_{-3}^{3}$$

$$= 6a + 54\left(\frac{c}{6} - \frac{e}{72} + \frac{g}{540}\right) + 486\left(\frac{e}{120} - \frac{g}{720}\right) + \frac{243}{280}g$$

$$= 6a + 9c + \tfrac{33}{10}e + \tfrac{41}{140}g.$$

Replacing a, c, e, g by the differences of u_x in Stirling's formula, we have

$$\int_{-3}^{3} u_x\, dx = 6a + 9c + \tfrac{33}{10}e + \tfrac{41}{140}g$$
$$= 6u_0 + 9\Delta^2 u_{-1} + \tfrac{33}{10}\Delta^4 u_{-2} + \tfrac{41}{140}\Delta^6 u_{-3}.$$

If now $\Delta^2 u_{-1}$, $\Delta^4 u_{-2}$ and $\Delta^6 u_{-3}$ are expressed in terms of $u_{-3}, u_{-2}, \ldots u_2, u_3$, we shall obtain a formula correct to seventh differences. It will be found, however, that the coefficients of the terms are large. This is due to the awkward fraction $\tfrac{41}{140}$ multiplying $\Delta^6 u_{-3}$. As sixth differences are usually small, the error involved in replacing $\frac{41}{140}\Delta^6 u_{-3}$ by $\frac{42}{140}\Delta^6 u_{-3}$, i.e. by $\frac{3}{10}\Delta^6 u_{-3}$, will, in general, be negligible. By this substitution the coefficients in the final formula will be much simplified. The modified formula will involve an error of $\frac{1}{140}\Delta^6 u_{-3}$ and will therefore be correct to fifth differences only.

The terms in the expression thus adjusted, namely,

$$6u_0 + 9\Delta^2 u_{-1} + \tfrac{33}{10}\Delta^4 u_{-2} + \tfrac{3}{10}\Delta^6 u_{-3},$$

may be collected as shown in the following table:

	u_{-3}	u_{-2}	u_{-1}	u_0	u_1	u_2	u_3
$6u_0$				6·0			
$9\Delta^2 u_{-1}$			9·0	−18·0	9·0		
$3·3\Delta^4 u_{-2}$		3·3	−13·2	19·8	−13·2	3·3	
$·3\Delta^6 u_{-3}$	·3	−1·8	4·5	− 6·0	4·5	−1·8	·3
Total ...	·3	1·5	·3	1·8	·3	1·5	·3

Therefore $\displaystyle\int_{-3}^{3} u_x\,dx$ is approximately equal to

$$·3u_{-3} + 1·5u_{-2} + ·3u_{-1} + 1·8u_0 + ·3u_1 + 1·5u_2 + ·3u_3$$
$$= \tfrac{3}{10}\left[(u_{-3} + u_3) + 5\,(u_{-2} + u_2) + (u_{-1} + u_1) + 6u_0\right]$$

or $\displaystyle\int_{0}^{6} u_x\,dx = \tfrac{3}{10}\left[(u_0 + u_6) + 5\,(u_1 + u_5) + (u_2 + u_4) + 6u_3\right].$

This is Weddle's rule.

(4) Hardy's formulae.

Certain approximate formulae due to G. F. Hardy have been used extensively in actuarial work.

Let $\qquad u_x = a + bx + cx^2 + dx^3 + ex^4 + fx^5$

so that $\qquad \displaystyle\int_{-3}^{3} u_x\,dx = 6a + 18c + \tfrac{486}{5}e;$

$u_0 = a;\ u_{-2} + u_2 = 2a + 8c + 32e;\ u_{-3} + u_3 = 2a + 18c + 162e.$

Solving for a, c and e, and substituting:

$$\int_{-3}^{3} u_x\,dx = 2·2u_0 + 1·62\,(u_{-2} + u_2) + ·28\,(u_{-3} + u_3)$$

or $$\int_0^6 u_x dx = 2 \cdot 2u_3 + 1 \cdot 62 \left(u_1 + u_5\right) + \cdot 28 \left(u_0 + u_6\right)$$

$$= \cdot 28 \left(u_0 + u_6\right) + 1 \cdot 62 \left(u_1 + u_5\right) + 2 \cdot 2u_3,$$

which is Hardy's "formula (37)."

If the interval of differencing be n, this becomes

$$\int_0^{6n} u_x dx = n \left\{ \cdot 28 \left(u_0 + u_{6n}\right) + 1 \cdot 62 \left(u_n + u_{5n}\right) + 2 \cdot 2u_{3n} \right\}.$$

Similarly

$$\int_{6n}^{12n} u_x dx = n \left\{ \cdot 28 \left(u_{6n} + u_{12n}\right) + 1 \cdot 62 \left(u_{7n} + u_{11n}\right) + 2 \cdot 2u_{9n} \right\},$$

and so on.

Since

$$\int_0^\infty u_x dx = \int_0^{6n} u_x dx + \int_{6n}^{12n} u_x dx + \int_{12n}^{18n} u_x dx + \dots,$$

$$\int_0^\infty u_x dx = n \left\{ \cdot 28 \left(u_0 + 2u_{6n} + 2u_{12n} + \dots\right) \right.$$

$$\left. + 1 \cdot 62 \left(u_n + u_{5n} + u_{7n} + \dots\right) + 2 \cdot 2 \left(u_{3n} + u_{9n} + \dots\right) \right\}.$$

This is Hardy's "formula (38)."

If we are dealing with functions derived from a mortality table, and we choose n so that $7n$ falls just within or just without the limits of the table—so that $7n$ is in fact about 100—we can write the above formula thus:

$$\int_0^\infty u_x dx = n \left(\cdot 28u_0 + 1 \cdot 62u_n + 2 \cdot 2u_{3n} + 1 \cdot 62u_{5n} + \cdot 56u_{6n} + 1 \cdot 62u_{7n} \right).$$

In this form the formula is known as Hardy's "formula (39a)." (See G. King, *Life Contingencies*, p. 488.)

Note. Since all these approximations give in effect the area of the curve bounded by u_x, the limiting ordinates and the x-axis, they are often termed "quadrature formulae," the word "quadrature" being defined as the exact or approximate calculation of the area of the square equal in area to that of the given figure.

6. Practical applications of the formulae.

Integration formulae of the above type may be used to advantage in obtaining approximations to the values of certain complicated forms of integral which occur in the theory of life contingencies.

Where the functions involved are such that the summation extends to the end of the life table, it is customary to calculate the values of the functions by Hardy's formula (39a). If, on the other hand, the upper limit is at an age-point short of the limiting age of the life table, any of the simpler integration formulae can be employed to advantage. (See, for example, Spurgeon, *Life Contingencies*, pp. 262, 263.)

It is evident that we can neither integrate the function u_x nor interpolate between given values of u_x if we are absolutely without information regarding the value of the function between the ordinates. For example, in a mortality table we may integrate between, say, l_{30} and l_{31}, assuming first differences constant, for we know that in general the decrements between ages 30 and 31 are small and may be fairly considered as being evenly distributed over the interval. We could not reasonably adopt the same assumption for interpolation between l_0 and l_1, since the deaths of infants in the first year of age are not evenly distributed over the year. Again, a reliable estimate of the population of a seaside resort in June of any calendar year would not be obtained by a first difference interpolation between the population figures for January and December of the same year. In the two latter illustrations further information would be necessary before we could proceed to interpolation or integration.

In applying the formulae of approximate integration to the solution of a problem it is therefore essential that we have sufficient knowledge of the function to justify our assumptions regarding the nature of the curve passing through the given points.

When the function to be integrated is one in which the slope of the curve is gradual between the limits of the integration, almost any of the above formulae will give satisfactory results. If the values of the function are changing rapidly between the limits there may be considerable differences between the approximate results. The following examples will show this clearly.

Example 2.

The formula for a continuous annuity-certain is

$$\bar{a}_{\overline{m}|} = \int_0^m e^{-\delta t}\, dt,$$

where δ is the force of interest corresponding to the rate of interest i at which the annuity is valued.

By means of an approximate integration formula find the value of $\bar{a}_{\overline{6}|}$ at 4 per cent.

Since we have to evaluate $\bar{a}_{\overline{6}|}$ we shall require some or all of the values of u_t from $t = 0$ to $t = 6$, where $u_t = e^{-\delta t}$.

By a well-known formula in the theory of interest,

$$e^{-\delta t} = v^t, \text{ where } v = (1 + i)^{-1}.$$

Values of v^t at 4 per cent. are available from any tables of interest. We have, therefore:

$$
\begin{aligned}
u_0 &= e^0 & &= 1, \\
u_1 &= e^{-\delta} &= v &= \cdot 96154, \\
u_2 &= e^{-2\delta} &= v^2 &= \cdot 92456, \\
u_3 &= e^{-3\delta} &= v^3 &= \cdot 88900, \\
u_4 &= e^{-4\delta} &= v^4 &= \cdot 85480, \\
u_5 &= e^{-5\delta} &= v^5 &= \cdot 82193, \\
u_6 &= e^{-6\delta} &= v^6 &= \cdot 79031.
\end{aligned}
$$

The following results will be obtained:

(i) Simpson's rule applied three times:

$$\tfrac{1}{3} (u_0 + 4u_1 + 2u_2 + 4u_3 + 2u_4 + 4u_5 + u_6)$$
$$= 5 \cdot 34630.$$

(ii) The three-eighths rule (with interval of differencing 2):

$$\tfrac{3}{8} \{2 (u_0 + 3u_2 + 3u_4 + u_6)\}$$
$$= 5 \cdot 34629.$$

(iii) Weddle's rule:

$$3 (u_0 + 5u_1 + u_2 + 6u_3 + u_4 + 5u_5 + u_6)$$
$$= 5 \cdot 34631.$$

The result obtained by integrating $\int_0^6 e^{-\delta t} \, dt$ will be $\left[\dfrac{1}{\delta} e^{-\delta t} \right]_0^6$ or $\dfrac{v^0 - v^6}{\delta}$, and since the value of δ at 4 per cent. as given by an interest table is $\cdot 039221$, the integral

$$= \frac{1 - \cdot 79031}{\cdot 039221} = \frac{\cdot 20969}{\cdot 039221} = 5 \cdot 34637 \ldots$$

The three approximate formulae all give results differing from this in the fourth or fifth place of decimals. The excellence of the approximations is due to the fact that the slope of the curve $y = u_t = e^{-\delta t}$ is gradual between the limits $t = 0$ and $t = 6$.

Example 3.

Evaluate $\int_0^6 \dfrac{dx}{(1 + \frac{1}{4}x)^2}$ (i) exactly, (ii) by an approximate integration formula.

(i) $\int_0^6 \dfrac{dx}{(1 + \frac{1}{4}x)^2} = \left[-\dfrac{4}{(1 + \frac{1}{4}x)} \right]_0^6 = 4\left(1 - \dfrac{1}{2\frac{1}{2}}\right) = 2\cdot4.$

(ii) By Simpson's rule applied three times, we obtain   2·37458;
   „ the three-eighths rule   „   2·43249;
   „ Weddle's rule   „   2·36382.

It will be seen that the differences between these results and the accurate result are considerable. None of the values is correct to more than the first place of decimals, and, moreover, the errors are not all in the same direction. The function $y = (1 + \frac{1}{4}x)^{-2}$ is changing rapidly over the given interval, and it is not to be expected that any of the above formulae will give a near approximation.

7. The Euler-Maclaurin expansion.

We have considered quadrature formulae in which the number of ordinates used is a simple multiple of the first two or three natural numbers, 2, 3, 4. We will now proceed to investigate the problem of approximate integration more generally.

The basic formula for expressing a definite integral in terms of given ordinates is the *Euler-Maclaurin expansion*. This expansion is in effect of similar form to the expressions already obtained, a greater degree of accuracy being ensured by the addition of functions, not of the ordinates themselves, but of derivatives of certain of the ordinates.

The formula may be derived by the expansion of operators, thus:

$$\sum_{x=0}^{x=n-1} f(x) = f(0) + f(1) + \dots + f(n-1)$$
$$= F(n) - F(0), \text{ where } f(x) \text{ is } \Delta F(x).$$

Since $f(x) = \Delta F(x)$,

$$F(x) = \Delta^{-1} f(x)$$
$$= (e^D - 1)^{-1} f(x) \text{ (since } 1 + \Delta \equiv e^D. \text{ Chap. XI, para. 13)}$$
$$= \left[\left(1 + D + \dfrac{D^2}{2!} + \dfrac{D^3}{3!} + \dots\right) - 1 \right]^{-1} f(x)$$

$$= D^{-1} \left[1 + \frac{D}{2!} + \frac{D^2}{3!} + \ldots \right]^{-1} f(x)$$

$$= D^{-1} \left[1 - \frac{D}{2} + \frac{D^2}{12} - \frac{D^4}{720} \ldots \right] f(x)$$

$$= \left[D^{-1} - \tfrac{1}{2} + \frac{D}{12} - \frac{D^3}{720} \ldots \right] f(x)$$

$$= D^{-1} f(x) - \tfrac{1}{2} f(x) + \frac{D}{12} f(x) - \frac{D^3}{720} f(x) \ldots$$

$$= \int f(x)\, dx - \tfrac{1}{2} f(x) + \frac{1}{12} \frac{df(x)}{dx} - \frac{1}{720} \frac{d^3 f(x)}{dx^3} \ldots.$$

Between limits o and n, we have therefore

$$F(n) - F(0) = \int_0^n f(x)\, dx - \tfrac{1}{2} \{ f(n) - f(0) \} + \tfrac{1}{12} \{ f'(n) - f'(0) \}$$
$$- \tfrac{1}{720} \{ f'''(n) - f'''(0) \} \ldots.$$

For $F(n) - F(0)$ we may write

$$\sum_{x=0}^{x=n-1} f(x) \quad \text{or} \quad f(0) + f(1) + f(2) + \ldots + f(n-1).$$

$$\therefore \int_0^n f(x)\, dx = f(0) + f(1) + f(2) + \ldots + f(n-1) + \tfrac{1}{2} \{ f(n) - f(0) \}$$
$$- \tfrac{1}{12} \{ f'(n) - f'(0) \} + \tfrac{1}{720} \{ f'''(n) - f'''(0) \} \ldots$$
$$= \tfrac{1}{2} f(0) + f(1) + f(2) + \ldots + f(n-1) + \tfrac{1}{2} f(n)$$
$$- \tfrac{1}{12} \{ f'(n) - f'(0) \} + \tfrac{1}{720} \{ f'''(n) - f'''(0) \} \ldots.$$

This is a simple form of the Euler-Maclaurin expansion.

A more general form can be obtained by changing the origin to the point a and the unit of measurement to r, thus:

$$\frac{1}{r} \int_a^{a+nr} f(x)\, dx = \tfrac{1}{2} f(a) + f(a+r) + f(a+2r) + \ldots$$

$$+ f(a + \overline{n-1}r) + \tfrac{1}{2} f(a+nr) - \frac{r}{12} \{ f'(a+nr) - f'(a) \}$$

$$+ \frac{r^3}{720} \{ f'''(a+nr) - f'''(a) \} \ldots.$$

It will be noted that, since

$$\frac{x}{e^x - 1} = 1 - \tfrac{1}{2} x + B_1 \frac{x^2}{2!} - B_2 \frac{x^4}{4!} + B_3 \frac{x^6}{6!} - \ldots$$

(Chap. XI, p. 185),

we can express the coefficients in $(e^D - 1)^{-1}$ in terms of Bernouilli's numbers. As, however, the resulting approximation formula is to be used for numerical computation, it is of advantage to give the coefficients their actual numerical values.

8. The following examples are illustrative of the use of the formula.

Example 4.

Evaluate $\int_0^1 \dfrac{dx}{1+x}$ to five places of decimals.

Choose a convenient unit, say 0·1. Then in the Euler-Maclaurin expansion we have

$$a = 0,\ n = 10,\ r = 0\cdot1,\ \text{and}\ u_x = \frac{1}{1+x}.$$

$$\frac{du_x}{dx} = -\frac{1}{(1+x)^2};\ \frac{d^3u}{dx^3} = -\frac{6}{(1+x)^4}.$$

$$\therefore\ \frac{1}{0\cdot1}\int_0^1 \frac{dx}{1+x} = \frac{1}{2}\cdot\frac{1}{1} + \frac{1}{1\cdot1} + \frac{1}{1\cdot2} + \frac{1}{1\cdot3} + \dots + \frac{1}{1\cdot9} + \frac{1}{2}\cdot\frac{1}{2}$$

$$- \frac{0\cdot1}{12}\left[-\frac{1}{2^2} + \frac{1}{1^2}\right] + \frac{0\cdot001}{720}\left[-\frac{6}{2^4} + \frac{6}{1^4}\right]\dots$$

$$= \cdot50000 - \frac{1}{120}\cdot\frac{3}{4} + \frac{1}{720000}\cdot6\cdot\frac{15}{16}$$

> ·90909
> ·83333
> ·76923
> ·71429
> ·66667
> ·62500
> ·58824
> ·55556
> ·52632
> ·25000

> 6·93773
> $= 6\cdot93773 - \cdot00625 + \cdot00001$
> $= 6\cdot93149.$

$$\therefore\ \int_0^1 \frac{dx}{1+x} = \cdot69315 \text{ to five places of decimals.}$$

This agrees with the true result ($\log_e 2$) to the required degree of accuracy.

Example 5.

Find the sum of the fourth powers of the first n natural numbers by means of the Euler-Maclaurin formula.

In the formula

$$\frac{1}{r} \int_a^{a+nr} u_x \, dx = \tfrac{1}{2} u_a + u_{a+r} + u_{a+2r} + \dots$$

$$+ \tfrac{1}{2} u_{a+nr} - \frac{r}{12} (u'_{a+nr} - u'_a) + \frac{r^3}{720} (u'''_{a+nr} - u'''_a) \dots ,$$

put $a = 0$, $r = 1$, $u_x = x^4$; then

$$\int_0^n x^4 \, dx = 1^4 + 2^4 + 3^4 + \dots$$

$$+ (n-1)^4 + \tfrac{1}{2} n^4 - \frac{1}{12} [4x^3]_{x=n} + \frac{1}{720} [4.3.2x]_{x=n},$$

since higher differential coefficients of u_x will be zero.

I.e.
$$\left[\frac{x^5}{5} \right]_0^n = \sum_{r=1}^{r=n} r^4 - \tfrac{1}{2} n^4 - \frac{1}{12} 4n^3 + \frac{1}{720} 24n.$$

$$\therefore \sum_{r=1}^{r=n} r^4 = \frac{1}{5} n^5 + \frac{1}{2} n^4 + \frac{1}{3} n^3 - \frac{1}{30} n.$$

By proceeding on the above lines it can easily be seen that the general formula for the sum of the pth powers of the first n natural numbers is

$$\sum_{r=1}^{r=n} r^p = \frac{1}{p+1} n^{p+1} + \tfrac{1}{2} n^p + \frac{1}{12} p n^{p-1} - \frac{1}{720} p(p-1)(p-2) n^{p-3}$$

$$+ \frac{p(p-1)(p-2)(p-3)(p-4)}{30{,}240} n^{p-5} \dots .$$

9. Lubbock's formula.

The previous formulae have been developed for the purpose of relating a definite integral to the sum of a number of ordinates at finite distances apart. We have, in effect, obtained approximate formulae for the value of

$$\underset{h \to 0}{\text{Lt}} \; h(u_a + u_{a+h} + u_{a+2h} + \dots + u_b).$$

In addition to formulae of this type we can find expressions which enable us to find the value of the sum of a number of ordinates at finite distances apart in terms of the sum of ordinates at greater or less intervals apart. Thus, if for the curve $y = u_x$ there are m unit intervals, so that we have Σu_x from $x = 0$ to $x = m - 1$, we may develop a relationship between this sum and the sum when the intervals are, say, h, where $nh = 1$.

In place of the sum $h (u_a + u_{a+h} + u_{a+2h} + \ldots + u_b)$, we may consider, without loss of generality, the simpler form when the series commences with u_0.

Let there be m ordinates at unit distance apart, and let each of these unit distances be divided into n equal parts, so that the new ordinates are

$$u_0, \; u_{1/n}, \; u_{2/n}, \; \ldots \, u_{r/n}, \; \ldots \, u_{m-1/n}.$$

Replace $1/n$ by h for convenience in working.

Then $h (u_0 + u_h + u_{2h} + \ldots + u_{m-h})$

$$= h (1 + E^h + E^{2h} + \ldots + E^{m-h}) u_0$$

$$= h \, \frac{E^m - 1}{E^h - 1} \, u_0$$

$$= h \, \frac{1}{E^h - 1} (u_m - u_0)$$

$$= h \, \frac{1}{(1 + \Delta)^h - 1} (u_m - u_0)$$

$$= h (h\Delta + h_2 \Delta^2 + h_3 \Delta^3 + \ldots)^{-1} (u_m - u_0)$$

$$= h . h^{-1} \Delta^{-1} \left(1 - \frac{h-1}{2} \Delta + \frac{h^2-1}{12} \Delta^2 \right.$$
$$\left. - \frac{h^2-1}{24} \Delta^3 \ldots \right) (u_m - u_0)$$

$$= \Delta^{-1} (u_m - u_0) - \frac{h-1}{2} (u_m - u_0) + \frac{h^2-1}{12} \Delta (u_m - u_0)$$
$$- \frac{h^2-1}{24} \Delta^2 (u_m - u_0) \ldots$$

$$= (u_0 + u_1 + u_2 + \ldots + u_{m-1}) - \frac{h-1}{2} (u_m - u_0)$$
$$+ \frac{h^2-1}{12} (\Delta u_m - \Delta u_0) - \frac{h^2-1}{24} (\Delta^2 u_m - \Delta^2 u_0) \ldots,$$

since $\Delta (u_0 + u_1 + u_2 + \ldots + u_{m-1}) = (u_1 + u_2 + \ldots + u_{m-1} + u_m)$
$$- (u_0 + u_1 + \ldots + u_{m-1})$$
$$= u_m - u_0.$$

But $h = 1/n$.

$$\therefore \ \frac{1}{n}\left(u_0 + u_{1/n} + u_{2/n} + \ldots + u_{m-1/n}\right) = \left(u_0 + u_1 + u_2 + \ldots + u_{m-1}\right)$$

$$- \frac{1/n - 1}{2}\left(u_m - u_0\right) + \frac{1/n^2 - 1}{12}\left(\Delta u_m - \Delta u_0\right)$$

$$- \frac{1/n^2 - 1}{24}\left(\Delta^2 u_m - \Delta^2 u_0\right) \ldots$$

or

$$u_0 + u_{1/n} + u_{2/n} + \ldots + u_{m-1/n} = n\left(u_0 + u_1 + \ldots + u_{m-1}\right)$$

$$- \frac{1 - n}{2}\left(u_m - u_0\right) + \frac{1 - n^2}{12n}\left(\Delta u_m - \Delta u_0\right) - \frac{1 - n^2}{24n}\left(\Delta^2 u_m - \Delta^2 u_0\right) \ldots$$

$$= n\left(u_0 + u_1 + \ldots + u_{m-1}\right) + \frac{n - 1}{2}\left(u_m - u_0\right) - \frac{n^2 - 1}{12n}\left(\Delta u_m - \Delta u_0\right)$$

$$+ \frac{n^2 - 1}{24n}\left(\Delta^2 u_m - \Delta^2 u_0\right) \ldots.$$

This is Lubbock's formula.

The coefficients of higher differences than the second are cumbersome, the terms in $\Delta^3 u$ and $\Delta^4 u$ being respectively

$$- \frac{\left(n^2 - 1\right)\left(19n^2 - 1\right)}{720 n^3}\left(\Delta^3 u_m - \Delta^3 u_0\right)$$

and

$$\frac{\left(n^2 - 1\right)\left(9n^2 - 1\right)}{480 n^3}\left(\Delta^4 u_m - \Delta^4 u_0\right).$$

If the interval of differencing be originally n instead of unity, Lubbock's formula becomes, on changing the unit,

$$u_0 + u_1 + u_2 + \ldots + u_{mn-1}$$

$$= n\left(u_0 + u_n + u_{2n} + \ldots + u_{(m-1)n}\right) + \frac{n - 1}{2}\left(u_{mn} - u_0\right)$$

$$- \frac{n^2 - 1}{12n}\left(\Delta u_{mn} - \Delta u_0\right) + \frac{n^2 - 1}{24n}\left(\Delta^2 u_{mn} - \Delta^2 u_0\right) \ldots.$$

10. Woolhouse's formula.

Although Lubbock's formula has the advantage that it may be used when the function is not capable of expression as a mathematical expansion—as for example when the data are based on a mortality table—there are disadvantages in adopting the formula. In the first place, if it is necessary to proceed further than second differences the calculations are heavy, and secondly it may happen that the differences converge slowly, so that if we stop at second or third differences we are likely to obtain a result differing considerably from the true value of the function. Where a mathematical function is available an alternative summation formula can be adopted in which differential coefficients replace the finite differences in Lubbock's formula.

The formula involving differential coefficients is due to Woolhouse, and may be developed directly from the Euler-Maclaurin expansion.

The Euler-Maclaurin expansion is

$$\int_0^m u_x dx = \tfrac{1}{2}u_0 + u_1 + u_2 + \dots + u_{m-1} + \tfrac{1}{2}u_m - \frac{1}{12}(u_m' - u_0')$$
$$+ \frac{1}{720}(u_m''' - u_0''')\dots$$

If the interval of differencing be $1/n$, the formula becomes

$$n\int_0^m u_x dx = (\tfrac{1}{2}u_0 + u_{1/n} + u_{2/n} + \dots + \tfrac{1}{2}u_m) - \frac{1}{12n}(u_m' - u_0')$$
$$+ \frac{1}{720n^3}(u_m''' - u_0''')\dots$$

If, however, we multiply both sides of the first expression by n we have

$$n\int_0^m u_x dx = n(\tfrac{1}{2}u_0 + u_1 + u_2 + \dots + \tfrac{1}{2}u_m) - \frac{n}{12}(u_m' - u_0')$$
$$+ \frac{n}{720}(u_m''' - u_0''')\dots$$

Equating the two values of $n\int_0^m u_x dx$:

$$\tfrac{1}{2}u_0 + u_{1/n} + u_{2/n} + \dots + \tfrac{1}{2}u_m - \frac{1}{12n}(u_m' - u_0') + \frac{1}{720n^3}(u_m''' - u_0''')\dots$$

$$= n(\tfrac{1}{2}u_0 + u_1 + u_2 + \dots + \tfrac{1}{2}u_m) - \frac{n}{12}(u_m' - u_0') + \frac{n}{720}(u_m''' - u_0''')\dots$$

F

20

or

$$u_0 + u_{1/n} + u_{2/n} + \ldots + u_m - \tfrac{1}{2}(u_0 + u_m) - \frac{1}{12n}(u_m{}' - u_0{}')$$

$$+ \frac{1}{720n^3}(u_m{}''' - u_0{}''') \ldots$$

$$= n(u_0 + u_1 + u_2 + \ldots + u_m) - \frac{n}{2}(u_0 + u_m) - \frac{n}{12}(u_m{}' - u_0{}')$$

$$+ \frac{n}{720}(u_m{}''' - u_0{}''') \ldots.$$

Re-arranging:

$$u_0 + u_{1/n} + u_{2/n} + \ldots + u_m = n(u_0 + u_1 + u_2 + \ldots + u_m)$$

$$- \frac{n-1}{2}(u_0 + u_m) - \frac{n^2-1}{12n}(u_m{}' - u_0{}') + \frac{n^4-1}{720n^3}(u_m{}''' - u_0{}''') \ldots.$$

If the unit of measurement be changed to n, we have

$$u_0 + u_1 + u_2 + \ldots + u_{mn} = n(u_0 + u_n + u_{2n} + \ldots + u_{mn})$$

$$- \frac{n-1}{2}(u_0 + u_m) - \frac{n^2-1}{12}(u_m{}' - u_0{}') + \frac{n^4-1}{720}(u_m{}''' - u_0{}''') \ldots,$$

the usual form of Woolhouse's formula.

It should be noted that, by replacing the derivatives of u by their values in finite differences, Lubbock's formula can be obtained directly from the above.

In applying these formulae to certain actuarial functions the values of u, $\dfrac{du}{dx}$, $\dfrac{d^3u}{dx^3}$, $\ldots$ at the end of the mortality table will disappear. Woolhouse's formula may then be written as

$$\frac{1}{n}(u_0 + u_{1/n} + u_{2/n} + \ldots)$$

$$= (u_0 + u_1 + \ldots) - \frac{n-1}{2n}u_0 + \frac{n^2-1}{12n}u_0{}' - \frac{n^4-1}{720n^3}u_0{}''' \ldots.$$

This is a convenient form for expressing the value of a benefit paid at $n$thly intervals in terms of the values at intervals of a year.

11. Other formulae for approximate integration.

It will have been observed that in the formulae of the type of Simpson's, Weddle's, etc., the function of the u's is symmetrical about the central value. If, however, a fixed number of ordinates be given and it is desired to obtain an approximation to the area of a curve in terms of these ordinates, the resulting form will not necessarily be symmetrical. Again, the formula for the area of the curve may be related not only to ordinates falling within the area to be measured, but to ordinates outside the area. It may be noted therefore that although standard formulae are available, it is not difficult to devise approximations to fit the particular problems under investigation.

Example 6.

If u_x is of the form $a + bx + cx^2$, find a convenient formula for $\int_0^1 u_x dx$ in terms of u_0, u_1 and u_2.

The interpolation formula which involves the terms u_0, u_1 and u_2 is

$$u_x = u_0 + x\Delta u_0 + \tfrac{1}{2}x(x-1)\Delta^2 u_0.$$

$$\therefore \int_0^1 u_x\, dx = \left[xu_0 + \tfrac{1}{2}x^2\Delta u_0 + (\tfrac{1}{6}x^3 - \tfrac{1}{4}x^2)\Delta^2 u_0 \right]_0^1$$

$$= u_0 + \tfrac{1}{2}\Delta u_0 - \tfrac{1}{12}\Delta^2 u_0$$

$$= u_0 + \tfrac{1}{2}(u_1 - u_0) - \tfrac{1}{12}(u_2 - 2u_1 + u_0)$$

$$= \tfrac{5}{12}u_0 + \tfrac{8}{12}u_1 - \tfrac{1}{12}u_2.$$

The required formula is therefore

$$\int_0^1 u_x\, dx = \tfrac{1}{12}(5u_0 + 8u_1 - u_2).$$

It should be noted that (i) the expression is unsymmetrical in the u's, and (ii) the ordinate u_2 falls without the area to be integrated.

It is obviously impossible to quote all the formulae that are in current use. Further examples and illustrations of various approximation integration formulae will be found in the following sources: Whittaker and Robinson's *Calculus of Observations*, chapter VII; C. H. Wickens, *J.I.A.* vol. LIV, pp. 209–13; A. E. King, *T.F.A.* vol. IX, pp. 218–31.

12. Alternative methods of proof of the formulae.

It has been stated above that the Euler-Maclaurin expansion is the basic quadrature formula. It will be instructive to develop Simpson's formula from this expansion.

$$\int_0^{2mn} u_x dx = n\left(\tfrac{1}{2}u_0 + u_n + u_{2n} + \ldots + u_{(2m-1)n} + \tfrac{1}{2}u_{2mn}\right) - \frac{n^2}{12}(u'_{2mn} - u'_0)$$

approximately.

Writing $2n$ for n, but preserving the same range o to $2mn$

$$\int_0^{2mn} u_x\,dx = 2n\left(\tfrac{1}{2}u_0 + u_{2n} + u_{4n} + \ldots + u_{(2m-2)n} + \tfrac{1}{2}u_{2mn}\right)$$
$$- \frac{4n^2}{12}\left(u'_{2mn} - u_0'\right).$$

Subtracting this from four times the first:

$$3\int_0^{2mn} u_x\,dx = 2n\left(\tfrac{1}{2}u_0 + 2u_n + u_{2n} + 2u_{3n} + \ldots + u_{(2m-2)n}\right.$$
$$\left. + 2u_{(2m-1)n} + \tfrac{1}{2}u_{2mn}\right);$$

i.e.

$$\int_0^{2mn} u_x\,dx = \frac{n}{3}\left(u_0 + 4u_n + 2u_{2n} + 4u_{3n} + \ldots + 2u_{(2m-2)n}\right.$$
$$\left. + 4u_{(2m-1)n} + u_{2mn}\right),$$

which is Simpson's formula.

Again, we have shown in para. 2 (p. 288) that we may adopt the expression for u_x in terms of u_0 and differences of u_0 as the assumed form of function. Since Lagrange's formula is based on the same assumption it is evident that we could obtain any approximate formula by the use of the Lagrange formula.

For example, given u_0, u_1, u_2,

$$u_x = u_0\frac{(x-1)(x-2)}{(-1)(-2)} + u_1\frac{x(x-2)}{1.(-1)} + u_2\frac{x(x-1)}{2.1}$$
$$= \tfrac{1}{2}u_0(x^2 - 3x + 2) + u_1(2x - x^2) + \tfrac{1}{2}u_2(x^2 - x),$$

so that

$$\int_0^2 u_x\,dx = \left[u_0\left(\frac{x^3}{6} - \frac{3x^2}{4} + x\right) + u_1\left(x^2 - \frac{x^3}{3}\right) + u_2\left(\frac{x^3}{6} - \frac{x^2}{4}\right)\right]_0^2$$
$$= \tfrac{1}{3}(u_0 + 4u_1 + u_2), \text{ which is Simpson's rule.}$$

If we integrate between o and 1 we shall obtain

$$\int_0^1 u_x\,dx = \tfrac{1}{12}(5u_0 + 8u_1 - u_2),$$

the formula given in Example 6.

EXAMPLES 17

1. Prove that

$$\int_0^{2a} u_x \, dx = \int_0^a (u_x + u_{2a-x}) \, dx,$$

and illustrate the result geometrically.

2. If $u_x = a + bx + cx^2$, prove that

$$\int_1^3 u_x \, dx = 2u_2 + \tfrac{1}{12} (u_0 - 2u_2 + u_4),$$

and hence find an approximate value for

$$\int_{-\frac{1}{2}}^{\frac{1}{2}} e^{-\frac{x^2}{10}} \, dx.$$

3. Show that $\int_0^1 u_x \, dx = \tfrac{1}{12} (5u_1 + 8u_0 - u_{-1})$ approximately.

Find the approximate mileage travelled between 12.0 and 12.30 by use of the above formula, from the following:

Time	Speed (m.p.h.)
11.50	24·2
12.0	35·0
12.10	41·3
12.20	42·8
12.30	39·2

4. Prove that, if u_x is a rational integral function of x, then

$$\int e^{\frac{x}{a}} u_x \, dx = ae^{\frac{x}{a}} (1 - aD + a^2 D^2 - a^3 D^3 + \ldots) u_x,$$

where $D \equiv \dfrac{d}{dx}$.

5. Show that the area of a curve, divided into n parts by $n + 1$ equidistant ordinates $u_0, u_1, \ldots u_n$, is given approximately by the series

$$nu_0 + \frac{n^2}{2} \Delta u_0 + \left\{ \frac{n^3}{3} - \frac{n^2}{2} \right\} \frac{\Delta^2 u_0}{1.2} + \left\{ \frac{n^4}{4} - n^3 + n^2 \right\} \frac{\Delta^3 u_0}{1.2.3} \ldots$$

to $n + 1$ terms.

6. Between the limits $x = 0$ and $x = n$ the functions u_x and du_x/dx are continuously increasing.

Show that $\int_0^n u_x \, dx$ is less than $\tfrac{1}{2}u_0 + \sum_1^{n-1} u_x + \tfrac{1}{2}u_n$.

7. Obtain the approximate formula

$$\int_{-1}^1 u_x \, dx = \frac{13 (u_1 + u_{-1}) - (u_3 + u_{-3})}{12},$$

showing up to what order of differences it holds.

8. Assuming u_x to be of the fourth degree in x, express $\int_0^5 u_x dx$ in terms of u_0, u_1, u_2, u_3 and u_4.

9. A plane area is bounded by a curve, the axis of x, and two ordinates. The area is divided into five figures by equidistant ordinates 2 inches apart, the lengths of the ordinates being 21·65, 21·04, 20·35, 19·61, 18·75 and 17·80 inches respectively. Apply the method of integration to obtain an approximate value of the area.

10. Prove the approximate formula

$$\int_0^{10} u_x dx = 2·5 \, (u_1 + u_4 + u_6 + u_9),$$

and show that the formula involves a small second difference error.

11. Find the value of $\int_0^6 (1 + x)^{-2} \, dx$.

Obtain approximations to the value by applying
(i) Weddle's rule:

$$\int_0^6 u_x dx = 0·3 \, (u_0 + 5u_1 + u_2 + 6u_3 + u_4 + 5u_5 + u_6),$$

(ii) Simpson's rule:

$$\int_0^2 u_x dx = \tfrac{1}{3} \, (u_0 + 4u_1 + u_2), \text{ applied three times.}$$

12. Which of the two following formulae would you expect to give the better approximation for $\int_0^4 u_x \, dx$?

    (a) $\tfrac{1}{9} \{5 \, (u_0 + u_4) + 4 \, (u_1 + u_3) + 18u_2\}$,

    (b) $\tfrac{2}{15} \{2 \, (u_0 + u_2 + u_4) + 12 \, (u_1 + u_3)\}$.

13. Prove that

$$\int_0^n u_x \, dx = n \, \{\tfrac{3}{8}u_0 + \tfrac{1}{24} \, (19u_n - 5u_{2n} + u_{3n})\},$$

and hence find $\int_0^1 u_x dx$ given the following table:

x	0	1	2	3
u_x	27,650	31,252	35,154	39,368

14. Prove that

$$\int_{-\frac{1}{2}}^{\frac{1}{2}} f(x) \, dx = \tfrac{1}{2} \{f(-\tfrac{1}{2}) + f(\tfrac{1}{2})\} + \tfrac{1}{24} \{\Delta f(-\tfrac{3}{2}) - \Delta f(\tfrac{1}{2})\} \text{ approximately.}$$

Hence find $\int_1^3 f(x) \, dx$, when $f(0) = 105$, $f(1) = 212$, $f(2) = 421$, $f(3) = 749$ and $f(4) = 1050$.

15. If u_x either increases continually or decreases continually as x increases, prove that $\int_1^n u_x\,dx$ differs from $\overset{n-1}{\underset{1}{\Sigma}}\,u_x$ by less than the difference between u_1 and u_n.

Prove that the difference between $\log n$ and

$$1 + \tfrac{1}{2} + \tfrac{1}{3} + \dots + 1/(n-1) < 1,$$

however great n may be.

16. If third differences are constant, prove that

$$\int_0^2 u_x\,dx = \tfrac{1}{24}\left(u_{-\frac{1}{2}} + 23u_{\frac{1}{2}} + 23u_{\frac{3}{2}} + u_{\frac{5}{2}}\right).$$

Adapt this formula to find the approximate value of $\log_e 2$ from the integral $\int_a^{2a} \dfrac{dx}{x}$.

17. Prove that, approximately,

$$\int_{-3}^3 u_x\,dx = 0\cdot3\,(1\cdot1u_{-3} + 4\cdot4u_{-2} + 2\cdot5u_{-1} + 4u_0 + 2\cdot5u_1 + 4\cdot4u_2 + 1\cdot1u_3).$$

18. $f(x)$ is a rational integral function of the fifth degree in x. Prove that

$$\int_{-1}^1 f(x)\,dx = \tfrac{1}{9}f(0) + \tfrac{5}{9}\{f(0\cdot6) + f(-0\cdot6)\}.$$

19. Use Simpson's rule to prove that $\log_e 7$ is approximately $1\cdot96$.

20. Apply the Euler-Maclaurin formula to find a formula for the sum of the fifth powers of the first n natural numbers.

21. Obtain Shovelton's integration formula:

$$\int_0^{10} u_x\,dx = \tfrac{5}{126}\{8\,(u_0 + u_{10}) + 35\,(u_1 + u_3 + u_7 + u_9)$$
$$+ 15\,(u_2 + u_4 + u_6 + u_8) + 36u_5\}.$$

22. By means of Hardy's formula

$$\int_0^6 u_x\,dx = \cdot28u_0 + 1\cdot62u_1 + 2\cdot2u_3 + 1\cdot62u_5 + \cdot28u_6,$$

calculate the value of

$$\int_0^{\frac{1}{2}}(1 - x^2)^{-\frac{1}{2}}\,dx$$

correct to four places of decimals.

23. If $f(x)$ be a function of the third degree in x, and if

$$u_{-1} = \int_{-3t}^{-t} f(x)\,dx, \quad u_0 = \int_{-t}^t f(x)\,dx, \quad u_1 = \int_t^{3t} f(x)\,dx,$$

show that

$$f(0) = \frac{1}{2t}\left\{u_0 - \frac{\Delta^2 u_{-1}}{24}\right\}.$$

24. AB is the base of a semicircle, centre O and radius unity. The points P and Q bisect OA and OB respectively. The area between the semicircle, the base PQ and the ordinates at P and Q is $\dfrac{\pi}{6} + \dfrac{\sqrt{3}}{4}$. Use Weddle's rule that

$$\int_0^6 f(x)\,dx = 0.3\,\{f(0) + 5f(1) + f(2) + 6f(3) + f(4) + 5f(5) + f(6)\}$$

to find an approximate value of π to three places of decimals.

25. The following values of u_x are given:

x	0	1	2	3	4	5	6
u_x	·146	·161	·176	·190	·204	·217	·230

Use an approximate integration formula to find the value of $\int_0^6 u_x\,dx$.

It is found that, for the values given, $y = \log_{10}(\cdot 05x + 1\cdot 4)$ fits the data. Verify that this is so by integrating $\log_{10}(\cdot 05x + 1\cdot 4)$ between the limits 0 and 6. ($\log_{10} e = \cdot 4343$; $\log_{10} 1\cdot 7 = \cdot 2304$; $\log_{10} 1\cdot 4 = \cdot 1461$.)

26. If u_x is a function whose fifth differences are constant, $\int_{-1}^{1} u_x\,dx$ can be expressed in the form

$$pu_{-a} + qu_0 + pu_a.$$

Find the values of p, q and a.

Use this formula, after making the necessary changes in the origin and scale, to find the value of $\log_e 2$ to four places of decimals from the equation

$$\int_0^1 \frac{1}{1+x}\,dx = \log_e 2.$$

27. Prove that

$$\int_a^{a+r} u_x\,dx = \tfrac{1}{2}u_0 + u_1 + u_2 + \dots + u_{r-1} + \tfrac{1}{2}u_r - \tfrac{1}{12}(\Delta u_{r-1} - \Delta u_0)$$

$$- \tfrac{1}{24}(\Delta^2 u_{r-2} + \Delta^2 u_0) - \tfrac{19}{120}(\Delta^3 u_{r-3} - \Delta^3 u_0)$$

$$- \tfrac{3}{160}(\Delta^4 u_{r-4} + \Delta^4 u_0)\dots.$$

If u_x be the function $(1 + x^2)^{-1}$ find an approximate value for π.

28. Obtain an approximate formula for $\int_{-3}^{3} u_x\,dx$ in the form

$$a(u_{-2} + u_2) + b(u_{-3} + u_3)$$

and find the values of a and b.

CHAPTER XVIII

PROBABILITY

1. Suppose that a bag contains a hundred balls of exactly the same size and shape, of which one is coloured and the remaining ninety-nine white. If one of these balls be drawn at random it is safe to say that there is a greater probability of drawing a white ball than of drawing the coloured ball. Again, of a number of men in a community, all subject to the same conditions, the probability that one aged 20 will survive 10 years is obviously greater than the probability that one aged 90 will survive the same period. These examples serve to illustrate what is understood by the term "probability." Many more such simple examples could be given, from which we could say that the probability that event A would happen is greater or less than that event B would happen. A difficulty arises, however, when we attempt to assign a measure to the probability that one of the events A or B might happen.

In the first of the above examples it is not unreasonable to argue that since there is one coloured ball among a hundred balls, the probability that this coloured ball would be drawn is one in a hundred. Whether this be so or not, we have used the data at our command and have given a measure to the probability. In the second example, however, we have no data immediately available to enable us to assign a numerical value to the probability in question. It would be necessary to collect statistics of the mortality of the men in the community, and to supplement the collection of these statistics by more or less elaborate calculations. In the application of the theory of probability to most actuarial problems the aggregation of statistics is necessary before the data are available, and it is not often that we are immediately in possession of such simple facts as are given in the first type of question. A complete answer to a problem in actuarial work would involve the collection and interpretation of the relevant statistics: these are matters which are outside the scope of this book, and in dealing with questions on probability it will be sufficient to assume that we have sufficient data to enable us to proceed without further analysis.

2. Numerical definitions of probability.

A simple definition of the measure of the probability that an event may happen is as follows:

(1) If an event can happen in a ways and fail to happen in b ways, all of these ways being equally likely and such that not more than one of them can occur, then the probability of the event happening is $\dfrac{a}{a+b}$.

The probability that the event does not happen is $\dfrac{b}{a+b}$, which is equal to $1 - \dfrac{a}{a+b}$.

Although this definition enables us to solve arithmetical problems in probability, it has, however, certain defects which render it unsatisfactory in general. In the first place we have to define the phrase "all of which are equally likely." It is difficult to say what this means without rendering the definition unintelligible, for if we define the words as equivalent to "there being no reason why one way should occur more than another" we should be involved in a further definition. Moreover, however we explain the phrase it may not be possible to say that the happenings of an event are equally likely: the probability of its occurrence cannot then be measured by the simple ratio $\dfrac{a}{a+b}$. The attempt that has been made to define "equally likely" events as those which occur equally often in the long run, i.e. when the number of occasions is very large, does not seem to solve the difficulty.

While the above definition—which is sometimes called the "unitary" definition—is sufficient for solving the questions involving probability that will be dealt with in this chapter, it will not be out of place to quote other definitions.

(2) If on taking any very large number N out of a series of cases in which an event A is in question, A happens on pN occasions, the probability of the event A is said to be p. (Chrystal, *Algebra*, chap. xxxvi.)

(3) If there be a large number N of a series in which an event M might occur and if, whenever it might occur it would necessarily

be associated with one of two or more mutually exclusive events
E, E', E'', ..., then if E would occur on pN occasions, E' on
$p'N$ occasions, ... and so on, p, p', p'', ... are said to be the probabilities of the event M being associated with E, E', E'', ..., and
$p + p' + p'' + ... = 1$. (Sheppard, *Ency. Brit.*, "Probability.")

The term "mutually exclusive" in the above definition means that
on each occasion one and only one of the events E, E', E'', ... can occur.

We can arrive at an approximate agreement between these definitions and the unitary definition thus. If an event occur on a
occasions out of $(a + b)$, we may say that the *frequency* of its occurrence is a, and the *relative frequency* will be $a/(a + b)$. Then the
probability of the event is the relative frequency when the number
of occasions is very large.

For example, we may revert to an illustration similar to the first
illustration in paragraph 1. If there be five exactly similar balls in
a bag, two coloured and three white, then by the unitary definition
the probability that a coloured ball will be drawn (supposing one
ball be drawn at random) is $\frac{2}{5}$. This does not mean that if a ball
were drawn five times, being replaced each time, two of the
draws would necessarily give coloured balls. The true interpretation of the fraction $\frac{2}{5}$ is that if the experiment were repeated a
large number of times a coloured ball would be drawn about twice
in five times. After many trials we should find that twice in five
times was approximately correct, and we might be said to have
confirmed our unitary result by experiment.

There are thus two distinct methods of ascertaining simple
probabilities, one from *a priori* considerations, and the other by
experiment. Usually only one of these methods is applicable to
any particular problem, and for the present purpose it will be unnecessary to consider statistical methods.

3. The basis for the solution of the problems that will be dealt
with later is, as has been remarked, the unitary definition. We may
amplify this definition by certain others.

    (*a*) The measure of certainty is unity. In other words, if an
        event is certain to happen the probability of its hap-
        pening is 1; if it is certain not to happen the probability
        of its happening is 0.

(b) If p is the probability that an event might happen, the probability of its failing is $1 - p$. This follows directly from the unitary definition.

(c) If the odds in favour of an event are $a : b$, the probability of its happening is $a/(a + b)$.

(d) If an event can happen in more than one way, all ways being mutually exclusive, the probability of its happening at all is the sum of the probabilities of its happening in the several ways.

This last proposition is known as the "addition" rule, and is fundamental in the application of the theory of probability. The rule may otherwise be stated thus:

If p and p' are the probabilities of two mutually exclusive events, the probability that one of these events happens on any occasion in which both events are in question is $p + p'$.

The words "mutually exclusive" in this definition are of the utmost importance. A proof of the addition rule depending on Chrystal's definition of probability will show that unless the events are mutually exclusive we cannot add the simple probabilities p and p'. Thus, if there be a large number N out of a series in which the two events are in question, the first will happen on pN occasions and the second on $p'N$ occasions respectively. Since the events are mutually exclusive, one and only one of the events can occur on any one occasion. Therefore out of N occasions one or other of the events will happen on $pN + p'N$ occasions, i.e. on $(p + p') N$ occasions. The probability that one of the events happens is therefore $p + p'$. It will be seen that this proof breaks down if the second event happens on any of the pN occasions that the first happens, i.e. if the events are not mutually exclusive.

4. The simplest problems in probability are those in which both the number of favourable ways and the total number of ways in which the event may happen can be counted, either arithmetically or by the aid of elementary rules. The enumeration is often best performed by the application of the theorems of permutations and combinations, and a thorough knowledge of this branch of algebra is essential for the speedy solution of many of these questions.

Example 1.

An ordinary pack of cards contains 13 cards of each of four suits; spades, hearts, diamonds and clubs. Ten cards of each suit are numbered 1 (the ace), 2, 3, ... 10, the remaining three being "court cards," namely, king, queen, knave.

Find the chance that if a card be drawn at random from an ordinary pack it will be a heart.

Since there are 52 cards in a pack, the number of ways in which a card can be drawn (i.e. the total number of ways in which the event can happen) is 52.

The number of ways favourable to the event is 13, since there are 13 hearts in the pack.

The required probability is therefore $\frac{13}{52}$ or $\frac{1}{4}$.

Notes: (i) The above result means that over a long series of trials the proportion of favourable draws would approximate to one-fourth of the whole number of trials. It is convenient, however, to think in terms of a single trial, although the results of our calculations merely epitomize the experience of a long series of trials.

(ii) The word "chance" may be taken to be the same as the word "probability." There is a shade of difference between the two ideas, "probability" referring to past, present and future events, and "chance" to future events only. This distinction can be ignored.

Example 2.

In a given race, the odds against three horses A, B, C are $2:1$; $5:2$; $10:1$ respectively. Assuming that a dead-heat is impossible, find the chance that one of them will win the race.

The events are mutually exclusive, and we may therefore use the "addition" rule.

$$p' = \text{probability that } A \text{ wins} = \tfrac{1}{3},$$
$$p'' = \quad ,, \quad ,, \quad B \quad ,, \quad = \tfrac{2}{7},$$
$$p''' = \quad ,, \quad ,, \quad C \quad ,, \quad = \tfrac{1}{11}.$$

The probability that one of the horses wins is therefore

$$p' + p'' + p''' = \tfrac{164}{231}.$$

Example 3.

Out of $2n + 1$ tickets consecutively numbered, three are drawn at random. Find the chance that the numbers on them are in arithmetical progression.

This problem can be solved by virtually writing down the sets of numbers that can be in A.P. Consider, for example, the sets of three numbers in A.P. beginning with 4: they will be

$$4 ; 5 ; 6 \qquad 4 ; 6 ; 8 \qquad 4 ; 7 ; 10 \ldots 4 ; n + 1 ; 2n - 2 \qquad 4 ; n + 2 ; 2n,$$

where the highest number that can enter into any set is $2n$. There will evidently be $n - 2$ such sets of numbers (being the number of numbers from 5 to $n + 2$, both numbers inclusive). We can therefore write down the following schedule:

Lowest number of the three	Number of favourable ways
1	n
2	$n - 1$
3	$n - 1$
4	$n - 2$
5	$n - 2$
6	$n - 3$
.	.
.	.
.	.
$2n - 2$	1
$2n - 1$	1

The total number of favourable ways is $\dfrac{2n (n + 1)}{2} - n$ or n^2, and since the total number of ways of drawing three tickets is $\dfrac{(2n + 1) 2n (2n - 1)}{6}$, it is easily seen that the required probability is $\dfrac{3n}{4n^2 - 1}$.

Example 4.

If the letters of the word REGULATIONS be arranged at random, what is the chance that there will be exactly four letters between the R and the E?

The conditions are satisfied if

the R is in the first place and the E in the sixth,

or ,, R ,, second ,, E ,, seventh,

,, ,, R ,, third ,, E ,, eighth,

,, ,, R ,, fourth ,, E ,, ninth,

,, ,, R ,, fifth ,, E ,, tenth,

,, ,, R ,, sixth ,, E ,, eleventh,

or if the R and the E are transposed in any of the above.

Now there are 11 letters in the word; therefore the letters R and E can jointly occupy 11 × 10 positions. Since there are 6 × 2 favourable positions (as above) the chance that the R and the E are in the favourable position is $\frac{12}{110}$ or $\frac{6}{55}$.

Example 5.
Find the probability that the number 8 will be thrown in a single throw with two dice.

The total number of different numbers that can be thrown with two dice is 36, since each of the 6 ways of throwing the first die can be associated with each of the 6 ways of throwing the second.

The number of ways favourable to the event can be found by simple enumeration, thus:

First die	Second die
2	6
3	5
4	4
5	3
6	2

Total: 5 ways.

The required probability is therefore $\frac{5}{36}$.

5. The multiplication rule.

If there be a series of events such that the happening of any one of them in no way affects the happening of any other of them, the events are said to be *independent*.

The probability that two independent events happen on any one occasion on which they are both in question is the product of the chances of their happening severally.

For consider two independent events C and D, the probabilities of which are p and p' respectively. Out of a large number (N) in which the events are in question C will happen on pN occasions, and out of these pN occasions D will happen on $p'(pN)$ or $pp'N$ occasions. The probability that they both happen is therefore pp'.

This rule is known as the "multiplication" rule, and its application to the probabilities of happening or otherwise of two independent events may be seen from a consideration of the following schedule.

Let the probabilities of happening of two independent events be p and p' respectively. Then

(i) the chance that they both happen $= pp'$;

(ii) the chance that the first happens and the second fails
$$= p\,(1 - p');$$

(iii) the chance that the second happens and the first fails
$$= p'\,(1 - p);$$

(iv) the chance that they both fail $= (1 - p)\,(1 - p')$.

The total of these chances

$$= pp' + p\,(1 - p') + p'\,(1 - p) + (1 - p)\,(1 - p')$$
$$= pp' + p - pp' + p' - pp' + 1 - p - p' + pp'$$
$$= 1,$$

which is obviously true, since we have exhausted all the possibilities.

If the two events are not independent, we may still apply the multiplication rule. Let p_1 be the chance of happening of an event, and p_2 the chance of happening of a second *when the first has happened*. The chance that they both should happen is $p_1 p_2$.

Care must be taken to distinguish between independent and dependent events. In considering independent events the happening of either event does not affect the happening of the other, and to find the probability that they both happen we multiply the simple probabilities of each event. Where the events are not independent, we must find the chance p_2 that the second happens when the first has happened before we can apply the multiplication rule. For example, if there be two urns, one containing one white and two coloured balls, and the other one white and three coloured balls, the probability that the combined result of two drawings, one from each urn, will give the two white balls is $\frac{1}{3} \times \frac{1}{4}$, since the drawing from the first urn in no way affects the drawing from the second. If, however, we were required to find the chance that in two successive drawings from an urn containing two white and five coloured balls the two white balls would be drawn (a ball drawn not being replaced) we should reason thus. The chance that a white ball is drawn at the first drawing is $\frac{2}{7}$; *after this has happened* there will be left one white and five coloured balls, and the chance of drawing the other white ball at the second drawing will be $\frac{1}{6}$. The combined chance is therefore $\frac{2}{7} \times \frac{1}{6}$.

6. The multiplication rule can be applied to the probability of happening of any number of independent events. If $p, p', p'', \ldots$ be the chances of the events happening severally, the chance that they all happen is $pp'p'' \ldots$.

Again, if the chance that an event happens in a single trial be p, the chance that it will happen in each of r trials is p^r, and the chance that it will fail in each of, say, $(n - r)$ trials is $(1 - p)^{n-r}$.

Suppose that it is desired to find the chance that an event will happen *exactly* r times in n trials.

Let the chance that in any one trial the event does not happen be $q (= 1 - p)$. Then if the event happen in r trials and fail in $n - r$, the combined chance is $p^r q^{n-r}$. But of the n trials we can select the r trials in which the event happens in n_r ways. The chance that the event happens in exactly r trials out of the n is the chance that it happens in these r trials and fails in the remaining $n - r$ trials. The required chance is therefore $n_r p^r q^{n-r}$.

Now it will be noted that $n_r p^r q^{n-r}$ is the term containing p^r in the expansion of $(p + q)^r$. The successive terms of this expansion will therefore give the probabilities of the event happening $n, n - 1, n - 2, \ldots n - r, \ldots$ times exactly in n trials.

7. The application of the above principles can best be appreciated by reference to actual examples.

Example 6.

Find the chance that (i) three heads, (ii) two heads and one tail will turn up in three successive spins of a coin.

    (i) The chance of a head at the first   spin $= \frac{1}{2}$

       ,,   ,,   second ,, $= \frac{1}{2}$

       ,,   ,,   third   ,, $= \frac{1}{2}$

          Total chance $= (\frac{1}{2})^3 = \frac{1}{8}$.

    (ii) The chance of a tail is the same as that of a head, so that the total chance might appear to be $(\frac{1}{2})^3$ as before. This is in fact the chance that 2 heads and 1 tail occur in a specified order, say, HTH. The conditions of the question would, however, be satisfied if the order were HHT or THH. These three favourable events are mutually exclusive. The chance that the two heads and tail are obtained in one of the three orders is found by adding the three probabilities. The required chance is therefore $3 \times (\frac{1}{2})^3 = \frac{3}{8}$.

Example 7.

Find the chance of drawing a king, a queen and a knave in that order from an ordinary pack in three consecutive draws, the cards drawn not being replaced.

This is an example of the application of the multiplication rule to dependent probabilities.

If p_1 be the chance of drawing a king;

p_2 „ „ „ a queen, a king having been drawn;

p_3 „ „ „ a knave, a king and a queen having been drawn,

then the chance of drawing a king, a queen and a knave in succession is $p_1 p_2 p_3$.

Now there are 4 kings in the pack, so that the chance of drawing a king is $\frac{4}{52}$. When the king has been drawn there are 51 cards left of which 4 are queens. The chance of drawing a queen is therefore $\frac{4}{51}$. Similarly, the chance of drawing a knave from the remaining 50 cards is $\frac{4}{50}$.

$$p_1 = \tfrac{4}{52}; \quad p_2 = \tfrac{4}{51}; \quad p_3 = \tfrac{4}{50}.$$

The required chance $= p_1 p_2 p_3 = \dfrac{4^3}{52 \cdot 51 \cdot 50}$.

Example 8.

A bag contains three balls, one red, one white and one blue. X and Y draw a ball at random alternately. If X draws the red ball or Y the white ball it is retained. Otherwise the ball drawn is immediately replaced. Find the chance that just before the fifth draw is made the blue ball only is in the bag.

Let R, W, B denote the red, white and blue ball respectively. Now the blue ball is the only one in the bag just before the fifth draw if any of the following have happened:

	X first draw	Y first draw	X second draw	Y second draw
(i)	R	B	B	W
(ii)	R	B	W	W
(iii)	B	W	R	B
(iv)	W	W	R	B
(v)	R	W	B	B
(vi)	B	R	R	W
(vii)	B	B	R	W
(viii)	W	R	R	W
(ix)	W	B	R	W

The chances of these events happening are: Product

(i)	$\frac{1}{3}$	$\frac{1}{2}$	$\frac{1}{2}$	$\frac{1}{2}$	$\frac{1}{24}$
(ii)	$\frac{1}{3}$	$\frac{1}{2}$	$\frac{1}{2}$	$\frac{1}{2}$	$\frac{1}{24}$
(iii)	$\frac{1}{3}$	$\frac{1}{3}$	$\frac{1}{2}$	1	$\frac{1}{18}$
(iv)	$\frac{1}{3}$	$\frac{1}{3}$	$\frac{1}{2}$	1	$\frac{1}{18}$
(v)	$\frac{1}{3}$	$\frac{1}{2}$	1	1	$\frac{1}{6}$
(vi)	$\frac{1}{3}$	$\frac{1}{3}$	$\frac{1}{3}$	$\frac{1}{2}$	$\frac{1}{54}$
(vii)	$\frac{1}{3}$	$\frac{1}{3}$	$\frac{1}{3}$	$\frac{1}{2}$	$\frac{1}{54}$
(viii)	$\frac{1}{3}$	$\frac{1}{3}$	$\frac{1}{3}$	$\frac{1}{2}$	$\frac{1}{54}$
(ix)	$\frac{1}{3}$	$\frac{1}{3}$	$\frac{1}{3}$	$\frac{1}{2}$	$\frac{1}{54}$

The total chance is therefore $\frac{2}{24} + \frac{2}{18} + \frac{1}{6} + \frac{4}{54} = \frac{47}{108}$.

Note. A systematic enumeration of possibilities is of great importance, and although in the above example the work may be shortened by alternative methods, for illustrative purposes the eventualities have been set out in full.

Example 9.

A bag contains three red and three green balls and a person draws out three at random. He then drops three blue balls into the bag and again draws out three at random. Show that he may just lay 8 to 3 with advantage to himself against the latter three balls being all of different colours.

After the insertion of three blue balls the bag may contain:

	Red	Green	Blue
(a)	3	--	3
(b)	2	1	3
(c)	1	2	3
(d)	-	3	3

The probability that the bag contains (a) is $\frac{3}{6}.\frac{2}{5}.\frac{1}{4}$ or $\frac{1}{20}$, for the chance that a green ball is drawn is obviously $\frac{3}{6}$, the chance that a second green ball is drawn is $\frac{2}{5}$ and the chance of a third green ball is then $\frac{1}{4}$. Similarly, the chances under (b), (c), (d) are $\frac{9}{20}, \frac{9}{20}, \frac{1}{20}$ respectively.

Now three different colours on the second draw can only be obtained if the six balls come under headings (b) and (c).

Under (b) the probability at the second draw of drawing three different coloured balls is $\frac{6}{20}$, and therefore the compound probability that this will happen is $\frac{6}{20}.\frac{9}{20}$. Under (c) the probability is the same.

The total chance is the sum of these and amounts to $\frac{27}{100}$. Therefore, since the odds against the favourable happening are 73 to 27, the person drawing the balls may lay 8 to 3 against his drawing three of different colours and obtain a slight advantage.

Example 10.

Q is the probability that a man aged x will die in a year. Find the probability that out of five men, A, B, C, D, E, each aged x, A will die in the year and be the first to die.

The chance that a given man dies in the year $= Q$.
The chance that a given man does not die in the year $= 1 - Q$.
The chance that none of the five dies in the year $= (1 - Q)^5$.
The chance that at least one man dies in the year $= 1 - (1 - Q)^5$.

Since the chance that A is the first to die is obviously $\frac{1}{5}$, and since this is independent of the chance that at least one man dies in the year, the required chance $= \frac{1}{5} \{1 - (1 - Q)^5\}$.

8. The methods for the solution of the above examples depend largely on the simple application of the formulae for permutations and combinations. It is safer as a general rule to use permutations rather than combinations. If repetitions are not allowed this is not very material, as each combination of r things forms $r!$ permutations. If, however, repetitions are allowed then in most instances it is *essential* to use arrangements.

Other algebraic devices are often useful. For example, in dealing with questions involving the sum of the numbers that can be thrown with dice and kindred problems dealing with homogeneous products, it is of advantage to employ the binomial theorem.

The following examples illustrate the use of this method.

Example 11.

Four dice are thrown. Find the chance that the sum of the numbers appearing will be 18.

Regard being had to the different ways of making up the same total, the number of numbers that can be thrown with four dice is the sum of the coefficients in the expansion

$$(x + x^2 + x^3 + x^4 + x^5 + x^6)^4.$$

The sum of the coefficients will be found by putting $x = 1$. The total number of possible numbers is therefore 6^4.

The number of ways of throwing 18 is the coefficient of x^{18} in the above expansion.

The coefficient of x^{18} in $(x + x^2 + x^3 + x^4 + x^5 + x^6)^4$

$=\quad$,, $\quad x^{18}$ in $x^4 (1 + x + x^2 + x^3 + x^4 + x^5)^4$

$=\quad$,, $\quad x^{14}$ in $(1 + x + x^2 + x^3 + x^4 + x^5)^4$

$=\quad$,, $\quad x^{14}$ in $\dfrac{(1 - x^6)^4}{(1 - x)^4}$

$=\quad$,, $\quad x^{14}$ in $(1 - x^6)^4 (1 - x)^{-4}$

$=\quad$,, $\quad x^{14}$ in $(1 - 4x^6 + 6x^{12} \ldots) \left(1 + 4x + 10x^2 + \ldots \right.$

$$\left. + \frac{9 \cdot 10 \cdot 11}{6} x^8 + \ldots + \frac{15 \cdot 16 \cdot 17}{6} x^{14} + \ldots \right)$$

$$= \frac{15 \cdot 16 \cdot 17}{6} - \frac{4 \cdot 9 \cdot 10 \cdot 11}{6} + 6 \cdot 10 = 80.$$

The required chance is therefore $\dfrac{80}{6^4}$.

Note. We are here dealing with arrangements which would be distinguishable if one die were red, one blue, one yellow and one green. Selections in an example of this type would give quite wrong results.

Example 12.

Nine cards are drawn at random from a set of cards. Each card is marked with one of the numbers 1, 0 or -1, and it is equally likely that any of the three numbers will be drawn. Find the chance that the sum of the numbers on the cards thus drawn is zero.

The number of favourable drawings will be the coefficient of x^0 in the expansion of $(x^{-1} + x^0 + x^1)^9$; the total number of possible drawings will be the sum of all the coefficients in the same expansion.

The coefficient of x^0 in $(x^{-1} + x^0 + x^1)^9$

$=\quad$,, $\quad x^0$ in $x^{-9} (1 + x + x^2)^9$

$=\quad$,, $\quad x^9$ in $(1 + x + x^2)^9$

$=\quad$,, $\quad x^9$ in $(1 - x^3)^9 (1 - x)^{-9}$.

Proceeding on the same lines as in Example 11, the required probability is found to be $\dfrac{3139}{3^9}$.

9. The theory of probability was evolved from a consideration of games of chance, and many problems dealing with these games can be solved by the elementary methods outlined above. No new principles are involved; all that is required in attacking these problems is a clear understanding of the particular happenings that may arise. The following examples are illustrative of the methods: the first of these examples is analysed fully, and the student should be able to solve problems of the same type by the application of similar reasoning.

Example 13.

A and B throw alternately with a pair of ordinary dice. A wins if he throws six before B throws seven, and B if he throws seven before A throws six. If A begins, show that his chance of winning is $\frac{30}{61}$. (Huyghens' Problem.)

First, let us consider the chances of throwing six or seven with two dice. We can find the number of ways of throwing these numbers either by actually counting the number of ways (as in Example 5) or by finding the coefficients of x^6 and x^7 in the expansion of $(x + x^2 + x^3 + x^4 + x^5 + x^6)^2$ (as in Example 11). Since the figures are small, the first way is simpler, and it is easily seen that six can be thrown in 5 ways, and seven in 6 ways. The chance of throwing six in one throw with the two dice is therefore $\frac{5}{36}$, and of throwing seven $\frac{6}{36}$.

A can win if he throws six the first time. His chance of throwing this number is $\frac{5}{36}$.

He may fail to throw six the first time. He can then win if B fails to throw seven at his first throw and A throws six with his second throw.

The chance that A fails to throw six is $1 - \frac{5}{36} = \frac{31}{36}$.

The chance that B throws seven is $\frac{6}{36}$ and the chance that he fails to throw this number is $1 - \frac{6}{36} = \frac{30}{36}$.

Therefore the chance that A wins at the second throw is $\frac{31}{36} \cdot \frac{30}{36} \cdot \frac{5}{36}$.

If A fails to win at the second throw, he can win at the third throw if B has not thrown seven at his second throw. The chance of this is

$$\frac{31}{36} \cdot \frac{30}{36} \cdot \frac{31}{36} \cdot \frac{30}{36} \cdot \frac{5}{36} \qquad \text{and so on.}$$

A's chance of winning in the long run, i.e. after a very large number of trials, is therefore

$$\frac{5}{36} + \frac{31}{36} \cdot \frac{30}{36} \cdot \frac{5}{36} + \frac{31}{36} \cdot \frac{30}{36} \cdot \frac{31}{36} \cdot \frac{30}{36} \cdot \frac{5}{36} + \dots$$
$$= \frac{5}{36} (1 + r + r^2 + r^3 + \dots),$$

where $r = \frac{31}{36} \cdot \frac{30}{36}$.

If we sum this geometrical progression to infinity, we find that A's chance

$$= \frac{5}{36} \frac{1}{1 - r} = \frac{5}{36} \cdot \frac{1296}{366} = \frac{30}{61}.$$

Example 14.

A and B play a match to be decided as soon as either has won two games. The chance of either winning a game is $\frac{1}{20}$ and of its being drawn $\frac{9}{10}$. What is the chance that the match is finished in 10 or less games?

If the match is *not* finished in 10 games, the following must occur:

  (i) All the games must be drawn; or

  (ii) A or B must win one game and the remaining 9 must be drawn; or

  (iii) A and B must each win one game and the remaining 8 must be drawn.

The chances of these mutually exclusive events are:

$$\text{(i)} \quad \left(\frac{9}{10}\right)^{10};$$

$$\text{(ii)} \quad \left(\frac{9}{10}\right)^{9} . \frac{1}{20} . 2 . 10,$$

since this result may occur in 10 different ways and either A or B may win;

$$\text{(iii)} \quad \left(\frac{9}{10}\right)^{8} . \left(\frac{1}{20}\right)^{2} . 10 . 9,$$

since the number of orders in which this may occur is $^{10}P_{2}$.

The chance that the match is not finished in 10 games is, by the addition rule,

$$\left(\frac{9}{10}\right)^{10} + \left(\frac{9}{10}\right)^{9} . \frac{1}{20} . 2 . 10 + \left(\frac{9}{10}\right)^{8} . \left(\frac{1}{20}\right)^{2} . 10 . 9$$

$$= \frac{9^{8} . 387}{2 . 10^{10}},$$

i.e. the chance that the match is finished in 10 games or less

$$= 1 - \frac{9^{8} . 387}{2 . 10^{10}} = \cdot17 \text{ approximately.}$$

Example 15.

A, B, C, D each throw two dice for a prize. The highest throw wins, but if equal highest throws are made by two or more players, those players continue. A throws 9, B throws 7. Find C's chance of winning the prize.

Consider the following scheme, showing the total number of possible ways in which C may win:

C may win if		Probability
C throws 12, D less than 12		$\dfrac{1}{6^2}\cdot\dfrac{35}{36}$
C throws 12, D 12, and C wins later ...		$\dfrac{1}{6^2}\cdot\dfrac{1}{6^2}\cdot\dfrac{1}{2}^*$
C throws 11, D less than 11		$\dfrac{2}{6^2}\cdot\dfrac{33}{36}$
C throws 11, D 11, and C wins later ...		$\dfrac{2}{6^2}\cdot\dfrac{2}{6^2}\cdot\dfrac{1}{2}^*$
C throws 10, D less than 10		$\dfrac{3}{6^2}\cdot\dfrac{30}{36}$
C throws 10, D 10, and C wins later ...		$\dfrac{3}{6^2}\cdot\dfrac{3}{6^2}\cdot\dfrac{1}{2}^*$
C throws 9, D less than 9 and C wins later (since A has thrown 9)		$\dfrac{4}{6^2}\cdot\dfrac{26}{36}\cdot\dfrac{1}{2}^*$
C throws 9, D 9, and C wins later ...		$\dfrac{4}{6^2}\cdot\dfrac{4}{6^2}\cdot\dfrac{1}{3}^*$

The total of these chances is $\frac{383}{1944}$.

10. Most probable value.

It is essential to distinguish between the absolute probability of an event, the average number of times that it may happen over a series of trials and the most probable number of times that it will occur. The *most probable value* is the value that occurs with greatest frequency, and in simple examples this value can be easily determined by considering separately the contingency of each event. Thus, in a single throw with two dice the numbers that may turn up and the chances of occurrence of these throws are given in the following table:

Possible numbers: 2 3 4 5 6 7 8 9 10 11 12
Chances of occurrence: 1 2 3 4 5 6 5 4 3 2 1 ($\div$ 36)

The most probable number to be thrown is therefore 7.

Again, in Example 17 below, a hasty conclusion would be that half the pack (i.e. 26 cards) would have to be turned up before two aces out of the four would appear. This is not so, however.

---

* The final factor in each of these terms expresses the chance that C will win after having equalled the number thrown by D and/or A.

The four aces divide the remaining 48 cards into 5 groups. If a large number of such divisions were made the average number in each of the 5 groups would be 48/5. The average number of cards which must be turned up before two aces appear is therefore 2 of these groups plus 2 aces, i.e. 96/5 + 2 or 21·2, as given below. The solution on p. 330 shows that 26 is neither the average number nor the most probable number, and, further, that there is a definite probability associated with each number of cards turned up. At the risk of labouring the point, it must be emphasized that these separate probabilities are only to be realized over a long series of trials.

Example 16.

A purse contains two half-crowns and three shillings; a second purse one half-crown and four shillings. A coin is drawn from the first and placed in the second, and then a coin is drawn from the second and placed in the first. Assuming that the chance of drawing a half-crown is twice that of drawing a shilling, find the most probable value of the coins in the first purse after the second operation.

At the end of the second operation the first purse may contain:

(i) 2 half-crowns and 3 shillings; or
(ii) 3 ,, ,, 2 ,, ,,
(iii) 1 half-crown ,, 4 ,,

The respective chances are found thus:

(i) In order to achieve this result, a coin of the same value must be taken from the second purse at the second draw as was placed in this purse as the result of the first draw.

Since the chance of drawing a half-crown is twice that of drawing a shilling, the chance that a half-crown is drawn from the first purse originally is $\frac{4}{7}$. The second purse will then contain 2 half-crowns and 4 shillings, and the chance of drawing a half-crown from this purse is $\frac{4}{8}$. The total chance that a half-crown is drawn on both occasions is therefore $\frac{4}{7} \cdot \frac{4}{8}$.

Similarly, the chance that a shilling is drawn both times is $\frac{3}{7} \cdot \frac{5}{7}$.

The total chance that the coins in the first purse have the same value at the end of the two operations is therefore

$$\frac{4}{7} \cdot \frac{4}{8} + \frac{3}{7} \cdot \frac{5}{7} = \frac{29}{49}.$$

By proceeding similarly, it can easily be shown that the respective chances under headings (ii) and (iii) are $\frac{6}{49}$ and $\frac{2}{7}$.

The greatest of these values is $\frac{29}{49}$.

The most probable value of the purse after the second draw is the value associated with this fraction, namely 8 shillings.

Example 17.

Cards are dealt one by one from an ordinary pack (without replacements) until two aces have appeared. Find (i) how many cards (on the average) will be turned up, (ii) the most probable number of cards to be turned up.

(i) Since two aces cannot appear until the second trial at the earliest, we have

Chance of success at the second trial $= \frac{4}{52} \cdot \frac{3}{51}$.

,, ,, third ,, $= 2 \cdot \frac{48}{52} \cdot \frac{4}{51} \cdot \frac{3}{50}$.

,, ,, fourth ,, $= 3 \cdot \frac{48}{52} \cdot \frac{47}{51} \cdot \frac{4}{50} \cdot \frac{3}{49}$.

.... ,

and generally

Chance of success at the xth trial $= \dfrac{(x - 1)(52 - x)(51 - x).4.3}{52.51.50.49}$.

The average number of cards to be turned up will be the sum of the series whose xth term is

$$x \left\{ (x - 1)(52 - x)(51 - x) \frac{4.3}{52.51.50.49} \right\}$$

for all values of x from 2 to 50 (since there must be two aces at least in the first 50 cards).

Summing this by ordinary algebraic or finite difference methods, it is found that the average number of cards to be turned up is 21·2.

(ii) The most probable number to be turned up will be the value of x which gives

$$\frac{(x - 1)(52 - x)(51 - x) 4.3}{52.51.50.49}$$

its greatest value.

The value for $x = r >$ the value for $x = r - 1$ so long as

$$(r - 1)(52 - r)(51 - r) > (r - 2)(53 - r)(52 - r),$$

i.e. so long as $\quad -r^2 + 52r - 51 > -r^2 + 55r - 106,$

i.e. so long as $\quad\quad\quad 55 > 3r,$

i.e. r is not greater than 18 (since r must be integral).

The most probable number of cards to be turned up is therefore 18.

11. Expectation and probable value.

The probability of happening of an event may be combined with a measure of the quantity depending on the event, thus producing an *expectation*. In other words, expectation is the product of an expected gain in actual value and the mathematical probability of obtaining such a gain. No special difficulty arises in this type of question, and the methods outlined above may equally well be applied to the solution of problems involving expectation. All that is necessary is to combine the respective chances with the gains in value should the events occur. Thus, if a player throwing an ordinary die is to receive $£\frac{1}{2^n}$, where n is the number of throws that he takes to throw the first 6, his expectation would be

$$\frac{1}{6}£\frac{1}{2} + \frac{5}{6}\cdot\frac{1}{6}£\frac{1}{2^2} + \frac{5}{6}\cdot\frac{5}{6}\cdot\frac{1}{6}£\frac{1}{2^3} + \dots + \left(\frac{5}{6}\right)\cdot\frac{1}{6}£\frac{1}{2^{r+1}} + \dots,$$

the sum of which is $£\frac{1}{7}$.

Probable value is the same as expectation, except that it refers to the things in question and not to the person. For example, in Example 16, the probable value of the coins in the purse at the end of the second operation (i.e. the expectation of the person drawing the coins) is

$$\tfrac{29}{49} \times 8 \text{ shillings} + \tfrac{6}{49} \times 9\tfrac{1}{2} \text{ shillings} + \tfrac{2}{7} \times 6\tfrac{1}{2} \text{ shillings}$$
$$= 7\tfrac{37}{49} \text{ shillings}.$$

In other words, it would be worth while to give about 7s. 9d. for the purse after the second draw.

The following example is instructive:

Example 18.

A table is divided into six squares numbered 1 to 6. A player places a coin on a certain square. Three dice are thrown. If the number thus backed appears once, twice or thrice, the player receives back his own coin together with one, two or three others respectively of the same value. In any other event he loses his stake. Does the advantage in the long run lie with the player or the "banker"?

(a) The chance that no die shows the number backed $= \left(\tfrac{5}{6}\right)^3$.

(b)   ,,   one die   ,,   ,, $= 3\cdot\left(\tfrac{5}{6}\right)^2\cdot\tfrac{1}{6}$.

(c)   ,,   two dice   ,,   ,, $= 3\cdot\tfrac{5}{6}\cdot\left(\tfrac{1}{6}\right)^2$.

(d)   ,,   three dice   ,,   ,, $= \left(\tfrac{1}{6}\right)^3$.

The net expectation of the player
$$= (b) + 2 (c) + 3 (d) - (a) = -\tfrac{17}{216},$$
and that of the banker
$$= - (b) - 2 (c) - 3 (d) + (a) = \tfrac{17}{216},$$
so that the advantage lies with the banker in the long run.

For a stake of a shilling it is easily seen that this advantage is just under a penny.

Here it might be contended that as the player is to receive back his own coin in addition to the prize, his expectation should be based on respective receipts of two, three or four units instead of one, two or three units, as appears in the above solution. His expectation on this basis might be argued as being $2 (b) + 3 (c) + 4 (d) - (a)$ or $\tfrac{74}{216}$, which would show a substantial advantage to the player. Further consideration would show, however, that if the return of the stake is treated as a *profit*, then the laying of the stake must be treated as a *payment* to the banker for the privilege of playing and that it is, accordingly, definitely paid away whether the player wins or loses. His expectation then becomes $2 (b) + 3 (c) + 4 (d) - 1 = -\tfrac{17}{216}$ as before.

12. In connection with mathematical expectation it is interesting to note the celebrated St Petersburg Problem, which has been a fruitful source of discussion for nearly two hundred years. Briefly stated, the problem is this: A coin is tossed until head turns up. If head turns up first A is to pay B one unit; if head does not turn up till the second throw B is to receive two units; if not until the third throw four units, and so on. How much must B pay A before the game, in order that the game may be considered fair? That is, what is B's expectation?

The theoretical solution is as follows:

At the first trial B's expectation is $\tfrac{1}{2} \times 1 \qquad = \tfrac{1}{2}$.

„ second „ „ $(\tfrac{1}{2})^2 \times 2 \quad = \tfrac{1}{2}$.

....

„ nth „ „ $(\tfrac{1}{2})^n \times 2^{n-1} = \tfrac{1}{2}$.

B's expectation is therefore $\tfrac{1}{2} + \tfrac{1}{2} + \tfrac{1}{2} + \dots$ to infinity, and as this is a divergent series, it appears that B could afford to pay an infinitely large sum before the game starts for his expectation.

Many explanations of this result have been given by eminent mathematicians, notably by d'Alembert, Bernouilli and de Morgan. An interesting account of the problem with an alternative solution depending upon the amount of money that B possesses at the outset is given by Whitworth in his *Choice and Chance*. This solution depends on a somewhat arbitrary assumption, and a more practical limitation of B's expectation arises from the fact that A's resources, however great, must be limited. Poincaré (*Calcul des Probabilités*, p. 42) shows that if A's total assets are 2^p, B's expectation is $1 + \frac{1}{2}p$. For example, if A possesses 2^{30}—which is more than a thousand millions—B's expectation is reduced from infinity to 16, and as Poincaré drily remarks, this is a considerable reduction!

13. The method of induction.

There is a certain type of problem in probability for which it is not possible to obtain a solution by the direct methods outlined in the preceding paragraphs. In these problems it is necessary to find a relation connecting the chance at any stage with that at succeeding stages and then to calculate the required probability by adopting an inductive process. The difficulty in these questions is to ascertain the fundamental relation: when this has been established the problem can be solved by the application of algebraic methods.

Since we have to obtain a relation connecting the probability of an event at the nth stage with those at succeeding stages, it is often of advantage to investigate the relation for simple numerical values of n and then to deduce the general result. The following is an excellent example of this method of solution.

Example 19.

Five green balls and sixteen red balls are placed in a bag. A ball is drawn at random n times in succession and replaced after each drawing. Find the chance that no two successive drawings shall have given green balls.

To satisfy the required conditions the events must have taken place as follows:

At the first draw either a red or a green ball must be drawn:

$$R$$
$$G$$

At the second draw one of the following draws must have taken place:

$$R \mid R \qquad\qquad R \ G$$
$$G \mid R$$

i.e. first drawing associated with R; or $R \ G$.

At the third draw:

$$\begin{array}{cc} R\ R\ |\ R & R\ |\ R\ G \\ G\ R\ |\ R & G\ |\ R\ G \\ R\ G\ |\ R & \end{array}$$

i.e. second drawing associated with R; or first drawing associated with $R\ G$.

At the fourth draw:

$$\begin{array}{cc} R\ R\ R\ |\ R & R\ R\ |\ R\ G \\ G\ R\ R\ |\ R & G\ R\ |\ R\ G \\ R\ G\ R\ |\ R & R\ G\ |\ R\ G \\ R\ R\ G\ |\ R & \\ G\ R\ G\ |\ R & \end{array}$$

i.e. third drawing associated with R; or second drawing associated with $R\ G$.

It is evident therefore that if we have attained success at the $(n-1)$th stage, i.e. if no two successive green balls have been drawn, we shall attain success at the nth stage provided that, either

(i) the nth draw gives a red ball;

or (ii) if the nth draw gives a green ball the drawing at the $(n-1)$th stage gave a red ball.

The chance of drawing a red ball $= \frac{16}{21}$, and the chance of drawing a green ball $= \frac{5}{21}$.

If therefore u_n be the required chance after n drawings, we shall have

$$u_n = \tfrac{16}{21} u_{n-1} + \tfrac{5}{21} \cdot \tfrac{16}{21} u_{n-2}.$$

This is a relation connecting three successive coefficients of the series

$$u_0 + u_1 x + u_2 x^2 + \ldots + u_{n-2} x^{n-2} + u_{n-1} x^{n-1} + u_n x^n + \ldots.$$

The series is therefore a recurring series with scale of relation

$$1 - \tfrac{16}{21} x - \tfrac{5}{21} \cdot \tfrac{16}{21} x^2.$$

Also $u_0 = 1$ and $u_1 = 1$, since the conditions are satisfied if no ball or one ball is drawn.

Proceeding in the usual way, we find that the generating function is

$$\frac{u_0 + x(u_1 - 16u_0/21)}{(1 + 4x/21)(1 - 20x/21)} \quad \text{or} \quad \frac{1 + 5x/21}{(1 + 4x/21)(1 - 20x/21)}$$

$$= \frac{25}{24} \cdot \frac{1}{1 - 20x/21} - \frac{1}{24} \cdot \frac{1}{1 + 4x/21}$$

$$= \frac{25}{24} \left(1 - \frac{20x}{21}\right)^{-1} - \frac{1}{24} \left(1 + \frac{4x}{21}\right)^{-1}.$$

The required chance, u_n, is the coefficient of x^n in these two expansions. This is easily seen to be

$$\tfrac{1}{24} \left[25 \left(\tfrac{20}{21} \right)^n - (-1)^n \left(\tfrac{4}{21} \right)^n \right].$$

Note. As an alternative method of obtaining the coefficients of $\left(\tfrac{20}{21} \right)^n$ and $\left(-\tfrac{4}{21} \right)^n$ we may say that $u_n = a \left(\tfrac{20}{21} \right)^n + b \left(-\tfrac{4}{21} \right)^n$. a and b can then be found from the conditions $u_0 = 1$ and $u_1 = 1$.

The following examples are illustrative of the same method of attack.

Example 20.

A player tosses a coin and is to score one point for every head turned up and two for every tail. He is to play on until his score reaches or passes n. If p_n is his chance of attaining exactly n, show that

$$p_n = \tfrac{1}{2} (p_{n-1} + p_{n-2})$$

and hence find the value of p_n.

There are two ways of reaching n exactly, namely, by throwing

(i) a tail when the score is $n - 2$; or

(ii) a head when the score is $n - 1$.

The respective chances are $\tfrac{1}{2} p_{n-2}$ and $\tfrac{1}{2} p_{n-1}$. Since these are mutually exclusive, we have

$$p_n = \tfrac{1}{2} (p_{n-1} + p_{n-2}).$$

The value of p_n may be found in either of two ways:

(a) $\qquad\qquad p_n = \tfrac{1}{2} (p_{n-1} + p_{n-2}),$

or $\qquad\qquad p_n + \tfrac{1}{2} p_{n-1} = p_{n-1} + \tfrac{1}{2} p_{n-2} \qquad \ldots\ldots(1).$

Also $\qquad\qquad p_1 = \tfrac{1}{2}$

and $\qquad\qquad p_2 = \tfrac{3}{4}$ } obviously $\qquad \ldots\ldots(2).$

By repetition of (1) and use of the facts in (2) we find that

$$p_n = 1 - \tfrac{1}{2} + \tfrac{1}{4} - \tfrac{1}{8} + \ldots + (-1)^{n-2} \frac{1}{2^{n-2}} + \tfrac{1}{2} (-1)^{n-1} \frac{1}{2^{n-1}},$$

which simplifies easily to

$$\frac{1}{3} \left\{ 2 + (-1)^n \frac{1}{2^n} \right\}.$$

(b) We may treat $1 - \tfrac{1}{2} x - \tfrac{1}{2} x^2$ as the scale of relation of a recurring series and proceed as in Example 19.

If the series is

$$p_0 + p_1 x + p_2 x^2 + p_3 x^3 + \ldots + p_{n-2} x^{n-2} + p_{n-1} x^{n-1} + p_n x^n + \ldots,$$

$$p_1 = \tfrac{1}{2}, p_2 = \tfrac{3}{4} \text{ and } p_0 = 1.$$

The generating function of the series is

$$\frac{1}{1 - \tfrac{1}{2} x - \tfrac{1}{2} x^2} = \frac{1}{(1 - x)(1 + \tfrac{1}{2} x)}.$$

By partial fractions this becomes

$$\frac{2}{3(1-x)} + \frac{1}{3(1+\frac{1}{2}x)}.$$

Expanding by the binomial theorem, we obtain for the value of p_n (the coefficient of x^n) the same result as is found by the first method.

Example 21.

A has 10 counters and B has 5; their chances of winning a single game are in the ratio 2 : 1. The loser in each game is to give a counter to his opponent. The game stops when one or the other has lost all his counters. Find A's chance of winning all B's counters.

Let u_n be A's chance of winning all B's counters when A has n counters. In the next game A must either win or lose a counter. His chances of these contingencies are $\frac{2}{3}$ and $\frac{1}{3}$ respectively. When he has lost the next game his chance of winning all B's counters is u_{n-1} and when he has won the next game it is u_{n+1}.

Hence $u_n = \frac{2}{3}u_{n+1} + \frac{1}{3}u_{n-1}$.

It is required to find u_n from the above relation, given that $u_{15} = 1$ (since A will then have won) and $u_0 = 0$ (since he will have lost).

The required relation for the recurring series is therefore

$$\tfrac{2}{3} - x + \tfrac{1}{3}x^2.$$

Since we may write this relation as

$$\tfrac{2}{3}\left(1 - \tfrac{3}{2}x + \tfrac{1}{2}x^2\right) = \tfrac{2}{3}\left(1 - \tfrac{1}{2}x\right)(1 - x),$$

we may put $u_n = a\left(\frac{1}{2}\right)^n + b$, and then obtain a and b from the values of u_0 and u_{15}.

This is a particular example of the problem of "duration of play." The problem in its general form gives m counters to A and n counters to B, and states that A's chances of winning, drawing and losing a single game are p, q, r respectively, where $p + q + r = 1$. The method of solution is precisely similar to that above.

The inductive method can be adapted to other types of question in probability. An excellent example will be found in *J.I.A.* vol. LVI, pp. 102–104, where a problem in direct probability is solved very simply by the inductive process.

14. We will conclude this chapter with some miscellaneous examples, including among them questions involving probabilities of living or dying. These problems require only a careful application of the ordinary methods, and no special comment is necessary.

Example 22.

Three men were known to be alive five years ago when their ages were 31, 48, 69. Assuming that of 98 males born together one dies annually until there are no survivors, find the chances that

(1) all are alive now;

(2) none are alive now;

(3) one, and only one, is alive now;

(4) two are alive and one dead.

The chance that a man aged x dies in five years is clearly $\dfrac{5}{98 - x}$.

The required probabilities are

(1) $\frac{62}{67} \cdot \frac{45}{50} \cdot \frac{24}{29}$;

(2) $\frac{5}{67} \cdot \frac{5}{50} \cdot \frac{5}{29}$;

(3) $\frac{62}{67} \cdot \frac{5}{50} \cdot \frac{5}{29}$ + two similar expressions;

(4) $\frac{62}{67} \cdot \frac{45}{50} \cdot \frac{5}{29}$ + two similar expressions.

As the above are the only possible events that can happen, the total of the chances is unity and the reader should verify this.

Example 23.

Three men, P, Q and R, are each of exact age 96. Find the chance that they will all die at different ages last birthday in the order P, Q, R given that

Exact age	Chance of dying before next exact age
96	$\frac{1}{2}$
97	$\frac{2}{3}$
98	$\frac{3}{4}$
99	1

We have to find the chance of their dying in a given order. There will be no need therefore to take into consideration the different orders in which the men may die.

(i) P may die at age 96   Chance $= \frac{1}{2}$.

Q may die at age 97, i.e. may survive a year and die in the following year   „ $= \left(1 - \frac{1}{2}\right) \frac{2}{3}$.

R may die at age 98 or later; i.e. may survive 2 years and die in the following year   „ $= \left(1 - \frac{1}{2}\right)\left(1 - \frac{2}{3}\right) 1$.

The total chance under this heading is therefore

$$\tfrac{1}{2} \times \left(1 - \tfrac{1}{2}\right) \tfrac{2}{3} \times \left(1 - \tfrac{1}{2}\right)\left(1 - \tfrac{2}{3}\right) 1 = \tfrac{1}{36}.$$

F   22

(ii) P may die at age 96   Chance $= \frac{1}{2}$.

Q ,,   98   ,, $= (1 - \frac{1}{2})(1 - \frac{2}{3})\frac{3}{4}$.

R ,,   99   ,, $= (1 - \frac{1}{2})(1 - \frac{2}{3})(1 - \frac{3}{4})\, 1$.

Total chance under heading (ii)

$$= \tfrac{1}{2} \times (1 - \tfrac{1}{2})(1 - \tfrac{2}{3})\tfrac{3}{4} \times (1 - \tfrac{1}{2})(1 - \tfrac{2}{3})(1 - \tfrac{3}{4})\, 1 = \tfrac{1}{384}.$$

(iii) P may die at age 97   Chance $= (1 - \frac{1}{2})\frac{2}{3}$.

Q ,,   98   ,, $= (1 - \frac{1}{2})(1 - \frac{2}{3})\frac{3}{4}$.

R ,,   99   ,, $= (1 - \frac{1}{2})(1 - \frac{2}{3})(1 - \frac{3}{4})\, 1$.

Total chance under heading (iii)

$$= (1 - \tfrac{1}{2})\tfrac{2}{3} \times (1 - \tfrac{1}{2})(1 - \tfrac{2}{3})\tfrac{3}{4} \times (1 - \tfrac{1}{2})(1 - \tfrac{2}{3})(1 - \tfrac{3}{4})\, 1 = \tfrac{1}{576}.$$

$$\text{Required chance} = \tfrac{1}{36} + \tfrac{1}{384} + \tfrac{1}{576} = \tfrac{37}{1152}.$$

Example 24.

The sum of two positive quantities is constant and equal to $2n$. Find the chance that the product of the two quantities is not less than $\frac{3}{4}$ their greatest product.

The product of two positive quantities whose sum is constant is greatest when the quantities are equal. The greatest product is therefore

$$\frac{2n}{2} \cdot \frac{2n}{2} = n^2.$$

If the two quantities are x and $2n - x$ we must have

$$x(2n - x) \geqslant \frac{3n^2}{4},$$

i.e. $4x^2 - 8nx + 3n^2 \leqslant 0,$

i.e. $(2x - 3n)(2x - n) \leqslant 0.$

Therefore x must lie between $\dfrac{3n}{2}$ and $\dfrac{n}{2}$.

The possible values of x range from 0 to $2n$, and the chance required is therefore

$$\frac{1}{2n}\left\{\frac{3n}{2} - \frac{n}{2}\right\} = \tfrac{1}{2}.$$

Example 25.

What is the chance that a hand of 5 cards contains a pair of 2 like cards of different suits?

This example is an excellent illustration of the manner in which a simple probability question can be capable of more than one reading. If the problem is to find the chance that of five cards two are to be like cards and the other three unlike, a result is obtained which is quite different from the chance that there are to be two like cards, it being immaterial what the other cards are. Moreover, this second reading is capable of two alternatives: there may be two like cards and two other like cards (e.g. two kings and two fours) in the five cards; or there may be three or more like cards—this is not expressly excluded by the question.

It will be instructive before setting down all the chances that are possible to examine what would seem to be the obvious solution.

Let N denote the number of ways of selecting five cards from 52.

Then
$$N = \frac{52 . 51 . 50 . 49 . 48}{5!}.$$

The probability of drawing exactly two like cards of given denomination (aces, say) will be

$$\frac{\frac{4 . 3}{2!} \times \frac{48 . 47 . 46}{3!}}{N} \text{ or } \frac{2162}{54145},$$

and since there are 13 different cards in each suit it might be thought that to multiply the above fraction by 13 would give the result. This answer is, however, incorrect, in that there is "overlapping," for the remaining three cards out of the five may be a pair of like cards which have already been counted.

The possible arrangements, with their respective chances, are

Arrangement	Chance	
(a) 4 like cards and 1 different	$\dfrac{48 \times 13}{N}$	or $\dfrac{1}{4165}$,
(b) 3 like cards and 2 like cards	$\dfrac{13 \times \frac{4 . 3 . 2}{3!} \times 12 \times \frac{4 . 3}{2!}}{N}$	or $\dfrac{6}{4165}$,
(c) 3 like cards and 2 different	$\dfrac{13 \times \frac{4 . 3 . 2}{3!} \times 4^2 \times \frac{12 . 11}{2!}}{N}$	or $\dfrac{88}{4165}$,
(d) 2 sets of 2 like cards, 1 different	$\dfrac{\frac{13 . 12}{2!} \times \frac{4 . 3}{2!} \times \frac{4 . 3}{2!} \times 44^{*}}{N}$	or $\dfrac{198}{4165}$,
(e) 2 like cards and 3 different	$\dfrac{13 \times \frac{4 . 3}{2!} \times 4^3 \times \frac{12 . 11 . 10}{3!}}{N}$	or $\dfrac{1760}{4165}$.

The reasoning to obtain these chances is straightforward, and it will be necessary to examine one only: the others are on the same lines.

* 44 because 8 cards are unallowable, being 4 of each of the previous numbers chosen. This avoids duplication with (b).

Consider the arrangement in which there are to be exactly two like cards and consequently three different ones. Having settled on the denomination of the like cards—which can be done in 13 ways—there remain 12 denominations from which to choose 3. This can be done in $\dfrac{12.11.10}{3!}$ ways. The two like cards can be selected from the four (one of each suit) in $\dfrac{4.3}{2}$ ways. This does not quite complete the selection, for the three different cards may be selected from any of the four suits, and this can be done in $4 \times 4 \times 4$ ways.

Returning now to the analysis above. If the problem is confined to the chance where exactly two like cards are to be chosen, the result will be (e); if there are not to be more than two like cards, two sets of two like cards being permitted, the chance will be $(d) + (e)$; if there are no restrictions, and we are given that two like cards at least are to be among the five, we shall require the total of the chances (a) to (e).

These results are respectively $\frac{1760}{4165}$, $\frac{1958}{4165}$, and $\frac{2053}{4165}$.

The above method of solution is designed to show, in full, the several probabilities of the various arrangements that may occur. If, however, it is known that there are no restrictions other than that there shall be at least two like cards, a simpler method of solving this problem obviously presents itself. It is sufficient to calculate the probability that there shall not be any like cards among the five; this probability is evidently the complement of that required. The probability that there are no like cards is

$$\dfrac{\dfrac{13.12.11.10.9}{5!}}{N} \times 4^5 \text{ or } \dfrac{2112}{4165},$$

the complement of which agrees with the third answer given above.

Example 26.

Ten clubs compete annually for a cup which is to become the absolute property of the club which wins it for three years in succession. Assuming that all the clubs are of equal skill, find the chance that last year's winners, not having won the previous year, will ultimately win the cup.

Let $\dfrac{x}{10}$ be A's chance of winning outright, A having won the previous year. Each of the others has a chance equal to

$$\dfrac{1 - \dfrac{x}{10}}{9},$$

since the clubs are of equal skill.

Now (a) A's chance of winning next year and the year after

$$= \left(\frac{1}{10}\right)^2.$$

(b) A's chance of winning, losing and then having the same chance as the other eight losing clubs

$$= \frac{1}{10} \cdot \frac{9}{10} \cdot \frac{1 - \dfrac{x}{10}}{9}.$$

(c) A's chance of losing and then having the same chance as the other eight losing clubs

$$= \frac{9}{10} \cdot \frac{1 - \dfrac{x}{10}}{9}.$$

A's total chance $= (a) + (b) + (c)$, and this we know to be $\dfrac{x}{10}$. Solving the resulting equation, we find that A's chance is $\frac{4}{37}$.

Note. The above solution assumes that the total probability of winning, for all the clubs, is unity, i.e. that the cup must eventually be won. It is easily seen that the cup must be won outright. If the chance that any particular club fails to win the cup outright after m trials is $1/n$ where n is greater than 1, then if there be an infinitely large number of sets of trials, the chance that the cup is never won outright by any particular club will not be greater than $\underset{k \to \infty}{\mathrm{Lt}} \left(\dfrac{1}{n}\right)^{km}$ which is obviously zero. In other words, if the contests be continued for a sufficient length of time, the chance that the cup is not won outright is zero, i.e. the cup must be won.

EXAMPLES 18

1. Explain how the probability of a compound event, consisting of two constituent simple events, is obtained. Illustrate your answer by examples.

2. The chance of one event happening is the square of the chance of a second event, but the odds against the first are the cube of the odds against the second. Find the chance of each.

3. If three squares are chosen at random on a chess board, show that the chance that they should be in a diagonal line is $\frac{7}{144}$.

4. A man has three current English coins. Find the chance that he can give change for half-a-crown.

5. *A* can hit a target four times in 5 shots; *B* three times in 4 shots; *C* twice in 3 shots. They fire a volley; what is the probability that two shots at least hit?

6. *A* and *B* stand in a ring with ten other persons. If the arrangement of the twelve persons is at random, find the chance that there are exactly three persons between *A* and *B*.

7. The first twelve letters of the alphabet are written down at random. What is the probability that there are four letters between the *A* and the *B*?

8. Find the chance of drawing two white balls in the first two draws from a bag containing five red and seven white balls, balls drawn not being replaced.

9. An experiment succeeds twice as often as it fails. Find the chance that in the next six trials there will be at least four successes.

10. If an experiment is equally likely to succeed or fail, find the chance that it will succeed exactly n times in $2n$ trials.

11. Find the chance of throwing ten with four dice.

12. If a die whose faces are numbered from 1 to 6 is thrown four times, what is the probability that the sum of the four throws is 14?

13. A five-figure number consisting of the digits 0, 1, 2, 3, 4 (no repetitions) is chosen at random. What is the chance that it is divisible by 4?

14. Out of a bag containing thirteen balls, six are drawn and replaced, and then seven are drawn. Find the chance that at least three balls were common to the two drawings.

15. If a die is thrown five times what is the probability that a six appears on at least two consecutive occasions?

16. What is the chance that a person with two dice will throw aces exactly four times in six trials?

17. There are m candidates taking an examination paper of n questions of equal difficulty; assuming that a candidate answers a question correctly or not at all, either being equally likely:

   (*a*) In how many different ways may a paper be answered?

   (*b*) How many different sets of answered papers are possible?

   (*c*) What is the chance that a set of papers is handed in in which a particular question is solved by not more than one candidate?

18. Six cards are chosen at random from a pack of 52. Find the chance that three will be black and three red.

19. A card is chosen at random from each of six packs of cards. Find the chance that three will be black and three red.

20. The 26 letters of the alphabet are placed in a bag. *A* and *B* alternately draw a letter from the bag, the letters drawn not being replaced. The winner is the one who draws most vowels. *A* starts and draws a vowel with his first draw. What is his chance of winning?

21. A book contains 1000 pages. A page is chosen at random. What is the chance that the sum of the digits of the number on the page is nine?

22. A bag contains three tickets marked with the numbers 00, 01, 10, and two tickets each marked with the number 11. A ticket is drawn at random eight times, being replaced each time. Find the probability that the sum of the numbers on the tickets thus drawn is 33.

23. If x be one of the first hundred numbers chosen at random, find the probability that $x + \dfrac{100}{x}$ is greater than 50.

24. In a lottery there are 1000 tickets numbered 1 to 1000. Three tickets are drawn. Find the chance that

    (1) the three tickets bear consecutive numbers;

    (2) two of the three bear consecutive numbers.

25. If m odd integers and n even integers be written down at random, prove that the chance that no two odd numbers are adjacent to one another is

$$\frac{n!\,(n+1)!}{(m+n)!\,(n-m+1)!},$$

m being not greater than $n + 1$.

26. The sum of two whole numbers is 100; find the chance that their product is greater than 1000.

27. There are ten tickets, five of which are numbered 1, 2, 3, 4, 5 and the other five are blank. What is the probability of drawing a total of 10 in three trials, one ticket being drawn and replaced at each trial?

28. If two of the first hundred numbers are chosen at random, what is the probability that their difference is greater than 10?

29. *A* and *B* have equal chances of winning a single game; *A* wants two games and *B* wants three games to win a match. Find the chance that *A* will win the match.

30. *A* and *B* play at a game which cannot be drawn. On the average *A* wins three games out of five. Show that it is more than 2 to 1 that *A* would win at least three games out of the first five.

31. *A*, *B*, *C* throw in order, each using three dice. Prove that *A*'s chance of throwing 10 first is $(\frac{8}{13})^2$ and find *C*'s chance.

32. *A* and *B* play for a prize. *A* is to throw a die first and is to win if he throws 6. If he fails, *B* is to throw and win if he throws 6 or 5. If he fails, *A* is to throw again and win if he throws 6 or 5 or 4, and so on. Find each player's chance of winning.

33. *A* and *B* play for a stake which is to be won by him who makes the highest score in four throws of a die. After 2 throws *A* has scored 12 and *B* 9. What is *A*'s chance of winning?

34. *A* and *B* play a set of games, to be won by the player who first wins four games, with the condition that if they each win three they are to play the best of three to decide the set. *A*'s chance of winning a single game is to *B*'s as 2 to 1. Find their respective chances of winning the set.

35. *A*, *B* and *C* draw in succession from a bag containing four white and eight black balls until a white ball is drawn. What is the probability that the white ball is drawn by *C*? Is his chance improved if each ball is replaced after drawing?

36. Three players of equal skill, *A*, *B* and *C*, play a series of games and the winner of each game scores one point. Each of the three keeps a separate score and the winner of the set is the one who first scores 4. *A* wins the first, *B* the second and *A* the third game. What is then *C*'s chance of winning the set?

37. *A* and *B* play a match of five games. *A*'s chances of winning, drawing and losing any game are in proportion to 3, 2 and 1 respectively. Two points are scored for a win and one for a draw. What is the chance that the match is drawn?

38. *A* and *B* play a match, the winner being the one who first wins two games in succession, no games being drawn. Their respective chances of winning any particular game are $p : q$. Find

(1) *A*'s initial chance of winning;

(2) *A*'s chance of winning after having won the first game.

39. Three players, *A*, *B*, *C*, play under the following conditions. In each turn the chance of success is the same for each of two contestants. *A* and *B* play together for the first turn, the winner plays with *C*, and

if he win again he wins the game; if not, C plays with the third man and so on until one man has won two turns in succession. Find each man's chance of winning the game.

40. The winner of a game is the one who first scores 4 points, but if both players score 3 points the game continues until one player has scored 2 points more than the other. A and B play; find A's chance of winning when the score is 2—0 in B's favour, being given that A is twice as skilful a player as B.

41. A, B, C, D each throw two dice for a prize. The highest throw wins, but if equal highest throws occur (thrown by two or more players) the players with these throws continue. A throws 10; find his chance of winning.

42. A and B cut a pack of cards, the player who wins the cut six times to be the winner. A, having won four times to B's once, cuts a five. Find the chance that A will be the winner.

43. A and B play a match consisting of a maximum of nine games. The chances that any game is won by A, won by B or drawn are equal. A win counts one point and a draw half a point (to each). The match ends when one of the players has a sufficient lead to leave him with an excess of points over his opponent even if the latter were to win all the remaining games. What is the chance that the match ends with the 7th game and not before?

44. Two persons throw an ordinary die alternately, and the first who throws 6 is to receive eleven shillings; find their expectations.

45. There are eleven tickets in a bag numbered 1, 2, 3, ... 11. A man draws two tickets together at random and is to receive a number of shillings equal to the product of the numbers he draws; find the value of his expectation.

46. A bag contains eighteen exactly similar counters. Ten counters are each of value a, four are each of value b and the remaining four are each of value $2b$. A man draws two counters at random. It is equally likely that any counter will be drawn. Find the ratio of a to b, if the value of the man's expectation is to be $4a/3$.

47. Each of two bags contains m sovereigns and n shillings. If a man draws a coin out of each bag, is he more or less likely to draw two sovereigns than if all the coins were in one bag and he drew two coins?

48. Purse A contains six shillings and two sovereigns, purse B seven shillings and one sovereign. Seven coins are transferred from A to B and then seven coins are transferred from B to A. Which purse is now likely to be the more valuable?

49. A bag contains thirteen counters marked with the squares of the first thirteen natural numbers respectively.

(1) A man draws a counter and is to receive the number of shillings equivalent to the number on the counter. Find his expectation.

(2) If the man is allowed to draw three counters and to reject the highest and lowest, find his expectation.

50. A purse contains five half-crowns and four shillings. A pays 5s. 3d. for the right to receive the value of three coins drawn at random. Criticize his bargain, and find the chance that, after two attempts, the second on the same terms as the first, he will be a winner.

51. A bag contains m white balls and two red balls. The balls are drawn from the bag one at a time without being replaced until a red ball is drawn. If $1, 2, 3, \dots$ white balls are drawn, A is to receive $1^2, 2^2, 3^2, \dots$ shillings respectively. Find his expectation.

52. A bag contains twenty shillings and three sovereigns. Coins are drawn in succession, one at a time, without being replaced, until two sovereigns have been drawn. What is the probable number of shillings left in the bag?

53. A bag contains a coin of value M, and a number of other coins whose aggregate value is m. A person draws one at a time till he draws the coin of value M. Assuming it is equally likely that any particular coin is drawn, find the value of his expectation.

54. A bag contains twenty white balls numbered 1 to 20 and ten unnumbered red balls. A ball is drawn at random and replaced, six times. Find the probability that

(1) at least three white balls are drawn;

(2) three white and three red balls are drawn;

(3) three red balls and Nos. 1, 2, 3 of the white balls are drawn.

What is the most probable number of white balls drawn, and what is the probability that this number is drawn?

55. A bag contains ten counters, numbered 1 to 10. One counter is drawn and replaced and this operation is repeated until four different numbers have appeared. Calculate the probability that success will be attained with the sixth draw.

56. If n is the product of any 69 integers taken at random, find, to the first significant place of decimals, the value of the probability that n is not a multiple of 5, given that $\log_{10} 2 = \cdot3010300$.

57. A bag contains counters marked with the digits 2, 4, 6, 8 and the number of times each digit occurs is equal to the value of the digit. Counters are drawn one at a time, each counter being replaced when drawn. What is the chance

(1) that the digit 2 is drawn before the digit 8;

(2) that the sum of the first three digits is 16;

(3) that the first five counters drawn contain one of those marked 4 or 6?

58. A and B have each eight pennies. Each tosses his set of pennies. Find to three places of decimals the chance that the number of heads obtained by A exceeds the number obtained by B by at least three.

59. At a certain age 99 per cent. of the persons alive at the beginning of the year will live to the end of the year. Find expressions for the probabilities that out of four persons of that age there will die within the year

(1) exactly 2;

(2) not more than 2;

(3) two specified persons;

(4) two specified persons and no others.

60. If the probability that exactly three lives out of six all aged x survive n years is $\cdot08192$, find the probability that at least three survive n years.

61. The probability that exactly one life out of three lives aged 20, 35 and 50, will survive 15 years is $\cdot092$; the probability that all will die within 15 years is $\cdot006$. If the probability that the life aged 20 will survive 15 years is $\cdot9$, find the probability that

(1) he will survive 30 years;

(2) he will survive 45 years.

62. Three men, A, B, C, are each aged 30. Given that the probability that a man aged 30 will survive 5 years is $\cdot974$ and the probability that he will survive 10 years is $\cdot940$, find the chance that between the end of the 5th year and the end of the 10th year from now

(1) one at least will die;

(2) all will die, A dying first and B second.

Find also the chance that A and B will die within this period and C will survive the 10th year.

63. Given that the probability that of three lives aged x one, and one only, will survive n years is 27 times the probability that all will die within n years, find the probability that

(a) at least two will survive n years;
(b) at least one will die within n years.

64. Given the following table, find the probability that of four persons aged 65 at least one will die between ages 75 and 85 and at least one after age 85:

Age	Probability of surviving 10 years
65	One-half
75	One-fifth

65. If m things are distributed amongst a men and b women, show that the chance that the number of things received by the group of men is odd is equal to

$$\frac{1}{2} \cdot \frac{(b + a)^m - (b - a)^m}{(b + a)^m}.$$

66. The sum of two positive quantities is constant and equal to $2n$. What is the chance that their product is less than $\frac{1}{2}n^2$?

67. A purse contains four half-crowns, three pennies and two shillings. Four coins are drawn at random. How many different sums can these amount to, and what is the most probable sum? (Assume that any one coin is as likely to be drawn as any other.)

68. How many times must a man be allowed to toss a penny so that the odds may be 100 to 1 that he gets at least one head?

69. A coin is tossed $m + n$ times $(m > n)$. Prove that the chance of at least m consecutive heads appearing is $\dfrac{(n + 2)}{2^{m+1}}$. Find also the chance of a run of exactly m consecutive heads.

70. If ten different things be distributed among three persons, show that the chance of a particular person having more than five of them is $\frac{1507}{19683}$.

71. If p be the chance that an odd number of aces turn up when n ordinary dice are thrown, show that $1 - 2p = (\frac{2}{3})^n$.

72. A pack of cards has been dealt in the usual way to four players. One player has just one ace; prove that the chance that his partner has the other three aces is $\frac{22}{703}$.

73. A bag contains a certain number of balls some of which are white. I am to get a shilling for every ball so long as I continue to draw white

only, the balls drawn not being replaced. An additional ball not being white is introduced and I claim as compensation to be allowed to replace every white ball that I draw. Is this fair?

74. There are three sets of cards, red, yellow and blue. Each set contains ten cards, numbered 1 to 10. Three cards are drawn at random. Find the chance that the sum of the numbers on them equals 15:

   (1) if the cards are all to be drawn from the red set;

   (2) if one card is to be drawn from each set;

   (3) if the cards are to be drawn from the three sets mixed indiscriminately.

75. From a bag containing ten red, ten white and ten blue balls one is to be drawn at random and replaced. The operation is to be repeated ten times. Find the chance that at least one ball of each colour will be drawn.

76. There are ten counters in a bag marked with consecutive numbers. Two counters are drawn from the bag. If the sum of the numbers drawn is odd, a man is to receive that number of shillings; if it is even, he is to pay that number of shillings. Find the man's expectation

   (1) if the counters are marked from 0 to 9;

   (2) if they are marked from 1 to 10;

   (3) if they are marked from 2 to 11.

77. Out of $3n$ consecutive integers three are selected at random. Find the chance that their sum is divisible by 3.

78. In a book of values of a certain function there is one error on the average in every m values. Find the number of times, r, a value must be turned up at random in order that you may have an even chance of turning up an erroneous value. Show that when m becomes large the ratio r/m tends to a fixed quantity and find this quantity.

79. A, B, C and five other football teams enter for a competition. The teams are of equal skill and are drawn by lot in pairs before each round, the winners of the previous round entering the next round. Find the chance that in the course of the competition A will beat B, having first beaten C.

80. A street consists of 24 houses numbered 1 to 24, odd numbers on one side, even on the other. Three houses are vacant. Assuming that the houses are all equally likely to be vacant, find the chances:

   (1) that the three houses are next to each other;

   (2) that all three are on the same side of the street;

   (3) that if they are all on the same side the sum of their numbers equals 42.

81. Find the chance that the sum of the numbers on three cards drawn at random from an ordinary pack of 52 cards amounts to 21, all the court cards counting as 10. How will the result be altered if an ace can count as 1 or 11?

82. If a coin be tossed 15 times, what is the probability of getting heads exactly as many times in the first 10 throws as in the last 5?

83. A bag contains eight counters numbered 1 to 8. Four are drawn at random. Find the chances that

   (1) the sum of the numbers on the four counters amounts to at least 17;

   (2) the counters numbered 2 and 3 are among the four;

   (3) the four counters contain at least two of the three numbers 3, 5, 7.

84. If $6n$ tickets numbered 0, 1, 2, ... $6n - 1$ are placed in a bag and 3 are drawn out, find the chance that the sum of the numbers on them is equal to $6n$.

85. From a bag containing nine red and nine blue balls nine are drawn at random, the balls being replaced. Show that the probability that four balls of each colour will be included is a little less than $\frac{1}{4}$.

86. A looks at a clock at some time between 2 and 5 p.m., all times within the limits being equally likely. He looks again when it strikes the next quarter hour. What is the chance that in the meantime the minute has overtaken the hour hand?

87. Four suits of cards, each suit consisting of 13 cards numbered from 1 to 13, are dealt to four persons. Find the chance that each person's cards contain all the numbers from 1 to 13.

88. There are four sets of calculations on one sheet which have to be made, then checked and finally scrutinized. A and B can calculate only, C and D can calculate or check, and E and F can scrutinize only. No person may check a calculation he has made and all work must be signed. Find the chance that when the sheet is finally completed each name of the above six appears exactly twice.

89. From an ordinary pack of cards a card is drawn and then six other cards at random. Find the chance that the card first drawn is the highest of its suit amongst all the cards drawn.

90. A coin is tossed until both head and tail have appeared twice.

   (1) On the average how many times will the coin have to be tossed?

   (2) What is the most likely of throws?

   (3) How many throws must a man be allowed if the odds in favour of success are to be 7 : 1?

91. A bag contains thirteen balls of which four are white and nine black. If a ball be drawn r times successively and replaced after each drawing, show that the chance that no two successive drawings shall have given white balls is

$$\frac{16 \cdot 12^r - (-3)^r}{15 \cdot 13^r}.$$

92. The reserved seats in a certain section of a concert-hall are numbered consecutively from 1 to 100. A man sends for five consecutive tickets for one concert and for eight consecutive tickets for another. Find the chance that there will be no number common to both sets of tickets.

93. In a cup draw there were four Southern and four Northern teams, the names being drawn one by one from a bag. Find the following probabilities:

(1) that each one of the four successive pairs consisted of one Southern and one Northern team;

(2) that each one of the four successive pairs consisted of two Southern or two Northern teams;

(3) that the first drawn in at least three of the pairs was a Southern team.

94. A number consists of seven digits whose sum is 59. Find the chance that it is divisible by 11.

95. Two dice are thrown and one of the players will win (a) if the sum be 7 or 11, or (b) if the sum be 4, 5, 6, 8, 9 or 10 and the same sum reappears before 7. Find the player's chance of success.

96. A and B cast alternately with two dice. It is agreed that, on each failure to win, the prize money is to be reduced by 3 per cent. of its value at the previous attempt. A wins if he throws 6 before B throws 7, and B wins if he throws 7 before A throws 6. A starts first. Compare the values of the respective chances of A and B.

97. A bag contains n counters marked 1, 2, 3, ... n. If two counters are drawn show that the chance that the difference of the counters exceeds m (less than $n - 1$) is

$$\frac{(n - m)(n - m - 1)}{n(n - 1)}.$$

Deduce from this result the chance that if two points are taken at random on a line the length between them exceeds half the length of the line.

98. A bag contains two white balls and one black ball. A drawing of two balls is made. If either is black, the two are replaced and another black ball is added. A second drawing of two balls is then made, and again if either is black, the two are replaced and another black ball is added and so on.

What is the chance that if the drawings are continued indefinitely two white balls will never be drawn together?

99. A's chance of scoring any point is $\frac{5}{4}$ of B's. A engages to score 14 in excess of B before B shall have scored 3 in excess of A. Show that A's chance of winning the match is equal to

$$\frac{1 - (\frac{4}{5})^3}{1 - (\frac{4}{5})^{17}}.$$

100. A and his wife engage in a "mixed doubles" tennis tournament in which each pair of players consists of one member of each sex. There are fourteen other persons, seven of each sex, also entered for the tournament and players are drawn by lot before each round in such a way that any person of one sex may be the partner of any person of the other sex. Only the winners in any one round enter the next round. Assuming that all the players of each sex are equal in skill, find the probability that in the final round A and his wife play together as partners.

101. All that is known about a quadratic equation is that the coefficients are all different and are positive integers less than 10. Find the chance that the roots of the equation are real, all the integral values of the coefficients satisfying the above conditions being equally likely, and zero values of the coefficients being excluded.

102. A pack of cards is dealt in the usual way to four players of whom two and two are partners and the dealer turns up his last card. Denoting by the term "honours" the ace, king, queen, knave of the suit to which the turned-up card belongs, find the chance that each pair of partners shall have two honours.

103. A number taken at random is squared. Find the chances that the following are even numbers:

        (1) the digit in the units place of the result;

        (2) the digit in the tens place of the result;

        (3) the digit in the hundreds place of the result.

104. Before commencing a game of cards four players cut for partners, i.e. the two highest play together and the two lowest together. All suits being of equal value, what is the chance that they will have to cut again?

105. *A* and *B* play a series of games to be won by the player who first wins two consecutive games. *A*'s chances of winning, losing or drawing any particular game are $\frac{1}{2}$, $\frac{1}{4}$ and $\frac{1}{4}$ respectively. Find *B*'s chance of winning the match (*a*) at the outset, (*b*) when he has just won one game, and (*c*) when he has just lost one game.

106. *A* and *B* have equal chances of winning a single game. *A* wants *n* games and *B* $n + 1$ games to win a match. Show that the odds on *A* are $1 + p$ to $1 - p$ where $p \equiv \dfrac{(2n)!}{n!\,n!\,2^{2n}}$.

107. Three posts are filled one after another by lot from amongst ten persons (*A, B, C, D*, and six others), the first by any one of the ten, the second by anyone except *A* and *B*, the third by anyone except *C* and *D*. What is the chance that *A* or *B* or both of them, and *C* or *D* or both of them, are chosen? No one can hold more than one post, and in drawing for the second and third posts the barred persons and any person previously chosen are excluded.

108. With a hand of thirteen cards a player is known to hold one ace. What is the chance that he has at least one other ace?

If it is known that the ace he holds is the ace of hearts, what is the chance that he has at least one other ace?

CHAPTER XIX

MEAN VALUE. THE APPLICATION OF THE CALCULUS TO THE SOLUTION OF QUESTIONS IN PROBABILITY

1. The ordinary arithmetical average of a number of quantities is the sum of the quantities divided by the number of the quantities. If there are n quantities $\phi(a), \phi(a + h_1), \phi(a + h_2), \ldots \phi(a + h_{n-1})$, then their average or *mean value* is

$$\frac{\phi(a) + \phi(a + h_1) + \phi(a + h_2) + \ldots + \phi(a + h_{n-1})}{n}.$$

Suppose that $y = \phi(x)$ is a function of x, and that x has the n successive values $a, a + h, a + 2h, \ldots a + (n-1)h$. Then the mean value of $\phi(x)$ for these n values from $x = a$ to $x = a + (n-1)h$ is, as above,

$$\frac{\phi(a) + \phi(a + h) + \phi(a + 2h) + \ldots + \phi(a + \overline{n - 1}h)}{n}.$$

Let $b = a + nh$ so that $nh = b - a$.

Then the mean value $= \dfrac{h}{nh} \sum_{r=0}^{r=n-1} \phi(a + rh)$

$$= \frac{h}{b - a} \sum_{r=0}^{r=n-1} \phi(a + rh).$$

If x varies continuously between a and b so that the number of values, n, tends to infinity, the mean value becomes

$$\underset{n \to \infty}{\mathrm{Lt}} \frac{h[\phi(a) + \phi(a + h) + \ldots + \phi(a + \overline{n - 1}h)]}{b - a}$$

$$= \frac{1}{b - a} \int_a^b \phi(x) \, dx.$$

It should be noted that the mean value depends on the law governing the selected values. For example, the mean value of the ordinate of a semicircle determined by ordinates passing through equidistant points along the diameter is different from the mean value determined by taking equidistant points along the circumference. It thus appears that the mean value of a continuous function $\phi(x)$ is not a definite quantity but a quantity varying according to the law assumed for the successive values of x.

2. This application of the integral calculus enables us to solve many problems involving mean values. The solution of these problems can generally be effected by the use of single integrals, although some of the more difficult questions necessitate the use of double integration. The two following examples illustrate the use of single integrals and, as will be seen, the solutions present little difficulty.

Example 1.

Find (i) the mean value of the ordinate, (ii) the mean value of the square of the ordinate of the curve $y = a \sin nx$ for the range $x = 0$ to $x = \dfrac{\pi}{n}$.

(i) We have to find the sum of the ordinates over the given range divided by the number of ordinates. Since the number of these ordinates will tend to infinity as the distance between them tends to zero, we shall have

$$\text{M.V.} = \frac{\displaystyle\int_0^{\frac{\pi}{n}} y\,dx}{\displaystyle\int_0^{\frac{\pi}{n}} dx} = \frac{\displaystyle\int_0^{\frac{\pi}{n}} a \sin nx\,dx}{\displaystyle\int_0^{\frac{\pi}{n}} dx}$$

$$= \frac{\left[-\dfrac{a}{n}\cos nx\right]_0^{\frac{\pi}{n}}}{\left[x\right]_0^{\frac{\pi}{n}}}$$

$$= \frac{-\dfrac{a}{n}\cos \pi + \dfrac{a}{n}\cos 0}{\dfrac{\pi}{n}}$$

$$= \frac{-\dfrac{a}{n}(-1) + \dfrac{a}{n}}{\dfrac{\pi}{n}}, \text{ since } \cos \pi = -1,$$

$$= \frac{2a}{\pi}.$$

(ii) Similarly

$$\text{M.V.} = \frac{\displaystyle\int_0^{\frac{\pi}{n}} a^2 \sin^2 nx\, dx}{\displaystyle\int_0^{\frac{\pi}{n}} dx}$$

$$= \frac{\displaystyle\int_0^{\frac{\pi}{n}} a^2 \tfrac{1}{2}\,(1 - \cos 2nx)\, dx}{\dfrac{\pi}{n}}$$

$$= \frac{\left[\tfrac{1}{2}u^2 x - \tfrac{1}{2}a^2\, \dfrac{1}{2n}\sin 2nx\right]_0^{\frac{\pi}{n}}}{\dfrac{\pi}{n}}$$

$$= a^2\,\frac{\pi}{2n}\Big/\frac{\pi}{n} = \tfrac{1}{2}a^2.$$

Example 2.

A straight line of length a is divided at random into two parts. Find the mean value of the rectangle contained by the two parts.

Let x be the length of one part; then $a - x$ is the length of the other part. The rectangle contained by the two parts is $x\,(a - x)$, and we have to integrate this function with respect to x. Also, since x may have any value from 0 to a, these values will be the limits of integration. Hence,

$$\text{M.V.} = \frac{\displaystyle\int_0^a x\,(a - x)\, dx}{\displaystyle\int_0^a dx}$$

$$= \frac{\displaystyle\int_0^a (ax - x^2)\, dx}{\displaystyle\int_0^a dx}$$

$$= \frac{\left[\dfrac{ax^2}{2} - \dfrac{x^3}{3}\right]_0^a}{\left[x\right]_0^a}$$

$$= \frac{\dfrac{a^3}{2} - \dfrac{a^3}{3}}{a}$$

$$= \frac{a^2}{6}.$$

Note. Since we are required to find the mean value of an area, the result must be of the second degree in a.

3. The use of double integrals.

Consider first a function, $\phi(x)$, involving a single variable x. Then the mean value of $\phi(x)$ between the limits $x = a$ and $x = b$ is

$$\sum_{x=a}^{x=b} \phi(x) \bigg/ \sum_{x=a}^{x=b} \mathbf{1}.$$

If there be a function $\psi(x, y)$ of two variables x and y, we may write similarly

$$\text{M.V.} = \sum_{x=a}^{x=b} \sum_{y=a}^{y=\beta} \psi(x, y) \bigg/ \sum_{x=a}^{x=b} \sum_{y=a}^{y=\beta} \mathbf{1},$$

where x and y proceed by small but finite intervals.

If these intervals, say $1/n$ and $1/m$ for x and y respectively, be very small, the numerator and denominator of this fraction will be very large.

Multiply both numerator and denominator by $(1/n \cdot 1/m)$, so that the fraction is

$$\sum_{x=a}^{x=b} \sum_{y=a}^{y=\beta} \psi(x, y) \frac{1}{n} \frac{1}{m} \bigg/ \sum_{x=a}^{x=b} \sum_{y=a}^{y=\beta} \mathbf{1} \frac{1}{n} \frac{1}{m}.$$

Replace the small quantities $1/n$ and $1/m$ by Δx and Δy, and find the limit when Δx and Δy each tend to zero. Then, since the limit of a quotient is the quotient of the limits of the numerator and denominator (provided that the limit of the denominator is not zero), we have

$$\text{M.V.} = \mathrm{Lt} \frac{\displaystyle\sum_{x=a}^{x=b} \sum_{y=a}^{y=\beta} \psi(x, y)\, \Delta y\, \Delta x}{\displaystyle\sum_{x=a}^{x=b} \sum_{y=a}^{y=\beta} \mathbf{1}\, \Delta y\, \Delta x}$$

when $\Delta x, \Delta y$ each tend to zero,

$$= \frac{\displaystyle\int_a^b \int_a^\beta \psi(x, y)\, dy\, dx}{\displaystyle\int_a^b \int_a^\beta dy\, dx}.$$

The following examples are illustrative of the method of application of double integrals.

Example 3.

A rod of length a is divided at random into three parts. Find the mean value of the sum of the squares on the three parts.

Let OP be the rod of length a. Take any point X in the rod distant x from O, and another point Y distant y from X. The squares on the three segments of the line will be x^2, y^2, $(a - x - y)^2$, respectively.

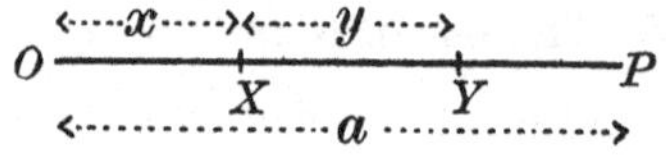

Fig. 39.

Let X be fixed. Then y will vary from o to $a - x$, so that the total values of the sum of the squares OX^2, XY^2, YP^2 will be

$$\Sigma \left[x^2 + y^2 + (a - x - y)^2 \right],$$

where y has every value from o to $a - x$.

Now let x vary. The limits of variation of x are evidently from o to a. Then

$$\text{M.V.} = \frac{\displaystyle\int_0^a \int_0^{a-x} \left[x^2 + y^2 + (a - x - y)^2 \right] dy\, dx}{\displaystyle\int_0^a \int_0^{a-x} dy\, dx}$$

$$= \frac{\displaystyle\int_0^a \int_0^{a-x} (2x^2 + 2y^2 + a^2 - 2ax - 2ay + 2xy)\, dy\, dx}{\displaystyle\int_0^a \int_0^{a-x} dy\, dx}$$

$$= \frac{\displaystyle\int_0^a \left[2x^2 y + \tfrac{2}{3} y^3 + a^2 y - 2axy - ay^2 + xy^2 \right]_0^{a-x} dx}{\displaystyle\int_0^a \left[y \right]_0^{a-x} dx}$$

$$= \frac{\displaystyle\int_0^a \left[2x^2 (a - x) + \tfrac{2}{3}(a - x)^3 + a^2(a - x) - 2ax(a - x) \right.}{\displaystyle\int_0^a (a - x)\, dx}, $$

$$\left. - a(a - x)^2 + x(a - x)^2 \right] dx$$

which becomes, on evaluating the integral,

$$\frac{\dfrac{a^4}{4}}{\dfrac{a^2}{2}} = \tfrac{1}{2} a^2.$$

It is important to note that if the sums of the required values can be obtained by considering separate sets of the values, the *total* sum must be found and divided by the total of the values. For example, if we could best solve a mean value problem by summing $\phi(x)$ for all values of x varying continuously from 0 to a, and $\psi(x)$ for all values from a to b, then we must write

$$\text{M.V.} = \frac{\int_0^a \phi(x)\,dx + \int_a^b \psi(x)\,dx}{\int_0^a dx + \int_a^b dx}$$

and not

$$\frac{\int_0^a \phi(x)\,dx}{\int_0^a dx} + \frac{\int_a^b \psi(x)\,dx}{\int_a^b dx}.$$

The fallacy in the second expression is easily seen when we consider that $\dfrac{A}{C} + \dfrac{B}{D}$ is not necessarily the same as $\dfrac{A+B}{C+D}$.

Example 4.

Find the mean value of the distance from one corner of a square to any point in the square.

Let $OABC$ be the square. Take any point X in the side OC distant x from O, and draw XM parallel to the side CB to meet the diagonal OB in M. Let Y be any point in XM distant y from X. The length $OY = \sqrt{x^2 + y^2}$ and

$$XM = OX = x.$$

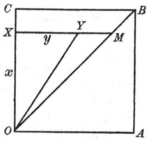

Fig. 40.

For a fixed value of x the sum of all values of OY, i.e. of $\sqrt{x^2 + y^2}$, will be

$$\overset{y=x}{\underset{y=0}{\Sigma}} \sqrt{x^2 + y^2},$$

since Y may take up all possible positions on the straight line XM. But x may have all values from 0 to a.

Therefore the sum of the distances from the corner O to any point in the triangle OBC

$$= \int_0^a \int_0^x \sqrt{x^2 + y^2}\,dy\,dx.$$

For the sum of the distances from O to any point in the square $OABC$ we must double this. The required mean value is therefore

$$\frac{2 \int_0^a \int_0^x \sqrt{x^2 + y^2}\, dy\, dx}{2 \int_0^a \int_0^x dy\, dx}$$

$$= \frac{1}{a^2} \int_0^a x^2 \left[\sqrt{2} + \log(1 + \sqrt{2})\right] dx,$$

on integrating with respect to y and inserting the limits o and x,

$$= \frac{a}{3} \left[\sqrt{2} + \log(1 + \sqrt{2})\right].$$

4. Application of the calculus to probability.

When we are dealing with problems in probability where the number of cases involved depends upon magnitudes varying continuously over a given range, the method of approach is similar to that outlined above for the solution of mean value problems. The general principle is to take the quotient of the number of favourable ways by the number of possible ways, where all ways are equally likely.

The application of the integral calculus to problems in probability is best illustrated by examples; as a general rule it is sufficient to employ single integrals, although in some instances it is of advantage to use double integration. Many problems can be solved by either method, and examples of both methods are given below.

Example 5.

A line of given length is divided into three parts by two points taken at random. Find the chance that no one part is greater than the sum of the other two.

We shall adopt the method of single integration for the solution of this question.

Let one of the random positions be at P distant x from the end A of the line, and let $AC = CB = \frac{1}{2}a$.

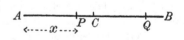

(i) Consider the favourable cases in which $AP\,(= x)$ is less than $\frac{1}{2}a$.

Fig. 41.

Take a point Q in the line such that $PQ = \frac{1}{2}a$. Then, for the conditions of the problem to be satisfied, the other random point R must lie in

CQ (otherwise PR will be greater than half the line and consequently greater than the sum of the other two parts AP, RB).

Now P lies in the small part dx between distances $x + dx$ and x from A, and since P has been taken at random, the chance that it falls in this small part is $\dfrac{dx}{a}$.

The chance that R lies in CQ is

$$\frac{CQ}{a} = \frac{AQ - AC}{a} = \frac{x + PQ - AC}{a} = \frac{x}{a},$$

since PQ and AC are each $\tfrac{1}{2}a$.

Therefore the total chance that P falls in dx and R in CQ is

$$\int_0^{\frac{1}{2}a} \frac{x}{a} \cdot \frac{dx}{a},$$

the limits of x being o and $\tfrac{1}{2}a$.

(ii) Consider the favourable cases in which AP $(= x)$ is greater than $\tfrac{1}{2}a$. Then, as above, R must lie in QC, the chance of which is

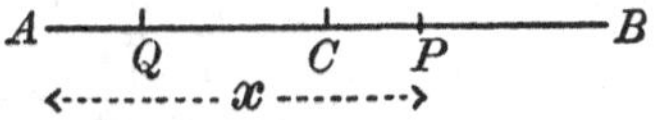

Fig. 42.

$$\frac{QC}{a} = \frac{PQ - CP}{a} = \frac{\tfrac{1}{2}a - x + \tfrac{1}{2}a}{a} = \frac{a - x}{a}.$$

Therefore, since the limits of x are now $\tfrac{1}{2}a$ and a, the chance that P falls in dx and R in CQ is

$$\int_{\frac{1}{2}a}^{a} \frac{a - x}{a} \cdot \frac{dx}{a}.$$

The total chance required

$$= \int_0^{\frac{1}{2}a} \frac{x}{a} \cdot \frac{dx}{a} + \int_{\frac{1}{2}a}^{a} \frac{a - x}{a} \cdot \frac{dx}{a}$$

$$= \frac{1}{a^2} \left[\tfrac{1}{2}x^2 \right]_0^{\frac{1}{2}a} + \frac{1}{a^2} \left[ax - \tfrac{1}{2}x^2 \right]_{\frac{1}{2}a}^{a}$$

$$= \frac{1}{a^2} \left(\frac{1}{2} \frac{a^2}{4} \right) + \frac{1}{a^2} (a^2 - \tfrac{1}{2}a^2 - \tfrac{1}{2}a^2 + \tfrac{1}{8}a^2)$$

$$= \tfrac{1}{4}.$$

Example 6.

Two points are selected at random on a line of length a. What is the probability that none of the three sections into which the line is thus divided is less than $\tfrac{1}{4}a$?

As an alternative this question will be solved by the use of double integrals.

Let AB be the given line divided into four equal parts at C, D, E. Now if P and Q be the random points, then to satisfy the required conditions neither can be in AC or EB.

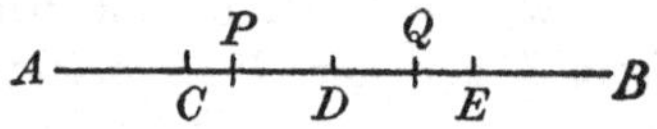

Fig. 43.

Let P be at distance x from A. Then the limits of x will evidently be $\frac{1}{4}a$ and $\frac{1}{2}a$. Let Q be at distance y from P; then Q can take up any position from $\frac{1}{4}a$ along the line from P to the point E. If the origin be at A, the limits of y will be $\frac{1}{4}a + x$ and $\frac{3}{4}a$.

Again, when P is fixed, all possible positions of Q will be from P to B, i.e. y can vary from x to a. Obviously x can vary from o to a.

Then by the unitary definition, the required chance is

$$
\frac{\int_{\frac{a}{4}}^{\frac{a}{2}} \int_{\frac{a}{4}+x}^{\frac{3}{4}a} dy\,dx}{\int_{0}^{a} \int_{x}^{a} dy\,dx} = \frac{\int_{\frac{a}{4}}^{\frac{a}{2}} \left[y\right]_{\frac{a}{4}+x}^{\frac{3}{4}a} dx}{\int_{0}^{a} \left[y\right]_{x}^{a} dx}
$$

$$
= \frac{\int_{\frac{a}{4}}^{\frac{a}{2}} [\frac{3}{4}a - \frac{1}{4}a - x]\,dx}{\int_{0}^{a} (a - x)\,dx}
$$

$$
= \frac{\left[\frac{3}{4}ax - \frac{1}{4}ax - \frac{1}{2}x^2\right]_{\frac{a}{4}}^{\frac{a}{2}}}{\left[ax - \frac{1}{2}x^2\right]_{0}^{a}}
$$

$$
= \tfrac{1}{16},
$$

on inserting the limits and simplifying.

Note. Each of the above two problems can be solved by the different methods here demonstrated. The two questions are exactly similar, and with the necessary alterations in the limits precisely the same working can be applied.

Example 7.

Two independent events, A and B, must each happen once and once only in the future. The chances of their happening in the interval from

t to $t + dt$ are proportionate to $a^t dt$ and $b^t dt$ respectively, where t is the time elapsed and a and b are constants (positive fractions). Find the chance that the two events happen in the order AB.

Let the chance that A happens at the moment of time dt be $ka^t dt$ and the chance that B happens be $lb^t dt$. Then, since the events must happen, we have

$$\int_0^\infty ka^t dt = 1 \quad \text{and} \quad \int_0^\infty lb^t dt = 1.$$

This gives $\quad k = -\log a \quad \text{and} \quad l = -\log b.$

Now the chance that B happens between now and time t from now

$$= \int_0^t lb^x dx.$$

Therefore the chance that B has not happened by that time

$$= 1 - \int_0^t lb^x dx.$$

The chance that A happens at the moment of time dt

$$= ka^t dt,$$

and the chance that A happens at that moment, B not having happened,

$$= \left(1 - \int_0^t lb^x dx\right) ka^t dt.$$

Therefore total chance that the events happen in the order AB

$$= \int_0^\infty \left(1 - \int_0^t lb^x dx\right) ka^t dt,$$

which becomes

$$\frac{\log a}{\log a + \log b}$$

on substituting for k and l and evaluating the integrals.

Example 8.

In a certain year A and B were in London for one period only in each case, A for one-third of a year, B for one-quarter of a year. Assuming that in the case of A any one period of one-third of a year and in the case of B any one period of one-quarter of a year is as likely as any other period, find the probabilities that

(1) A was in London the whole of the time that B was;

(2) A and B were not in London at any moment together;

(3) A and B were in London at some moment together;

(4) A came to London before B.

(1) The chance that A arrived in London at point of time between t and $t + dt$ from the beginning of the year is $\dfrac{dt}{\frac{2}{3}}$, since he must have arrived in the first two-thirds of the year.

The chance that B arrived in the one month permissible $= \dfrac{\frac{1}{12}}{\frac{3}{4}} = \dfrac{1}{9}$.

Therefore the chance that A was in London the whole of the time that B was $= \displaystyle\int_0^{\frac{2}{3}} \dfrac{1}{9} \dfrac{dt}{\frac{2}{3}} = \dfrac{1}{9}$.

(2) The chance that A and B were not in London together $=$ (a) the chance that B arrived after A had left $+$ (b) the chance that B left before A arrived.

For (a) B must have arrived between times $t + \frac{1}{3}$ and $\frac{3}{4}$, i.e. in the space of time $\frac{5}{12} - t$. The limits of t are 0 and $\frac{5}{12}$.

Therefore chance $= \displaystyle\int_0^{\frac{5}{12}} \dfrac{\frac{5}{12} - t}{\frac{3}{4}} \dfrac{dt}{\frac{2}{3}} = \dfrac{25}{144}$.

(b) B must have left between the times 0 and $t - \frac{1}{4}$, and the chance of event (b)

$$= \int_{\frac{1}{4}}^{\frac{2}{3}} \dfrac{t - \frac{1}{4}}{\frac{3}{4}} \dfrac{dt}{\frac{2}{3}} = \dfrac{25}{144}.$$

Total chance under this head $= \frac{25}{72}$.

(3) This is evidently the complement of (2) and is

$$1 - \tfrac{25}{72} \text{ or } \tfrac{47}{72}.$$

(4) If A came to London before B the chance is evidently

$$\int_0^{\frac{2}{3}} \dfrac{\frac{3}{4} - t}{\frac{3}{4}} \dfrac{dt}{\frac{2}{3}} = \dfrac{5}{9}.$$

5. Geometrical solutions.

Many of the above types of question can be solved by the aid of geometry. Since a definite integral represents an area, the ratio of the number of favourable ways to the total number of ways when there is continuous variation between the limits can evidently also be solved by relating the areas enclosed by parts of curves.

These curves or parts of curves may take the form of rectilinear figures, and in this event the problem can often be solved in a

simpler manner by the use of geometry than by having recourse
to the methods of the calculus.

Consider for instance Example 6 above:

If the straight line be divided at random into three parts
$x, y, a - x - y$, the following must hold to satisfy the conditions
of the problem:

$$x + y < a; \quad x, y, a - x - y \text{ each} > \tfrac{1}{4}a.$$

We have
$$\left. \begin{array}{c} x > \tfrac{1}{4}a \\ y > \tfrac{1}{4}a \end{array} \right\}$$

and
$$a - x - y > \tfrac{1}{4}a,$$

giving
$$x + y < \tfrac{3}{4}a.$$

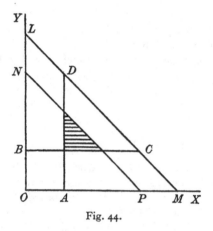

Fig. 44.

Draw the straight lines LM, $x + y = a$ and NP, $x + y = \tfrac{3}{4}a$
and complete the diagram as shown:

$$OM = a = OL; \quad OA = \tfrac{1}{4}a; \quad OB = \tfrac{1}{4}a; \quad AP = \tfrac{1}{2}a.$$

Then the above conditions may be illustrated thus:

$x > \tfrac{1}{4}a$ means that the points must be to the right of AD;
$y > \tfrac{1}{4}a$ means that the points must be above BC;
$x + y < \tfrac{3}{4}a$ means that the points must be below the line NP.

The only points satisfying all these conditions are contained in
the shaded area.

Similarly, for the total possible positions governed by the condition $x + y < a$, it will be seen that all possible points lie in the triangle LOM.

The required chance is therefore

$$\frac{\text{Shaded area}}{LOM} = \frac{\frac{1}{2}(\frac{1}{4}a)^2}{\frac{1}{2}a^2} = \frac{\frac{1}{32}a^2}{\frac{1}{2}a^2} = \frac{1}{16}, \text{ as before.}$$

6. We will conclude this chapter by solving a further problem by integral calculus and by plane geometry. The alternative solutions by integral calculus are given in order to show that there may be more than one method of approaching the question, and the geometrical solution is an excellent example of the application of elementary methods to a seemingly difficult problem.

Example 9.

X starts between 2.30 and 3 o'clock to walk at a uniform rate of 4 miles per hour from A through B and C to D. Y starts from D in the reverse direction between 2 and 3 o'clock and walks at a uniform rate of 3 miles per hour. From A to B is 2 miles, B to C 1 mile, C to D 3 miles. What is the chance that they meet between B and C assuming that between the given limits any time of starting is equally likely?

Method (i).

The chance that Y leaves D between t and $t + dt$ past 2 is $\dfrac{dt}{60}$. He arrives at C at t minutes past 3, and at B at $t + 20$ minutes past 3. The chance that he meets X between B and C is that X has not reached C by t minutes past 3, i.e. that Y has not started after $t + 15$ minutes past 2 and that X has reached B by $t + 20$ minutes past 3.

If X has reached B by $t + 20$ minutes past 3, he must have started by $t + 50$ minutes past 2.

In order to meet, X must have started between $(t + 15)$ and $(t + 50)$ minutes past 2; the earliest time cannot be before 2.30 and the latest after 3.

Therefore if t is 10 or less, X can start at any time between 30 and $t + 50$;

$$\text{chance} = \frac{t + 20}{30}.$$

If t is 10 to 15, X can start anywhere from 30 to 60;

$$\text{chance} = \frac{30}{30}.$$

If t is 15 to 45, X can start anywhere from $t + 15$ to 60;

$$\text{chance} = \frac{45 - t}{30}.$$

Required probability

$$= \int_0^{10} \frac{t + 20}{30} \frac{dt}{60} + \int_{10}^{15} \frac{30}{30} \frac{dt}{60} + \int_{15}^{45} \frac{45 - t}{30} \frac{60}{60}$$

$$= \tfrac{17}{36} \text{ (on evaluating the integrals)}.$$

Method (ii).

The chance that they *miss* is the sum of the chances that Y starts too early and Y starts too late.

(a) Y starts too early.

The chance that X reaches B between t and $t + dt$ minutes past 3 is $\dfrac{dt}{30}$.

As Y cannot reach B until 3.20, t must be greater than 20.

Therefore chance that Y is too early $= \displaystyle\int_{20}^{30} \frac{t - 20}{60} \frac{dt}{30} = \frac{1}{36}$.

(b) Y starts too late.

The chance that X reaches C between t and $t + dt$ minutes past 3 is $\dfrac{dt}{30}$, and the limits of these times are evidently 3.15 and 3.45.

The chance that Y has not arrived at C by t minutes past $3 = \dfrac{60 - t}{60}$.

Therefore chance that Y is too late $= \displaystyle\int_{15}^{45} \frac{60 - t}{60} \frac{dt}{30} = \frac{1}{2}$.

Therefore the chance that they *miss* $= \tfrac{1}{36} + \tfrac{1}{2} = \tfrac{19}{36}$.

Therefore the chance that they *meet* $= 1 - \tfrac{19}{36}$

$$= \tfrac{17}{36}.$$

Method (iii).

Let the straight line $ABCD$ represent the route.

Draw two straight lines at right angles to AD at A and D respectively and choose a suitable unit on both these straight lines to represent an hour. Then if X starts from A at 2.30 he would cover the distance AD by 4 o'clock; if he starts at 3.0 he would reach D by 4.30. Similarly, if Y starts at 2 o'clock he would reach A by 4 o'clock; if at 3 o'clock by 5 o'clock.

If, therefore, we join these points by the straight lines $A_1 D_1$; $A_2 D_2$ and DA_3; $D_4 A_4$, the rhombus $KLMN$ represents graphically the space of time over which it is possible for X and Y to meet.

Draw BB_1 perpendicular to AD meeting DA_3 and A_2D_2 in b_1, b_2 respectively, and CC_1 perpendicular to AD meeting A_1D_1 and A_2D_2

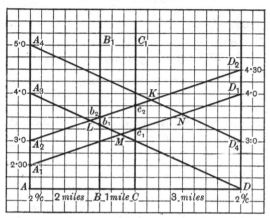

Fig. 45.

in c_1, c_2 respectively. Then the space of time over which X and Y can meet between the points B and C on their journey is represented by the area $b_2b_1Mc_1c_2$.

The required chance $= \dfrac{\text{area } b_2b_1Mc_1c_2}{\text{area } KLMN}$.

By simple geometrical methods the value of this is found to be $\frac{17}{36}$.

EXAMPLES 19

1. There are m posts in a straight line at equal distances of a yard apart. A man starts from any one and walks to any other; prove that the average distance which he will travel after doing this at random a great many times is $\frac{1}{3}(m+1)$ yards.

2. If two milestones be selected on a straight road n miles long, what is their average distance apart?

3. Two quantities are taken at random from 0 to a; find, by means of the integral calculus, the chance that the greater of the two is less than a given value b.

4. Find the mean value of the reciprocals of all quantities from n to $2n$.

5. A ladder of length x can be safely used, without its being secured, at any angle to the ground between $\dfrac{\pi}{4}$ and $\dfrac{\pi}{3}$. If any angle between these limits is equally likely, find the mean vertical height reached by the ladder in an infinite number of placings.

6. OP is a straight line of length p. A fixed point Q is taken in OP such that $OQ = q$. Two other points are taken at random in OP. Find the chance that they both fall in OQ.

7. A point is taken at random on a given finite straight line of length a. Find the mean value of the sum of the squares on the two parts of the line. Find also the chance of the sum being less than this mean value.

8. A semicircle, APB, stands on a base, AB, of length $2r$. P is a point on the circumference, and AP, BP are joined to form the right-angled triangle, APB. Find the mean value of the area of the triangle:

(1) if P is a point chosen on the circumference at random;

(2) if P is fixed by choosing a point N at random in the base AB, and erecting a perpendicular from N, to meet the circumference at P.

9. Find the mean value of the ordinate of a semicircle, the points along the diameter at which the ordinates are taken being equidistant.

10. In two opposite sides of a square, whose side is of length a, points P and Q are taken at random and are joined by the line PQ which thus divides the square into two pieces. Find the mean value of the area of the smaller of the two pieces.

11. Find the mean of the square of the distance of a point within a given square of side $2a$ from the centre of the square.

12. A straight line of length a is divided at random at two points. Find the mean value of the product of the three segments.

13. A point is taken at random within the area bounded by $y = x \log x$, the x-axis and the ordinates $x = 1$, $x = 4$. Find the probability that the distance of the point from the y-axis is less than 2.

14. Three points are taken at random on the circumference of a circle. Find the chance that the sum of any two of the arcs thus cut off is greater than the third.

15. A straight line is divided into three parts by two points taken at random. Find the chance that none of the three parts is greater than five-eighths of the line.

16. There are two clerks in an office, each of whom goes out for an hour for lunch. One may start at any time between 12 and 1 o'clock,

the other at any time between 1 and 2. All times within these limits are equally likely. Find the chance that they are not out together.

17. Find the chance that the roots of the equation $x^2 - 2ax + b = 0$ are real, where a and b are positive proper fractions chosen at random.

18. The point M is the centre of a line LMN of length $4a$. Two points P, Q on the line are chosen at random. Find the chance that the sum of the two distances MP and MQ is greater than a.

19. If on a straight line of length $(a + b)$ two lengths a and b are cut off at random, find the chance that the common part does not exceed a length c.

20. In a line AB of length $3a$, a point P is taken at random and then in AP a point Q is taken at random. What is the probability that PQ exceeds a?

21. The sides of a rectangle are taken at random each less than an inch and all lengths are equally likely. Find the chance that the diagonal is less than an inch.

22. Three points are taken at random on the circumference of a circle. Find the probability that they lie in the same semicircle.

23. Two points are taken at random on a given straight line of length a. Prove that the probability of their distance exceeding a given length c $(< a)$ is equal to $\left\{1 - \dfrac{c}{a}\right\}^2$.

24. OA and OB are straight lines of length a at right angles to one another. P and Q are points taken at random in OA and OB respectively. Find the chance that the area of the triangle OPQ is less than $\frac{1}{4}a^2$.

25. A starts to walk from X to Y 3 miles apart at 3 miles per hour. On the journey he unknowingly drops his handkerchief, but discovers his loss when he has covered half the remaining distance. He then proceeds to retrace his steps at 4 miles per hour. B starts on the same journey at 3 miles per hour 5 minutes after the handkerchief is dropped. Find his chance of reaching the place where it was dropped before A does.

Assuming that B picks it up, find the mean distance he would have to carry it to restore it to A if the series of events were to take place a large number of times.

26. Find the mean distance between two points on opposite sides of a square whose side is unity.

MISCELLANEOUS EXAMPLES

1. Find the sum of n terms of the series 1, 2, 4, 9, 19, 36, 62, ...

2. A person writes four letters and four envelopes. If the letters are placed in the envelopes at random, what is the chance that not more than one letter is placed in its correct envelope?

3. Make a rough sketch of the curve $y^2 = x^2 (1 - x^2)$. Find the maximum and minimum values of y and the area enclosed by the curve.

4. Given $u_0 = 1027$, $u_6 = 1212$, $u_{12} = 1469$, $u_{18} = 2014$, explain
   (i) how you would complete the series from u_0 to u_6;
   (ii) how you would proceed if you were asked to complete the series from u_6 to u_{12} supposing that it were unnecessary to find u_1, u_2, u_3, u_4 and u_5.

5. Differentiate (i) $\left(x + \dfrac{a}{x}\right)^{\frac{2}{3}}$; (ii) $\sin^{-1}(\sin^{-1}x)$.

6. Evaluate (i) $\underset{x \to 1}{\mathrm{Lt}} \dfrac{x^4 - 2x^3 + 2x^2 - 2x + 1}{x^3 - x^2 - x + 1}$;

   (ii) $\underset{\theta \to 0}{\mathrm{Lt}} \dfrac{\operatorname{cosec} \theta - \cot \theta}{\theta}$.

7. The faces of a cubical die are marked 1, 2, 2, 4, 6, 6. Find the chance that in ten throws, four 2's, two 4's, four 6's are thrown.

8. Integrate $\displaystyle\int \dfrac{x^2 + 4}{x^2 + 2x + 3}\, dx$ and $\displaystyle\int \dfrac{a^2 + b^2 \cos^2 x}{\cos x}\, dx$.

9. Find the tenth term of the series:
   (a) 1, 4, 13, 36, 97, 268, 765, ...;
   (b) 2, 12, 36, 98, 270, 768, ...

10. Show that $\Delta u_x v_x = v_x \Delta u_x + u_{x+1} \Delta v_x$ and hence prove by *mathematical induction* that

$$\Delta^n u_x v_x = v_x \Delta^n u_x + n\Delta v_x \Delta^{n-1} u_{x+1} + n_2 \Delta^2 v_x \Delta^{n-2} u_{x+2}$$
$$+ n_3 \Delta^3 v_x \Delta^{n-3} u_{x+3} + ...$$

11. A policy register of 384 pages contains particulars of 1920 policies, an equal number being entered on each page. 640 of the whole number are policies for £500, and 480 of the whole number have terminated. On how many pages of the register would you expect to find
   (a) at least one policy for £500 in force;
   (b) exactly one policy for £500 in force;
   (c) more than one policy for £500 in force?

12. Differentiate

$$\tan^{-1}\frac{bx-a}{ax+b}; \quad \sin^{-1}\frac{3+4x}{5\sqrt{1+x^2}}; \quad \cos^{-1}\frac{1-x^2}{1+x^2}.$$

13. Prove that in the process of obtaining divided differences of the function u_x, given u_a, u_b, u_c, ..., the last divided difference is numerically the same whatever the order of the arguments and the corresponding u's.

14. Given that

(1) $u_{-1} = 4$; $u_1 = 6$;

(2) the area between the curve $y = u_x$, the x-axis and the ordinates u_{-1} and u_0 is 4·7;

(3) the tangent to the curve $y = u_x$ at the point $(0, u_0)$ makes an angle θ with the x-axis such that $\tan\theta = \cdot 8$;

find an approximate value for u_0.

15. Show that

(1) $\Sigma x^m = C + \dfrac{x^{(2)}}{2!}\Delta o^m + \dfrac{x^{(3)}}{3!}\Delta^2 o^m + ...;$

(2) $\Sigma u_x = C + x^{(1)}u_0 + \dfrac{x^{(2)}}{2!}\Delta u_0 + \dfrac{x^{(3)}}{3!}\Delta^2 u_0 + ...$

16. Two Companies A and B make simultaneous issues each of 1000 bonds. Those of Company A are redeemable by equal drawings spread over 20 years, and those of B by equal drawings spread over 40 years. Find, in the case of two definite bonds, one of each issue:

(1) the probability that the bond of Company B is redeemed before the bond of Company A;

(2) the probability that the bond of Company B is redeemed before the bond of Company A and within 15 years of issue.

17. Prove that $\displaystyle\int_0^{\frac{\pi}{2}} \frac{dx}{1+2\cos x} = \frac{1}{\sqrt{3}}\log(2+\sqrt{3}).$

18. If u_0, u_5, u_{10}, u_{15} be four values of a function at equidistant points, find expressions true to third differences for u_6 and u_8, solely in terms of u_0, u_5, u_{10} and u_{15}.

19. The area of a curve is given by $A = y\sqrt{(25+4y)(4-y)}$. Plot A against y on squared paper and hence obtain the maximum value of A and the value of y for which A is a maximum. Verify your results by the methods of the calculus.

20. Define the following types of functions, giving examples: Inverse function; Rational Integral function; Multiple-valued function; Algebraic function.

$$\phi(x) = \frac{a^x - a^{-x}}{a^x + a^{-x}}. \quad \text{Prove that} \quad \frac{\phi(x) + \phi(y)}{1 + \phi(x)\phi(y)} = \phi(x + y).$$

21. Two throws are made, the first with three dice and the second with two. What is the probability both that the first throw is not less than 11 and that the second throw is not less than 8?

22. Prove that $\log(1 - x) + x(1 - x)^{-\frac{1}{2}}$ is positive for all values of x between 0 and unity.

23. A horizontal trough with vertical ends is of V-shaped cross-section, the angle between the sides being 60°, and the length of the trough 6 feet. If water enters at the rate of 4 cu. ft. per min., find the rate at which the surface is rising when the depth is 1 foot.

24. Show that the series whose nth term is

$$\frac{(-1)^{n-1}}{8^{n-1}} \frac{1 \cdot 3 \cdot 5 \cdots (2n - 3)}{(n - 1)!} \Delta^{2(n-1)} u_{x-2n+\frac{1}{2}}$$

is equivalent to

$$2(u_x - u_{x+1} + u_{x+2} - u_{x+3} + \ldots).$$

25. Obtain the approximate quadrature formula

$$\int_{-\frac{1}{2}}^{1\frac{1}{2}} u_x \, dx = \tfrac{1}{24}(27u_0 + 17u_1 + 5u_2 - u_3).$$

26. The numbers of members in a Friendly Society were available for the following years:

Year	1922	1923	1924	1925	1928
Number of members	995	998	1003	996	976

It was desired to obtain estimates for the years 1926 and 1927. This was effected on the assumption of a constant fourth difference. Subsequently it was discovered that the numbers for 1926 were actually 1002, and a fresh estimate for the year 1927 had to be prepared. Calculate the original estimates for 1926 and 1927, and find the revised figure for the year 1927.

27. If b and c are positive quantities ($b > c$) and if $\dfrac{3x^2 - bc}{6x - b - 3c}$ may have any value between b and c, all such values being equally likely, find the probability that x is real.

28. If m and n are positive integers, find by successive integration by parts the value of $\int_0^1 (1 - x^{\frac{1}{n}})^m \, dx$.

By expanding the integrand and integrating each term, deduce the value of the sum of the series

$$\frac{1}{n} - \frac{m_1}{n+1} + \frac{m_2}{n+2} - \frac{m_3}{n+3} + \ldots + (-1)^m \frac{m_m}{n+m},$$

where $m_r \equiv m!/r!\,(m-r)!$.

29. If $\log \theta = n \log t - \dfrac{x^2 + y^2}{4t}$, find what value of n will make

$$\frac{\partial^2 \theta}{\partial x^2} + \frac{\partial^2 \theta}{\partial y^2} = \frac{\partial \theta}{\partial t}.$$

30. If $\displaystyle\sum_{x=a}^{x=a+4} u_x = w_a$ for all integral values of a, prove that, to the third order of differences, $u_7 = \cdot 2w_5 - \cdot 008\,(w_{10} - 2w_5 + w_0)$.
Given the following table, find u_7, u_{12} and u_{17}:

a	$\displaystyle\sum_{x=a}^{x=a+4} u_x$
0	·0427
5	·1467
10	·2459
15	·3408
20	·4317

31. Transform the integral $\displaystyle\int_0^a x^2\,(a^2 - x^2)^{\frac{1}{2}}\,dx$ by the substitution $x = a \cos \phi$; and find its value, explaining by reference to a diagram what are the new limits of integration.

32. A reservoir has plane sloping sides and ends; its top and base are horizontal rectangles of sides 24 ft., 16 ft. and 12 ft., 8 ft. respectively, and its depth is 40 ft. If water flows into it at the uniform rate of 30 cu. ft. per minute, at what rate is the surface rising when the depth of the water is 10 ft.?

33. The lengths of day on March 19, April 18, May 18 and June 17 are 12 hours, 14 hours, 15 hours 40 minutes and 16 hours 30 minutes respectively. Obtain an equation in the form $y = f(x)$, where y is the length of day and x is the number of days elapsed since March 19, and apply it to ascertain the mean length of day from March 19 to June 17, both days inclusive.

34. If events A, B and C are independent of each other, and events E and F are mutually exclusive and are both contingent upon the happening of A, give an expression for the probability that either E or F will happen and that neither B nor C will happen.

35. The following formulae for approximate integration are correct to third differences:

$$\int_{-3}^{3} u_x dx = \tfrac{3}{4}(3u_{-2} + 2u_0 + 3u_2),$$

$$\int_{-3}^{3} u_x dx = (u_{-3} + 4u_0 + u_3).$$

Prove that if these formulae are applied to a function whose fifth differences are constant, the respective errors involved in the approximations are in the ratio 7 : 18, and are in opposite directions.

By a combination of the two formulae obtain an expression, correct to fifth differences, for $\int_{-3}^{3} u_x dx$.

36. Draw the graph of $y = x^3 - 3x + 1$. By reference to the graph, supplemented by arithmetical trials, find approximately the value of the negative root of the equation $x^3 - 3x + 1 = 0$, correct to two places of decimals.

37. Define a differential coefficient. If Δx is a finite increment, is it ever true that $\dfrac{\Delta y}{\Delta x}$ is equal to $\dfrac{dy}{dx}$?

If V be the volume of a regular polyhedron, and x the length of an edge, what is the meaning of $\dfrac{dV}{dx}$, and of $\dfrac{d^2V}{dx^2}$? Illustrate with a regular tetrahedron.

38. $u_1 = 3$; $u_2 = 44$; $\left(\dfrac{du}{dx}\right)_{x=1} = 25$; $\int_0^1 u_x dx = -\tfrac{71}{12}$. Find u_0.

39. A and B throw in turn with two dice, A having the first throw. A is to win either (1) if he throws a double six in his first six throws or (2) if he throws a double six before B has a throw scoring 9 or more. Find an expression for A's chance of winning.

40. Find the mean length of a straight line drawn from one of the angular points of an equilateral triangle to a point taken at random in any one of the sides.

41. Find an expression, correct to fourth differences, for the value of $\dfrac{du_x}{dx}$ when $x = 1$, in terms of $u_{-2}, u_{-1}, u_0, u_1, u_2$.

42. Evaluate $\int_0^1 x^2 \tan^{-1} x\, dx$ and $\int_0^{\frac{\pi}{2}} \sin^4 x\, dx$.

43. Three numbers are selected at random, one at a time, from the five numbers 1, 2, 3, 4 and 5, repetitions being allowed. Find the probability that the third number selected is not less than the second and the second is not less than the first.

44. By means of the formula (taking $n = 10$)

$$\sum_{x=0}^{x=mn} u_{a+x} = n \sum_{x=0}^{x=m} u_{a+nx} - \frac{n-1}{2} (u_{a+mn} + u_a)$$

$$- \frac{n^2 - 1}{12} \left[\left(\frac{du_x}{dx} \right)_{x=a+mn} - \left(\frac{du_x}{dx} \right)_{x=a} \right] \text{approx.,}$$

find the approximate value of $\log_{10} \dfrac{50!}{9!}$, given that $\log_{10} 2 = \cdot 3010$, $\log_{10} 3 = \cdot 4771$, $\log_{10} e = \cdot 4343$.

45. If $x = \tan \phi - \phi$ and $y = \sec \phi$, prove that $\left(\dfrac{dy}{dx} \right)^4 + y^3 \left(\dfrac{d^2y}{dx^2} \right) = 0$.

46. Prove that $\displaystyle\int \frac{dx}{x \sqrt{x+a}} = \frac{2}{\sqrt{a}} \log \frac{\sqrt{x}}{\sqrt{x+a} + \sqrt{a}} + K$.

Hence prove that

$$\int \frac{(1 + x^2)\, dx}{(1 - x^2) \sqrt{1 + x^4}} = \frac{1}{\sqrt{2}} \log \frac{\sqrt{1 + x^4} + x \sqrt{2}}{1 - x^2} + K.$$

47. Show that $x^2 - 2x + 4 \log (x + 2)$ increases with x from $x = -2$ to $x = -1$, then diminishes from $x = -1$ to $x = 0$ and then increases.

48. Given that

$u_0 = 16;\ u_1 + u_2 = 64;\ u_3 + u_4 + u_5 = 266;\ u_6 + u_7 + u_8 + u_9 = 1029$, find the values of u_4 and u_5, on the assumption that $\Delta^3 u_x$ is constant.

49. Through two points taken at random in a diagonal of a square, two straight lines are drawn parallel to one of the sides and to each other. Find the probability that the area of that part of the square between the two lines is not less than one-third of the area of the whole square.

50. If n be a positive integer find the limit when $n \to \infty$ of

$$\left[\left(1 + \frac{1}{n} \right) \left(1 + \frac{2}{n} \right) \left(1 + \frac{3}{n} \right) \cdots \left(1 + \frac{n}{n} \right) \right]^{1/n}.$$

51. Two straight roads meet at X at an angle of $\sin^{-1} \frac{3}{5}$. A is travelling in the direction of X along one of the roads at 40 miles an hour, and B is walking along the other road, also towards X, at the rate of 4 miles an hour. When A is 62 miles from X, B is 81 miles from X. Find their minimum distance apart.

52. *A* and *B* play a match of seven games. *A*'s chances of winning, drawing and losing any game are as $5 : 3 : 2$. One point is scored for a win and half a point for a draw. Find the chance that the match is drawn.

53. Prove that $u_1 - u_2 + u_3 - \ldots = \tfrac{1}{2}u_1 - (\tfrac{1}{2})^2\Delta u_1 + (\tfrac{1}{2})^3\Delta^2 u_1 - \ldots$, where u_n is a real positive quantity which diminishes as n increases, and $\underset{n \to \infty}{\text{Lt}}\, u_n = 0$.

In the series $1 - \tfrac{1}{3} + \tfrac{1}{5} - \tfrac{1}{7} + \ldots$ find the value of $\Delta^r u_n$ and prove that this series is equivalent to the series

$$\frac{1}{2}\left[1 + \frac{1}{3} + \frac{1 \cdot 2}{3 \cdot 5} + \frac{1 \cdot 2 \cdot 3}{3 \cdot 5 \cdot 7} + \ldots\right].$$

54. Use the conception of finite differences to prove that the general term in the recurring series $u_0 + u_1 x + u_2 x^2 + u_3 x^3 + \ldots$ (scale of relation $1 - px - qx^2$) is of the form $Aa^n + Bb^n$, where a and b are functions of p and q, and A and B are constants.

Prove that every series whose coefficients form an arithmetical progression is a recurring series, and that the generating function is

$$\frac{a + (d - a)\,x}{(1 - x)^2},$$

where a is the first term and d the common difference of the progression.

55. Given $u_{-2} = 4$, $u_0 = 6 \cdot 5$, $u_2 = 6 \cdot 3$, and that u_x has a maximum value when $x = 1$, find an approximate value for u_1.

56. A bag contains four black balls and eight white balls. Two balls are drawn at a time and replaced, this operation being performed six times. Calculate the probability that two black balls are not drawn four times consecutively.

57. Find the value of $\displaystyle\int\frac{P\,dx}{1 + e^x}$, where P has the values

(i) e^x;   (ii) 1;   (iii) e^{2x};   (iv) e^{-x}.

58. If $x = y^3 + 3a^2 y$ for real values of y, find by means of Maclaurin's theorem the expansion of y in powers of x as far as the term involving x^3.

59. Obtain a formula for the finite integration of any rational integral function of x and apply it to find the sum to n terms of the series whose rth term is $(r^2 + 1)(r - 2)$.

60. $a_{25:30} = 16 \cdot 311$; $a_{30:30} = 15 \cdot 784$; $a_{25:35} = 15 \cdot 660$;

$a_{35:30} = 14 \cdot 420$; $a_{25:40} = 14 \cdot 824$; $a_{30:35} = 15 \cdot 209$.

Find as accurately as possible $a_{27:32}$.

61. A and B toss a coin in turn, a head counting two and a tail one. The winner is the person who first scores a total of exactly three. If either tosses a head when his score is already two, his score is reduced to one. Calculate A's chance of winning the game if he has the first toss.

62. Two points are chosen at random on the circumference of a circle of radius r. Find the chance that the length of the chord joining them is less than $r\sqrt{3}$.

63. Find the value of $\dfrac{d}{dt}\displaystyle\int_0^{\log t} e^{tx}\,dx$, where t is independent of x.

64. If $A = x/(2x + z)$ and $B = -A^2 y/x$, prove that
$$\frac{\partial^2 A}{\partial z^2} = \frac{\partial^2 B}{\partial z\,\partial y}.$$

65. A person X walks along the diagonal of a square field $ABCD$ from B to D at the uniform rate of 5 feet per second. A second person Y proceeds along the side of the field from B to C at such a rate that the positions of X and Y at any moment lie on a straight line which, when produced, would pass through A. At what speed is Y moving when X has walked one-fourth of the distance from B to D?

66. A die whose sides are marked 1, 2, 3, 4, 5, 6 is thrown five times. Find the probabilities:

    (a) that the product of the five throws is 432;

    (b) that the sum of the first three throws is exactly three more than the sum of the last two throws.

67. Show that the infinite series $1 - \frac{1}{5} + \frac{1}{7} - \frac{1}{11} + \frac{1}{13} - \frac{1}{17} + \ldots$ can be expressed in the form
$$\int_0^1 \frac{1 - x^4}{1 - x^6}\,dx$$
and hence deduce its value.

68. Complete the series u_5 to u_{15} by means of Everett's formula:

x	-5	0	5	10	15	20	25
u_x	61·0	91·4	113·6	134·2	179·4	238·0	296·2

69. If $\qquad u_0 + u_1 x + u_2 x^2 + u_3 x^3 + \ldots = f(x)$,
show that
$$u_0 v_x + u_1 v_{x+1} + u_2 v_{x+2} + \ldots = f(1)\,v_x + f'(1)\,\Delta v_x + \frac{f''(1)}{2!}\,\Delta^2 v_x + \ldots.$$

70. The probability that A will die within ten years is ·2 and the probability that A, B, C will all be alive ten years hence is ·42. The probability that at least one of the three will be alive ten years hence is ·985. Find the probability that A and B alone will be living at the end of the tenth year.

71. Integrate

$$\text{(i) } \int x \, (1 + x)^{-\frac{1}{3}} \, dx; \qquad \text{(ii) } \int \frac{3 \sin x - 5 \cos x}{4 \sin x + \cos x} \, dx.$$

72. A closed circular cylinder of height h is to be inscribed in a given sphere of radius R. If the whole surface of the cylinder, including the base and the lid, is to be a maximum, prove that

$$\frac{h^2}{R^2} = 2 \left(1 - \frac{1}{\sqrt{5}} \right).$$

73. Show that $\dfrac{d}{dx} \{(1 + 1/x)^x\} = e/2x^2$ approximately, if x is large.

74. A man constantly stakes a fixed proportion of his property in a fair wager in which if he wins he will increase his property by $1/m$th part, and if he loses he will decrease it by $1/n$th part. Show that in the long run he will lose.

75. The equation $x^3 + 2x - 20 = 0$ has a root between 2·4 and 2·5. Determine the value of this root correct to four decimal places by a method of inverse interpolation.

76. A large army consists of men between ages 20 and 40, the number at age x being proportionate to $a + bc^x$, where a, b and c are constants. If the numbers at ages 20, 30 and 40 are proportionate to 100, 68 and 20 respectively, find, correct to one decimal place, the average age of the men in the army. Given

$$\log_{10} 2 = \cdot 301, \quad \log_{10} 3 = \cdot 477 \quad \text{and} \quad \log_{10} e = \cdot 4343.$$

77. Show that

$$\frac{d^n}{dx^n} \left\{ \frac{\log x}{x^m} \right\} = \frac{(-1)^n \, n!}{(m-1)! \, x^{m+n}} \left\{ \frac{(m+n-1)!}{n!} \log x - \sum_{r=0}^{r=n-1} \frac{(m+r-1)!}{r! \, (n-r)} \right\}.$$

78. The winner of a game is the one who first scores four points with the proviso that if two players score three points, the game continues until one player has scored two points more than the other. A's skill is to B's as 2 : 1. Find A's chance of winning the game if he owes one point and B receives a start of one point.

79. (i) Prove that $e^x = \left(\dfrac{\Delta^2}{E} \right) e^x \cdot \dfrac{E e^x}{\Delta^2 e^x}$ (interval of differencing h).

(ii) If u_x be a function of the form

$$b_1 x + b_2 x^2 + b_3 x^3 + \dots \text{ to infinity,}$$

show that it can be expressed in the form

$$u_x = \frac{b_1 x}{1 - x} + \frac{\Delta b_1 x^2}{(1 - x)^2} + \frac{\Delta^2 b_1 x^3}{(1 - x)^3} + \dots.$$

80. (i) If $K/(y - u) = Kv/(t - x) = (1 + v^2)^{\frac{1}{2}}$, where $v = du/dt$ and K is a constant, find the differential coefficient of y with respect to x.

(ii) Given that $be^{x/a} = \sin(y/a - c)$, find the value of
$$Dy\,[1 + (Dy)^2]/D^2y.$$

81. The following data are available:

Age x	32	37	42	47	52	57
e_x	35·36	33·25	30·72	27·23	23·16	19·11

It is desired to obtain $e_{57\frac{1}{2}}$ with as little labour as possible, and it is suggested that 18·71 would be a reasonable approximation. Do you agree with this? Give reasons.

From the above data, obtain a value for $e_{44\frac{1}{2}}$.

82. Evaluate $\displaystyle\int x^3 (\log x)^2\, dx$ and $\displaystyle\int \sin^2 x \cos^3 x\, dx$.

83. If u_x be a function whose differences, when the increment of x is unity, are denoted by $\delta u_x, \delta^2 u_x, \delta^3 u_x, \ldots$ and by $\Delta u_x, \Delta^2 u_x, \Delta^3 u_x, \ldots$ when the increment of x is n; then if $\delta^2 u_x, \delta^2 u_{x+1}, \ldots$ are in geometric progression with common ratio q, show that
$$\frac{\Delta u_x - n\delta u_x}{(q^n - 1) - n(q-1)} = \frac{\delta^2 u_x}{(q-1)^2}.$$

84. Show that
$$n_1 . 1^4 + n_2 . 2^4 + n_3 . 3^4 + \ldots + n^4 = 2^{n-4}\, n\,(n+1)\,(n^2 + 5n - 2).$$

85. A thin closed rectangular box is to have one edge n times the length of another edge and the volume is to be V. Prove that the least surface S is given by
$$nS^3 = 54\,(n+1)^2\,V^2.$$

86. Two men throw for a guinea, equal throws to divide the stake. A uses an ordinary die, but B uses a die marked 2, 3, 4, 5, 6, 6. Show that B thereby increases his expectation by 5/18ths.

87. Prove that if the polar coordinates of two points on the curve $r = f(\theta)$ be (r_1, θ_1) and (r_2, θ_2), the area contained by the curve and the two radii r_1 and r_2 is $\frac{1}{2}\displaystyle\int_{\theta_1}^{\theta_2} r^2 d\theta$.

Hence prove that the whole area of the curve $r^2 = a^2 \cos 2\theta$ is a^2.

88. Integrate $\displaystyle\int \frac{dx}{\sqrt{k} + \sqrt{x}}$ according as

    (i) k is a constant;

    (ii) $k = x - a$, where a is independent of x;

    (iii) $1/k = \sqrt{x}$.

89. Evaluate $\quad \underset{x \to 0}{\mathrm{Lt}} \dfrac{\log\left(1 + e^x\right) - \log 2 - \frac{1}{2}x}{x \log\left(x + \sqrt{1 + x^2}\right)}$,

and find the limit of

$$\frac{\log x + \log y}{x + y - 2} \quad \text{when } x \text{ and } y \text{ each} \to 1.$$

90. Explain the difference, if any, between $\Delta_x\Delta_y$ and Δ_{xy}.
Find $a_{44:51}$, given

$$a_{40:50} = 10\text{·}894 \qquad\qquad a_{40:55} = 9\text{·}796 \qquad\qquad a_{40:60} = 8\text{·}553$$
$$a_{45:50} = 10\text{·}591 \qquad\qquad a_{45:55} = 9\text{·}583$$
$$a_{50:50} = 10\text{·}059$$

91. A certain type of tag consists of a "bootlace" with a cylinder at one end into which the tag at the other end fits. If any number N of exactly similar tags be held in the middle so that the cylinder ends hang down at one side and the tag ends at the other:

    (*a*) what is the chance that if, say, n tags be fitted into n cylinders at random, both ends have been chosen from the same "bootlace," so that n loops are formed?

    (*b*) if all the N tags be fitted into all the N cylinders, what is the chance that one large loop is formed?

92. Differentiate with respect to x:

$$x \sin^{-1} x \log ae/x + \sqrt{1 - x^2} \log a/x + \log\{x/(1 + \sqrt{1 - x^2})\}.$$

93. Three metal discs are numbered 1, 2, 4 respectively on one side: the other side of each disc is blank. The discs are tossed three times, and the numbers showing up are added. A is to win a stake from B if the total is 8 to 13 inclusive, while B wins if the total is less than 8 or more than 13. Find the odds in favour of B's winning.

94. Prove that, if $y = \cos\left(m \cos^{-1} nx\right)$, then

$$\left(1 - n^2x^2\right) \frac{d^2y}{dx^2} - n^2x \frac{dy}{dx} + m^2n^2y = 0.$$

95. If interpolated values are found in the interval $x = 0$ to $x = 1$ from the values u_{-1}, u_0, u_1, u_2, by means of the formula

$$u_x = \xi u_0 + \frac{\xi^2\left(\xi - 1\right)}{2} \Delta^2 u_{-1}$$
$$+ xu_1 + \frac{x^2\left(x - 1\right)}{2} \Delta^2 u_0 \quad \text{(where } \xi = 1 - x\text{),}$$

and in the next interval $x = 1$ to $x = 2$ by the corresponding formula based on the values u_0, u_1, u_2 and u_3, show that:

    (1) The given values u_0, u_1 and u_2 will be reproduced by the interpolation.

(2) The two interpolation curves have the same differential coefficient when $x = 1$.

(3) The interpolated values for $u_{\frac{1}{2}}$ and $u_{\frac{3}{2}}$ agree with those given by the ordinary third difference interpolation formula based on the same values of u_x.

Given the following values:

$$u_{-5} = 1000, \qquad u_{10} = 2609,$$
$$u_0 = 1403, \qquad u_{15} = 3487,$$
$$u_5 = 1931,$$

complete the table for unit intervals from u_0 to u_{10} by the above formulae and calculate the value of the differential coefficient of the interpolated curves when $x = 5$.

96. Prove that the limit of the series

$$\frac{n}{(n+1)\sqrt{2n+1}} + \frac{n}{(n+2)\sqrt{2(2n+2)}} + \frac{n}{(n+3)\sqrt{3(2n+3)}} + \cdots$$
$$+ \frac{n}{2n\sqrt{n(3n)}}$$

when $n \to \infty$ is $\frac{1}{3}\pi$.

97. If $y^{1/p} + y^{-1/p} = 2x$, prove that
$$(x^2 - 1)D^{n+2}y + (2n+1)xD^{n+1}y + (n^2 - p^2)D^n y = 0.$$

98. Solve the equation $u_{x+1}u_{x-1} = u_x(u_x + xu_{x-1})$.

99. Prove that

$$\frac{d}{dx}\{x^{m-2}(1 - 2x^2)^{p+1}\} = Ax^{m-3}(1 - 2x^2)^p + Bx^{m-1}(1 - 2x^2)^p,$$

where A and B are constants.

Find A and B and hence show that $\int x^6(1 - 2x^2)^{\frac{9}{2}}\,dx$ can be expressed in the form $aI - \{f(x).(1 - 2x^2)^{\frac{7}{2}}\}$, where $I \equiv \int (1 - 2x^2)^{\frac{5}{2}}\,dx$ and a is a constant.

100. If a is a first approximation to a root of an equation $f(x) = 0$, show that $a - f(a)/f'(a)$ is likely to be a better approximation.

Apply the method to determine, correct to three places of decimals, the root of $x^4 - 8x - 60 = 0$ which is nearly equal to 3.

101. If in an examination six men are bracketed, the extreme difference between their marks being 6, find the chance that they have all obtained different marks.

102. The xth term of the series 1, 2, 17, 72, 243, 754, ... is of the form $a + bx + c^x + d^x$. Determine a, b, c, d and find the sum of n terms of the series.

ANSWERS TO THE EXAMPLES

Examples 1.

1. $\dfrac{1}{2}, -\dfrac{\sqrt{3}}{2}, -\dfrac{1}{\sqrt{3}}; \dfrac{1}{\sqrt{2}}, -\dfrac{1}{\sqrt{2}}, -1; \dfrac{1}{2}, \dfrac{\sqrt{3}}{2}, \dfrac{1}{\sqrt{3}}; -\dfrac{1}{2}, -\dfrac{\sqrt{3}}{2}, \dfrac{1}{\sqrt{3}}.$

2. $\dfrac{5\pi}{6}, \dfrac{3\pi}{4}, \dfrac{25\pi}{6}, \dfrac{7\pi}{6}.$

4. (a) $\dfrac{\pi}{6}$; (b) $\dfrac{2\pi}{3}$; (c) $\dfrac{\pi}{16}$; (d) $\dfrac{\pi}{4}$; (e) 0.

5. (a) $1\cdot008$; (b) $1\cdot006$; (c) $2\cdot233$.

7. (i) $n\pi + (-1)^n \dfrac{\pi}{4}$; (ii) $2n\pi \pm \dfrac{\pi}{3}$; (iii) $n\pi + 5\dfrac{\pi}{6}$; (iv) $2n\pi \pm \dfrac{\pi}{4}$;

   (v) $n\pi + \dfrac{\pi}{4}$.

8. (i) $\dfrac{\pi}{2}$; (ii) $\dfrac{\pi}{2}$; (iii) $\dfrac{\pi}{2}$; (iv) 2π; (v) $\dfrac{2\pi}{3}$; (vi) $\dfrac{\pi}{4}$; (vii) 4π;

   (viii) $\dfrac{8\pi}{3}$; (ix) 2π; (x) $\dfrac{19\pi}{6}$.

9. (i) $\dfrac{\pi}{18}$; (ii) $\dfrac{\pi}{22}$; (iii) $\dfrac{\pi}{8}$; (iv) $\dfrac{5\pi}{2}$; (v) $(3n - \frac{1}{2})\dfrac{\pi}{7}$.

10. $-\cos\theta$; $-\sin\theta$; $-\tan\theta$; $\tan\theta$; $\operatorname{cosec}\theta$; $-\operatorname{cosec}\theta$; $-\cot\theta$; $\sin\theta$; $\sin\theta$.

12. $\dfrac{56}{65}$; $\dfrac{13}{85}$; $\dfrac{19}{13\sqrt{5}}$; $\dfrac{29}{13\sqrt{5}}$; $\dfrac{240}{289}$; $\dfrac{3}{5}$; $\dfrac{56}{33}$; $\dfrac{2}{11}$

33. $(4n + 1)\dfrac{\pi}{2}$ or $(2n + 3)\dfrac{\pi}{2} + \tan^{-1}\dfrac{20}{21}$.

34. $(2n - \frac{1}{4})\pi - a.$

35. $2n\pi \pm \cos^{-1}\dfrac{3}{\sqrt{10}}.$

36. $n\pi + (-1)^n \sin^{-1}\left\{\dfrac{-1 \pm \sqrt{5}}{4}\right\}.$

37. $\dfrac{n\pi}{4}$ or $-\dfrac{n\pi}{8}.$

38. Solving in the ordinary way, $x = 2$. On substitution, however, $x = 2$ gives a positive value to the left-hand side of the equation, whereas the right-hand side is negative. Strictly speaking, therefore, there is no solution.

39. $2n\pi \pm \dfrac{\pi}{2}$, $4n\pi \pm \pi$ or $\frac{1}{3}(4n\pi \pm \pi).$

40. $x = \dfrac{\pi}{4}.$

46. $\{\frac{1}{2}n + \frac{1}{6}\}\pi$ or $\{n - \frac{1}{6}\}\pi.$

48. $\pm\dfrac{\sqrt{3}}{2}.$

49. $a = \frac{1}{2}n\pi + (-1)^n \frac{1}{2}\pi$; $\beta = \frac{1}{2}n\pi + (-1)^n \frac{1}{4}\pi.$

50. $\dfrac{\sin a + (n - 1)\,\beta \sin n\beta}{\sin \frac{1}{2}\beta}.$

Examples 2.

1. 58. 2. 30, 42. 3. 15.

4. 1·9, 4·9. 5. 1110. 8. $6ah^3$.

9. $\frac{1}{6}(-11x^3 + 252x^2 - 1051x + 1344)$. 10. $abcd.10!$.

11. $ab^{cx}(b^c - 1)$; $ab^{cx}(b^c - 1)^2$; $ab^{cx}\dfrac{(b^c - 1)[(b^c - 1)^{10} - 1]}{b^c - 2}$.

12. (i) $\frac{1}{2}x(x-1) + k$, (ii) $c^x/(c-1) + k$,
(iii) $3x(x-1)(x-2) + \frac{3}{2}x(x-1) + 3x + k$, where k is a constant.

13. $-\dfrac{2}{(x+2)(x+3)} - \dfrac{3}{(x+3)(x+4)}$;

$\dfrac{4}{(x+2)(x+3)(x+4)} + \dfrac{6}{(x+3)(x+4)(x+5)}$.

14. $\dfrac{2}{x(x-1)(x-2)}$. 15. -2 or 109.

16. (1) $an!$; (2) $e^{ax+b}(e^a - 1)^n$. 18. 55. 19. $a^{2x} + (a^2 + 1)^2 a^{4x}$.

20. $\frac{1}{4}x(x-1)(x-2)(x-3) + 2x(x-1)(x-2) + \frac{3}{2}x(x-1) + 12x + k$.

21. 1225. 22. 20. 23. -161. 24. 1093. 25. 1261.

28. $x^{(4)} - 6x^{(3)} + 13x^{(2)} + x^{(1)} + 9$; $4x^{(3)} - 18x^{(2)} + 26x^{(1)} + 1$;
$12x^{(2)} - 36x^{(1)} + 26$; $24x^{(1)} - 36$; 24.

29. (i) $(m+1)m(m-1) \ldots (m-n+2) a^{m+1} (b/a + x + m)^{(m-n+1)}$;
(ii) $(-1)^n (m+1)(m+2) \ldots (m+n) a^{-\overline{m+1}} (b/a + x)^{(-\overline{m+n+1})}$.

30. $2\cos(x + \frac{1}{2}a)\sin\frac{1}{2}a$; $\sin a/\{\cos(x+a)\sin x\}$; $a - 2\sin(x + \frac{1}{2}a)\sin\frac{1}{2}a$.

31. $6x$; $6x/(x-1)^3$. 42. $\gamma^2 + 4a\gamma = \beta^2$. 43. $2(x-2)^n - 2(x-3)^n$.

Examples 3.

1. 465. 2. 441; 653. 3. 300.

4. 182; 343. 5. 5414. 6. 89,920; 89,073.

7. 205. 8. 94; 396; 662. 9. 194·3; 279·9.

10. 97,357. 11. 844; 746. 12. ·98127.

13. 69,215. 14. 2·37223. 15. $-·432$; $-·337$; $-·195$.

17. 14·73658. 18. 3·708; 3·711. 19. 5281; 6504.

20. ·5479. 21. 2153; 1705.

22. 2459; 2424; 2359; 2268; 2153; 2018; 1868; 1705; 1534; 1357; 1180.

23. ·017; ·035; ·052; ·070; ·087; ·104; ·122; ·139; ·157.

24. 23·1234; 23·2039; 23·2914; 23·3865; 23·4898; 23·6019; 23·7234.

26. 1·000. 27. ·020660; ·020625; ·020628. 28. 58,844.

29. 1; 2·10; 3·31; 4·64; 6·11; 7·73; 9·51; 11·47; 13·62; 15·97.

31. 117·7; 114·2; 110·5; 106·7; 102·7; 98·6; 94·3; 89·8; 85·2; 80·3; 75·4.

32. ·22643. 33. Third degree: 275. 34. 459.

35. $u_2 = 218$; $u_4 = 0$; $u_5 = 19$; $u_x = 1876 - 1429x + 360x^2 - 30x^3$.

Examples 4.

1. 5745. 2. 47,983. 3. 2·8169. 4. 1·7243. 5. 2300. 6. 460.

7. $-\dfrac{l+m}{l^2m^2}$; $\dfrac{lm+mn+nl}{l^2m^2n^2}$; $\dfrac{lmn+mnp+npl+plm}{l^2m^2n^2p^2}$.

8. 13·18. 9. 14·942. 10. 20·43. 11. 162.

12. $659 + 22\frac{1}{4}x + \frac{29}{72}x^2 - \frac{1}{72}x^3$. 13. 32. 16. 1; 25.

18. 33 and 67 to the nearest integer. 19. 37·2.

20. 7·37. 21. 130,326.

Examples 5.

1. 15. 2. 6. 3. 47,692. 4. 3251. 5. 16·9216

6. 2·85807; 2·86305; 2·86157; 2·86155. 7. 2017.

8. 3·5283. 9. 2196, 2108, 2022, 1939; 1786, 1718, 1657, 1604.

10. ·3165. 11. 2290·1. 14. 4·034.

Examples 6.

1. 471·5; 2·7. 2. 13·3. 3. 5·0113...; 5·012.

4. 43·1. 5. 3·67. 6. 2·751. 7. 16·9.

8. 1·1576.... 9. 1·2134. 10. 45·70. 11. 1·85.

12. 3·091. 13. 3·667 per cent. 14. 1·3713. 15. 37·2.

Examples 7.

1. $\frac{1}{6}n(-2n^2 + 27n + 17)$. 2. $\frac{1}{12}n(n+1)(3n^2 + 7n + 2)$.

3. -4195. 4. $2^{21} + 628$. 5. $3^{n+1} + \frac{1}{2}(n^2 + 7n - 6)$.

6. $\frac{1}{5}\{\frac{1}{2}(3^n - 1) + 5n + \frac{1}{3}n(n+1)(2n+1)\}$.

7. $2^{2k+1} - 2 - \frac{1}{3}k(2k+1)(4k+1)$. 8. $\frac{1}{3}(n^4 - 10n^3 + 29n^2 + 10n)$.

9. $2n^4 + 16n^3 + 47n^2 + 60n$. 10. $2^{19} - 2095$.

11. $\frac{1}{4}(n+3)(n+4)(n+5)(n+6) - 90$.

12. $\frac{1}{4}n(n+1)(n+4)(n+5)$.

13. $\frac{1}{12}\{(3n-2)(3n+1)(3n+4)(3n+7) + 56\}$.

14. $\frac{1}{12}n(n+1)(n+2)(3n+13)$.

15. $\frac{1}{30}n(n+1)(n+2)(6n^2 + 57n + 137)$.

16. $\frac{1}{10}\{(2n+3)(2n+5)(2n+7)(2n+9)(2n+11) - 10395\}$.

17. $\dfrac{n}{4(n+4)}$. 18. $\dfrac{n(5n+13)}{12(n+2)(n+3)}$. 19. $\dfrac{n(n+1)}{6(n+3)(n+4)}$.

F

25

20. $\dfrac{n(3n+5)}{8(3n+1)(3n+4)}$.

21. $\dfrac{n(5n+11)}{4(n+1)(n+2)}$.

22. $\frac{1}{18}n(n+1)(n+2)(3n^2+36n+101)$.

23. $\dfrac{19}{168} - \dfrac{12n^2+33n+19}{6(3n+1)(3n+4)(3n+7)}$; $\dfrac{19}{168}$.

24. $\frac{1}{12}n(n+1)(3n^2+31n+74)$.

25. $\frac{1}{4}(n+3)(n+2)(n+1)n$; $\frac{1}{4}n(n-1)(n-2)(n-3)$.

26. $3^n - 1 - n$.

27. $\dfrac{a^x}{a-1}\left\{x^2 - \dfrac{2ax}{a-1} + \dfrac{a(a+1)}{(a-1)^2}\right\} + C$.

28. $1 - 3(n+1)! + (n+2)!$.

29. $\frac{1}{15}\{(3n-1)(3n+2)(3n+5)(3n+8)(3n+11) + 880\}$.

30. $\frac{1}{8}n(6n^3+16n^2+9n-4)$.   **31.** $\frac{1}{24}n(7n^3-34n^2+89n-254)$.

33. $\frac{1}{12}n(n+1)(9n^2+17n+4)$; $\{2^{n+1}(n^3-3n^2+10n-14)\} + 28$.

34. $\dfrac{2}{3} + \dfrac{4^{n+1}}{3}\left\{\dfrac{n-1}{n+2}\right\}$.   **35.** $\dfrac{11}{768}$.   **36.** $34 - (4n^2+12n+17)/2^{n-1}$.

37. $(x-2)3^x$.   **38.** $\frac{5}{2}(3^n-1) + \frac{1}{12}(42n+17n^2+n^4)$.

39. $\dfrac{(n+2)x^n - 2}{x-1} - \dfrac{x^{n+1}-x}{(x-1)^2}$.   **40.** $C - \dfrac{12n^3+36n^2+28n+3}{12n(n+1)(n+2)(n+3)}$.

42. $\dfrac{1}{54}\left\{\dfrac{39}{10} - \dfrac{36n+39}{(3n+2)(3n+5)}\right\}$.   **43.** 23.   **44.** $n^2 2^{n+1}$.

45. $\dfrac{2-(n+1)(n+2)x^n}{1-x} + \dfrac{2x}{(1-x)^2}\{2-(n+2)x^n\} + \dfrac{2x^2}{(1-x)^3}(1-x^n)$.

46. $C - 2^{x-2}\dfrac{(x-1)!}{(2x-1)!}$.

47. $\frac{5}{4} + \frac{1}{60}(2n-1)(2n+1)(2n+3)(24n+54n+25)$.

48. $\frac{1}{5}ax^4 - (\frac{1}{2}a - \frac{1}{3}b)x^3 + (\frac{1}{4}a - \frac{1}{4}b + \frac{1}{2}c)x^2 + (\frac{1}{6}b - \frac{1}{2}c + d)x + K$.

49. $(1-x)^{r+1}$.

Examples 8.

2. $20\cdot796875$; $-\frac{1}{64}$.   **10.** $5\cdot254$.   **13.** $13\cdot094$.

14. $5\cdot319$.   **15.** $3\cdot9634$.   **16.** $10\cdot389$; $10\cdot475$.

Examples 9.

1. $\dfrac{p}{q}a^{p-q}$.   **3.** $\frac{1}{2}(\log a)^2$.   **5.** $\frac{1}{2}(a-k)$.   **7.** o.

8. $\frac{1}{2}a^2$.   **9.** $\dfrac{2\sqrt{3}}{9}$.   **10.** $\frac{1}{2}$.   **11.** $-\frac{3}{2}$.

12. $\dfrac{a-b}{e(\log a - \log b)}$.   **13.** $\dfrac{m}{n}$.   **14.** 1.   **15.** $\dfrac{1}{\sqrt{2a}}$.

16. ∞.   **17.** o.   **20.** $\frac{3}{2}$.

Examples 10.

5. $\sqrt{a^2 - x^2} - \dfrac{x^2}{\sqrt{a^2 - x^2}}$; $e^{x \log x} (\log x + 1)$.

6. $5x^4$; $an (ax + b)^{n-1}$; $x^x (1 + \log x)$.

7. $bn (a + bx)^{n-1}$; $na^{nx} \log a$; $\dfrac{2x}{n} (a^2 + x^2)^{1 - \frac{1}{n}}$; $\dfrac{1}{x} - \log a$.

8. $\dfrac{2x (x^2 + 1)}{x^2 - 1}$; $x^{m-1} (1 - x)^{n-1} (m - \overline{m + n}x)$; $x^{m-1} e^x (x + m)$;

$x^{n-1} (1 + n \log x)$.

9. $- \dfrac{\log_x a}{x \log_e x}$; $x (1 + 2 \log x)$; $10^{10^x} (\log_e 10)^2 \, 10^x$; $\dfrac{1 - \log x}{x^2}$.

10. $2 \sin x \cos x$; $2 \cos 2x$; $- 3 \cos^2 x \sin x$; $x \sec x (2 + x \tan x)$.

11. $\dfrac{2x}{\sqrt{1 - x^4}}$; $\dfrac{\sin x + x \cos x}{2 \sqrt{x \sin x}}$; $\sec^2 x \tan 2x + 2 \sec^2 2x \tan x$.

12. $\cos^{-1} x - \dfrac{x}{\sqrt{1 - x^2}}$; $2x \tan^{-1} x + \dfrac{x^2}{1 + x^2}$;

$\cos x (\tan^{-1} x)^2 + \dfrac{2 \sin x \tan^{-1} x}{1 + x^2}$.

13. $(5 + 4x)^{\log x} \left\{ \dfrac{1}{x} \log (5 + 4x) + \dfrac{4}{5 + 4x} \log x \right\}$;

$\dfrac{- mx^{m-1}}{\sqrt{1 - x^2} \{1 - \sqrt{1 - x^2}\}^m}$; $\dfrac{1}{x \log x}$.

14. $a^x \log a + ax^{a-1}$; $x^x (1 + \log x) - 2mx (1 - x^2)^{m-1}$;

$x^{x^n} x^{n-1} (x \log x + 1)$.

15. $\dfrac{3 (1 - 4x^2)}{(1 + x^2) (1 + 16x^2)}$; $\dfrac{3}{2} \sqrt{x} \sqrt{\cos^{-1} x} - \dfrac{1}{2} \dfrac{1}{\sqrt{1 - x^2} \sqrt{\cos^{-1} x}}$.

18. $\dfrac{y^2}{x - xy \log x}$.   **19.** $\dfrac{1}{x} - \dfrac{1}{e^x - 1}$.   **20.** $\frac{5}{8}$ feet per second.

21. (i) $\dfrac{x^4 - 2a^2 x^2 + 4a^4}{(x^2 - a^2)^{\frac{3}{2}} (x^2 - 4a^2)^{\frac{1}{2}}}$; (ii) $\dfrac{na^{\frac{1}{2}}}{2x (a + bx^n)^{\frac{1}{2}}}$.

23. $- \dfrac{4x}{4x^4 + 1} \left\{ \tan^{-1} \left(\dfrac{2x^2 + a}{2ax^2 - 1} \right) \right\}^{-1}$.

24. (i) $e^x x^{e^x} \left\{ \log x + \dfrac{1}{x} \right\}$; (ii) $\left\{ \log \dfrac{y}{1 + x} - \dfrac{x}{1 + x} \right\} \Big/ \left\{ 1 - \dfrac{x}{y} \right\}$.

26. $\dfrac{3}{x} (\log x)^2 \, x^{(\log x)^2}$.   **27.** $\frac{1}{2}$.

28. $\dfrac{2 (1 - t^2)}{(1 + t^2)^2}$; $\dfrac{- 4t}{(1 + t^2)^2}$; $\dfrac{8t}{(1 - t^2)^4}$; $\dfrac{2}{(1 + t^2)}$.

29. $\dfrac{1}{3}\dfrac{3a^2x^2 + 2ax^3 + x^4}{(a + x)(a^2 + x^2)(a^2 + ax + x^2)}$.

30. $\dfrac{1}{2x^2 \log_e 10}$; $\dfrac{1 + \sqrt{1 - x^4}}{x^6}$. **32.** $\dfrac{2e^x}{\sqrt{e^{2x} - a^2}}$.

33. $\dfrac{1 - 2xy}{x^2 + 3y^2 - 1}$. **34.** (i) $\cot x$; (ii) $\dfrac{4}{1 + x^2}$.

35. $a_r = -\dfrac{n!}{(n - r)!}$. **36.** $\dfrac{a}{2x^2} \cdot \dfrac{\sin a/x - \cos a/x}{1 + \sin a/x \cos a/x}$.

37. (i) $\dfrac{a}{y}$; (ii) $2y - \dfrac{c}{y}$. **38.** $\dfrac{2x^4 + y^2}{x^3}$.

39. (i) $e^{x^x} x^x (1 + \log x)$; (ii) $\dfrac{e^{x^x} x^x (1 + \log x)}{e^x}$; (iii) e^{x^x}.

41. (i) $6c^2 \dfrac{(ad - bc)}{(cx + d)^4}$; (ii) $\dfrac{11 - 6 \log x}{x^4}$.

44. $4x^2 - 4x$. **46.** $\dfrac{2 \log a}{a}$. **50.** 0.

51. $(- 1)^n n! \left\{ \dfrac{pa + q}{(a - b)(a - c)} \cdot \dfrac{1}{(x - a)^{n+1}} + \dfrac{pb + q}{(b - c)(b - a)} \cdot \dfrac{1}{(x - b)^{n+1}} \right.$
$\left. + \dfrac{pc + q}{(c - a)(c - b)} \cdot \dfrac{1}{(x - c)^{n+1}} \right\}$.

52. $(- 1)^n n! \left\{ \dfrac{6}{(x - 2)^{n+1}} - \dfrac{2}{(x - 1)^{n+1}} \right\}$.

53. $\dfrac{(- 1)^n n!}{c - d} \left\{ \dfrac{(c - a)(c - b)}{(x - c)^{n+1}} - \dfrac{(d - a)(d - b)}{(x - d)^{n+1}} \right\}$.

54. $\dfrac{8}{(1 - x)^5} + \dfrac{256}{(1 + 2x)^5}$.

57. (i) $(- 1)^{n-1} \dfrac{2(n - 3)!}{x^{n-2}}$; (ii) $(- 1)^n n! \left\{ \dfrac{5 \cdot 3^n}{(3x + 1)^{n+1}} + \dfrac{1}{(x - 1)^{n+1}} \right\}$.

59. $a^{n+2} x^2 e^{ax}$.

60. $(- 1)^n \dfrac{n!}{(b - a)^2} \left\{ \dfrac{1}{(x - b)^{n+1}} - \dfrac{1}{(x - a)^{n+1}} \right\} - (- 1)^n \dfrac{(n + 1)!}{(b - a)} \dfrac{1}{(x - a)^{n+2}}$.

70. $p = (\log s)^2$; $q = \log c \log g (\log cs^2)$; $r = (\log g \log c)^2$.

71. (i) $\dfrac{- \cot \theta}{\sqrt{\cos 2\theta - \mathrm{cosec}^2 \theta \cos^2 2\theta}}$; (ii) $\dfrac{1}{2 \sqrt{1 + x^2}}$.

73. 3. **74.** $(0, 0)$ and $(2a, - 4a^3/3b^2)$.

75. (i) $(- 2, 3)(- 2, - 1)$; (ii) $(1, 1)(- 5, 1)$.

Examples 11.

2. $\log 2 + \dfrac{x}{2} + \dfrac{x^2}{8} - \dfrac{x^4}{192} \ldots$ **4.** $1 + x^2 - \dfrac{x^3}{2} + \dfrac{5x^4}{6} \ldots$

6. $1 + \dfrac{x}{2} - \dfrac{x^2}{12} + \dfrac{x^3}{24} \ldots$ **7.** $1 + 2x + \dfrac{3x^2}{2} + \dfrac{x^3}{6} + \dfrac{x^4}{12} + \dfrac{x^5}{40} + \dfrac{x^6}{720} \ldots$

9. $x - \dfrac{x^3}{3} + \dfrac{x^5}{5} - \dfrac{x^7}{7} \ldots$ 10. $\dfrac{\pi}{4} + \dfrac{x}{2} + \dfrac{x^2}{4} - \dfrac{5x^3}{12} \ldots$ 12. $-\frac{1}{45}$.

13. $1 + \dfrac{x}{3a} - \dfrac{x^3}{81a^3} \ldots$ 14. $x - \frac{7}{6}x^3 + \frac{27}{40}x^5 \ldots$ 17. $-\frac{11}{24}$.

18. $1 + \frac{3}{2}x + \frac{11}{8}x^2 + \frac{23}{16}x^3 \ldots$ 20. $\dfrac{1}{e^x + 1} = \dfrac{1}{2} - \dfrac{x}{4} + \dfrac{x^3}{48} - \dfrac{x^5}{480} \ldots$

22. $px - \frac{1}{6}p\,(p^3 + 6)\,x^3 + \frac{1}{120}p\,(p^4 + 20p^2 + 60)\,x^5 \ldots$

Examples 12.

1. Max. 1; Min. $-\frac{1}{11}$.   2. Max. $9a^3$; Min. $-\dfrac{5a^3}{3}$.

3. Max. 3; Min. $\frac{1}{3}$.   4. Max. $\frac{4}{27}, \frac{4}{27}$; Min. 0.

5. Max. 73; Min. $69, 69$.   6. Max. $\dfrac{2}{6^3}, \dfrac{2}{6^3}$; Min. $-\frac{1}{27}$.

7. Max. 13; Min. -10; Point of inflexion where $x = 0$.

8. Max. $\dfrac{2\sqrt{ab} + a + b}{2\sqrt{ab} - a - b}$; Min. $\dfrac{2\sqrt{ab} - a - b}{2\sqrt{ab} + a + b}$.   9. Max. $\frac{1}{4}$; Min. 0.

10. Max. $-2c\sqrt{ab}$; Min. $2c\sqrt{ab}$.   11. $-\dfrac{a}{n}$.

12. Max. $4\frac{1}{3}$; Min. 3.   13. $207\cdot8$.   14. $e^{\frac{1}{e}}$.

16. $3 - 3\log_e 3$.   17. $a = -6$; $\beta = 9$.

18. 125 yards from A along AB and then across the grass to C.

19. $\dfrac{c}{2\sqrt{3}}$.   20. n parts.   21. $\frac{1}{6}\{(a + b) - \sqrt{a^2 - ab + b^2}\}$.

22. $(a^{\frac{2}{3}} + b^{\frac{2}{3}})^{\frac{3}{2}}$.   23. 66 minutes.

24. Max. $\dfrac{c}{\sqrt{ab} + h}$; Min. $-\dfrac{c}{\sqrt{ab} - h}$.

27. $\dfrac{a}{\sqrt{\lambda^2 - 1}}$.   30. $2\sqrt{ab}$.   31. $\frac{1}{2}(a + b)^2$.

32. 165 feet.   33. $y = 2x^3 + \dfrac{3}{x^2}$.   34. Max. 2; Min. $\frac{2}{3}$.

35. Max. -6; Min. 0.   36. Max. -100; Min. $8, 12$.

38. $x = 0$.   39. $\pm\dfrac{1}{\sqrt{2}}$.   40. $\pm\dfrac{1}{\sqrt{3}}$.

43. Max. $\frac{8}{3}$; Min. 0.   44. Max. $4\cdot317$; Min. $4\cdot183$.

45. Max. $\frac{10}{9}$; Min. $\frac{18}{5}$.   46. -5.   47. $(a + b)^2$.

Examples 13.

1. o.   2. o.   3. $\frac{1}{6}$.   4. $\log_b a$.

5. $\frac{m}{n}$.   6. $\frac{1}{\sqrt{2a}}$.   7. -1.   8. $\sqrt{\dfrac{m}{n}}\, a^{\frac{1}{2}(m-n)}$.

9. $\frac{3}{2}$.   10. I.   11. I.   12. $\frac{1}{n}$.

13. $\log_e a$.   14. $\frac{11e}{24}$.   15. I.   16. $\frac{1}{30}$.

17. $\frac{1}{6}$.   18. $\frac{1}{2}\dfrac{b+a}{b-a}\log\dfrac{b}{a}$.   20. ∞.

21. $a = 120$; $b = 60$; $c = 180$.   23. o.   24. o.

25. $3u$.   26. $\frac{1}{30}u$.   28. $-\dfrac{x^2+y}{y^2+x}$.   30. $u - uy$.

33. $\cdot 02455$; $-\cdot 0003$; o.   34. $\cdot 109$.   36. $ke^{ax+\lambda c^x}$.   38. 48; 24.

Examples 14.

Note. In the answers to questions on indefinite integrals, the presence of the constant of integration is to be inferred.

2. $\dfrac{3x^{n+1}}{n+1}$; $\dfrac{x^{-n+1}}{3(-n+1)}$; $\frac{1}{2}e^{2x}$.

3. $\frac{1}{5}x^5 + \frac{2}{3}x^3a^2 + xa^4$; $ax + \frac{1}{2}bx^2 + \frac{1}{3}cx^3$.   4. $-\cos x$; $\sin x$; $-\cot x$.

5. $\dfrac{a^x}{\log_e a}$; $\dfrac{a^x}{\log_e a} + bx$; $\dfrac{a^x}{\log_e a} + \frac{1}{2}bx^2 + cx$.

6. $-\frac{1}{2}\cos 2x$; $\frac{1}{3}\sin 3x$; $\frac{1}{4}\tan 4x$.

7. $\log(x+1)$; $\dfrac{1}{1-x}$; $-\dfrac{1}{12}\cdot\dfrac{1}{(a+3x)^4}$.

8. $3\log x + \dfrac{2}{x}$; $-\left[\dfrac{a}{(n-3)x^{n-3}} + \dfrac{b}{(n-2)x^{n-2}} + \dfrac{c}{(n-1)x^{n-1}}\right]$.

9. $\frac{1}{2}\log\dfrac{x-1}{x+1}$; $\log x - \tan^{-1}x$.

10. $a\sin^{-1}x$; $\dfrac{1}{a}\sin^{-1}ax$.   11. $\frac{1}{12}\sin 3x + \frac{3}{4}\sin x$.

12. $-\left[\dfrac{1}{(n-3)y^{n-3}} - \dfrac{2}{(n-2)y^{n-2}} + \dfrac{1}{(n-1)y^{n-1}}\right]$;

$-\left[\dfrac{1}{(n-3)(1+x)^{n-3}} - \dfrac{2}{(n-2)(1+x)^{n-2}} + \dfrac{1}{(n-1)(1+x)^{n-1}}\right]$.

13. $\dfrac{1}{m}\displaystyle\int_1^{1+m}\dfrac{dy}{y}$.   14. $\displaystyle\int_0^1\dfrac{dx}{1+x^2}$.   15. $\log\left\{\dfrac{\sqrt{x^2-2x}}{x-1}\right\}$.

16. $-\log(1-x) - \tan^{-1} x.$ **17.** $\frac{1}{4}\log(1-x^2) - \dfrac{1}{2(1+x)}.$

23. $e^x + ax^2 + bx + c.$ **25.** $\dfrac{11a}{6}.$

26. $l_x = ke^{-Ax - Bc^x/\log_e c}.$ **27.** $\frac{1}{2}\log\dfrac{1+t}{1-t}.$ **28.** $\log\dfrac{1}{1-x^4}.$

Examples 15.

Note. In the answers to questions on indefinite integrals, the presence of the constant of integration is to be inferred.

1. $\dfrac{1}{n-1}\cdot\dfrac{1}{(1+x)^{n-1}} - \dfrac{1}{n-3}\cdot\dfrac{1}{(1+x)^{n-3}}$; $2\sqrt{x} + \dfrac{4}{\sqrt{x}}$; $\frac{2}{3}(x-1)(x+2)^{\frac{1}{2}}.$

2. $2\log(x-3) - \log(x-1)$; $3x + 11\log(x-2) - 2\log(x-1)$;

$\dfrac{2\sqrt{x-1}}{35}(5x^3 + 6x^2 + 8x + 16).$

3. $\dfrac{1}{4a^2}\log\dfrac{x^2-a^2}{x^2+a^2}$; $-\dfrac{1}{x-1} + \frac{1}{4}\log\dfrac{x-1}{x+3}.$

4. $\frac{1}{4}\log(3+4\sin x)$; $\log(4x^2+3)$; $\log(e^x + \cos x).$

5. $\sin^{-1}\dfrac{2x+1}{3}$; $\log(x+\frac{1}{2} + \sqrt{2+x+x^2}).$

6. $-3\log\{\frac{1}{2} + \frac{1}{3}\cos x\}$; $\frac{1}{6}\log\dfrac{1+x+x^2}{(1-x)^2} + \dfrac{1}{\sqrt{3}}\tan^{-1}\dfrac{2x+1}{\sqrt{3}}.$

7. $\log\sqrt{\dfrac{x^2-x+1}{x^2+x+1}}$; $\dfrac{1}{6a^3}\log\dfrac{x^3-a^3}{x^3+a^3}.$

8. $\sqrt{1+x^2}$; $\frac{3}{8}\log(4x^2+3) + \dfrac{2}{\sqrt{3}}\tan^{-1}\dfrac{2x}{\sqrt{3}}.$

9. $\frac{1}{2}\{\cos x - \frac{1}{5}\cos 5x\}$; $\sin\frac{1}{2}x + \frac{1}{3}\sin\frac{3}{2}x.$

10. $\frac{1}{3}(x^2-2a^2)\sqrt{a^2+x^2}$; $\dfrac{1}{n}\log\dfrac{\sqrt{1+x^n}-1}{\sqrt{1+x^n}+1}.$

11. $\dfrac{1}{2k}\log\dfrac{cx+b-k}{cx+b+k}$ or $\dfrac{1}{k}\tan^{-1}\dfrac{cx+b}{k}.$ **12.** $-\dfrac{1}{2}\sqrt{\dfrac{2+x^2}{x^2}}.$

13. (i) $\sqrt{x^2-1}$; (ii) $\frac{1}{2}\{x\sqrt{x^2-1} + \log(x+\sqrt{x^2-1})\}$;

(iii) $\frac{1}{3}(x^2-1)^{\frac{3}{2}} + \sqrt{x^2-1}.$

14. $-\frac{3}{2}\log(x-1) - \dfrac{5}{2(x-1)} - \dfrac{1}{2(x-1)^2} - \tan^{-1}x + \frac{3}{4}\log(1+x^2).$

15. $\log t$; t; $\log\dfrac{t}{1-t^2}.$ **16.** $\frac{1}{2}x^2\log x - \frac{1}{4}x^2$; $\dfrac{e^{ax}}{a^3}(2 - 2ax + a^2x^2).$

17. $e^x(x^2-2x+2)$; $\frac{1}{3}(x^3\log x - \frac{1}{3}x^3).$

18. $\sin x - x \cos x$; $x^3 \sin x + 3x^2 \cos x - 6x \sin x - 6 \cos x$.

19. $\frac{1}{2}\{(x^2 + 1) \tan^{-1} x - x\}$; $e^x/(x + 1)$.

20. $e^{ax} (a \cos bx + b \sin bx)/(a^2 + b^2)$.

21. $\frac{1}{2} \log (2x + \sqrt{4x^2 - 7})$.
22. $\log \tan (\frac{1}{4}\pi + \frac{1}{2}x)$.

23. $- \frac{1}{2}\{\log (1 - x)\}^2$.
24. $\log x \{\log (\log x) - 1\}$.

25. $\dfrac{x (3a^2 + 2x^2)}{3a^4 (a^2 + x^2)^{\frac{3}{2}}}$.
26. $\dfrac{(x^2 + 2bx + c)^{n+1}}{2 (n + 1)}$.

27. $\dfrac{1}{\sqrt{3}}\{\log (6x + 1) + 2 \sqrt{3} \sqrt{3x^2 + x + 8}\}$.

28. $x - \log_e (1 + c^x)/\log_e c$.

29. $\log \sqrt{x^2 + x + 1} + \dfrac{1}{\sqrt{3}} \tan^{-1}\{(2x + 1)/\sqrt{3}\}$.

30. $\sqrt{5 + 2x + x^2} - \log (1 + x + \sqrt{5 + 2x + x^2})$.

31. $\log x - \frac{1}{3} \log (1 + x^3)$.
32. $\frac{1}{20} \tan^{-1} (\frac{4}{5} \tan \frac{1}{2}x)$.

33. $\dfrac{1}{\sqrt{2}} \log \dfrac{x - \sqrt{2} + \sqrt{1 + x^2}}{x + \sqrt{2} + \sqrt{1 + x^2}}$.
34. $- \dfrac{1}{\sqrt{3}} \sin^{-1} \dfrac{3 - x}{2x}$.

35. $- \dfrac{1}{\sqrt{2}} \log \{x + 4 + \sqrt{2} \sqrt{2 + x - x^2}\} - \dfrac{1}{\sqrt{2}} \log x$.

36. $\dfrac{1}{2 (a - b)} \log \dfrac{\sec^2 x}{a + b \tan^2 x}$.
37. $a \sin^{-1} (x/a) - \sqrt{a^2 - x^2}$.

38. $\dfrac{2}{3a} \{(x + a)^{\frac{3}{2}} - x^{\frac{3}{2}}\}$.
39. $\frac{1}{25} \{3x - 4 \log (4 \cos x + 3 \sin x)\}$.

40. $\dfrac{1}{\sqrt{a^2 + ab}} \tan^{-1} \left\{\dfrac{\sqrt{a}}{\sqrt{a + b}} \tan x\right\}$.

42. (a) $y (\log y - 1)$;   (b) $y \cos^{-1} y - \sqrt{1 - y^2}$.

43. $- \frac{1}{4} (2x^2 + 1)/(x^2 + 1)^2$ + a constant.
45. $\frac{1}{2} \tan^{-1} x^2$.

46. $\log (x + \sqrt{x^2 - 1}) - \sec^{-1} x$.
47. $\dfrac{2}{\sqrt{a^2 - b^2}} \tan^{-1} \left\{\dfrac{\sqrt{a - b}}{\sqrt{a + b}} \tan \frac{1}{2}x\right\}$.

48. $- \frac{1}{3} (a^2 + x^2)^{-\frac{3}{2}} (2a^2 + 3x^2)$.
49. $e^{qx} (x/q - 1/q^2)$.

50. $I_m = \dfrac{1}{(2 - 2m) a^2} \dfrac{x}{(x^2 - a^2)^{m-1}} - \dfrac{3 - 2m}{(2 - 2m) a^2} I_{m-1}$;

$- \dfrac{1}{2a^2} \dfrac{x}{x^2 - a^2} - \dfrac{1}{4a^3} \log \dfrac{x - a}{x + a}$.

51. $\frac{1}{4}x^4 (\log x)^2 - \frac{1}{8}x^4 \log x + \frac{1}{32} x^4$.

53. $- \frac{1}{2}\{a (a - x) \sqrt{2ax - x^2} + a^3 \sin^{-1} (a - x)/a\} - \frac{1}{3} (2ax - x^2)^{\frac{3}{2}}$.

54. $\dfrac{1}{\sin (a - b)} \log \dfrac{\sin (x - a)}{\sin (x - b)}$.

55. $\frac{1}{3}x^3 \sin^{-1} x + \frac{1}{9}(2 + x^2)\sqrt{1 - x^2}$.　　　**56.** $\tan^{-1}(-\cos 2\theta)$.

57. $\frac{1}{4}\left\{\tan^{-1}\sqrt{\dfrac{x-2}{3-x}} - (5 - 2x)\sqrt{(x-2)(3-x)}\right\}$.

58. $ke^{-Ax}x^{pc^x}$, where $p \equiv B/\log c$.

59. $\log x - \log\{(x + 1) + \sqrt{3x^2 + 2x + 1}\}$.

60. $\frac{1}{2}\log\tan\frac{1}{2}x - \dfrac{\cos x}{2\sin^2 x}$.　　　**61.** $\dfrac{9}{\sqrt{2}}\tan^{-1}\left(\dfrac{1}{\sqrt{2}}\tan x\right) - x$.

62. $-\dfrac{2x^2 + 1}{4(x^2 + 1)^2}$.　　　**63.** $\dfrac{\sqrt{x^4 + x^2 + 1}}{x}$.

65. $\frac{1}{16}z^{-\frac{2}{3}} - \frac{1}{4}z^{\frac{1}{3}} - \frac{1}{32}z^{\frac{4}{3}}$, where $z \equiv (2 - x^3)/x^3$.

66. $\frac{8}{5}(2 + x^{-\frac{3}{4}})^{\frac{5}{3}} - \frac{1}{2}(2 + x^{-\frac{3}{4}})^{\frac{8}{3}}$.

67. $6(\frac{1}{9}z^9 - \frac{1}{8}z^8 + \frac{1}{7}z^7 - \frac{1}{6}z^6 + \frac{1}{5}z^5 - \frac{1}{4}z^4)$, where $z \equiv (x + 1)^{\frac{1}{6}}$.

68. $\frac{1}{2}\sqrt{a - b}\left(t + \dfrac{1}{3t^3}\right)$.

69. $\dfrac{1}{a^4 n(b - 1)}(z - 4b\log z - 6b^2 z^{-1} + b^3 z^{-2} - \frac{1}{3}b^4 z^{-3})$,

　　　where $z \equiv ax^{-n} + b$.

70. $\frac{1}{24}\log\{(x^4 - 1)^2/(x^8 + x^4 + 1)\} + \dfrac{1}{4\sqrt{3}}\tan^{-1}\{(2x^4 + 1)/\sqrt{3}\}$.

71. $\dfrac{1}{\sqrt{3}}\cos^{-1}\left(\dfrac{1 + 2\cos\theta}{2 + \cos\theta}\right)$.

Examples 16.

2. $n^{n+1}/(n + 1)$;　$12a + 41\frac{1}{3}b$.

3. $(1 - e^{-a^2 k})/a^2$;　$2[5^{\frac{1}{2}(m+n+2)} - (-5)^{\frac{1}{2}(m+n+2)}]/(m + n + 2)$.

4. $1 - \dfrac{1}{\sqrt{2}}$;　$\frac{1}{4}\pi - \frac{1}{2}\log 2$.　　　**5.** $\log\frac{81}{80}$;　$2 - \frac{3}{2}\log 3 + \frac{1}{12}\pi$.

6. $\frac{2}{27}\log 2 + \frac{13}{72}$;　$\pi/\sqrt{3}$.　　　**7.** $\frac{4}{3}\sqrt{a}(\sqrt{2} - 1)$;　$\sqrt{2} - 1$.

8. $3\pi/16$;　$\pi/15$.　　　**9.** $\frac{1}{324}$;　$\frac{32}{3003}$.

10. $\frac{1}{2}(b^2\log b - a^2\log a) - \frac{1}{4}(b^2 - a^2)$;　$\frac{1}{2}(e^{\frac{\pi}{2}} + e^{-\frac{\pi}{2}})$.

11. $\pi - 2$;　$26e^{-\frac{1}{2}} + 16$.　　　**13.** $\frac{1}{2}\log\frac{5}{4}$.

15. $\frac{1}{4}(b - a - 1)(3b - 3a - 1) - \frac{1}{2}(a - b)^2\log(b - a)$.　　　**16.** $3\pi/16$.

18. $\frac{1}{2}\log 2 - \frac{1}{4}$.　　　**19.** $e^2\log 2$.　　　**24.** $\log(\frac{3}{2}) - \frac{5}{8}$.

26. $\frac{1}{2} + \frac{1}{8}\log\frac{2}{7} + \frac{1}{8}\tan^{-1}\frac{6}{7}$.　　　**28.** $72a^2$.

29. $\frac{4}{3}a^2(c^3 - b^3)$.　　　**30.** $\frac{8}{15}$.　　　**31.** $8a^2/3$.　　　**32.** $\frac{32}{105}$.

33. $\frac{1}{2}(e^9 - e^{-9} - e + e^{-1})$.　　　**34.** $24\sqrt{3}/5$.　　　**35.** $1 - \log\frac{3}{2}$.

36. $(8\pi/3 - 3\sqrt{3})a^2$;　$(4\pi/3 + 3\sqrt{3})a^2$.　　　**37.** 4π.

39. $16a^2/3$.   **40.** $\frac{2}{3}(2^{\frac{3}{2}} - 1) - \log 2$; $\frac{2}{3}(2^{\frac{3}{2}} + 1) + \log 2$.

41. $-\dfrac{1}{\sqrt{x^2 + a^2}\,(x + \sqrt{x^2 + a^2})}$.   **42.** $\dfrac{\pi(a - \sin a \cos a)}{\sin^3 a}$.

44. $n!/a^{n+1}$; $\pi \log(a + 1)$.   **45.** $y = \frac{1}{2}a \sin^{-1}\sqrt{2x/a} + \frac{1}{2}\sqrt{2ax - 4x^2}$.

47. $3\sqrt{2}/8 + \frac{7}{8}\log(\sqrt{2} + 1)$.

49. $x^2\left\{\dfrac{1}{\sqrt{2}} + \frac{1}{2}\log(1 + \sqrt{2})\right\}$; $\dfrac{1}{3}\left\{\dfrac{1}{\sqrt{2}} + \frac{1}{2}\log(1 + \sqrt{2})\right\}$.   **50.** $\frac{1}{3}a^2$.

Examples 17.

2. $\cdot9921$.   **3.** $20\cdot4$ miles.

8. $\frac{1}{144}(95u_0 - 50u_1 + 600u_2 - 350u_3 + 425u_4)$.

9. 200 square miles.   **11.** $\cdot8571\ldots$; (i) $\cdot8806\ldots$; (ii) $\cdot8946\ldots$

12. The second.   **13.** 29,426.   **14.** 888.   **16.** $\cdot6942$.

22. $\cdot5236$.   **24.** $3\cdot142\ldots$ **25.** $1\cdot1358\ldots$

26. $\cdot6931\ldots$ **27.** $3\cdot142\ldots$

Examples 18.

2. $\frac{1}{9}$; $\frac{1}{3}$.   **4.** $\frac{1}{12}$.   **5.** $\frac{5}{8}$.   **6.** $\frac{2}{11}$.   **7.** $\frac{7}{66}$.

8. $\frac{7}{22}$.   **9.** $\frac{496}{729}$.   **10.** $\dfrac{(2n)!}{n!\,n!}\left(\dfrac{1}{2}\right)^{2n}$.   **11.** $\frac{5}{81}$.

12. $\frac{146}{1296}$.   **13.** $\frac{5}{16}$.   **14.** $\frac{679}{858}$.   **15.** $\dfrac{751}{6^5}$.   **16.** $\dfrac{15 \times 35^2}{6^{12}}$.

17. (a) 2^n;   (b) 2^{mn};   (c) $\dfrac{(m+1)}{2^m}$.   **18.** $\frac{13000}{39151}$.   **19.** $\frac{5}{16}$.

20. $\frac{773}{1150}$.   **21.** $\frac{55}{1000}$.   **22.** $\dfrac{138 \times 56}{5^5}$.   **23.** $\frac{11}{20}$.

24. (1) $\frac{1}{166500}$; (2) $\frac{997}{166500}$.   **26.** $\frac{7}{9}$.   **27.** $\frac{33}{1000}$.   **28.** $\frac{89}{100}$.

29. $\frac{11}{16}$.   **31.** $(\frac{7}{13})^2$.   **32.** $\frac{169}{324}$; $\frac{155}{324}$.   **33.** $\frac{493}{648}$.

34. $\frac{16592}{19683}$; $\frac{3091}{19683}$.   **35.** $\frac{7}{33}$; $\frac{4}{19}$.   **36.** $\frac{83}{729}$.   **37.** $\frac{263}{1944}$.

38. (i) $\dfrac{p^2(p+2q)}{(p+q)(p^2+pq+q^2)}$; (ii) $\dfrac{p(p+q)}{p^2+pq+q^2}$.   **39.** $\frac{5}{14}$; $\frac{5}{14}$; $\frac{2}{7}$.

40. $\frac{208}{405}$.   **41.** $\frac{1547}{2304}$.   **42.** $\frac{711}{832}$.   **43.** $\frac{380}{2187}$.

44. 6s. 0d.; 5s. 0d.   **45.** 35s. 0d.   **46.** 6:1.   **48.** Purse A.

49. (i) 63s. 0d.; (ii) 56s. 0d.   **50.** $\frac{775}{1764}$.   **51.** $\frac{1}{2}m(m+1)$.

52. 10.   **53.** $M + \frac{1}{2}m$.

54. (1) $\frac{656}{729}$; (2) $\frac{160}{729}$; (3) $\frac{1}{6075}$: Most probable number is 4; $\frac{240}{729}$.

55. $\cdot126$.   **56.** $2\cdot06 \times 10^{-7}$.   **57.** (1) $\frac{1}{5}$; (2) $\frac{87}{500}$; (3) $\frac{31}{32}$.

58. $\cdot105$.   **60.** $\cdot09888$.   **61.** (1) $\cdot72$; (2) $\cdot504$.

62. (1) $\cdot099\ldots$; (2) $\cdot000007\ldots$, $\cdot001\ldots$ **63.** (a) $\cdot972$; (b) $\cdot271$.

64. $\frac{173}{625}$.   66. $1 - \dfrac{1}{\sqrt{2}}$.   67. 11; $6s.$ $1d.$ 68. 7.   69. $\dfrac{n+3}{2^{m+2}}$.

74. (1) $\frac{1}{12}$;   (2) $\frac{73}{1000}$;   (3) $\frac{307}{1000}$.   75. $\frac{8220}{6561}$.

76. (1) 1 shilling;   (2) $1\frac{2}{9}$ shillings;   (3) $1\frac{4}{9}$ shillings.

77. $\dfrac{3n^2 - 3n + 1}{9n^2 - 9n + 2}$.   78. $-\dfrac{\log_e 2}{\log_e\left(1 - \dfrac{1}{m}\right)}$; $\log_e 2$.   79. $\frac{1}{84}$.

80. (1) $\frac{5}{506}$;   (2) $\frac{5}{28}$;   (3) $\frac{3}{44}$.   81. $\frac{443}{3525}$; $\frac{503}{5525}$.   82. $\dfrac{3003}{2^{15}}$.

83. (1) $\frac{23}{35}$;   (2) $\frac{3}{14}$;   (3) $\frac{1}{2}$.   84. $\dfrac{3n}{36n^2 - 18n + 2}$.   86. $\frac{7}{66}$.

87. $\dfrac{(4!)^{13}\,(13!)^4}{52!}$.   88. $\frac{1}{96}$.   89. $\cdot506\ldots$.

90. (1) Between 5 and 6;   (2) 4;   (3) 7.   92. $\frac{979}{1116}$.

93. (1) $\frac{8}{35}$;   (2) $\frac{3}{35}$;   (3) $\frac{17}{70}$.   94. $\frac{4}{21}$.   95. $\frac{244}{495}$.

96. 3000 : 3007.   97. $\frac{1}{4}$.   98. $\frac{1}{8}$.   100. $\frac{1}{32}$.   101. $\frac{5}{21}$.

102. $\frac{325}{833}$.   103. (1) $\frac{1}{2}$;   (2) $\frac{4}{5}$;   (3) $\frac{59}{100}$.   104. $\frac{461}{4165}$.

105. (a) $\frac{3}{13}$;   (b) $\frac{5}{13}$;   (c) $\frac{2}{13}$.   107. $\frac{38}{245}$.   108. $\frac{5359}{14498}$; $\frac{11086}{20825}$.

Examples 19.

2. $\frac{1}{3}(n+2)$.   3. $\dfrac{b^2}{a^2}$.   4. $\dfrac{1}{n}\log_e 2$.   5. $\dfrac{6l}{\pi}(\sqrt{2}-1)$.

6. $\dfrac{q^2}{p^2}$.   7. $\frac{2}{3}a^2$; $\dfrac{1}{\sqrt{3}}$.   8. (1) $\dfrac{2r^2}{\pi}$;   (2) $\dfrac{r^2\pi}{4}$.   9. $\dfrac{\pi r}{4}$.

10. $\frac{1}{3}a^2$.   11. $\dfrac{2a^2}{3}$.   12. $\frac{1}{4}a^2$.   13. $\dfrac{8\log 2 - 3}{64\log 2 - 15}$.

14. $\frac{1}{4}$.   15. $\frac{37}{64}$.   16. $\frac{1}{2}$.   17. $\frac{1}{3}$.   18. $\frac{7}{8}$.   19. $\dfrac{c^2}{ab}$.

20. $\frac{2}{3} - \frac{1}{3}\log_e 3$.   21. $\dfrac{\pi}{4}$.   22. $\frac{3}{4}$.   24. $\frac{1}{2} + \frac{1}{2}\log_e 2$.

25. $\frac{19}{45}$; $\frac{19}{28}$ miles.   26. $\frac{1}{3}(2 - \sqrt{2}) + \log(1 + \sqrt{2})$.

Miscellaneous Examples.

1. $\dfrac{n}{12}(n^3 - 4n^2 + 11n + 4)$.   2. $\frac{11}{24}$.   3. Max.$\frac{1}{2}$; Min.$-\frac{1}{2}$; Area $\frac{4}{3}$.

5. (i) $\dfrac{2}{3}\left(1 - \dfrac{a}{x^2}\right)\left(x + \dfrac{a}{x}\right)^{-\frac{1}{3}}$;   (ii) $\dfrac{1}{\sqrt{(1 - x^2)\{1 - (\sin^{-1}x)^2\}}}$.

6. (i) 1;   (ii) $\frac{1}{2}$.   7. $\frac{175}{13122}$.

8. $x - \log(x^2 + 2x + 3) + \dfrac{3}{\sqrt{2}}\tan^{-1}\dfrac{x+1}{\sqrt{2}}$; $a^2\log\tan(\frac{1}{4}\pi + \frac{1}{2}x) + b^2\sin x$.

9. (a) 19,764; (b) 59,156. **10.** (a) 293; (b) 152; (c) 141.

12. $\dfrac{1}{1+x^2}$; $\dfrac{1}{\sqrt{1+x^2}}$; $\dfrac{2}{1+x^2}$. **14.** 5·225. **16.** (1) $\frac{19}{40}$; (2) $\frac{9}{40}$.

19. $A = 18$, $y = 2\cdot8$. **21.** $\frac{5}{24}$. **23.** 0·577... ft. per min.

26. 977, 961; 1023. **27.** $\dfrac{2b}{3(b-c)}$. **28.** $\dfrac{m!\,n!}{(m+n)!}$; $\dfrac{m!\,(n-1)!}{(m+n)!}$.

29. − 1. **30.** ·0294; ·0492; ·0682. **31.** $\dfrac{\pi a^4}{16}$.

32. $\frac{1}{6}$ ft. per min. **33.** 14 hr. 41 min. **36.** − 1·88.

38. − 12. **39.** $1 - (\frac{35}{36})^6 + (\frac{35}{36})^6 (\frac{25}{36})^2 \frac{18}{193}$. **40.** $\frac{1}{2}a + \frac{1}{8}a \log_e 3$.

42. $\dfrac{\pi}{12} + \frac{1}{8}\log 2 - \frac{1}{8}$; $\dfrac{3\pi}{16}$. **43.** $\frac{7}{25}$. **44.** 58·9321....

48. 86; 121. **49.** $\frac{4}{5}$. **50.** $4e^{-1}$. **51.** 48·48... miles.

52. 0·109.... **55.** 7·04.... **56.** $1 - \dfrac{31}{11^5}$.

57. (i) $x - \log(1 + e^x)$; (ii) $\log(1 + e^x)$; (iii) $e^x - \log(1 + e^x)$;
(iv) $\log(1 + e^x) - x - e^{-x}$.

58. $\dfrac{x}{3a^2} - \dfrac{x^3}{81a^8}$ .... **59.** $\frac{1}{12}\{3n^4 - 2n^3 - 3n^2 - 22n\}$. **60.** 15·975.

61. $\frac{2}{3}$. **62.** $\frac{2}{3}$. **63.** $\dfrac{1}{t^2}\{t^{t+1}(\log t + 1) - t^t + 1\}$.

65. $\dfrac{40\sqrt{2}}{9}$ ft. per sec. **66.** $\dfrac{180}{6^5}$; $\dfrac{780}{6^5}$. **67.** $\dfrac{\pi}{2\sqrt{3}}$.

68. 113·6, 117·0, 120·4, 124·2, 128·8, 134·2, 141·4, 149·4, 158·6, 168·6, 179·4. **70.** ·14 or ·18.

71. (i) $\frac{3}{10}(2x - 3)(1 + x)^{\frac{2}{3}}$; (ii) $\frac{1}{17}[7x - 23 \log(4 \sin x + \cos x)]$.

75. 2·4695.... **76.** 28·0.... **78.** $\frac{448}{125}$. **80.** (i) v; (ii) a.

81. 29·08. **82.** $\dfrac{x^4}{4}\{\frac{1}{8} + (\log x)^2 - \frac{1}{2}\log x\}$; $\frac{1}{3}\sin^3 x - \frac{1}{5}\sin^5 x$.

88. (i) $2\sqrt{x} - 2\sqrt{k}\log\{\sqrt{k} + \sqrt{a}\}$; (ii) $\frac{2}{3}\{x^{\frac{3}{2}} - (x-a)^{\frac{3}{2}}\}$;
(iii) $2\sqrt{x} - 2\tan^{-1}\sqrt{x}$.

89. $\frac{1}{8}$; 1. **90.** 10·476. **91.** $\dfrac{(N-n)!}{n!}$; $\dfrac{1}{N}$.

92. $\sin^{-1} x \log\left(\dfrac{a}{x}\right) + \dfrac{2x}{\sqrt{1 - x^2}}$. **93.** 15 : 17.

95. 1403, 1498, 1598, 1703, 1814, 1931, 2054, 2182, 2316, 2458, 2609; 120.

98. $2^{-x}k[x(x-1) + c][(x-1)(x-2) + c] ... [2.1 + c]$, where k and c are arbitrary constants.

100. 3·030.... **101.** $\frac{3600}{39962}$. **102.** $\frac{1}{2}\{2^{n+2} + 3^{n+1} - 7n^2 - n - 7\}$.

INDEX

The numbers refer to the pages

Printed in the United States
By Bookmasters